Mirjam Augstein, Eelco Herder, Wolfgang Wörndl (Eds.)
Personalized Human-Computer Interaction

Also of Interest

AutomationML
A Practical Guide
Rainer Drath, 2021
ISBN 978-3-11-074622-8, e-ISBN (PDF) 978-3-11-059937-4

Mathematics of Deep Learning
An Introduction
Leonid Berlyand, Pierre-Emmanuel Jabin, 2023
ISBN 978-3-11-102431-8, e-ISBN (PDF) 978-3-11-102555-1

Advances in Systems, Signals and Devices
ISSN 2364-7493, e-ISSN 2364-7507

De Gruyter Series on the Applications of Mathematics in Engineering and Information Sciences
Edited by Mangey Ram
ISSN 2626-5427, e-ISSN 2626-5435

Personalized Human-Computer Interaction

Edited by
Mirjam Augstein, Eelco Herder, and Wolfgang Wörndl

2nd edition

DE GRUYTER
OLDENBOURG

Editors

Mirjam Augstein
University of Applied Sciences Upper Austria
Softwarepark 11
4232 Hagenberg
Austria
mirjam.augstein@fh-hagenberg.at

Eelco Herder
Utrecht University
Department of Information and Computing
Sciences
Princetonplein 5
3584 CC Utrecht
The Netherlands
eelcoherder@acm.org

Wolfgang Wörndl
Technical University of Munich
Department for Informatics
Boltzmannstr. 3
85748 Garching b. München
Germany
woerndl@in.tum.de

ISBN 978-3-11-099960-0
e-ISBN (PDF) 978-3-11-098856-7
e-ISBN (EPUB) 978-3-11-098877-2

Library of Congress Control Number: 2023936467

Bibliographic information published by the Deutsche Nationalbibliothek
The Deutsche Nationalbibliothek lists this publication in the Deutsche Nationalbibliografie;
detailed bibliographic data are available on the Internet at http://dnb.dnb.de.

© 2023 Walter de Gruyter GmbH, Berlin/Boston
Cover image: ipopba / iStock / Getty Images
Typesetting: VTeX UAB, Lithuania
Printing and binding: CPI books GmbH, Leck

www.degruyter.com

Introduction

Decades of research on user modeling, personalization and recommender systems have led to a solid body of general approaches, principles, algorithms and tools. Personalization has become a core functionality in search engines, online stores and social media feeds.

In the area of Human-Computer Interaction (HCI), personalization plays a prominent role as well. For instance, interaction with computer-based devices requires users to exhibit a wide range of physical and cognitive abilities, which differ from person to person. Further, most users have their own preferred interaction styles, modalities, devices and user interfaces, which raises the need for personalization in all aspects of HCI. Even though personalization is a commonly adopted technology, many principles and insights from the research community have not yet sufficiently been applied.

User modeling refers to the process of collecting data about users, inferring a user model in order to apply this model to customize and personalize systems. Personalized systems use this model to adapt the interaction with the users to their requirements, preferences, background knowledge, restrictions, usage contexts and/or goals. The adaptation can be carried out in different manners, e. g., modifying a user interface according to the user's capabilities or knowledge about the system, or proposing interesting and relevant items to a user in a recommender system to reduce information overload. In this book, core researchers present the state-of-the-art in research and practice on adaptation and personalization from the perspective of HCI in a wide range of areas.

The book chapters of the first edition were elicited via a public call for chapters. We received 24 abstracts and accepted 11 full-chapter submissions after a thorough selection and reviewing process. For the second edition, we invited experts to write four additional chapters on current and emerging topics in personalized human-computer interaction. Existing chapters have been revised to reflect developments in the years in between both editions. We have grouped the chapters into the following parts: (1) Foundations of personalization, (2) User input and feedback, (3) Personalization purposes and goals and (4) Personalization domains.

Foundations of personalization (Chapters 1–3)

The first chapter, *"Theory-driven user models for personalization"* by Mark P. Graus and Bruce Ferwerda presents a literature overview of models from psychological theory that can be used in personalization. The motivation is to leverage the theoretical understanding between behavior and user traits that can be used to characterize individual users. They propose a step-by-step approach on how to design personalized systems that take users' traits into account.

The second chapter focuses on principles for *"User-centered recommender systems."* It has been recognized that optimizing recommender systems in terms of algorithm ac-

https://doi.org/10.1515/9783110988567-201

curacy often does not result in corresponding levels of user satisfaction. Jürgen Ziegler discusses the use of visualizing and explaining recommendations, as well as methods for eliciting preferences and critiquing. Also in the chapter quality factors are discussed that are important from a user point of view, including novelty, serendipity, diversity and trustworthiness.

Finally, Markus Schedl and Elisabeth Lex introduce principles of *"Fairness of Information Access Systems."* They discuss various sources of bias and methods to measure this. Further, the chapter gives an overview on methods to mitigate harmful bias during pre-processing, in-processing and post-processing. The chapter ends with conclusions and open challenges.

User input and feedback (Chapters 4–7)

The second part of the book focuses on user input and feedback options in adaptive systems.

Mirjam Augstein and Thomas Neumayr discuss personalized interaction in their chapter *"Personalization and user modeling for interaction processes."* They provide a concise overview of literature on personalized interaction and the underlying user modeling activities, and domains that have been in the focus of related research. Further, they describe the developments in this field throughout the past decades based on their targeted literature review.

Tobias Moebert, Jan Schneider, Dietmar Zoerner and Ulrike Lucke look at cause-and-effect models behind adaptive training systems in the chapter *"How to use socio-emotional signals for adaptive training."* They explain mechanisms for implementing the models and also empirical results from a study on the training of emotion recognition by people with autism as an example. They present two approaches; one is to extend the algorithm regarding dimensions of difficulty in social cognition. The second approach is to make use of socio-emotional signals of the learners in order to further adapt the training system.

"Explanations and user control in personalized systems" by Dietmar Jannach, Michael Jugovac and Ingrid Nunes review explanations and feedback mechanisms in recommender systems. Often, these systems are black boxes for users and do not provide information on why items were recommended. In addition, users frequently have very limited means to control the recommendations, which may lead to limited trust and acceptance.

Building upon insights in the previous chapters, Eelco Herder and Claus Atzenbeck describe *"Feedback loops and mutual reinforcement in personalized interaction."* The chapter focuses on how computers support human decision-making and the role that persuasive techniques play in this process. It is shown how human-system feedback loops lead to short-term as well as long-term mutual reinforcement, with several negative effects that can be observed in current commercial recommender systems and social media. The authors discuss several techniques to stimulate active, conscious decision making to overcome these issues.

Personalization purposes and goals (Chapters 8–10)

Following the foundations of personalization and the principles of user input and feedback, the third part of this book is dedicated to selected purposes and goals for personalized human-computer interaction.

The chapter *"Personalizing the user interface to people with disabilities"* by Julio Abascal, Olatz Arbelaitz, Xabier Gardeazabal, Javier Muguerza, Juan E. Pérez, Xabier Valencia and Ainhoa Yera deals with user interface personalization for people with disabilities. The authors present methods and techniques that are being applied to research and practice in this important application area for personalized human-computer interaction. They outline possible approaches for diverse application fields where personalization is required, for example, accessibility to the web using transcoding or personalized eGovernment.

In *"Personalized persuasion for behavior change,"* Judith Masthoff and Julita Vassileva give a comprehensive introduction to persuasive technology. The chapter provides theory on behavioral economics and behavioral determinants, followed by frameworks and techniques for personalization for behavior change. Further, the authors introduce selected application domains, including healthy living, sustainability and participation in communities. The chapter concludes with evaluation techniques and ethical issues in the domain of persuasion.

Chiara Luisa Schleu and Mirjam Augstein further focus on *"Personalization approaches for remote collaborative interaction."* The chapter starts with an overview of systems and approaches for Computer-Supported Collaborative Work (CSCW). The authors continue with an empirical study in which they identify critical situations, support measures and design implications for personalized interaction support in collaborative settings. The results are wrapped up in a taxonomy that is extensively discussed in the final part of this chapter.

Personalization domains (Chapters 11–13)

The fourth part of the book is about the application of adaptation and personalization in interactive systems in the domains of music recommendation and tourism.

Music recommender systems represent a widely adopted application area for personalized systems and interfaces. In their chapter, *"User awareness in music recommender systems,"* Peter Knees, Markus Schedl, Bruce Ferwerda and Audrey Laplante focus on the listener's aspects of music recommender systems. The authors review different factors that influence relevance for music recommendation, for example, the individual listener's background and context. This is complemented by a discussion on user-centric evaluation strategies for music recommender systems and a reflection on current barriers as well as on strategies to overcome them.

"Tourist trip recommendations – foundations, state- of-the-art and challenges" by Daniel Herzog, Linus W. Dietz and Wolfgang Wörndl surveys the field of Tourist Trip Design Problems (TTDP). TTDP deals with the task of supporting tourists in creating personalized trips with sets or sequences of points of interest or other travel-related items. The authors present trip recommender systems with a focus on recommendation techniques, data analysis and user interfaces.

Continuing the tourism domain, Wilfried Grossmann, Julia Neidhardt and Hannes Werthner present their chapter *"Pictures as a tool for matching tourist preferences with destinations."* They introduce a so-called Seven Factor Model for characterizing the preferences of tourists by assigning values in this model with a picture-based approach. For this purpose, users select pictures that represent various personality aspects and destination descriptions. The authors evaluated their profile acquisition method with a study using data from a travel agency.

Contents

List of Contributing Authors

Julio Abascal
Egokituz: Laboratory of Human-Computer Interaction for Special Needs University of the Basque Country/Euskal Herriko Unibertsitatea Informatika Fakultatea
Donostia
Spain

Olatz Arbelaitz
ALDAPA: ALgorithms, DAta mining and Parallelism University of the Basque Country/Euskal Herriko Unibertsitatea Informatika Fakultatea
Donostia
Spain

Claus Atzenbeck
Institute for Information Systems (iisys)
Hof University
Hof
Germany

Mirjam Augstein
Research Group for Personalized Environments and Collaborative Systems
University of Applied Sciences Upper Austria
Hagenberg
Austria

Linus W. Dietz
Department of Informatics
Technical University of Munich
Munich
Germany

Bruce Ferwerda
Department of Computer Science and Informatics, School of Engineering
Jönköping University
Jönköping
Sweden

Xabier Gardeazabal
Egokituz: Laboratory of Human-Computer Interaction for Special Needs University of the Basque Country/Euskal Herriko Unibertsitatea Informatika Fakultatea
Donostia
Spain

Mark P. Graus
Department of Human-Technology Interaction
Eindhoven University of Technology
Eindhoven
The Netherlands
Department of Marketing and Supply Chain Management, School of Business and Economics
Maastricht University
Maastricht
The Netherlands

Wilfried Grossmann
Faculty of Computer Science
University of Vienna
Vienna
Austria

Eelco Herder
Department of Information and Computing Sciences
Utrecht University
Utrecht
The Netherlands

Daniel Herzog
Department of Informatics
Technical University of Munich
Munich
Germany

Dietmar Jannach
University of Klagenfurt
Klagenfurt
Austria

Michael Jugovac
Technical University of Dortmund
Dortmund
Germany

Peter Knees
Institute of Information Systems Engineering, Faculty of Informatics
TU Wien
Vienna
Austria

Audrey Laplante
École de bibliothéconomie et des sciences de l'information
Université de Montréal
Quebéc
Canada

Elisabeth Lex
Graz University of Technology
Graz
Austria

Benedikt Loepp
University of Duisburg-Essen
Duisburg
Germany

Ulrike Lucke
Department of Computer Science
University of Potsdam
Potsdam
Germany

Judith Masthoff
Department of Information and Computing Sciences
Utrecht University
Utrecht
The Netherlands

Tobias Moebert
Department of Computer Science
University of Potsdam
Potsdam
Germany

Javier Muguerza
ALDAPA: ALgorithms, DAta mining and Parallelism
University of the Basque Country/Euskal Herriko
Unibertsitatea Informatika Fakultatea
Donostia
Spain

Julia Neidhardt
Christian Doppler Laboratory for Recommender Systems
TU Wien
Vienna
Austria

Thomas Neumayr
Research Group for Personalized Environments and Collaborative Systems
University of Applied Sciences Upper Austria
Hagenberg
Austria

Ingrid Nunes
Federal University of Rio Grande do Sul
Porto Alegre
Brazil

Markus Schedl
Johannes Kepler University Linz and Linz Institute of Technology
Linz
Austria
Institute of Computational Perception
Johannes Kepler University Linz
Linz
Austria

Chiara Luisa Schleu
Research Group for Personalized Environments and Collaborative Systems
University of Applied Sciences Upper Austria
Hagenberg
Austria

Jan N. Schneider
Berlin School of Mind and Brain
Humboldt-Universität zu Berlin
Berlin
Germany

Mete Sertkan
Christian Doppler Laboratory for Recommender Systems
TU Wien
Vienna
Austria

Anna Tscherejkina
Department of Computer Science
University of Potsdam
Potsdam
Germany

Julita Vassileva
Department of Computer Science
University of Saskatchewan
Saskatoon
Canada

Hannes Werthner
Research Unit of E-Commerce, Institute of Information Systems Engineering
University of Vienna
Vienna
Austria

Wolfgang Wörndl
Department of Informatics
Technical University of Munich
Munich
Germany

Ainhoa Yera
ALDAPA: ALgorithms, DAta mining and Parallelism
University of the Basque Country/Euskal Herriko Unibertsitatea Informatika Fakultatea
Donostia
Spain

Jürgen Ziegler
University of Duisburg-Essen
Duisburg
Germany

Dietmar Zoerner
Department of Computer Science
University of Potsdam
Potsdam
Germany

Part I: **Foundations of personalization**

Mark P. Graus and Bruce Ferwerda

1 Theory-grounded user modeling for personalized HCI

Abstract: Personalized systems are systems that adapt themselves to meet the inferred needs of individual users. The majority of personalized systems mainly rely on data describing how users interacted with these systems. A common approach is to use historical data to predict users' future needs, preferences and behavior to subsequently adapt the system to cater to these predictions. However, this adaptation is often done without leveraging the theoretical understanding between behavior and user traits that can be used to characterize individual users or the relationship between user traits and needs that can be used to adapt the system. Adopting a more theoretical perspective can benefit personalization in three ways: (i) relying on theory can reduce the amount of data required to train compared to a purely data-driven system, (ii) interpreting the outcomes of data-driven analysis (such as predictive models) from a theoretical perspective can expand our knowledge about users and (iii) provide means for explanations and transparency. However, in order to incorporate theoretical knowledge in personalization a number of obstacles need to be faced. In this chapter, we review literature that taps into aspects of (i) psychological models from traditional psychological theory that can be used in personalization, (ii) relationships between psychological models and online behavior, (iii) automated inference of psychological models from data, and (iv) how to incorporate psychological models in personalized systems. Finally, we propose a step-by-step approach on how to design personalized systems that take users' traits into account.

Keywords: Personalization, psychological models, cognitive models, psychology, user modeling, theory-driven

1.1 Introduction

Personalization is performed by adapting aspects of systems to match individual users' needs in order to improve the user experience by making it more easy for the user to reach their goals in the system. Examples are recommender systems that make it easy to find relevant content in a library [94], or adaptive interfaces that make it easier for users to achieve their goals [91]. Current personalization strategies are mainly data-driven in the sense that they are based on the way users have been and are interacting with a system, after which the system is dynamically adapted to match inferred user needs. The more theory-driven counterparts of personalization are often designed based on general knowledge about how user traits influence user needs, and how these needs in-

https://doi.org/10.1515/9783110988567-001

fluence the requirements of a system. Systems are adapted to individual users based on a set of rules. Although both strategies are used separately, combining the knowledge gained from both strategies could be used to achieve greater personalization possibilities.

In order to provide approaches to personalization, current research has primarily focused on using historical data that describes interaction behavior. Using this data, personalization strategies are developed that predict users' future interactions. The prediction of these future interactions is often done without leveraging the understanding of the relationship between user behavior and user traits. In other words, predictions are made without considering the root cause of certain behavior that users are showing. A prominent direction using this approach is the field of recommender systems in which historical behavioral data is used to alter the order of items in a catalog (from highest predicted relevance to lowest predicted relevance), with the goal of making users consume more items or helping them to find relevant items more easily [73].

By adopting a more theoretical perspective (often based on psychological literature), the root cause of behavior can be identified and thereby benefit personalization opportunities. Using a theoretical perspective can benefit personalization in two ways: (i) a large body of theoretical work can be used to inform personalized systems without the need of extensive data-driven analysis. For example, research has shown that it might be beneficial to adapt the way course material is presented to match students' working memory capacity [45], and (ii) including theory can help to interpret the results gained from the data-driven perspective and thereby meaningfully expand our knowledge about users. For example, research on music players has demonstrated that different types of people base their decisions on what to listen to on different sources of information [31].

Although personalization has been shown to benefit from adopting a more theoretical perspective by considering the relationship between user behavior and user traits, this theoretical perspective comes with theoretical and methodological challenges. A first challenge is to identify and measure user traits that play a role in the needs for personalization (e. g., cognitive style [82], personality [16] or susceptibility to persuasive strategies [21]) and to capture these traits in a formal user model. A second challenge is to infer the relevant user traits from interaction behavior (e. g., inferring user preferences from historical ratings or inferring a person's personality from the content they share on social media). A third challenge is to identify the aspects of a system that can or should be altered based on these user traits that can improve the user experience. In certain cases, this is straightforward (e. g., altering the order of a list of items based on predicted relevance), while in other cases the required alterations can be more intricate and require more thought to implement (e. g., altering the way in which information is presented visually to match a user's cognitive style).

While the aforementioned challenges are interconnected, they are often addressed in isolation. The current chapter provides an overview of work that relied on user traits for several (system) aspects:

- introduction of psychological models that are currently used in personalization
- psychological models that have been linked to online behavior
- automatic inference of psychological models from behavioral data
- incorporating psychological models in personalized systems or systems for personalization

The literature discussed throughout the chapter can serve as starting points for theory-grounded personalization in certain applications (e. g., e-learning, recommendations) and content domains (e. g., movies, music). Finally, the chapter concludes with a blueprint for designing personalized systems that take user traits into consideration.

1.2 Psychological models in personalization

Psychological models serve to explain how aspects of the environment influence human behavior and cognition. Since these models provide information on how people react to their surroundings, they can also be used to anticipate how people will react to aspects of technological systems and can thus provide insight in people's needs in technological contexts. The proposition to use psychological models for personalization is not a new concept. Rich [95] already proposed in 1979 the use of psychological stereotypes for personalizing digital systems. A more recent overview provided by Lex et al. [78] similarly elaborates on how psychological theory can be applied in specifically recommender systems, or personalized systems that aid people in finding relevant items based on their interaction behavior.

While the concept of incorporating psychological theory into personalization is not new, the current abundance of available user data have made personalization strategies adopt more data-driven approaches and move away from incorporating theoretical knowledge. While the availability of user data obviously benefits data-driven approaches, there are opportunities for theory-driven approaches as well to exploit the available data (e. g., the implicit acquisition of user traits). In the following section, we will lay out different models that are currently used in personalization. We will then continue with providing an overview of prior research that has focused on the relationship between psychological models and online behavior, then continue with work that has looked at the automated inference of psychological models and then discuss work that have been personalizing systems based on psychological models.

1.2.1 Personality

Personality is a long lasting research area in psychology [2]. Personality is considered to reflect behavior through the coherent patterning of affect, cognition and desires. Aside from this patterning, personality has shown to be a stable construct over time [66]. Through the construct of personality, research has aimed to capture observable individual behavioral differences [23]. Traditional personality psychology has established numerous associations between personality and concepts such as happiness, physical and psychological health, spirituality and identity at an individual level; the quality of relationships with peers, family and romantic others at an interpersonal level; and occupational choice, satisfaction and performance, as well as community involvement, criminal activity and political ideology at a social institutional level (for an overview see [89]).

Different models have been developed to express personality of people. The most commonly used model is the five-factor model (FFM; mostly used in academic research). The FFM found its roots in the lexical hypothesis, which proposes that personality traits and differences that are the most important and relevant to people eventually become a part of their language. Thus the lexical hypothesis relies on the analysis of language to derive personality traits [2]. The notion of the lexical hypothesis was used by Cattell [16] to lay out the foundation of the FFM by identifying 16 distinct factors. Based on the identified 16 factors, Tupes and Christal [113] found recurrences among the factors that resulted in clusters that represent the five personality traits that make up the FFM (see Table 1.1). The FFM thus describes personality in five factors (also called the big five personality traits): openness to new experiences, conscientiousness, extraversion, agreeableness and neuroticism.[1] Different measurements were created to assess the five personality factors of which the big five inventory (BFI: 44-item) [66] and the ten item personality inventory (TIPI: 10-item) [50] are two commonly used surveys.

Table 1.1: Five-factor model adopted from John, Donahue, and Kentle [66].

General dimensions	Primary factors
Openness to experience	Artistic, curious, imaginative, insightful, original, wide interest
Conscientiousness	Efficient, organized, planful, reliable, responsible, thorough
Extraversion	Active, assertive, energetic, enthusiastic, outgoing, talkative
Agreeableness	Appreciative, forgiving, generous, kind, sympathetic, trusting
Neuroticism	Anxious, self-pitying, tense, touchy, unstable, worrying

1.2.2 Cognitive styles

Cognitive styles refer to the psychological dimensions that determine individuals' modes of perceiving, remembering, thinking and problem-solving [59, 82]. Different cognitive styles have been identified to indicate individual processes, such as analytic-holistic and

---

1 also called the OCEAN model due to the acronym of the five factors.

verbal-visual. In an attempt to make sense out of the fuzziness of different kinds of cognitive styles, Miller [83] proposed a hierarchal framework for systematizing cognitive styles (particularly the analytical-holistic dimension) by connecting them to different stages of cognitive processes[2] (see Figure 1.1).

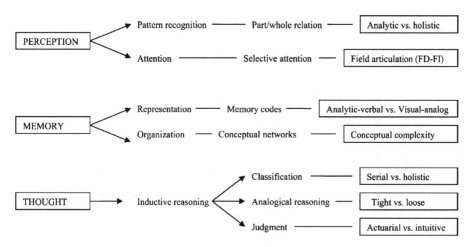

Figure 1.1: A model of cognitive styles and processes adopted from Miller [83].

To measure general cognitive styles, multiple questionnaires have been developed. The cognitive style index (CSI; Hayes and Allinson [59]) is often used. The CSI consists of 38 items and assigns a score along a single dimension ranging from intuitive to analytical. The items are based on the cognitive style dimensions: active-passive, analytic-holistic and intuitive-systematic. An alternative measurement to the CSI is the cognitive style analysis (CSA; [96]), which assigns scores to the analytic-holistic and verbal-visual dimensions.

Although it is recognized that individual differences exist in general cognitive functioning, their effects are often diluted by overlapping characteristics of humans. Cognitive styles have been shown to be a better predictor of influence for particular situations and tasks rather than general functioning [74].

For example, cognitive styles have been shown to be related to academic achievements among students (see for an overview Coffield et al. [22]). Despite the domain-dependent variations of cognitive styles that adhere to their own measurements (e. g., learning style questionnaire [60] to assess learning styles), studies have shown that correlations between learning styles and cognitive styles exist (see for an overview Allinson

---

2 We acknowledge the existence of basic, higher and complex cognitive processes. However, since this chapter focuses on personalization strategies, the focus will be put on individual differences (i. e., cognitive styles) rather than the generic cognitive processes (e. g., perception, memory, thought).

and Hayes [1]). In the following sections, we discuss the domain-dependent cognitive styles that are currently used for the purpose of personalization.

1.2.2.1 Learning styles

The educational field has given much attention to identifying individual differences based on a subset of cognitive styles, namely learning styles. Messick [82] discussed the merit of using cognitive styles to characterize people in an educational setting. Related to people having different preferences regarding processing information as described by cognitive styles, people have different preferences for acquiring knowledge, which are captured in learning styles. In applications that have as goal to assist people in learning, learning styles are a logical candidate to base personalization on. Coffield et al. [22] provide an extensive overview of these learning styles, comprising a selection 350 papers from over 3,000 references, in which they identify 13 key models of learning styles. Aside from this overview, they provide references to surveys to measure learning styles, together with a list of studies in which these surveys are validated. Two notable models are the learning style inventory (LSI) by Kolb [71] and the learning styles questionnaire (LSQ) by Honey and Mumford [60]. The LSI assesses learning styles through a 100-item self-report questionnaire indicating preferences for environment (e. g., temperature), emotional (e. g., persistence), sociological (e. g., working alone or with peers), physical (e. g., modality preferences) and psychological factors (e. g., global-analytical). The LSQ uses an 80-item checklist to assess learning styles on four dimensions: activist, reflector, theorist and pragmatist.

1.2.2.2 Personal styles

Whereas the previously described FFM of personality (see Section 1.2.1) found its ground in the lexical hypothesis, the Myers–Briggs model is based on cognitive styles. The Myers–Briggs model of personality is commonly used in the consultancy and training world. People's scores on the Myers–Briggs model is measured by the Myers–Briggs Type Indicator (MBTI) [88], consisting of 50 questions to measure personality types. The MBTI describes a person's personality across four dimensions:

1. Extraversion–introversion (E vs. I): how a person gets energized
2. Sensing–intuition (S vs. N): how a person takes in information
3. Thinking–feeling (T vs. F): the means a person uses to make decisions
4. Judging–perceiving (J vs. P): the speed with which a person makes decisions

The combinations of these four dimensions result in one of 16 personality types that are based on Jung's personality theory from the early 1920s [67] (see Figure 1.2).

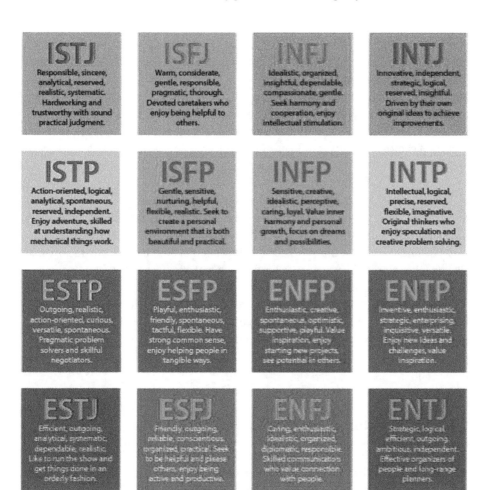

Figure 1.2: The 16 MBTI personality-type combinations based on the four personality dimensions. Reprinted from Wikipedia, by Jake Beech, 2014, retrieved from https://commons.wikimedia.org/wiki/File: MyersBriggsTypes.png Licensed under a Creative Commons Attribution-ShareAlike 3.0 Unported license.

1.2.2.3 Cognitive models

The previous models all described sets of traits, dimensions or factors that capture an individual's characteristics related to the user experience. Another type of cognitive models describe how thinking, reasoning or deciding is done in the user's psyche and how this is related to the user experience. For example, memory affects how people interact with movie recommender systems [10], resulting in people expressing their preferences differently depending on how much time has passed since they have watched the movie. While these effects can be observed in the data itself, cognitive models of memory (e. g., models making the distinction between sensory, working, short-term and long-term memory) provide ways to understand and opportunities to anticipate on these effects so that they can be taken into consideration when designing and implementing systems.

Another cognitive model that describes how people interact with (personalized) systems is that of attention. People differ in the ways in which they process information presented to them as a result of how they direct their attention. Paying attention to certain aspects of choice alternatives influences people's preferences. For example, Busemeyer and Townsend [12] describe that when people have to make a choice between three options they compare these alternatives in terms of individual attributes. When a decision maker pays attention to an attribute, the expected outcome of choosing the alternative that is superior in terms of that attribute increases. After this, the decision maker continues selecting relevant item attributes to pay attention to until the information that is processed has reached a threshold for the decision maker to make a satisfactory decision. In other words, the way in which a decision maker guides attention influences the decision-making process.

As this process relates to preferences and decision-making, it has an effect on how people interact with personalized systems that aid in decision-making, such as recommender systems. Considering these kinds of models has shown to improve, for example, predictions of what movies a user will enjoy [122] or what reading resources to recommend [72].

1.2.3 Relationship between models

Psychological models all have their foundation in either behavioral or cognitive assessments of people. As behavior and cognition are so interconnected, the different models are expected to be related as well. Busato et al. [11] found distinct correlations between several personality traits and the type of learning styles people adhere to. Zhang [121] showed relationships between personality traits and cognitive styles and found that creativity-generating and more complex cognitive styles were related to extraversion and openness. Also, other models from traditional psychology that have not been used yet for personalization purposes have shown to correlate with personality traits. For example, Greenberg et al. [56] found correlations between personality traits and people's "music sophistication" (Gold-MSI; [87]); a measurement to indicate the musical expertise of people.

An extensive literature review that summarizes the findings of how cognitive styles correlate with other psychological models is given in Allinson and Hayes [1]. In multiple studies, cognitive styles have been shown to correlate with other measures of learning, thinking or teaching, such as the Learning Style Questionnaire [60]. This indicates that models are related and user traits according to one model can be indicative of their traits in another model.

1.3 The relationship between psychological traits and online behavior

Aside from using psychological traits defined by traditional psychology to explain the root cause of online behavior, there is an uncharted terrain evolving with the advancement of technologies. Especially as technologies are becoming increasingly ubiquitous and pervasive, new ways of interaction become available between technologies and users. These new ways of interaction may reduce how straightforward the relationship between online behavior and traditional psychological traits is. Hence, there is an increased importance to verify to what extent results from traditional psychology still hold in computer-mediated scenarios before implementation. Aside from that, there is a need for critical reflection on the findings of new relationships between psychological traits and online behavior (e. g., the differentiation between correlation and causation) and the implications for implementation of such findings in personalized systems. In this section, we lay out the related work that has focused on verifying relationships between behaviors and traits based on results from traditional psychology, and work that has focused on identifying new relationships between psychological traits and online behaviors. Subsequently Section 1.5 discusses work that focused on incorporating psychological traits in personalized systems.

1.3.1 Personality

The way we communicate with others is becoming increasingly mediated through technology in the form of social networking sites (SNSs), such as Facebook, Instagram and Twitter [26, 114]. Just like personalities are found to be related to many behaviors in the social or physical world, the digital footprint that people leave behind on these SNSs can be a reflection of people's personalities as well. Factors such as images (e. g., profile pictures), expressions of thoughts (e. g., content postings) and content preferences (e. g., reactions on content) are in general the information that people leave behind digitally. Similar factors in the real world have already shown to consist of information that people use to generate impressions about others [43]. Back et al. [6] showed that the personalities we express online have resemblances with the personalities that we express in the real world. In other words, it seems that how people express themselves online is an extension of their personality-based behavior, preferences and needs in the real world.

The notion of extended personality has led to different studies that investigated the digital footprint of users in relation to their personality traits. In particular, Facebook has received a lot of attention in the search for personality related behaviors. To exemplify the abundance of research on online personalities, we highlight some of the work that has been done. Some of the results that are found indicate a direct interpretation of personality characteristics to certain online behaviors. For example, one of the findings of Ross et al. [99] showed that extroverts on average belong to more Facebook groups, which is argued to relate to the social nature of extroverts that leverage Facebook as a social tool. Neurotics (less emotionally stable) were found to spend more time on Facebook, allegedly in an attempt to try to make themselves look as attractive as possible [86]. Conscientiousness has shown to relate to an increased usage of Twitter although this is not the case for Facebook. Hughes et al. [64] explains this finding to the limitation of the characters that can be used in a Tweet, which causes conscientious people to still able to partake in social networking without it becoming a temporal distraction.

Although most research in online behavior has been done in the context of SNSs, in which attempts are made to find relationships between personality traits and online behavior, research has also been conducted in other areas focusing on how to infer personality from different sources. For example, Biel, Aran, and Gatica-Perez [9] found that personality can be successfully inferred from auditory and visual cues in video logs (vlogs). An overview of current research on personality related to online behaviors can be found in Table 1.2.

1.3.2 Cognitive styles: learning styles

Whereas personality research has mainly focused on the relationship in SNSs, the research on cognitive styles has influenced other application areas, such as online learning environments. The research in this area has mainly been focusing on identifying whether the cognitive styles as known from traditional psychology have the same effects in an online setting. The findings that can be drawn from the research that has been done on cognitive styles and online learning environments are inconclusive. The disposition of the various results sketches the importance to validate the effect of psychological traits in relation to online behavior. For example, Zacharis [120] looked at 161 students in which the difference of learning styles was investigated between online and offline participation of students, but no differences between the two different groups were found. Huang, Lin, and Huang [63] found differences between online and offline students, such as sensing learners (i. e., those who were patient with details and were good at practical work) engaged online more frequently and for a longer duration. Similarly, Wang et al. [116] showed that online achievements are influenced by the learning styles of students.

As mentioned previously, the majority of research on cognitive styles has focused on investigating to what extent understanding of offline learning translates to online learning environments. Prior research that has looked at adapting content delivery based on cognitive styles in these environments. Also, the results are mainly inconclusive in whether cognitive styles can explain individual behavior. For example, Graf and Liu [53] identified different navigational strategies based on learning styles, information that

Table 1.2: An overview of current research on the relationship between personality traits and online behavior.

Study	Domain
Ellison et al. [26]	Facebook
Valkenburg and Peter [114]	Facebook
Moore and McElroy [86]	Facebook
Ross et al. [99]	Facebook
Back et al. [5]	Facebook
Seidman [105]	Facebook
Gosling, Gaddis, Vazire, et al. [49]	Facebook
Gosling et al. [51]	Facebook
Rosenberg and Egbert [98]	Facebook
Bachrach et al. [4]	Facebook
Carpenter [14]	Facebook
Skues, Williams, and Wise [107]	Facebook
Stieger et al. [108]	Facebook
Lee, Ahn, and Kim [77]	Facebook
Ljepava et al. [80]	Facebook
Eftekhar, Fullwood, and Morris [25]	Facebook
Winter et al. [117]	Facebook
Chen and Marcus [19]	Facebook
Jenkins-Guarnieri, Wright, and Hudiburgh [65]	Facebook
Wu, Chang, and Yuan [119]	Facebook
Ryan and Xenos [100]	Facebook
Amichai-Hamburger and Vinitzky [3]	Facebook
Quercia et al. [93]	Facebook
Davenport et al. [24]	Facebook & Twitter
Hughes et al. [64]	Facebook & Twitter
Qiu et al. [92]	Twitter
Ferwerda and Tkalcic [36]	Instagram
Lay and Ferwerda [76]	Instagram
Schrammel, Köffel, and Tscheligi [103]	Online communities
Ferwerda, Tkalcic, and Schedl [38, 39]	Online music listening
Ferwerda, Schedl, and Tkalcic [31]	Online music listening
Ferwerda et al. [40]	Online music listening
Tkalčič et al. [110]	Online music listening
Marcus, Machilek, and Schütz [81]	Personal website
Ferwerda et al. [41]	Recommender system
Chen, Wu, and He [20]	Recommender system
Hu and Pu [61]	Recommender system
Golbeck and Norris [46]	Recommender system
Biel, Aran, and Gatica-Perez [9]	Video logs

can potentially be used to create adaptive interfaces. However, Mitchell, Chen, and Macredie [85] showed that adaptive interfaces based on cognitive styles do not have an advantageous effect on student performance.

One of few studies that investigated differences based on cognitive styles in a different domain than a learning environment is Belk et al. [7]. They found that people with different cognitive styles differ in preferences with regards to CAPTCHA (acronym for "Completely Automated Public Turing test to tell Computers and Humans Apart").[3] They found that the cognitive processing style (i. e., verbal or visual) plays a role in the speed of the CAPTCHA completion: those that possess a more verbal cognitive style showed a faster completion of textual CAPTCHAs (e. g., text-recognition: deciphering a scrambled text), whereas those adhering to a visual cognitive style showed a faster completion of visual CAPTCHAs (e. g., image-recognition: finding a matching set of pictures).

1.4 Automated inference of psychological traits or styles

By investigating how psychological knowledge from the offline world transfers to online environments, research has turned to personalization opportunities based on psychological traits and/or styles. The research on personalization has not only focused on implementing psychological traits and styles in systems, but also on how to implicitly infer these traits and styles. By being able to implicitly infer relevant psychological traits and styles, personalization strategies based on these traits and styles can be implemented without the use of extensive questionnaires that are normally used to assess psychological models. Although the use of questionnaires has its advantages (e. g., increased validity and reliability), it also has apparent drawbacks (e. g., time consuming and interrupting the flow between user and system). Moreover, the data for implicit inference does not necessarily need to come from the system directly. Thus, inference and implementation of psychological traits/styles can be achieved across different (connected) platforms [13].

1.4.1 Personality

As personality has shown to be related to online behavior, attempts have been made to infer personality traits from online behavior. Although all kinds of data can be exploited for personality prediction, research has primarily focused on data retrieved from SNSs. Especially Facebook, Twitter and Instagram have received a lot of attention in attempts to infer personality from users' information and generated content (see Table 1.3 for an overview).

---

3 commonly used as a security defense mechanism to determine whether an entity interacting with a system is a human and not, for example, an automated bot.

Table 1.3: An overview of current personality predictors.

Study	Domain
Golbeck, Robles, and Turner [47]	Facebook
Celli, Bruni, and Lepri [17]	Facebook
Segalin et al. [104]	Facebook
Ferwerda, Schedl, and Tkalcic [32]	Facebook
Quercia et al. [93]	Twitter
Golbeck et al. [48]	Twitter
Ferwerda, Schedl, and Tkalcic [33, 34]	Instagram
Ferwerda and Tkalcic [35]	Instagram
Skowron et al. [106]	Twitter & Instagram

Golbeck, Robles, and Turner [47] looked at how language features expressed in Facebook profiles can be used to infer personality traits. They were able to create a personality predictor with mean absolute errors (MAE) between 0.099 and 0.138 (on a normalized 0–1 scale) across the five personality traits. Similarly, Celli, Bruni, and Lepri [17] and Segalin et al. [104] showed that compositions of Facebook profiles can be used to infer users' personalities. However, these approaches rely on content that people share on their Facebook page. With extensive privacy options available, users may limit the content they share on their profile. Ferwerda, Schedl, and Tkalcic [32] showed that by the decisions users make with regards to what sections of their Facebook profile they disclose is indicative of their personality information as well. They were able to create a personality predictor with a root-mean-square error (RMSE) between 0.73 and 0.99 for each personality trait (on a 1–5 scale).

Other attempts to infer personality from online behavioral data have been done on Twitter. Quercia et al. [93] looked at traits of Twitter profiles (e. g., number of followers and following) and found that these characteristics could be used to infer personality. Their personality predictor achieved an RSME between 0.69 and 0.88 for each personality trait (on 1–5 scales) with openness to experience as the trait that could be predicted most accurately and extraversion as the least accurately predictable one. Golbeck et al. [48] analyzed language features (e. g., use of punctuation, sentiment) of Twitter feeds and that they could predict personality with mean absolute errors ranging from 0.119 to 0.182 (on a normalized 0–1 scale).

Ferwerda, Schedl, and Tkalcic [33, 34] analyzed the picture sharing social network Instagram. More specifically, they investigated how users manipulate the pictures they upload with filters. They found that personality could be inferred from hue saturation valence (HSV) properties of the uploaded pictures. Skowron et al. [106] combined information of Twitter and Instagram. By using linguistic and meta data from Twitter and linguistic and image data from Instagram, personality prediction could be significantly improved. They were able to achieve RMSE personality scores between 0.50 and 0.73.

Aside of extracting personality traits from SNSs, Ferwerda and Tkalčič [37] explored the extraction of personality traits from drug consumption profiles to facilitate personalized treatments plans. They found that they could achieve RMSE personality scores between 0.83 and 0.93 based on how people consume drugs.

1.4.2 Cognitive styles

Although inference of cognitive styles (e. g., learning styles) has mostly been done within a learning environment (see Section 1.4.2.1), there is a limited amount of work that has focused on general cognitive styles in other domains. One type of applications in which this has been studied is digital libraries. Frias-Martinez, Chen, and Liu [42] investigated to what extent behavior in digital libraries can be used to make inferences about users' cognitive styles and how these inferences can be used to personalize these digital libraries. They outline the steps to construct a predictive model that infers cognitive styles from clickstreams and show how this can be done successfully. Similarly, Hauser et al. [57] inferred cognitive styles from the way users interacted with an advice tool for mobile phone contracts and showed that incorporating these cognitive styles improved the buying propensity of users. Belk et al. [8] argued that the cognitive style of users (i. e., the way people organize and perceive information) influences their navigational behaviors in Web 2.0 interactive systems. To investigate the effects of cognitive styles, their study consisted of three steps: (i) investigating the relationship between cognitive styles and navigational behaviors, (ii) investigating whether clustering techniques can group users based on their cognitive style, and (iii) investigating which navigational metrics can be used to predict users' cognitive style.

1.4.2.1 Learning styles

Learning styles are thought to be reflected in the way students acquire knowledge. Specifically, online learning environments provide students with a variety of ways to learn and the possibility to log the way students behave within the system. As such, they provide large amounts of data that enable the possibility to build models that can infer learning styles. On average, the algorithms that are developed to are able to achieve a 66 % to 80 % precision. For example, Sanders and Bergasa-Suso [101] developed a system that allowed teachers to help their students study. They collected information related to how students used this system and subsequently conducted a study to investigate how well this information could be used to infer students' learning styles expressed in the Felder–Silverman Learning Styles Model (FSLSM [27]) and measured through surveys. The FSLSM defines learning styles by four dimensions: active/reflective (A/R), sensing/intuitive (S/I), verbal/visual (V/V) and sequential/global (S/G). Sanders and Bergasa-Suso [101] was able to make significantly better predictions over naive best guesses, which indicates that the way students interact with a learning environment can indeed be used to infer their learning styles.

Similarly, García et al. [44] used a Bayesian network to infer students' learning styles as expressed by the FSLSM from how intensively the students interacted with the different elements (e. g., chat, mail, revising exam questions) in the learning system. They found that they could predict students' learning styles with around 77 % accuracy, permitted that the students had prior experience with online learning systems. An overview of other current research on inference of the FSLSM dimensions can be found in Table 1.4.

Table 1.4: An overview of learning style inferences based on the FSLSM by García et al. [44]. Percentages are represented, reported precision measures for the four dimensions of the FSLSM: active/reflective (A/R), sensing/intuitive (S/I), verbal/visual (V/V) and sequential/global (S/G).

Study	Algorithm	A/R	S/I	V/V	S/G
Cha et al. [18]	Decision tree	66.70 %	77.80 %	100 %	71.40 %
García et al. [44]	Bayesian network	58 %	77 %	N/A	63 %
Graf and Liu [54]	Rule-based	79 %	77 %	77 %	73 %
Latham et al. [75]	Rule-based	86 %	75 %	83 %	72 %
Özpolat and Akar [90]	NB tree classification	70 %	73.30 %	73.30 %	53.30 %
Villaverde, Godoy, and Amandi [115]	Artificial neural network	69.30 %	69.30 %	N/A	69.30 %
	Hidden Markov model	66.70 %	77.80 %	85.70 %	85.70 %

1.5 Incorporating psychological models in personalized systems

In Section 1.3, we discussed work that focused on identifying differences/similarities between offline and online behaviors as well as work identifying new relationships between psychological traits in online environments. Section 1.4 presented prior work on the implicit inference of psychological traits and styles from online behavior. Whereas the majority of previous work has focused on identifying relationships between behavior and psychological traits and the implicit inference of said psychological traits, limited work has incorporated psychological traits and styles in personalized systems. In this section, we illustrate work that has incorporated psychological traits in systems to create personalized experiences to users.

1.5.1 Personality

Several studies have shown how incorporating users' personalities can improve prediction accuracy in the domain of recommender systems. Hu and Pu [62] demonstrated that personality can be used to overcome the new-user, cold-start problem that arises when no or insufficient information about a user is available to make predictions on. By relying on new users' personality scores expressed in the FFM, predictions could be made without the need for any additional rating data. Similarly, Fernández-Tobías et al. [29] showed that incorporating personality data in a recommender algorithm allowed for more easily recommending across domains. By considering users' personality scores in conjunction with ratings across domains (i. e., books, movies and music), they found that they were better able to predict users' ratings in one domain based on another if they considered personality on top of rating information. Similarly Ferwerda and Schedl [30] and Ferwerda, Schedl, and Tkalcic [32] showed how personality information can be integrated and exploited to improve music recommender systems, whereas Tkalcic, Delic, and Felfernig [109] proposes to incorporate personality to better serve individual needs in group recommendations by taking into account different personality types.

1.5.2 Cognitive styles

Personalization strategies based on cognitive styles have been primarily been applied in a learning context (Section 1.5.2.1 discusses work in a learning context that specifically used cognitive learning styles instead of the general cognitive styles). Karampiperis et al. [68] adapted the cognitive trait model of Lin [79], focusing on the inductive reasoning ability of participants (next to the basic cognitive trait: working memory) to personalize learning environments in which they dynamically adapted the content presentation based on different learners' navigational behavior. Triantafillou et al. [111] proposed the Adaptive Educational System based on Cognitive Styles system (AES-CS); a system based on the cognitive field dependency and independency style of Witkin et al. [118]. Different navigational organization, amount of control and navigational support tools were adapted based on this cognitive style. The dynamic adaptation of the interaction elements based on field dependency and independency showed a significant increase in performance then when a static version of the system was presented. In a similar fashion, Tsianos et al. [112] used Riding's Cognitive Style Analysis [97] to categorize users: imager/verbal and wholist/analyst. Based on the measured categorization, they provided users with an adaptive content presentation and navigational organization. An overview of the studies that applied cognitive styles for adaptation can be found in Table 1.5.

1.5.2.1 Learning styles

Knowing a student's learning styles can be used to alter online learning environments to provide students with information in line with the way they prefer to process information. This is shown to lead to improved learning. Although there is debate about

Table 1.5: An overview of studies in which *cognitive styles* were adopted for personalization.

Study	Personalization
Karampiperis et al. [68] Triantafillou et al. [111]	– Adaptive presentation of content – Navigation organization – Amount of user control – Navigation support tools
Tsianos et al. [112]	– Adaptive presentation of content – Navigation organization

the merit of matching a learning environment to learning styles, there are indications that personalizing learning environments improves the learning effectiveness. Related to learning styles, the working memory capacity has shown to be a trait that influences what the best learning environments [45, ch. 4]. Students for whom the instructional style matched their learning style scored higher in tests and expressed lower levels of anxiety.

Graf et al. [52] proposed a framework using the FSLSM [27]. The framework consists of adaptation strategies using the sequence as well as the amount of examples and exercises. The same FSLSM [27] was used by Papanikolaou et al. [91] in which interaction preferences were investigated in two educational systems (i. e., FLexi-OLM and INSPIRE) to provide personalized learner support.

Carver, Howard, and Lane [15] used the B. S. Solomon's Inventory of Learning Styles [28] to create an interface with adaptive content presentation based on the learning style. Milosevic et al. [84] used the LSI [71] in addition to capture preferences, knowledge, goals, and navigational histories of users to adapt the learning environment. An overview of the studies that applied learning styles for adaptation can be found in Table 1.6.

Table 1.6: An overview of studies in which *learning styles* were adopted for personalization.

Study	Personalization
Carver, Howard, and Lane [15] Germanakos and Belk [45] Graf et al. [52]	– Adaptive presentation of content – Instructional style – Sequence of content – Amount of content
Milosevic et al. [84]	– Different course material sequencing
Papanikolaou et al. [91]	– Adaptive navigation support (i. e., sequential, global) – Adaptive content presentation (i. e., visual/verbal)

1.5.2.2 Cognitive models

Cognitive models have similarly been incorporated in personalized systems. As attention is closely linked to preferences, work has been conducted on using models of attention to improve the prediction of what items are relevant to an individual user over time. Zhao et al. [122] propose to model the user's temporal interactions (e. g., paying attention) with recommender systems to produce better and more accurate recommendations for users. They demonstrated that by modeling temporal interactions of users create a significant accuracy improvement of more conventional models (e. g., RNN) that only models the sequence of positive items.

Kopeinik et al. [72] used an unsupervised human category learning model to mimic nonlinear user-resource dynamics that are the basis of attention and interpretation. By mimicking these nonlinear user-resources dynamics (i. e., attention-interpretation dynamics), they were able to substantially improve collaborative filtering approaches that treats users just as another entity in the computation. Moreover, their approach is able to compete against a more computationally, expensive, matrix factorization approach.

1.6 Combining trait inference and trait-based personalization

The examples in the previous sections (Sections 1.4 and 1.5) all address two sub-problems related to using psychological traits in personalization. They either aim to infer user traits or styles from online behavioral data, or they aim to use already measured user traits or styles to improve personalization approaches. However, these two problems can be addressed in conjunction. Relevant domain-dependent psychological traits can be identified from psychological theory, measured through surveys to serve as ground-truth and incorporated in user models in a personalized system. The current section presents two studies in which this is done and describes the steps in the approach.

1.6.1 Adapting a comparison tool based on cognitive styles

Hauser et al. [57] hypothesized that cognitive styles would be traits that influence how users of an online comparison tool would best be helped. They developed and tested a tool to compare cell phone contracts that relied on two subsystems for personalization. The first subsystem was a Bayesian inference loop, which was used to infer users' cognitive styles based on what elements of the system they interacted with. The second subsystem was an automatic Gittins loop, which was used to learn how to adapt the content and form of the system to match the cognitive style. There were immediate feedback loops, where the Bayesian inference loop was updated with each click users made and the Gittins loop updated after each time a user finished using the system. If the user exhibited the desired behavior, the systems' predictions were reinforced. Similarly, if the system did not manage to convince the user to make a purchase, the prediction parameters were changed. The study showed that people expressed a higher propensity to buy, which indicates that incorporating the cognitive styles for personalization indeed improved the system. The system was initially not tested in an actual field study but the system was not tested in an actual field study so no conclusions in terms of behavior could be made. In a follow-up study, they conducted a field study and found that their approach improves the purchase likelihood in a more natural setting [58].

1.6.2 Library personalization based on parenting styles

Graus, Willemsen, and Snijders [55] personalized a digital library for new parents, or parents with children younger than 2 years old. When designing personalized systems for young parents, an additional challenge arises from the fact that not only can the users be new to a system, the users themselves are most likely new to the domain of parenting. As such, they may not be aware of what type of content is relevant to them and a mismatch may exist between interests and interaction behavior. Information about how to get babies to sleep appears relevant to everyone, but in practice is more relevant for people that raise their kids according to a schedule than it is for parents allow their children to decide when they go to bed. Parents however might beforehand not know whether they want to raise their children according to a schedule or be more flexible, and thus incorrectly judge the relevance of content on getting kids to sleep.

Graus, Willemsen, and Snijders [55] compared user experience and behavior in a library personalized based on reading behavior against a library personalized based on survey responses to measure parenting styles. Their study consisted of an initial data collection that served to gather interaction and survey data to measure parenting styles. They used this data to create personalized relevance predictions, which were used to reorder the articles in the library for each individual user. In a second session, the same users were reinvited to the now personalized library and data regarding their behavior and user experience was collected. The data showed that personalizing the order of articles based on the survey responses resulted in a higher user experience than relying on reading behavior, despite the fact that the former had lower objective prediction accuracy.

1.7 Conclusion

Over the years, personalization strategies have applied different methods. Whereas in the past, personalization took a more theoretical approach (e. g., by developing systems that require explicit authoring [70, 95] or by leveraging different psychological models as discussed in this chapter), the abundance of behavioral data and computational power nowadays have caused a shift to a more data-driven perspective (e. g., collaborative filtering [73]). Although these two different perspectives on personalization are often used in isolation, they could be used together to maximize each other's potential and mitigate each other's limitations.

The way users interact with systems can in part be explained through psychological models of the users and incorporating these same psychological models in personalized systems may be a way to improve these systems in terms of effectiveness, efficiency or user satisfaction over considering interaction behavior alone. The current chapter illustrates the possible advantages of combining psychological theory with more naive, data-driven methods for personalization. Doing so leverages the potential of data describing interaction behavior, with the benefits of having interpretable, meaningful user models.

The current chapter presented a number of psychological models that are used in personalization and how they can complement approaches that rely on behavioral data only. Furthermore, the chapter presents a number of ways in which user traits in terms of these models can be inferred from their interaction behavior, and presents ways in which users' inferred traits can be used to improve how systems are personalized. The benefit of this approach is illustrated with two studies that created a full system by incorporating the inference of psychological models as well as implementing them to personalize systems.

The current chapter considers mainly stable user traits, but more dynamic user characteristics can be considered as well. In principle, any latent trait or characteristic that is related to how users interact with systems and their needs of a system can be used. For example, expertise or experience with a system has shown to have an effect on how people prefer interacting with a system [69]. Similarly, in adaptive hypermedia the inferred level of knowledge dictates what information the system presents [70]. These characteristics are more prone to change, and (can) even change during the interaction with the system, which brings additional challenges with it. As they are related to both the way people interact with a system and what they need from a system, they are logical candidates for being incorporated in user models.

In summary, the chapter demonstrates that adopting a more theoretical perspective by incorporating user traits into personalized systems can lead to improvements of existing systems [29, 62], and that this approach can be used to build new systems [55, 57]. The presented findings warrant future research to focus on incorporating theoretical knowledge about users in personalized systems, instead of solely relying on behavioral data. Apart from providing directions for future research, the literature can be used to generate a blueprint that captures the idea of combining the theory and data-driven perspective on personalization (See Section 1.7.1).

1.7.1 Theory-driven personalization blueprint

The approach of incorporating psychological traits into personalization approaches can be formulated into a blueprint. The proposed multidisciplinary approach comprises both theoretical and methodological challenges.

Designing a theory-driven personalized system involves four steps. The first step (Section 1.7.1.1) is the identification of the right user traits and the right model to measure those. There is a virtually unlimited freedom of choice and making the right choice can be daunting. A model's suitability depends on the application, domain and the users. After identifying the right model, the second step (Section 1.7.1.2) consists of collecting data regarding the users' traits through surveys or through existing inference methods. After collecting this data, the third step (Section 1.7.1.3) is to find methods to infer the user traits measured in the previous step from natural interaction behavior with the target system. This third step is optional, as in some cases user traits might readily be available. The fourth step (Section 1.7.1.4) is incorporating the user traits in the personalized systems through formal user models. This section serves to explain these four steps in more detail.

1.7.1.1 Step 1: identifying the right psychological model

The first step consists of identifying the right user traits that can be used to improve systems through personalization. Two aspects play a role: first, the level of generality or specificity. The more specific, the more likely it is that the user traits can be inferred reliably and the more likely that they can be used to improve the system.

Another challenge is the availability of measurement instruments. Regardless of how the user traits will be measured, collecting ground-truth to incorporate in the personalization is essential. If validated measurement instruments are available, the chance of success is much higher as there is no need to develop and validate a new measurement instrument.

A drawback of generic models such as personality is that they are not necessarily strongly related to what a user needs from a system. More specific models are more likely to be related to users' needs. If no specific model is available, another possibility is that of developing an instrument to measure relevant user traits, either by designing it from scratch, or by combining existing instruments that measure relevant aspects. This step however then requires designing and validating a survey.

1.7.1.2 Step 2: collecting data regarding individual user traits

After identifying the right model, the second step is collecting data regarding the user traits of the individual users of a system. This can be done in two ways. On the one hand, this can be done through surveys as part of the system. Measurement instruments already exist for most psychological models. Collecting data then becomes a matter of administering surveys to users of the system. However, using surveys can be time consuming and interrupts the user from interacting with the system. An alternative way to acquire user data can be done by using inference methods through the use of external data sources (e. g., through the connectedness of single sign-on mechanisms).[4] If traits can be inferred from external data, collecting this data suffices to start personalizing the system without the need to interrupt the interaction flow between the user and the system.

1.7.1.3 Step 3: inferring individuals' user traits from interaction behavior

The data collected on the user traits in the second step can be used as ground- truth to build models that can infer user traits from natural behavior with the system. Section 1.4 describes for different models how user traits can be inferred.

Hauser et al. [57] performed this step in what they called a priming study. This priming study served to create a baseline model that inferred cognitive styles from clickstream behavior. Later on they relied on a Bayesian inference loop to relate certain aspects of behavior (e.g,. what elements users interacted with) to cognitive styles. Similarly, Frias-Martinez, Chen, and Liu [42] trained a neural network to infer cognitive styles from navigation behavior in a digital library.

As mentioned in Step 2, this inference from interaction behavior is in some cases not needed. When using, for example, single sign-on mechanisms, data from an external system can be used to make inferences as the interconnectedness can indefinitely provide information regarding the systems' users. A problem that occurs is that not all data from the external system is necessarily readily useful for personalization. By relying on psychological models, this data can be exploited through methods as described by Golbeck et al. [48] and Ferwerda, Schedl, and Tkalcic [33], resulting in information useful for personalization. The use of psychological models thus allows for maximum usage of data as even data that is not directly related to the system of interest can be exploited for the inference. Acquiring data from external sources can mitigate the cold-start problem that occurs when users use a system for the first time and no historical interaction behavior is available to base predictions on [102].

1.7.1.4 Step 4: incorporating user traits in personalization models

The third and final step consist of incorporating these traits in the personalization models. Most straightforwardly, this can be done in business rules (similar to as described

---

4 Buttons that allow users to register with or log into a system with accounts from other applications. For example, social networking services: "Login with your Facebook account."

in Rich [95]). If we know, for example, that a user has a visual cognitive style, a system might start putting more emphasis on visual information. In a more data-driven way, this can be done following Hauser et al. [57], who used a Gittins loop to decide what way of presenting content resulted in the desired behavior (purchasing). In such a way, the system learned how to adapt the content to the users' cognitive styles.

An additional advantage of incorporating user traits is that the user cold-start problem can be (partially) alleviated. If we rely on external data or surveys to infer user traits, the system can be personalized even for users for whom no interaction behavior is available. Hu and Pu [62] did this by using personality information for calculating predictions during the user cold-start stage. Personality information made it possible to calculate rating predictions even for users for whom no rating information was available.

References

[1]   Christopher Allinson and John Hayes. The cognitive style index: Technical manual and user guide. *Retrieved January* 13 (2012) 2014.

[2]   Gordon W. Allport and Henry S. Odbert. Trait-names: A psycho-lexical study. In: *Psychological monographs*, volume 47.1, 1936, p. i.

[3]   Yair Amichai-Hamburger and Gideon Vinitzky. Social network use and personality. *Computers in Human Behavior* 26(6) (2010) 1289–1295.

[4]   Yoram Bachrach et al. Personality and patterns of Facebook usage. In: *Proceedings of the 4th Annual ACM Web Science Conference*. ACM, 2012, pp. 24–32.

[5]   Mitja D. Back et al. Facebook Profiles Reflect Actual Personality, Not SelfIdealization. *Psychological Science* 21(3) (2010) 372–374. ISSN: 0956-7976. https://doi.org/10.1177/0956797609360756.

[6]   Mitja D. Back et al. Facebook profiles reflect actual personality, not selfidealization. *Psychological Science* 21(3) (2010) 372–374.

[7]   Marios Belk et al. Do human cognitive differences in information processing affect preference and performance of CAPTCHA? *International Journal of Human-Computer Studies* 84 (2015) 1–18.

[8]   Marios Belk et al. Modeling users on the World Wide Web based on cognitive factors, navigation behavior and clustering techniques. *The Journal of Systems and Software* 86(12) (2013) 2995–3012.

[9]   Joan-Isaac Biel, Oya Aran, and Daniel Gatica-Perez. You Are Known by How You Vlog: Personality Impressions and Nonverbal Behavior in YouTube. In: *ICWSM*, 2011.

[10]   Dirk Bollen, Mark Graus, and Martijn C. Willemsen. Remembering the Stars? Effect of Time on Preference Retrieval from Memory. In: *Proceedings of the Sixth ACM Conference on Recommender Systems. RecSys '12*. Dublin, Ireland: Association for Computing Machinery, 2012, pp. 217–220. ISBN: 9781450312707. https://doi.org/10.1145/2365952.2365998.

[11]   Vittorio V. Busato et al. The relation between learning styles, the Big Five personality traits and achievement motivation in higher education. *Personality and Individual Differences* 26(1) (1998) 129–140.

[12]   Jerome R. Busemeyer and James T. Townsend Decision field theory: a dynamic-cognitive approach to decision making in an uncertain environment. *Psychological Review* 100(3) (1993) 432–459.

[13]   Iván Cantador, Ignacio Fernández-Tobias, and Alejandro Bellogin. Relating personality types with user preferences in multiple entertainment domains. In: Shlomo Berkovsky, editor, *CEUR Workshop Proceedings*, 2013.

[14]   Christopher J. Carpenter. Narcissism on Facebook: Self-promotional and anti-social behavior. *Personality and Individual Differences* 52(4) (2012) 482–486.

[15]   Curtis A. Carver, Richard A. Howard, and William D. Lane. Enhancing student learning through hypermedia courseware and incorporation of student learning styles. *IEEE Transactions on Education* 42(1) (1999) 33–38.

[16]   Raymond B. Cattell. *Personality and motivation structure and measurement*, 1957.

[17]   Fabio Celli, Elia Bruni, and Bruno Lepri. Automatic personality and interaction style recognition from facebook profile pictures. In: *Proceedings of the 22nd ACM international conference on Multimedia*. ACM, 2014, pp. 1101–1104.

[18]   Hyun Jin Cha et al. Learning styles diagnosis based on user interface behaviors for the customization of learning interfaces in an intelligent tutoring system. In: *International Conference on Intelligent Tutoring Systems*. Springer, 2006, pp. 513–524.

[19]   Baiyun Chen and Justin Marcus. Students' self-presentation on Facebook: An examination of personality and self-construal factors. *Computers in Human Behavior* 28(6) (2012) 2091–2099.

[20]   Li Chen, Wen Wu, and Liang He. How personality influences users' needs for recommendation diversity? In: *CHI'13 Extended Abstracts on Human Factors in Computing Systems*. ACM, 2013, pp. 829–834.

[21]   Robert B. Cialdini. *Influence*, volume 3. A. Michel Port Harcourt, 1987.

[22]   Frank Coffield et al. *Learning styles and pedagogy in post-16 learning: A systematic and critical review*, 2004.

[23]   Philip J. Corr and Gerald Matthews. *The Cambridge handbook of personality psychology*. Cambridge University Press Cambridge, 2009.

[24]   Shaun W. Davenport et al. Twitter versus Facebook: Exploring the role of narcissism in the motives and usage of different social media platforms. *Computers in Human Behavior* 32 (2014) 212–220.

[25]   Azar Eftekhar, Chris Fullwood, and Neil Morris. Capturing personality from Facebook photos and photo-related activities: How much exposure do you need? *Computers in Human Behavior* 37 (2014) 162–170.

[26]   Nicole B. Ellison et al. Social network sites: Definition, history, and scholarship. *Journal of Computer-Mediated Communication* 13(1) (2007) 210–230.

[27]   Richard M. Felder, Linda K. Silverman, et al. Learning and teaching styles in engineering education. *Engineering Education* 78(7) (1988) 674–681.

[28]   Richard M. Felder and B. Solomon. Inventory of learning styles. *Retrieved January* 8 (1998) 1998.

[29]   Ignacio Fernández-Tobías et al. Alleviating the new user problem in collaborative filtering by exploiting personality information. *User Modeling and User-Adapted Interaction* 26(2–3) (2016) 221–255. ISSN: 0924-1868. https://doi.org/10.1007/s11257-016-9172-z.

[30]   Bruce Ferwerda and Markus Schedl. Enhancing Music Recommender Systems with Personality Information and Emotional States: A Proposal. In: *UMAP Workshops*, 2014.

[31]   Bruce Ferwerda, Markus Schedl, and Marko Tkalcic. Personality & Emotional States: Understanding Users' Music Listening Needs. In: *UMAP Workshops*, 2015.

[32]   Bruce Ferwerda, Markus Schedl, and Marko Tkalcic. Personality traits and the relationship with (non-) disclosure behavior on facebook. In: *Proceedings of the 25th International Conference Companion on World Wide Web*. International World Wide Web Conferences Steering Committee, 2016, pp. 565–568.

[33]   Bruce Ferwerda, Markus Schedl, and Marko Tkalcic. Predicting personality traits with instagram pictures. In: *Proceedings of the 3rd Workshop on Emotions and Personality in Personalized Systems 2015*. ACM, 2015, pp. 7–10.

[34]   Bruce Ferwerda, Markus Schedl, and Marko Tkalcic. Using instagram picture features to predict users' personality. In: *International Conference on Multimedia Modeling*. Springer, 2016, pp. 850–861.

[35]   Bruce Ferwerda and Marko Tkalcic. Predicting Users' Personality from Instagram Pictures: Using Visual and/or Content Features? In: *The 26th Conference on User Modeling, Adaptation and Personalization, Singapore*. 2018.

[36]   Bruce Ferwerda and Marko Tkalcic. You Are What You Post: What the Content of Instagram Pictures Tells About Users' Personality. In: *Companion Proceedings of the 23rd International on Intelligent User Interfaces: 2nd Workshop on Theory-Informed User Modeling for Tailoring and Personalizing Interfaces (HUMANIZE)*, 2018.

[37]   Bruce Ferwerda and Marko Tkalčič. Exploring the prediction of personality traits from drug consumption profiles. In: *Adjunct Publication of the 28th ACM Conference on User Modeling, Adaptation and Personalization*, 2020, pp. 2–5.

[38]   Bruce Ferwerda, Marko Tkalcic, and Markus Schedl. Personality Traits and Music Genre Preferences: How Music Taste Varies Over Age Groups. In: *Proceedings of the 1st Workshop on Temporal Reasoning in Recommender Systems (RecTemp) at the 11th ACM Conference on Recommender Systems, Como, August 31, 2017.*

[39]   Bruce Ferwerda, Marko Tkalcic, and Markus Schedl. Personality Traits and Music Genres: What Do People Prefer to Listen To? In: *Proceedings of the 25th Conference on User Modeling, Adaptation and Personalization*. ACM, 2017, pp. 285–288.

[40]   Bruce Ferwerda et al. Personality traits predict music taxonomy preferences. In: *Proceedings of the 33rd Annual ACM Conference Extended Abstracts on Human Factors in Computing Systems*. ACM, 2015, pp. 2241–2246.

[41]   Bruce Ferwerda et al. The Influence of Users' Personality Traits on Satisfaction and Attractiveness of Diversified Recommendation Lists. In: *EMPIRE@ RecSys*, 2016, pp. 43–47.

[42]   Enrique Frias-Martinez, Sherry Y. Chen, and Xiaohui Liu. Automatic cognitive style identification of digital library users for personalization. *Journal of the American Society for Information Science and Technology* 58(2) (2017) 237–251. https://doi.org/10.1002/asi.20477.

[43]   David C. Funder. *Personality judgment: A realistic approach to person perception*. Academic Press, 1999.

[44]   Patricio García et al. Evaluating Bayesian networks' precision for detecting students' learning styles. *Computers and Education* 49(3) (2007) 794–808.

[45]   Panagiotis Germanakos and Marios Belk. *Human-Centred Web Adaptation and Personalization*. Human-Computer Interaction Series. Cham: Springer International Publishing, 2016, pp. 336. ISBN: 978-3-319-28048-6. https://doi.org/10.1007/978-3-319-280509.

[46]   Jennifer Golbeck and Eric Norris. Personality, movie preferences, and recommendations. In: *Advances in Social Networks Analysis and Mining (ASONAM), 2013 IEEE/ACM International Conference on*. IEEE, 2013, pp. 1414–1415.

[47]   Jennifer Golbeck, Cristina Robles, and Karen Turner. Predicting personality with social media. In: *CHI'11 extended abstracts on human factors in computing systems*. ACM, 2011, pp. 253–262.

[48]   Jennifer Golbeck et al. Predicting personality from twitter. In: *Privacy, Security, Risk and Trust (PASSAT) and 2011 IEEE Third International Conference on Social Computing (SocialCom), 2011 IEEE Third International Conference on*. IEEE, 2011, pp. 149–156.

[49]   Samuel D. Gosling, Sam Gaddis, Simine Vazire et al. Personality impressions based on facebook profiles. In: *ICWSM 7*, 2007, pp. 1–4.

[50]   Samuel D. Gosling, Peter J. Rentfrow, and William B. Swann Jr. A very brief measure of the Big-Five personality domains. *Journal of Research in Personality* 37(6) (2003) 504–528.

[51]   Samuel D. Gosling et al. Manifestations of personality in online social networks: Self-reported Facebook-related behaviors and observable profile information. *Cyberpsychology, Behavior, and Social Networking* 14(9) (2011) 483–488.

[52]   Sabine Graf et al. Advanced adaptivity in learning management systems by considering learning styles. In: *Proceedings of the 2009 IEEE/WIC/ACM International Joint Conference on Web Intelligence and Intelligent Agent Technology-Volume 03*. IEEE Computer Society, 2009, pp. 235–238.

[53]   Sabine Graf and T.-C. Liu. Analysis of learners' navigational behaviour and their learning styles in an online course. *Journal of Computer Assisted Learning* 26(2) (2010) 116–131.

[54]   Sabine Graf and Tzu-Chien Liu. Supporting Teachers in Identifying Students' Learning Styles in Learning Management Systems: An Automatic Student Modelling Approach. *Journal of Educational Technology & Society* 12(4) (2009).

[55]   Mark P. Graus, Martijn C. Willemsen, and Chris C. P. Snijders. Personalizing a Parenting App: Parenting-Style Surveys Beat Behavioral Reading-Based Models. In: *Joint Proceedings of the ACM IUI 2018 Workshops*, 2018.

[56]   David M. Greenberg et al. Personality predicts musical sophistication. *Journal of Research in Personality* 58 (2015) 154–158.

[57]   J. R. Hauser et al. Website Morphing. *Marketing Science* 28(2) (2009) 202–223. ISSN: 0732-2399. https://doi.org/10.1287/mksc.1080.0459.

[58]   J. R. Hauser, G. L. Urban, and G. Liberali. Website Morphing 2.0: Technical and Implementation Advances Combined with the First Field Experiment of Website Morphing (2011). http://web.mit.edu/hauser/www/HauserArticles5.3.12/Hauser_Urban_Liberali_Website_Morphing_20_September2011.pdf.

[59]   John Hayes and Christopher W. Allinson. Cognitive style and the theory and practice of individual and collective learning in organizations. *Human Relations* 51(7) (1998) 847–871.

[60]   Peter Honey and Alan Mumford. *The learning styles helper's guide*. Peter Honey Publications Maidenhead, 2000.

[61]   Rong Hu and Pearl Pu. Exploring Relations between Personality and User Rating Behaviors. In: *UMAP Workshops*, 2013.

[62]   Rong Hu and Pearl Pu. Using Personality Information in Collaborative Filtering for New Users. In: *2nd ACM RecSys'10 Workshop on Recommender Systems and the Social Web*, 2010, pp. 17–24. URL: http://www.dcs.warwick.ac.uk/~ssanand/RSWeb_files/Proceedings_RSWEB-10.pdf#page=23.

[63]   Eugenia Y. Huang, Sheng Wei Lin, and Travis K. Huang. What type of learning style leads to online participation in the mixed-mode e-learning environment? A study of software usage instruction. *Computers and Education* 58(1) (2012) 338–349.

[64]   David John Hughes et al. A tale of two sites: Twitter vs. Facebook and the personality predictors of social media usage. *Computers in Human Behavior* 28(2) (2012) 561–569.

[65]   Michael A. Jenkins-Guarnieri, Stephen L. Wright, and Lynette M. Hudiburgh. The relationships among attachment style, personality traits, interpersonal competency, and Facebook use. *Journal of Applied Developmental Psychology* 33(6) (2012) 294–301.

[66]   Oliver P. John, Eileen M. Donahue, and Robert L. Kentle. *The big five inventory—versions 4a and 54*. 1991.

[67]   Carl Jung. *Psychological types*. Taylor & Francis, 2016.

[68]   Pythagoras Karampiperis et al. Adaptive cognitive-based selection of learning objects. *Innovations in Education and Teaching International* 43(2) (2006) 121–135.

[69]   Bart P. Knijnenburg, Niels J. M. Reijmer, and Martijn C. Willemsen. Each to his own. In: *Proceedings of the fifth ACM conference on Recommender systems – RecSys '11, New York*. New York, USA: ACM Press, 2011, p. 141. ISBN: 9781450306836. https://doi.org/10.1145/2043932.2043960.

[70]   Evgeny Knutov, Paul De Bra, and Mykola Pechenizkiy. AH 12 years later: a comprehensive survey of adaptive hypermedia methods and techniques. *New Review of Hypermedia and Multimedia* 15(1) (2009) 5–38. ISSN: 1361-4568. https://doi.org/10.1080/13614560902801608.

[71]   David A. Kolb. *Learning-style inventory: Self-scoring inventory and interpretation booklet: Revised scoring*. TRG, Hay/McBer, 1993.

[72]   Simone Kopeinik et al. Improving Collaborative Filtering Using a Cognitive Model of Human Category Learning. *The Journal of Web Science* 2(4) (2017) 45–61. https://doi.org/10.1561/106.00000007.

[73]   Yehuda Koren, Robert Bell, and Chris Volinsky. Matrix Factorization Techniques for Recommender Systems. *IEEE Computer* (2009) 42–49.

[74]   Maria Kozhevnikov. Cognitive styles in the context of modern psychology: Toward an integrated framework of cognitive style. *Psychological Bulletin* 133(3) (2007) 464.

[75]   Annabel Latham et al. A conversational intelligent tutoring system to automatically predict learning styles. *Computers and Education* 59(1) (2012) 95–109.

[76] Alixe Lay and Bruce Ferwerda. Predicting users' personality based on their 'liked' images on Instagram. In: *Companion Proceedings of the 23rd International on Intelligent User Interfaces: 2nd Workshop on Theory-Informed User Modeling for Tailoring and Personalizing Interfaces (HUMANIZE)*, 2018.

[77] Eunsun Lee, Jungsun Ahn, and Yeo Jung Kim. Personality traits and selfpresentation at Facebook. *Personality and Individual Differences* 69 (2014) 162–167.

[78] Elisabeth Lex et al. Psychology-informed Recommender Systems. *Foundations and Trends® in Information Retrieval* 15(2) (2021) 134–242. ISSN: 1554-0669. https://doi.org/10.1561/1500000090.

[79] Taiyu Lin. Cognitive profiling towards formal adaptive technologies in web-based learning communities. *International Journal of Web Based Communities* 1(1) (2004) 103–108.

[80] Nikolina Ljepava et al. Personality and social characteristics of Facebook non-users and frequent users. *Computers in Human Behavior* 29(4) (2013) 1602–1607.

[81] Bernd Marcus, Franz Machilek, and Astrid Schütz. Personality in cyberspace: Personal web sites as media for personality expressions and impressions. *Journal of Personality and Social Psychology* 90(6) (2006) 1014.

[82] Samuel Messick. The nature of cognitive styles: Problems and promise in educational practice. *Educational Psychologist* 19(2) (1984) 59–74.

[83] Alan Miller. Cognitive styles: An integrated model. *Educational Psychology* 7(4) (1987) 251–268.

[84] Danijela Milosevic et al. Adaptive learning by using scos metadata. *Interdisciplinary Journal of E-Learning and Learning Objects* 3(1) (2007) 163–174.

[85] T. J. F. Mitchell, Sherry Y. Chen, and R. D. Macredie. Cognitive styles and adaptive web-based learning. *Psychology of Education Review* 29(1) (2005) 34–42.

[86] Kelly Moore and James C. McElroy. The influence of personality on Facebook usage, wall postings, and regret. *Computers in Human Behavior* 28(1) (2012) 267–274.

[87] Daniel Müllensiefen et al. The Musicality of Non-Musicians: An Index for Assessing Musical Sophistication in the General Population. *PLOS ONE* 9(2) (2014). https://doi.org/10.1371/journal.pone.0089642.

[88] Isabel Briggs Myers. The Myers-Briggs Type Indicator: Manual (1962).

[89] Daniel J. Ozer and Veronica Benet-Martinez. Personality and the prediction of consequential outcomes. *Annual Review of Psychology* 57 (2006) 401–421.

[90] Ebru Özpolat and Gözde B. Akar. Automatic detection of learning styles for an e-learning system. *Computers and Education* 53(2) (2009) 355–367.

[91] Kyparisia A. Papanikolaou et al. Personalizing the Interaction in a Web-based Educational Hypermedia System: the case of INSPIRE. *User Modeling and User-Adapted Interaction* 13(3) (2003) 213–267.

[92] Lin Qiu et al. You are what you tweet: Personality expression and perception on Twitter. *Journal of Research in Personality* 46(6) (2012) 710–718.

[93] Daniele Quercia et al. The personality of popular facebook users. In: *Proceedings of the ACM 2012 conference on computer supported cooperative work*. ACM, 2012, pp. 955–964.

[94] Francesco Ricci, Lior Rokach, and Bracha Shapira. Recommender systems: introduction and challenges. In: *Recommender systems handbook*, 2015, pp. 1–34.

[95] Elaine Rich. User modeling via stereotypes. *Cognitive Science* 3(4) (1979) 329–354.

[96] Richard Riding and Indra Cheema. Cognitive Styles—an overview and integration. *Educational Psychology* 11(3–4) (1991) 193–215. https://doi.org/10.1080/0144341910110301.

[97] Richard Riding and Indra Cheema. Cognitive styles—an overview and integration. *Educational Psychology* 11(3–4) (1991) 193–215.

[98] Jenny Rosenberg and Nichole Egbert. Online impression management: Personality traits and concerns for secondary goals as predictors of self-presentation tactics on Facebook. *Journal of Computer-Mediated Communication* 17(1) (2011) 118.

[99] Craig Ross et al. Personality and motivations associated with Facebook use. *Computers in Human Behavior* 25(2) (2009) 578–586.

[100] Tracii Ryan and Sophia Xenos. Who uses Facebook? An investigation into the relationship between the Big Five, shyness, narcissism, loneliness, and Facebook usage. *Computers in Human Behavior* 27(5) (2011) 1658–1664.

[101] David Adrian Sanders and Jorge Bergasa-Suso. Inferring learning style from the way students interact with a computer user interface and the WWW. *IEEE Transactions on Education* 53(4) (2010) 613–620.

[102] Andrew I. Schein et al. Methods and metrics for cold-start recommendations. In: *Proceedings of the 25th annual international ACM SIGIR conference on Research and development in information retrieval SIGIR 02 46.Sigir*, 2002, pp. 253–260. ISSN: 01635840. https://doi.org/10.1145/564376.564421.

[103] Johann Schrammel, Christina Köffel, and Manfred Tscheligi. Personality traits, usage patterns and information disclosure in online communities. In: *Proceedings of the 23rd British HCI group annual conference on people and computers: Celebrating people and technology*. British Computer Society, 2009, pp. 169–174.

[104] Cristina Segalin et al. What your Facebook profile picture reveals about your personality. In: *Proceedings of the 2017 ACM on Multimedia Conference*. ACM, 2017, pp. 460–468.

[105] Gwendolyn Seidman. Self-presentation and belonging on Facebook: How personality influences social media use and motivations. *Personality and Individual Differences* 54(3) (2013) 402–407.

[106] Marcin Skowron et al. Fusing social media cues: personality prediction from twitter and instagram. In: *Proceedings of the 25th international conference companion on world wide web*. International World Wide Web Conferences Steering Committee, 2016, pp. 107–108.

[107] Jason L. Skues, Ben Williams, and Lisa Wise. The effects of personality traits, selfesteem, loneliness, and narcissism on Facebook use among university students. *Computers in Human Behavior* 28(6) (2012) 2414–2419.

[108] Stefan Stieger et al. Who commits virtual identity suicide? Differences in privacy concerns, internet addiction, and personality between Facebook users and quitters. *Cyberpsychology, Behavior, and Social Networking* 16(9) (2013) 629–634.

[109] Marko Tkalcic, Amra Delic, and Alexander Felfernig. *Personality, Emotions, and Group Dynamics*. Springer, 2018.

[110] Marko Tkalčič et al. Personality correlates for digital concert program notes. In: *International Conference on User Modeling, Adaptation, and Personalization*. Springer, 2015, pp. 364–369.

[111] Evangelos Triantafillou et al. The value of adaptivity based on cognitive style: an empirical study. *British Journal of Educational Technology* 35(1) (2004) 95106.

[112] Nikos Tsianos et al. User-Centric Profiling on the Basis of Cognitive and Emotional Characteristics: An Empirical Study. In: *International Conference on Adaptive Hypermedia and Adaptive Web-Based Systems*. Springer, 2008, pp. 214–223.

[113] Ernest C. Tupes and Raymond E. Christal. Recurrent personality factors based on trait ratings. *Journal of Personality* 60(2) (1992) 225–251.

[114] Patti M. Valkenburg and Jochen Peter. Social consequences of the Internet for adolescents: A decade of research. *Current Directions in Psychological Science* 18(1) (2009) 1–5.

[115] James E. Villaverde, Daniela Godoy, and Analıa Amandi. Learning styles' recognition in e-learning environments with feed-forward neural networks. *Journal of Computer Assisted Learning* 22(3) (2006) 197–206.

[116] Kua Hua Wang. et al. Learning styles and formative assessment strategy: enhancing student achievement in Web-based learning. *Journal of Computer Assisted Learning* 22(3) (2006) 207–217.

[117] Stephan Winter et al. Another brick in the Facebook wall-How personality traits relate to the content of status updates. *Computers in Human Behavior* 34 (2014) 194–202.

[118] Herman A. Witkin et al. Field-dependent and field-independent cognitive styles and their educational implications. *Review of Educational Research* 47(1) (1977) 1–64.

[119] Yen-Chun Jim Wu, Wei-Hung Chang, and Chih-Hung Yuan. Do Facebook profile pictures reflect user's personality? *Computers in Human Behavior* 51 (2015) 880–889.

[120] Nick Z. Zacharis. The effect of learning style on preference for web-based courses and learning outcomes. *British Journal of Educational Technology* 42(5) (2011) 790–800.

[121] Li-Fang Zhang. Thinking styles and the big five personality traits. *Educational Psychology* 22(1) (2002) 17–31.

[122] Qian Zhao et al. From Preference into Decision Making: Modeling User Interactions in Recommender Systems. In: *Proceedings of the 13th ACM Conference on Recommender Systems. RecSys'19*. Copenhagen, Denmark: Association for Computing Machinery, 2019, pp. 29–33. ISBN: 9781450362436. https://doi.org/10.1145/3298689.3347065.

Jürgen Ziegler and Benedikt Loepp

2 User-centered recommender systems

Abstract: Recommender systems aim at facilitating users' search and decision-making when they are faced with a large number of available options, such as buying products online or selecting music tracks to listen to. A broad range of machine learning models and algorithms has been developed that aim at predicting users' assessment of unseen items and at recommending items that best match their interests. However, it has been shown that optimizing the system in terms of algorithm accuracy often does not result in a correspondingly high level of user satisfaction. Therefore, a more user-centric approach to developing recommender systems is needed that better takes into account users' actual goals, the current context and their cognitive demands. In this chapter, we discuss a number of techniques and design aspects that can contribute to increasing transparency, user understanding and interactive control of recommender systems. Furthermore, we present methods for evaluating systems from a user perspective and point out future research directions.

Keywords: Recommender systems, visualization, interactive recommending, explanations, evaluation

2.1 Introduction

Recommender systems (RS) aim at supporting users in their search and decision-making process when interacting with online systems in a variety of application domains, such as e-commerce, media streaming or social media. Due to the very large number of items typically available on such platforms, RS have become widespread, almost indispensable tools for counteracting the choice overload problem that often results from such large sets of options. In contrast to other types of AI-based systems, RS address the task of preferential choice where there is not a single correct outcome but a ranking of options that may match the user's preferences to different degrees and that is, therefore, mostly personalized.

The development of RS has in the past been largely driven from an algorithmic perspective, focusing on algorithm effectiveness and accuracy, defined as correctly predicting the user's likely choices based on signals collected from past user interactions with the system [51]. These signals may stem from the target user's interactions with items and their features in content-based filtering methods, whereas in the popular collaborative filtering approach, both data obtained from the target user and from other, similar users are leveraged to generate recommendations. The signals exploited may consist in explicit user feedback such as ratings submitted for products chosen or implicitly collected data such as item clicks, viewing time or other interaction data, from which a per-

https://doi.org/10.1515/9783110988567-002

sonalized user model is constructed. In the prevalent algorithmic perspective, users are mostly only treated as sources of such preference signals. The content of the stored user model and the working of the recommendation process can neither be inspected nor controlled by the user. Most RS can therefore be described as black boxes that prevent users from understanding which data are used and how the output is created. Moreover, the training of RS algorithms is typically based on historical data sets of preference signals with the aim of accurately predicting user feedback that has happened in the past, not taking into account the user's current goals, which may be context-dependent and short-term [40]. As a consequence, users may find it difficult to assess the suitability of the recommendations, feel dominated by the system or distrust the RS altogether [33].

The purely algorithmic perspective with its focus on accuracy has increasingly been criticized as insufficient for achieving user-centric quality criteria such as perceived recommendation quality, diversity or trustworthiness of the recommendations [50]. The turn to a more user-centric development and evaluation of RS has produced a considerable number of studies in recent years that aim at making RS user-controllable and more transparent. One implication of this user-centric turn is that aspects of the RS user interface, e. g., the visual presentation of the items, have been receiving more attention. Also, RS mostly do not provide means for the user to influence the recommendation process and the resulting recommendations, which are typically presented in an all-or-none fashion. To increase user control, various interactive techniques have been proposed that change the recommendation process into a multiturn dialog between user and system [46]. Interacting with a RS can involve various aspects of the process, such as interactively specifying one's preferences [59], selecting appropriate recommendation methods or influencing their functioning [20, 27], and critiquing, i. e., modifying the attributes of an item to receive updated recommendations [18].

Adding to the lack of control, conventional RS are typically not transparent, and their outcome is hard to understand due to their black-box characteristics. Users are mostly not able to understand why a certain item is recommended and whether it really matches their needs and preferences. One way to address the lack of transparency is to provide explanations. Various explanation methods have been proposed in recent years, aiming at promoting transparency and intelligibility of the RS [81], factors that can also increase trust in the system [69]. Beyond explaining recommendations, providing users with means for interactive control can also increase transparency and user comprehension. Techniques that allow users to interactively explore the available options, to modify their user model or to influence the recommendation algorithm and its input may all foster understanding. These techniques can help to answer what-if questions and to gain a better understanding through counterfactual exploration [90]. Such techniques, however, are very rarely used in real-world applications yet.

The present chapter does not aim at providing a complete account of the large number of recommendation techniques and HCI-related aspects. For a more complete treatment, the reader is referred to comprehensive sources such as the Recommender Systems Handbook by Ricci et al. [73].

In this chapter, we provide an overview of design aspects of RS that are pertinent from a user-centric perspective without aiming at a comprehensive coverage of the large range of recommendation techniques and their implications for users. The rest of the chapter is organized as follows: In the next section, we address the presentation and visualization of recommendations. Subsequently, we present a range of interactive methods for increasing user control. We begin this section by discussing methods for eliciting user preferences, followed by an overview of methods for controlling the recommendation process. Furthermore, conversational recommenders are discussed as an increasingly important interactive recommendation technique. In the next section, we briefly review explanation methods for RS, followed by a section on metrics and methods for evaluating RS from a user-centric perspective. Finally, we sketch out some future research directions.

2.2 Presentation and visualization of recommendations

An increasing body of research has provided evidence that informativeness and style of presenting recommendations can have a large influence on user choices. In the simplest case, recommendations are shown as short textual list entries containing only very limited descriptive information. Yet, the availability of more detailed product information appears to positively influence users' perception of RS and can enhance user trust in the system [79].

As one of the few works addressing presentation issues with regards to the recommended items, Beel and Dixon [9] compared seven variants of a recommendation panel, varying the visibility of thumbnails, abstracts and additional information. They found that already small changes can have a large effect on click-through rate, and that the best performance was achieved with the version where additional information could be obtained on mouseover. In document retrieval and recommending, short snippets or summaries extracted from the source documents are often presented to allow users to predict the utility of an item for their current search task [19]. Also, nontextual material, such as movie poster images, can help users predict the quality of recommended items [57]. Explanatory information related to other users' ratings or reviews has also been found helpful for assessing the value of recommendations (see Section 2.4 as well as Chapter 6 (Explanations and user control in recommender systems) in this volume).

2.2.1 Recommendation lists

Recommended items are conventionally presented as lists, either displayed with a vertical or horizontal orientation. Jugovac and Jannach [46] discuss a variety of design aspects, such as item ordering, list label, list length and item descriptions, which may influence users' perception and acceptance of the recommendations. The position of an item is one of the strongest predictors for the probability that the user clicks on the item. This position bias [7] has long been shown for search result pages in information retrieval, but it is also present in recommendation lists [34]. Usually, items are positioned based on their predicted relevance score, where the item with the highest score is placed at the beginning of the list. However, taking additional factors such as attractiveness, diversity or novelty into account when producing the final ordering may increase click-through rate and lead to higher user satisfaction [85, 92].

List length is also a critical factor. Several studies in physical choice settings have shown that increasing the number of available products too much may result in choice overload, i. e., increased decision time and decreased satisfaction with the product finally chosen or may even prevent users from making a decision [37]. However, as Scheibehenne, Greifeneder and Todd [77] show in their meta-analysis, the occurrence of choice overload may depend on users' domain knowledge and the distinctiveness of their goals, as well as on the presence of dominant items in the choice set. Bollen et al. [10] compared recommendation lists of 5 and 20 items. While the larger list increased the attractiveness of the recommendations, it also increased choice difficulty; yet these opposing effects seemed to neutralize each other, resulting in the same level of choice satisfaction as for the shorter list. In addition, the authors found that higher diversity of the contained items increased the perceived attractiveness of the list. They conjecture there might be a U-shaped relation between list length and user satisfaction with an optimal number in the medium range. In general, however, striking the right balance between an overly constrained choice set and choice overload may depend on a number of factors, including product domain, used device and psychological characteristics of the user, e. g., whether he or she tends to make decisions based on intuition rather than reason.

2.2.2 List layouts and multilists

It has often been argued that the typical presentation as a ranked list is not optimal in several regards, e. g., because it may intensify position bias. Different layouts were compared by Chen and Tsoi [17], who found that in list and grid layouts users more often clicked on the top recommendations, while in a circular layout, also lower-ranked items were frequently clicked. Single lists also have the disadvantage of not conveying a meaningful organization of the items beyond their ranking. Grouping items by factors such as semantic similarity or closeness to user preferences and presenting them in separate lists can support the user's search and understanding of the recommendations. In an eye-tracking study, Chen and Pu [16] found that in a grouped layout, attention was more equally dispersed among the items and users more often made a choice.

In recent years, carousel interfaces have become a popular means. For instance, Netflix and Amazon show multiple lists of recommendations one below the other, each containing items with common characteristics. Thus, users can explore a more diverse range of recommendations and find items that better match their current needs [39]. Carousels have also been found to reduce the number of interaction steps [71]. The semantic organization is usually conveyed by adding a label to each list. For the grouping, various concepts may be used, such as item features (e. g., movie genres), popularity, or user preference. Defining a suitable set of categories is an important design challenge [21]. Moreover, carousels increase the complexity of the ranking problem, since not only the ranking within a list has to be considered, but also the vertical ranking of the lists.

2.2.3 Visualization of recommendations

Graphical methods offer a number of advantages that can help overcome the limitations of a listwise presentation of recommendations. For instance, they can present large sets of items more effectively and reveal relationships among items. Various techniques from the area of information visualization have been adopted for RS, which can be classified according to the following dimensions:
- Visual structure, e. g., sequence, set or cluster, graph, multidimensional layout, map
- Scope, i. e., only recommended items, parts of the item space, entire item space
- Interactivity, e. g., rating, weighting, filtering

Venn diagrams are examples that allow users to inspect the overlap of sets of recommended items filtered by different criteria [65]. Hence, users can explore items that either fully or partially match their filter settings, which has been found to be more engaging than lists and to improve user experience. Venn diagrams have also been used to explain similarity between users in social recommendations [83]. In this area, graphs presented as node-link diagrams constitute another useful visualization method. For example, Gretarsson et al. [25] use a multilayer graph in which users, their preferences, social peers and recommendations are displayed as nodes. Users can manipulate the position of these nodes, thus influencing their relevance for the recommendations. In a user study, the authors found that users experienced a higher level of control and better understood the underlying collaborative filtering process. Petridis et al. [68] proposed the music recommender *TastePaths*, which displays artists as nodes in a graph. They found that the system can educate users about relationships between artists, thus helping them discover content they were not aware of.

Scatterplots combine a two-dimensional layout of items with interactive filtering. In *MusiCube* [76], users can select musical features (e. g., tempo, acoustic texture) to change the axes of a scatterplot of songs, where recommendations are highlighted by coloring. *Scatter Viz* [82] is a social RS that recommends academic scholars based on a research profile. In a user study, the proposed interface performed better than a list-wise presentation on several user-centric dimensions such as trust, supportiveness and intention to reuse.

Maps have been found especially useful for providing an overview of large item sets while conveying information about the item similarity, i. e., similar items are usually closer together. In RS, maps are mostly automatically generated projections of latent dimensions, e. g., derived from collaborative rating data, onto a 2D or 3D space. This can provide a global context for the recommendations by positioning them in relation to the other available items, thus fostering user exploration and comprehension. For instance, in *TVLand* [22], clusters of TV shows are displayed as a map with a heatmap overlay to indicate recommendations. In *MoodPlay* [5], paths shown on the map additionally display the user's previous or suggested future interactions.

However, only a few works have addressed interactive preference manipulation in maps. *MovieLandscape* is a 3D map that offers means for changing preferences through "landscape engineering" [53]. Users can raise the elevation of areas they are interested in, while "digging" indicates lower interest in items located in this area (Figure 2.1). Consequently, users can express their preferences for a range of items, instead of being limited to rating single items, as is usually the case. In a user study, the authors found that the map helped users understand their user profile in relation to the rest of the item space and become aware of the complete set of choice options. Treemaps are a more abstract form of maps, which have been used to display clusters of items in rectangular areas sized by the number of items in a category [74]. These maps have also been extended with interactive means for modifying preferences [54].

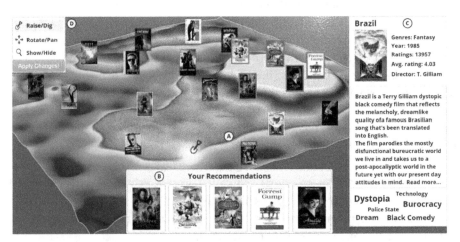

Figure 2.1: Example of a visualization of the item space: (A) Map with representative movie samples illustrating the different areas. Elevations represent the active user's preferences. Current recommendations are shown with colored border. (B) Additional recommendation panel. (C) Details of currently selected movie. (D) Palette of tools to modify the view and to reshape the landscape, leading to immediate recalculation of recommendations [53].

2.3 Preference elicitation and interactive control

Conventional RS computes recommendations and presents them in a single-shot fashion without users being able to influence the process. However, users often want to have more real-time control over the process to adapt the recommendations better to their situational needs. A higher sense of control has shown to be strongly related to user experience and to contribute considerably to user satisfaction [46, 50]. More recently, several interactive approaches to recommending have been proposed that address different aspects or phases of the process. Among these aspects are methods for eliciting user preferences, weighing the influence of different data sources or algorithms or critiquing recommended items. Also, conversational techniques, using either GUI interfaces or natural language dialogs have gained considerable attention recently.

2.3.1 Item ratings and comparisons

To provide personalized recommendations, RS must be able to learn about the users' preferences. In many RS, including successful commercial examples such as the ones used by Amazon and Netflix [23, 56], the only way for users to explicitly inform the RS about their preferences is to rate single items they have consumed or bought, an action which mostly only takes effect in later sessions. In experimental research settings, ratings for a set of items are often collected prior to using the RS for establishing a user model, but this approach is not practical in real-world applications. Ratings are usually provided in the form of unary (e. g., "likes"), binary (e. g., "thumbs up" or "thumbs down"),or ordinal (e. g., 1–5 stars scale) feedback [41].

Ideally, methods for eliciting preferences should motivate users to respond, help them formulate their preferences precisely and truthfully, handle conflicts and also allow them to revise what they told the system in earlier sessions [69]. These goals are often hard to achieve with single-item post-consumption ratings. The examples of *YouTube* and *Netflix* illustrate that the different rating types have different strengths and weaknesses.[1] For instance, when 5-star ratings were still in use on these platforms, users almost exclusively provided extreme ratings, resulting in bimodal rating distributions. This led the two RS providers years ago to shift to binary ratings. Recently, however, an opposite trend can be observed, e. g., on *Netflix*, where the "super like" was introduced to obtain richer preference data. Rating-based feedback has also been the subject of many experiments, showing that ratings may be noisy, inaccurate or unstable over time (Amatriain et al. [4]; Jones, Brun and Boyer [45]). In addition, the different types of feedback differ in terms of usage effort and cognitive load [62]. For these reasons, many

---

1 https://youtube.googleblog.com/2010/01/video-page-gets-makeover.html, https://media.netflix.com/en/company-blog/goodbye-stars-hello-thumbs/

real-world RS rely on *implicit* user-item feedback such as product page views, duration of page visits or purchases [41]. Since these data are often correlated with explicit feedback, and at the same time, much easier to obtain from a provider perspective [64], implicit feedback is widely adopted today for generating personalized recommendations [46]. In these cases, however, users have even less control over the recommendations and the interpretation of the results becomes more difficult.

Implicit or explicit user feedback mostly refers to single, complete items. Only a few authors have investigated approaches where users can express their preferences toward a number of item attributes, e. g., based on predefined metadata [2]. This is particularly useful in complex product domains, where certain features of a product are of particular relevance for the user, but it is also cognitively demanding and increases data sparsity. In general, providing ratings as *absolute* values have shown to be cognitively demanding and unreliable. As an alternative, expressing item preferences in a *relative* manner is inspired by consumer behavior in physical settings, where purchase decisions are usually made after comparing the products. Accordingly, comparison-based preference elicitation, which is often used in marketing research, has also been found to make ratings easier and to increase recommendation quality [75]. Jones, Brun and Boyer [45] were the first to present RS users with pairwise item comparisons as an alternative to asking them to rate single items one at a time (Figure 2.3, left). In a user study, they showed that decision-making can thus be facilitated, and preferences become more stable. Rokach and Kisilevich [75] proposed a similar method specifically for modern collaborative filtering approaches. The approach considers interdependencies between the items that are otherwise ignored and may therefore promote a more accurate modeling of user preferences.

A few authors have suggested to sample the items directly from a latent factor space as derived in state-of-the-art collaborative filtering algorithms such as matrix factorization. Loepp, Hussein and Ziegler [59] select representative items factor by factor, which enables users to choose between groups of items in a number of dialog steps, where each step corresponds to one factor of the underlying model (Figure 2.2). In a user study, the authors found that this approach provides a good trade-off between manual filtering mechanisms and a largely automated processing of item ratings. The approach proposed by Graus and Willemsen [24] confronts users in a number of steps with sets of recommended items, asking them to choose one item at a time. The diversity of the item sets is maximized in order to present users with the full set of choices and to learn as much as possible from their decisions. Several user experiments have shown that users prefer comparisons over rating items and find them easier for providing feedback on items from different parts of the item space. Moreover, comparisons turned out to be particularly useful for cold-start situations, where it may be difficult to motivate users to rate a sufficiently large number of items, which is needed for generating meaningful recommendations.

Figure 2.2: Example of a comparison-based preference elicitation, where users are presented with sets of items sampled from an underlying latent factor space [59].

2.3.2 Controlling the recommendation process and output

Some recent works aim more generally at providing user control over the recommendation methods and related RS components, or at producing output users can directly interact with. While still rare in real-world applications, the range of methods proposed in academia is relatively large. In the simplest forms, interactive widgets are provided that enable users to modify algorithm parameters [27] or choose from different algorithms [20]. In hybrid systems, which combine several algorithms to benefit from their individual advantages, the influence of each algorithm can be manipulated. A prominent example is the *TasteWeights* music RS proposed by Bostandjiev, O'Donovan and Höllerer [11]. As visible in Figure 2.3, sliders allow users to control the individual influence of preferred artists as well as of the data sources associated with the different recommendation methods. The connections between these entities and the resulting recommendations are highlighted graphically. A user experiment showed that this process of generating recommendations was perceived as more transparent, and that the visualization helped to understand the system's behavior. Moreover, the additional interaction capabilities led to considerable gains in perceived recommendation quality and overall satisfaction. Similar results were achieved with several successor systems of *TasteWeights* (see, e. g., Bostandjiev, O'Donovan and Höllerer [12]) as well as with other systems (see, e. g., Cardoso et al. [14]).

Other works focus on providing users control over the system's output. Example critiquing is one of the most prominent techniques [18], allowing them to iteratively change attribute values of the recommended items (the examples), either by selecting

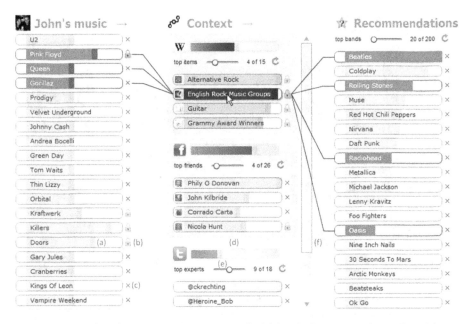

Figure 2.3: Screenshot of the TasteWeights system: On the left-hand side, users can change the weight of artists in their profile. In addition, they can adjust the influence of the different sources in the center column and immediately observe the effects on the recommendations, which are shown on the right-hand side ([11], used with permission of ACM, conveyed through Copyright Clearance Center, Inc.).

a different value or by indicating the direction of the desired change (e. g., higher or lower). Applying the critiques results in an immediate update of the recommendations. This way, users can start from a recommended item that already matches their needs (to some extent), but then indicate, e. g., a preference for cheaper products, products by another manufacturer or of a different color. This relies on the assumption that telling the system what is wrong with the results is easier than stating precise requirements in advance. Especially without being provided with cognitive clues, this is a particular problem in case of insufficient domain knowledge [88]. While early variants such as the *FindMe* system by Burke et al. [13] only allowed users to critique a single item property at a time, Reilly et al. [72] introduced compound critiques as a means to provide feedback simultaneously with respect to multiple item properties.

Example critiquing is mostly implemented based on predefined metadata, which may be costly to obtain. However, this is not necessarily a prerequisite. For example, tags generated by the user community can also be leveraged for implementing a critiquing mechanism [87]. In addition, Xie et al. [88] proposed a graph-based structure to represent past critiquing sessions, which allows them to suggest items that are compatible to the user's critique *and* similar to the items other users previously accepted in a similar situation. In a simulation study based on real-world data sets, this reduced the number of rounds in the critiquing process. Loepp et al. [58] combined this form of content-based critiquing with collaborative filtering, and found that with their *TagMF* method, users rate the recommendations significantly better in a number of dimensions than in the case of critiquing based exclusively on tags. Moreover, they provided a mechanism to let users adjust the system's output by selecting tags and applying individual weights to each selected tag. Using sliders to adjust the recommendations has received attention by other authors as well, in particular, in the music domain. For instance, Jin et al. [43] proposed an interface similar to the *TasteWeights* system, but with sliders that allow users to adjust the weight of selected artists or genres. Liang and Willemsen [55] use specific features such as energy and valence of songs to improve user control. In addition, they use a contour plot visualization to foster exploration of new genres. In general, several authors have suggested using information visualization techniques to present the system output in a way that allows users to manipulate how the recommendations are generated. These works have shown their potential in a number of user studies, but are often too complex to apply them widely. For an overview, we refer to Section 2.2.3 and to the survey paper by He, Parra and Verbert [28].

Finally, there exist a few approaches that aim at increasing the interactivity of other RS components. For example, interactive quizzes and gamification mechanisms have been proposed to extend the user model to capturing the user's personality [35, 80]. The systems by Baltrunas et al. [8] and Najafian, Wörndl and Braunhofer [61] are some of the few exceptions where users can decide which context information is taken into account—regardless of the fact maintaining a context model is increasingly considered essential for the success of RS [1].

2.3.3 Conversational recommendation approaches

Due to the recent advances in natural language processing based on deep learning techniques, natural language conversation has become another popular way of interacting with RS. Conversational recommender systems (CRS) try to detect the intentions of users in their textual or spoken utterances, e. g., expressing a preference or asking for a recommendation. In addition, the systems keep track of the conversation state. For instance, a dialog graph that describes (predefined) dialog states and the transitions between them can be used for "slot filling," i. e., the system asks questions about the user's preferences with respect to a certain set of item features. Alternatively, dialog engines such as the one used in Google's *Dialogflow* employ machine learning techniques to model a set of user intents, detect the most probable one and subsequently either ask a question or show a recommendation [38]. For a more detailed overview of the algorithms used in CRS, we refer to the survey paper by Jannach et al. [38].

Although CRS can use different modalities including speech, the dominant form of interaction is simply text-based. Only a few authors have investigated how to support users in answering the questions of a chatbot. Iovine et al. [36] present the *ConveRSE* framework, and found that users were less efficient in a purely text-based interface, in particular, in situations in which precise input was required. They conclude that when users need to choose from a set of options, other interaction strategies must be made available. Accordingly, Jin et al. [42] also implement buttons into a chatbot interface, but specifically for critiquing the recommendations. A user study showed that system-suggested critique dimensions increased user efficiency and recommendation variety, whereas critiquing in general led to higher user engagement. Moreover, the authors observed several effects of personal characteristics, e. g., participants with high domain knowledge and need for control were more likely to provide feedback. In another experiment, Jin et al. [44] studied the key qualities of CRS, taking into account important characteristics of conversations. They found that the adaptability of a chatbot and whether it understands the user positively affect the perceived trustworthiness and the intention to use the system again. Since this effect was mediated by user control, the authors attribute this to the fact that the interaction with a CRS is more natural and flexible than with a traditional RS. Alkan et al. [3] show that any noninteractive RS can be turned into a CRS. Two online user studies confirmed that users prefer the additional options to provide feedback they were thus able to provide over traditional ratings and likes. Nevertheless, one should keep in mind that users do not necessarily want to interact with a chatbot, e. g., because of a general reluctance to engage with virtual agents [84].

2.4 Explaining recommendations

Conventional RS suffer from the black-box problem since they do not provide users with the information necessary to understand and assess the recommendation process, the underlying data and the outcomes. Explaining recommendations is therefore increasingly considered an important means for making RS more transparent and intelligible for users. In this section, we will focus on selected user-centric aspects of explanations. For a more comprehensive treatment of the topic, we refer to Chapter 6 (Explanations and user control in recommender systems) in this volume as well as to recent surveys (Nunes and Jannach [63] and Zhang and Chen [93]).

Providing explanations for recommended items can serve different purposes [81]. For instance, explanations enable users to understand the suitability of the recommendations or why an item was recommended, and they may assist users in their decision-making. Providing explanations can also increase users' perception of transparency and their trust in the RS [69]. Also, personalizing the explanations has been found to positively affect their effectiveness.

The methods for generating explanations may be categorized based on the recommendation model used, the information provided and the style of presentation [93]. Among the most popular explanation approaches are the methods based on collaborative filtering, e. g., explanations like "based on your neighbors' ratings for this movie" [29], as well as on content-based methods that allow feature-based explanations, showing users how well certain item features match their preferences [86]. Explanations created in the collaborative filtering approach have mainly been based on ratings or implicit feedback of similar users. With the rapid advancements in natural language processing techniques in recent years, also textual feedback, and especially customer reviews, have been leveraged for explaining recommendations based on other users' assessments of the products. Review-based methods allow providing:

1) verbal summaries of reviews, using abstractive summarization through natural language generation [89],
2) a selection of helpful reviews (or excerpts) that might be relevant to the user, detected using deep learning techniques and attention mechanisms [15], and
3) an account of the pros and cons of item features, usually using topic modeling or aspect-based sentiment analysis [94]. This information can also be integrated into collaborative filtering algorithms like matrix factorization to generate both recommendations and aspect-based explanations.

The presentation format of explanations also plays an important role in fostering explanation helpfulness. Explanations can be provided in different forms of text (e. g., canned text, template-based, structured language), visualizations or other media formats [63]. Kouki et al. [52] proposed a series of explanations in a hybrid music RS, and tested, among others, the influence of the presentation format on users' perception. In this study, the authors found that textual explanations were perceived as more persuasive than the explanations provided using a visual format. However, users with greater visual familiarity perceived one of the visual format explanations more positively (a Venn diagram). Hernandez-Bocanegra and Ziegler [30] compared bar charts, tables and text providing statistical information about positively and negatively rated aspects in hotel reviews. They also manipulated the level of interactivity, i. e., whether users could click on links that led them to more detailed explanations and the original review text, if requested. While no main effect of presentation style was found, interactivity significantly increased the perceived explanation quality, effectiveness of the recommendations and trust. It was also found that psychological user characteristics influenced the perception of the explanations. More rational decision makers as well as more socially aware participants rated explanations higher in several dimensions. This influence of psychological characteristics was also found in other studies.

These findings indicate that users may prefer a high level of interactive control not only over the recommendation process but also over the explanations. In this respect, conversational recommending approaches (see Section 2.3.3) offer interesting possibilities, where users can more freely express their preferences, but may also query the system for information depending on their current explanatory needs. A limited number of developments have begun providing explanatory information in a conversational style, either embedded in the dialog flow of a CRS [67] or in the form of a separate conversational explainer based on information extracted from customer reviews [31]. In this study, questions that users asked about hotel recommendations generated by the system were collected, resulting in a data set consisting of 1806 questions. It was found that the questions could be classified into two main types: domain-related intents (regarding hotels and their features) and system-related intents (regarding the algorithm or the system input). Interestingly, only 24 out of 1,806 questions could be classified as system-related questions [32]. This indicates that users are much more interested in obtaining a deeper understanding of the recommended items and their features than in learning about the recommendation process or the input to the process.

To further explore explanatory needs for the dominant class, domain-related questions were further classified according to the following dimensions:

–   Scope: Is the question about a single item, several items or indefinite (not referring to specific items)?
–   Comparison: Do users ask for comparative information about two or more items?
–   Assessment: Does the question refer to facts about an item, or to users' subjective assessments? Furthermore, questions about why the system recommended an item were included in this category.
–   Detail: Does the question refer to specific features or aspects of an item, or to an item in its entirety?

The classification results showed that the majority of questions referred to facts about a hotel (e. g., "does hotel X have a pool?"), followed by subjective assessment questions (e. g., "how is the food at hotel X?"). Overall, these results indicate that users want to obtain information that helps them to form their own opinion about the recommended items, rather than to understand the inner workings of the algorithm. This also suggests that providing means for interactively exploring the recommendations under a variety of perspectives might be helpful to satisfy users' explanatory needs, an aspect that deserves more attention in future research.

2.5 Evaluation of recommender systems

Conventional evaluation methods for RS are focused on gauging the accuracy of the recommendations, which is often considered an objective measurement approach. The recommendation task consists in either predicting missing ratings or in learning a ranking of the items that is supposed to reflect their relevance for the user. Metrics such as mean absolute error (MAE) and root mean squared error (RMSE) measure the difference between the ratings predicted by the system and those actually provided by the users for the items. For ranking-based methods, metrics such as mean average precision (MAP) and normalized discounted cumulative gain (NDCG) are typically used. These metrics apply to entire recommendation lists and also take positional effects into account. For an overview of metrics, we refer to the overview provided by Gunawardana, Shani and Yogev [26].

From a user-centric perspective, however, accuracy-focused techniques are limited by several shortcomings. First, these evaluations are mostly performed in offline experiments, which are retrospective because they are based on user feedback already collected in the past and represented in static data sets. Therefore, they may not reflect the user's expected assessment of the items in the current context of use, which may create specific or transient needs different from the user's long-term preferences. Second, user satisfaction with the recommendations does not only depend on accuracy, as measured by the methods mentioned above, but also on a number of other, subjective factors that influence users' experience with the system [49, 50]. Accordingly, online A/B tests and user studies have gained increasing attention in recent years, which capture users' behavior and assessment of the recommendations and the entire system in a more timely and comprehensive manner. A limitation that is difficult to overcome in experimental studies is that actual consumption or usage of the recommendations is rarely possible, even though this has shown to strongly affect the assessment of recommendations. In two user studies, Loepp et al. [57] compared the subjective perception of recommendations before and after participants listened to the recommended songs or watched the recommended movies. The results suggest that users may have difficulties in gauging the value of recommendations reasonably well before actually having experienced it. For instance, prior to consuming the items, they underrated songs and were less satisfied with their choices, which they made from a list containing only descriptive information. This effect was less visible in the movie domain where additional material such as pictures of movie posters was shown. For experimental studies, this implies that it is important to present sufficient information about the items, allowing participants to provide ratings that approximate their assessment after having experienced the items.

2.5.1 User-centric quality factors

Beyond offline accuracy, a large number of other factors have been considered at least equally important for evaluating a RS from a user-centric perspective [26, 47, 50]. Among the most frequently discussed factors are the following:

–   *Novelty:* An inherent goal of RS is to suggest items that users do not know about. In user experiments, this is easy to measure by asking participants about the perceived novelty of recommended items, but it is also possible in offline experiments, e. g., by using accuracy metrics that reward systems differently depending on whether they recommend popular items [26].
–   *Serendipity:* A serendipitous recommendation, in contrast, refers to an item that is not only novel, but also pleasantly surprising as the user did not actively look for it [47]. Without serendipity, users may be trapped in a filter bubble [66], i. e., recommendations limited to items similar to what the user has rated positively in the past, which is often the case in content-based approaches. However, there is no real consensus on how to define serendipity, which makes it difficult to measure in a standardized way [47].

- *Diversity:* The variety of the items in a recommendation set is another important recommendation quality. Studies have shown that high diversity can increase user satisfaction and make it easier to settle on one of the recommended items [10]. In contrast to other metrics, this can be measured well even in offline experiments, namely, by calculating item-item similarity based on item metadata or latent factors as derived from collaborative filtering data [47].
- *Trustworthiness:* Trusting the recommendations is an important success factor for RS. However, trust does not only depend on the quality of the recommendations but also on the experience with the entire system in which they are embedded and the trustworthiness of its provider. Increasing confidence in the recommendations themselves can be a reason for including items in the recommendations list that are *not* novel, as they can provide an anchor to determine whether or not a system produces meaningful results [26]. Providing effective explanations for the recommendations given (see Section 2.4) can also increase user trust. Trust can be measured by asking participants in a user study or by considering recommendations accepted by users in online studies trustworthy. However, it is difficult to gain insights from offline experiments since trust depends on the user's interaction and experience with the system.

Various other factors may also influence user experience with a RS. Usability of the system or its esthetic appeal generally impact user perception for which user experience questionnaires such as UEQ-S [78] can be applied. For interactive recommending techniques, assessing the quality of the interface and the interaction are very relevant factors. The controllability and transparency factors are of particular importance for interactive techniques [28]. Only a few works have yet addressed criteria for the increasingly important class of conversational recommenders based on natural language dialogs. The understanding of users' written or spoken utterances and the quality of system responses are primary quality aspects in such systems, but factors relating to the communication process may be of similar importance. Jin et al. [44] propose several factors particularly relevant for recommenders using conversational user interfaces (CUI), including positivity, attentiveness and coordination, which can be summarized under the concept of rapport. Positivity refers to the friendliness and mutual caring of the communication partners while attentiveness describes a focused and cohesive interaction, and coordination of a synchronous and harmonious communication.

2.5.2 Evaluation frameworks and questionnaires

To assess RS quality in a more reliable and standardized form, several evaluation frameworks have been proposed that provide a statistically proven set of questionnaire items organized according to a number of quality factors. Such frameworks are an important means for comparing systems against baselines and alternative design options. Dimensional frameworks organize the questionnaire items around a set of high-level dimensions, each of which is hierarchically decomposed into a set of constructs that are measured by concrete items, often using Likert scales. A well-known example of this type is ResQue [70], which is organized according to the dimensions perceived system qualities, users' beliefs resulting from these qualities, their subjective attitudes and their behavioral intentions. The dimension perceived system qualities, for example, is decomposed into the constructs: recommendation quality (comprising constructs such as perceived accuracy, novelty, attractiveness and diversity), interface adequacy (covering information provided and presentational aspects), interaction adequacy (related to preference elicitation and modification) and information sufficiency and explicability. Further subordinate factors comprise, among others, perceived usefulness and ease of use, control and transparency, overall satisfaction and trust, as well items related to usage and purchase intentions.

In ResQue, it is already assumed that there are influencing relationships among the constructs of the framework. This notion is extended by the framework proposed by Knijnenburg, Willemsen and Kobsa [48], Knijnenburg and Willemsen [49], which is based on a structural model representing relationships that can be causally interpreted. The model proposes a chain of relationships leading from objective system properties to subjectively perceived system aspects, which in turn influence user experience and interaction. The framework has been validated in a number of user studies, which confirmed that objective system aspects such as the recommendation or preference elicitation method, influence the assessment of subjective system aspects, including general usability, and, in particular, dimensions such as perceived recommendation quality and diversity. The assessment of these aspects, in turn, affects user experience, e. g., regarding the perceived system effectiveness, the perceived effort during the recommendation process, and the user's satisfaction with the items finally chosen. Finally, the user experience is strongly related to the user's interaction behavior, whereas all these dimensions are moderated by personal and situational characteristics. This high-level structural model can be populated by different constructs and concrete items depending on the purpose of the study. A major advantage of this model is that it can be tested statistically by structural equation modeling, which can provider deeper insights than simple, single-level evaluation questionnaires.

2.5.3 Evaluation methods

Accuracy-related evaluations mostly use either user-item feedback data that have been collected from the target RS in use, or existing data sets. If such data are available, a new or optimized recommendation method can be investigated in a relatively simple and inexpensive manner through offline experiments [26], which can be especially helpful for choosing an appropriate recommendation algorithm. However, user-centric evaluation requires the involvement of humans in the evaluation procedure.

In industry, A/B testing is a popular approach for evaluating the effectiveness of different variants of a system in production. Through A/B testing, the effects a modification may have on users' behavior, and to a limited extent, on their actual satisfaction, e. g., when click-through rates or purchases increase, can be analyzed. To perform an A/B test, one or more groups of randomly selected users are presented with the modified system, usually without being aware that they are in an experimental condition. The modified system may implement a new recommendation method, present recommendations differently or provide a novel interaction mechanism. The log data is then compared with the control group, i. e., users who see the original system variant. Large companies are known to run several hundred A/B tests simultaneously on their platforms. A/B testing is an exploratory approach based on objective interaction data that can yield important insights, especially when large numbers of users are involved. Its explanatory power, however, is limited since users' subjective assessments are not captured. Further challenges arise, for example, a specific technical infrastructure is required, which is well illustrated by Xu et al. [91] for the example of LinkedIn.

Conducting user studies (either in the lab or online) allows performing deeper analyses of users' perceptions and judgements of the system, which may elucidate reasons for their interaction behavior and provide more generalizable insights than can be gained from log data. Lab studies are typically done with smaller numbers of participants but can yield more extensive feedback by applying think-aloud techniques or perceptual data captured through eye tracking. Much larger numbers of participants, typically several hundred, are needed for advanced analyses such as structural equation modeling, e. g., when using the framework by Knijnenburg, Willemsen and Kobsa [48]. Crowdsourced online experiments are therefore often performed to recruit a sufficiently large number of participants. They also enable performing studies in a short period of time, since participants can work in parallel. However, they also have limitations since it is harder to control the composition and background of the sample, and the usage of the system. Also, special care needs to be taken in formulating the tasks to be performed. For a discussion of the pros and cons of crowdsourcing, we refer to the overview provided by Archambault, Purchase and Hoßfeld [6].

An interesting alternative approach to evaluating RS lies in simulation studies, which, however, have only recently begun to attract attention in RS research [60]. Here, users' exposure to recommendations and their corresponding choice behavior are simulated. This is less costly than studies with actual users, allows testing different RS configurations and can help investigate long-term effects.

2.6 Summary and future directions

There is increasing awareness in research and industry that RS need to be designed and evaluated from a user-centric perspective. Beyond algorithmic performance, users' perceptions of and attitudes toward RS are of critical importance for the success of RS. Transparency and control have shown to be important desiderata for user-centric system design. Although there exist now numerous works that have proposed methods for achieving these goals, the one optimal strategy is not yet in sight, and may never be.

User-centered design, in general, requires a thorough understanding of users' goals, their capabilities and limitations, as well as of the context of use, which is also true for the development of user-centric RS. Research under this perspective is, however, still much more limited than algorithm-related work. One of the many open HCI-related questions is the design of RS in their application context. RS are not used in isolation but usually form part of a larger system such as an online shop. Here, the interplay of different forms of interaction, such as browsing, searching and exploring recommendations needs to be better understood. To support users who need to accomplish tasks that are more complex than choosing a movie or song, more domain knowledge should be incorporated in RS, for facilitating search as well as for explaining candidate items. Novel forms of recommending such as conversational approaches promise to offer more interactive and flexible ways of expressing one's needs and preferences. The recent advances in large language models promise interesting future opportunities, at the same time raising a multitude of open questions, including the acceptance and trustworthiness of systems with seemingly human-level capabilities.

Finally, many questions are still open concerning what constitutes a good recommendation. A wide range of methods, metrics and evaluation techniques has been proposed, but the question of how to really support users in making better decisions has not been ultimately answered yet.

References

[1]   Gediminas Adomavicius, Konstantin Bauman, Alexander Tuzhilin, and Moshe Unger. Context-Aware Recommender Systems: From Foundations to Recent DevelopmentsContext-Aware Recommender Systems. In: Francesco Ricci, Lior Rokach, and Bracha Shapira, editors. *Recommender Systems Handbook*. New York, NY: Springer US, 2022, pp. 211–250. https://doi.org/10.1007/978-1-0716-2197-4_6.

[2]   Gediminas Adomavicius and Youngok Kwon. Multi-Criteria Recommender Systems. In: *Recommender Systems Handbook, edited by Francesco Ricci, Lior Rokach, and Bracha Shapira*, 2nd edition. Springer, 2015.

[3]   Öznur Alkan, Massimiliano Mattetti, Elizabeth M. Daly, Adi Botea, Inge Vejsbjerg, and Bart P. Knijnenburg. IRF: A Framework for Enabling Users to Interact with Recommenders through Dialogue. In: *Proceedings of the ACM on Human-Computer Interaction 5 (CSCW1)*, 2021, pp. 163:1–163:25.

[4]   Xavier Amatriain, Josep M. Pujol, Nava Tintarev, and Nuria Oliver. Rate It Again: Increasing Recommendation Accuracy by User Re-Rating. In: *RecSys'09: Proceedings of the 3rd ACM Conference on Recommender Systems*. New York, NY, USA: ACM, 2009, pp. 173–180.

[5]   Ivana Andjelkovic, Denis Parra, and John O'Donovan. Moodplay: Interactive Mood-Based Music Discovery and Recommendation. In: *Proceedings of the 2016 Conference on User Modeling Adaptation and Personalization, UMAP'16*. New York, NY: Association for Computing Machinery, 2016, pp. 275–279. https://doi.org/10.1145/2930238.2930280.

[6] Daniel Archambault, Helen Purchase, and Tobias Hoßfeld. Evaluation in the Crowd. In: *Crowdsourcing and Human-Centered Experiments: Dagstuhl Seminar 15481, Dagstuhl Castle, Germany, November 22–27, 2015. Revised Contributions*, Lecture Notes in Computer Science, volume 10264. Cham: Springer International Publishing, 2017. https://doi.org/10.1007/978-3-319-66435-4.

[7] Ricardo Baeza-Yates. Bias on the Web. *Communications of the ACM* 61(6) (2018) 54–61. https://doi.org/10.1145/3209581.

[8] Linas Baltrunas, Bernd Ludwig, Stefan Peer, and Francesco Ricci. Context-Aware Places of Interest Recommendations and Explanations. In: *Joint Proceedings of the 1st Workshop on Decision Making and Recommendation Acceptance Issues in Recommender Systems (DEMRA'11) and the 2nd Workshop on User Models for Motivational Systems: The Affective and the Rational Routes to Persuasion (UMMS'11)*, volume 740, 2011, pp. 19–26.

[9] Joeran Beel and Haley Dixon. The 'Unreasonable' Effectiveness of Graphical User Interfaces for Recommender Systems. In: *Adjunct Proceedings of the 29th ACM Conference on User Modeling, Adaptation and Personalization*. New York, NY: Association for Computing Machinery, 2021, pp. 22–28. https://doi.org/10.1145/3450614.3461682.

[10] Dirk Bollen, Bart P. Knijnenburg, Martijn C. Willemsen, and Mark Graus. Understanding Choice Overload in Recommender Systems. In: *Proceedings of the Fourth ACM Conference on Recommender Systems, RecSys'10*. New York, NY: Association for Computing Machinery, 2010, pp. 63–70. https://doi.org/10.1145/1864708.1864724.

[11] Svetlin Bostandjiev, John O'Donovan, and Tobias Höllerer. TasteWeights: A Visual Interactive Hybrid Recommender System. In: *Proceedings of the Sixth ACM Conference on Recommender Systems, RecSys'12*. New York, NY, USA: Association for Computing Machinery, 2012, pp. 35–42. https://doi.org/10.1145/2365952.2365964.

[12] Svetlin Bostandjiev, John O'Donovan, and Tobias Höllerer. LinkedVis: Exploring Social and Semantic Career Recommendations. In: *Proceedings of the 18th International Conference on Intelligent User Interfaces, IUI'13*. New York, NY, USA: Association for Computing Machinery, 2013, pp. 107–116. https://doi.org/10.1145/2449396.2449412.

[13] Robin Burke, Kristian J. Hammond, and Benjamin Young. The FindMe Approach to Assisted Browsing. *IEEE Expert* 12(4) (1997) 32–40.

[14] Bruno Cardoso, Gayane Sedrakyan, Francisco Gutiérrez, Denis Parra, Peter Brusilovsky, and Katrien Verbert. IntersectionExplorer, a Multi-Perspective Approach for Exploring Recommendations. *International Journal of Human-Computer Studies* 121 (2019) 73–92. https://doi.org/10.1016/j.ijhcs.2018.04.008.

[15] Chong Chen, Min Zhang, Yiqun Liu, and Shaoping Ma. Neural Attentional Rating Regression with Review-Level Explanations. In: *Proceedings of the 2018 World Wide Web Conference, WWW'18*. Republic and Canton of Geneva: International World Wide Web Conferences Steering Committee, 2018, pp. 1583–1592. https://doi.org/10.1145/3178876.3186070.

[16] Li Chen and Pearl Pu. Eye-Tracking Study of User Behavior in Recommender Interfaces. In: Paul De Bra, Alfred Kobsa, and David Chin, editors. *User Modeling, Adaptation, and Personalization*. Lecture Notes in Computer Science. Berlin, Heidelberg: Springer, 2010, pp. 375–380. https://doi.org/10.1007/978-3-642-13470-8_35.

[17] Li Chen and Ho Keung Tsoi. Users' Decision Behavior in Recommender Interfaces: Impact of Layout Design. In: *RecSys'11 Workshop on Human Decision Making in Recommender Systems*, 2011. http://ceur-ws.org/Vol-811/paper4.pdf.

[18] Li Chen and Pearl Pu. Critiquing-Based Recommenders: Survey and Emerging Trends. *User Modeling and User-Adapted Interaction* 22(1–2) (2012) 125–150. https://doi.org/10.1007/s11257-011-9108-6.

[19] Wei-Fan Chen, Shahbaz Syed, Benno Stein, Matthias Hagen, and Martin Potthast. Abstractive Snippet Generation. In: *Proceedings of The Web Conference 2020*. New York, NY: Association for Computing Machinery, 2020, pp. 1309–1319. https://doi.org/10.1145/3366423.3380206.

[20] Michael D. Ekstrand, Daniel Kluver, F. Maxwell Harper, and Joseph A. Konstan. Letting Users Choose Recommender Algorithms: An Experimental Study. In: *Proceedings of the 9th ACM Conference on Recommender Systems, RecSys'15*. New York, NY, USA: Association for Computing Machinery, 2015, pp. 11–18. https://doi.org/10.1145/2792838.2800195.

[21] Nicolò Felicioni, Maurizio Ferrari Dacrema, and Paolo Cremonesi. Measuring the User Satisfaction in a Recommendation Interface with Multiple Carousels. In: *ACM International Conference on Interactive Media Experiences, IMX'21*. New York, NY: Association for Computing Machinery, 2021, pp. 212–217. https://doi.org/10.1145/3452918.3465493.

[22] Emden Gansner, Yifan Hu, Stephen Kobourov, and Chris Volinsky. Putting Recommendations on the Map: Visualizing Clusters and Relations. In: *Proceedings of the Third ACM Conference on Recommender Systems, RecSys'09*. New York, NY: Association for Computing Machinery, 2009, pp. 345–348. https://doi.org/10.1145/1639714.1639784.

[23] Carlos A. Gomez-Uribe and Neil Hunt. The Netflix Recommender System: Algorithms, Business Value, and Innovation. *ACM Transactions on Management Information Systems* 6(4) (2015) 13:1–13:19. https://doi.org/10.1145/2843948.

[24] Mark P. Graus and Martijn C. Willemsen. Improving the User Experience during Cold Start through Choice-Based Preference Elicitation. In: *Proceedings of the 9th ACM Conference on Recommender Systems, RecSys'15*. New York, NY, USA: Association for Computing Machinery, 2015, pp. 273–276. https://doi.org/10.1145/2792838.2799681.

[25] Brynjar Gretarsson, John O'Donovan, Svetlin Bostandjiev, Christopher Hall, and Tobias Höllerer. SmallWorlds: Visualizing Social Recommendations. *Computer Graphics Forum* 29(3) (2010) 833–842. https://doi.org/10.1111/j.1467-8659.2009.01679.x.

[26] Asela Gunawardana, Guy Shani, and Sivan Yogev. Evaluating Recommender Systems. In: Francesco Ricci, Lior Rokach, and Bracha Shapira, editors. *Recommender Systems Handbook*, New York, NY: Springer US, 2022, pp. 547–601. https://doi.org/10.1007/978-1-0716-2197-4_15.

[27] F. Maxwell Harper, Funing Xu, Harmanpreet Kaur, Kyle Condiff, Shuo Chang, and Loren Terveen. Putting Users in Control of Their Recommendations. In: *Proceedings of the 9th ACM Conference on Recommender Systems, RecSys'15*. New York, NY, USA: ACM, 2015, pp. 3–10. https://doi.org/10.1145/2792838.2800179.

[28] Chen He, Denis Parra, and Katrien Verbert. Interactive Recommender Systems: A Survey of the State of the Art and Future Research Challenges and Opportunities. *Expert Systems with Applications* 56 (2016) 9–27. https://doi.org/10.1016/j.eswa.2016.02.013.

[29] Jonathan L. Herlocker, Joseph A. Konstan, and John Riedl. Explaining Collaborative Filtering Recommendations. In: *Proceedings of the 2000 ACM Conference on Computer Supported Cooperative Work, CSCW'00*. New York, NY: Association for Computing Machinery, 2000, pp. 241–250. https://doi.org/10.1145/358916.358995.

[30] Diana C. Hernandez-Bocanegra and Jürgen Ziegler. Explaining Review-Based Recommendations: Effects of Profile Transparency, Presentation Style and User Characteristics. *i-Com – Journal of Interactive Media* 19(3) (2020) 181–200. https://doi.org/10.1515/icom-2020-0021.

[31] Diana C. Hernandez-Bocanegra and Jürgen Ziegler. Conversational Review-Based Explanations for Recommender Systems: Exploring Users' Query Behavior. In: *CUI 2021 – 3rd Conference on Conversational User Interfaces, CUI'21*. New York, NY: Association for Computing Machinery, 2021, pp. 1–11. https://doi.org/10.1145/3469595.3469596.

[32] Diana C. Hernandez-Bocanegra and Jürgen Ziegler. Explaining Recommendations Through Conversations - Dialog Model and the Effects of Interface Type and Degree of Interactivity. *The ACM Transactions on Interactive Intelligent Systems* (2023). https://doi.org/10.1145/3579541.

[33] Mireille Hildebrandt. The Issue of Proxies and Choice Architectures. Why EU Law Matters for Recommender Systems. *Frontiers in Artificial Intelligence* 5 (2022). https://www.frontiersin.org/articles/10.3389/frai.2022.789076.

[34] Katja Hofmann, Anne Schuth, Alejandro Bellogín, and Maarten de Rijke. Effects of Position Bias on Click-Based Recommender Evaluation. In: Maarten de Rijke, Tom Kenter, Arjen P. de Vries, ChengXiang Zhai, Franciska de Jong, Kira Radinsky, and Katja Hofmann, editors. *Advances in Information Retrieval*. Lecture Notes in Computer Science. Cham: Springer International Publishing, 2014, pp. 624–630. https://doi.org/10.1007/978-3-319-06028-6_67.

[35] Rong Hu and Pearl Pu. A Comparative User Study on Rating vs. Personality Quiz Based Preference Elicitation Methods. In: *Proceedings of the 14th International Conference on Intelligent User Interfaces, IUI'09*. New York, NY, USA: Association for Computing Machinery, 2009, pp. 367–372. https://doi.org/10.1145/1502650.1502702.

[36] Andrea Iovine, Fedelucio Narducci, and Giovanni Semeraro. Conversational Recommender Systems and Natural Language: A Study Through the ConveRSE Framework. *Decision Support Systems* 131 (2020) 113250.

[37] Sheena S. Iyengar and Mark R. Lepper. When Choice Is Demotivating: Can One Desire Too Much of a Good Thing?. *Journal of Personality and Social Psychology* 79(6) (2000) 995–1006. https://doi.org/10.1037/0022-3514.79.6.995.

[38] Dietmar Jannach, Ahtsham Manzoor, Wanling Cai, and Li Chen. A Survey on Conversational Recommender Systems. *ACM Computing Surveys* 54(5) (2021) 105:1–105:36. https://doi.org/10.1145/3453154.

[39] Dietmar Jannach, Mathias Jesse, Michael Jugovac, and Christoph Trattner. Exploring Multi-List User Interfaces for Similar-Item Recommendations. In: *Proceedings of the 29th ACM Conference on User Modeling, Adaptation and Personalization, UMAP'21*. New York, NY: Association for Computing Machinery, 2021, pp. 224–228. https://doi.org/10.1145/3450613.3456809.

[40] Dietmar Jannach, Lukas Lerche, and Michael Jugovac. Adaptation and Evaluation of Recommendations for Short-term Shopping Goals. In: *Proceedings of the 9th ACM Conference on Recommender Systems, RecSys'15*. New York, NY: Association for Computing Machinery, 2015, pp. 211–218. https://doi.org/10.1145/2792838.2800176.

[41] Gawesh, Jawaheer, Peter Weller, and Patty Kostkova. Modeling User Preferences in Recommender Systems: A Classification Framework for Explicit and Implicit User Feedback. *The ACM Transactions on Interactive Intelligent Systems* 4(2) (2014) 8:1–8:26. https://doi.org/10.1145/2512208.

[42] Yucheng Jin, Wanling Cai, Li Chen, Nyi Nyi Htun, and Katrien Verbert. MusicBot: Evaluating Critiquing-Based Music Recommenders with Conversational Interaction. In: *CIKM'19: Proceedings of the 28th ACM International Conference on Information and Knowledge Management*, New York, NY, USA: ACM, 2019, pp. 951–960.

[43] Yucheng Jin, Nava Tintarev, Nyi Nyi Htun, and Katrien Verbert. Effects of Personal Characteristics in Control-Oriented User Interfaces for Music Recommender Systems. *User Modeling and User-Adapted Interaction* 30(2) (2020) 199–249. https://doi.org/10.1007/s11257-019-09247-2.

[44] Yucheng Jin, Li Chen, Wanling Cai, and Pearl Pu. Key Qualities of Conversational Recommender Systems: From Users' Perspective. In: *HAI'21: Proceedings of the 9th International Conference on Human-Agent Interaction*. New York, NY, USA: ACM, 2021, pp. 93–102.

[45] Nicolas Jones, Armelle Brun, and Anne Boyer. Comparisons Instead of Ratings: Towards More Stable Preferences. In: *Proceedings of the 2011 IEEE/WIC/ACM International Conferences on Web Intelligence and Intelligent Agent Technology - Volume 01, WI-IAT'11*. USA: IEEE Computer Society, 2011, pp. 451–456. https://doi.org/10.1109/WI-IAT.2011.13.

[46] Michael Jugovac and Dietmar Jannach. Interacting with Recommenders—Overview and Research Directions. *The ACM Transactions on Interactive Intelligent Systems* 7(3) (2017) 10:1–10:46. https://doi.org/10.1145/3001837.

[47] Marius Kaminskas and Derek Bridge. Diversity, Serendipity, Novelty, and Coverage: A Survey and Empirical Analysis of Beyond-Accuracy Objectives in Recommender Systems. *The ACM Transactions on Interactive Intelligent Systems* 7(1) (2016) 2:1–2:42.

[48] Bart P. Knijnenburg, Martijn C. Willemsen, and Alfred Kobsa. A Pragmatic Procedure to Support the User-Centric Evaluation of Recommender Systems. In: *Proceedings of the Fifth ACM Conference on Recommender Systems, RecSys'11*, New York, NY: Association for Computing Machinery, 2011, pp. 321–324. https://doi.org/10.1145/2043932.2043993.

[49] Bart P. Knijnenburg and Martijn C. Willemsen. Evaluating Recommender Systems with User Experiments. In: Francesco Ricci, Lior Rokach, and Bracha Shapira, editors. *Recommender Systems Handbook*. Boston, MA, USA: Springer US, 2015, pp. 309–352.

[50] Joseph A. Konstan and John Riedl. Recommender Systems: From Algorithms to User Experience. *User Modeling and User-Adapted Interaction* 22(1–2) (2012) 101–123. https://doi.org/10.1007/s11257-011-9112-x.

[51] Joseph A. Konstan and Loren G. Terveen. Human-Centered Recommender Systems: Origins, Advances, Challenges, and Opportunities. *AI Magazine* 42 (2021) 31–42.

[52] Pigi Kouki, James Schaffer, Jay Pujara, John O'Donovan, and Lise Getoor. Personalized Explanations for Hybrid Recommender Systems. In: *Proceedings of the 24th International Conference on Intelligent User Interfaces, IUI'19*. New York, NY: Association for Computing Machinery, 2019, pp. 379–390. https://doi.org/10.1145/3301275.3302306.

[53] Johannes Kunkel, Benedikt Loepp, and Jürgen Ziegler. A 3D Item Space Visualization for Presenting and Manipulating User Preferences in Collaborative Filtering. In: *IUI'17: Proceedings of the 22nd International Conference on Intelligent User Interfaces, IUI'17*. New York, NY: Association for Computing Machinery, 2017, pp. 3–15. https://doi.org/10.1145/3025171.3025189.

[54] Johannes Kunkel, Claudia Schwenger, and Jürgen Ziegler. NewsViz: Depicting and Controlling Preference Profiles Using Interactive Treemaps in News Recommender Systems. In: *Proceedings of the 28th ACM Conference on User Modeling, Adaptation and Personalization, UMAP'20*, New York, NY: Association for Computing Machinery, 2020, pp. 126–135. https://doi.org/10.1145/3340631.3394869.

[55] Yu Liang and Martijn C. Willemsen. Interactive Music Genre Exploration with Visualization and Mood Control. In: *Proceedings of the 26th International Conference on Intelligent User Interfaces, IUI'21*, New York, NY, USA: Association for Computing Machinery, 2021, pp. 175–185. https://doi.org/10.1145/3397481.3450700.

[56] Greg Linden, Brent Smith, and Jeremy York. Amazon.Com Recommendations: Item-to-Item Collaborative Filtering. *IEEE Internet Computing* 7(1) (2003) 76–80.

[57] Benedikt Loepp, Tim Donkers, Timm Kleemann, and Jürgen Ziegler. Impact of Item Consumption on Assessment of Recommendations in User Studies. In: *Proceedings of the 12th ACM Conference on Recommender Systems, RecSys'18*. New York, NY: Association for Computing Machinery, 2018, pp. 49–53. https://doi.org/10.1145/3240323.3240375.

[58] Benedikt Loepp, Tim Donkers, Timm Kleemann, and Jürgen Ziegler. Interactive Recommending with Tag-Enhanced Matrix Factorization (TagMF). *International Journal of Human-Computer Studies* 121 (2019) 21–41.

[59] Benedikt Loepp, Tim Hussein, and Jürgen Ziegler. Choice-Based Preference Elicitation for Collaborative Filtering Recommender Systems. In: *CHI 2014: Proceedings of the SIGCHI Conference on Human Factors in Computing Systems, CHI'14*. New York, NY: Association for Computing Machinery, 2014, pp. 3085–3094. https://doi.org/10.1145/2556288.2557069.

[60] James McInerney, Ehtsham Elahi, Justin Basilico, Yves Raimond, and Tony Jebara. Accordion: A Trainable Simulator for Long-Term Interactive Systems. In: *RecSys'21: Proceedings of the 15th ACM Conference on Recommender Systems*. New York, NY, USA: ACM, 2021, pp. 102–113.

[61] Shabnam Najafian, Wolfgang Wörndl, and Matthias Braunhofer. Context-Aware User Interaction for Mobile Recommender Systems. In: *HAAPIE'16: Proceedings of the 1st International Workshop on Human Aspects in Adaptive and Personalized Interactive Environments*, 2016.

[62] Syavash Nobarany, Louise Oram, Vasanth Kumar Rajendran, Chi-Hsiang Chen, Joanna McGrenere, and Tamara Munzner. The Design Space of Opinion Measurement Interfaces: Exploring Recall Support for Rating and Ranking. In: *Proceedings of the SIGCHI Conference on Human Factors in Computing Systems, CHI'12*. New York, NY, USA: Association for Computing Machinery, 2012, pp. 2035–2044. https://doi.org/10.1145/2207676.2208351.

[63] Ingrid Nunes and Dietmar Jannach. A Systematic Review and Taxonomy of Explanations in Decision Support and Recommender Systems. *User Modeling and User-Adapted Interaction* 27(3) (2017) 393–444. https://doi.org/10.1007/s11257-017-9195-0.

[64] Denis Parra and Xavier Amatriain. Walk the Talk: Analyzing the Relation between Implicit and Explicit Feedback for Preference Elicitation. In: *Proceedings of the 19th International Conference on User Modeling, Adaption, and Personalization, UMAP'11*. Berlin, Heidelberg: Springer-Verlag, 2011, pp. 255–268.

[65] Denis Parra, Peter Brusilovsky, and Christoph Trattner. See What You Want to See: Visual User-Driven Approach for Hybrid Recommendation. In: *Proceedings of the 19th International Conference on Intelligent User Interfaces, IUI'14*. New York, NY: Association for Computing Machinery, 2014, pp. 235–240. https://doi.org/10.1145/2557500.2557542.

[66] Eli Pariser. *The Filter Bubble: What the Internet is Hiding From You*. New York, NY, USA: Penguin Press, 2011.

[67] Florian Pecune, Shruti Murali, Vivian Tsai, Yoichi Matsuyama, and Justine Cassell. A Model of Social Explanations for a Conversational Movie Recommendation System. In: *Proceedings of the 7th International Conference on Human-Agent Interaction, HAI'19*. New York, NY: Association for Computing Machinery, 2019, pp. 135–143. https://doi.org/10.1145/3349537.3351899.

[68] Savvas Petridis, Nediyana Daskalova, Sarah Mennicken, Samuel F. Way, Paul Lamere, and Jennifer Thom. TastePaths: Enabling Deeper Exploration and Understanding of Personal Preferences in Recommender Systems. In: *27th International Conference on Intelligent User Interfaces, IUI'22*. New York, NY: Association for Computing Machinery, 2022, pp. 120–133. https://doi.org/10.1145/3490099.3511156.

[69] Pearl Pu and Li Chen. Trust Building with Explanation Interfaces. In: *Proceedings of the 11th International Conference on Intelligent User Interfaces, IUI'06*. New York, NY: Association for Computing Machinery, 2006, pp. 93–100. https://doi.org/10.1145/1111449.1111475.

[70] Pearl Pu, Li Chen, and Rong Hu. A User-Centric Evaluation Framework for Recommender Systems. In: *Proceedings of the Fifth ACM Conference on Recommender Systems, RecSys'11*. New York, NY: Association for Computing Machinery, 2011, pp. 157–164. https://doi.org/10.1145/2043932.2043962.

[71] Behnam Rahdari, Branislav Kveton, and Peter Brusilovsky. The Magic of Carousels: Single vs. Multi-List Recommender Systems. In: *Proceedings of the 33rd ACM Conference on Hypertext and Social Media, HT'22*. New York, NY: Association for Computing Machinery, 2022, pp. 166–174. https://doi.org/10.1145/3511095.3531278.

[72] James Reilly, Kevin McCarthy, Lorraine McGinty, and Barry Smyth. Explaining Compound Critiques. *Artificial Intelligence Review* 24(2) (2005) 199–220.

[73] Francesco Ricci, Lior Rokach, and Bracha Shapira, *Recommender Systems Handbook*. New York, NY: Springer, 2022. https://doi.org/10.1007/978-1-0716-2197-4.

[74] Christian Richthammer and Günther Pernul. Explorative Analysis of Recommendations Through Interactive Visualization. In: Derek Bridge and Heiner Stuckenschmidt, editors. *E-Commerce and Web Technologies*. Lecture Notes in Business Information Processing. Cham: Springer International Publishing, 2017, pp. 46–57. https://doi.org/10.1007/978-3-319-53676-7_4.

[75] Lior Rokach and Slava Kisilevich. Initial Profile Generation in Recommender Systems Using Pairwise Comparison. *IEEE Transactions on Systems, Man and Cybernetics Part C* 42 (2012) 1854–1859. https://doi.org/10.1109/TSMCC.2012.2197679.

[76] Yuri Saito and Takayuki Itoh. MusiCube: A Visual Music Recommendation System Featuring Interactive Evolutionary Computing. In: *Proceedings of the 2011 Visual Information Communication - International Symposium, VINCI'11*. New York, NY: Association for Computing Machinery, 2011, pp. 1–6. https://doi.org/10.1145/2016656.2016661.

[77] Benjamin Scheibehenne, Rainer Greifeneder, and Peter M. Todd. Can There Ever Be Too Many Options? A Meta-Analytic Review of Choice Overload. *Journal of Consumer Research* 37(3) (2010) 409–425. https://doi.org/10.1086/651235.

[78] Martin Schrepp, Andreas Hinderks, and Jörg Thomaschewski. Design and Evaluation of a Short Version of the User Experience Questionnaire (UEQ-S). *International Journal of Interactive Multimedia and Artificial Intelligence* 4 (2017) 103. https://doi.org/10.9781/ijimai.2017.09.001.

[79] Kirsten Swearingen and Rashmi Sinha. Beyond Algorithms: An HCI Perspective on Recommender Systems. In: *ACM SIGIR Workshop on Recommender Systems*, 2001, pp. 11.

[80] Feben Teklemicael, Yong Zhang, Yongji Wu, Yanshen Yin, and Chunxiao Xing. Toward Gamified Personality Acquisition in Travel Recommender Systems. In: *International Conference on Human Centered Computing*, 2016, pp. 385. https://doi.org/10.1007/978-3-319-31854-7_34.

[81] Nava Tintarev and Judith Masthoff. Effective Explanations of Recommendations: User-Centered Design. In: *Proceedings of the 2007 ACM Conference on Recommender Systems, RecSys'07*. New York, NY: Association for Computing Machinery, 2007, pp. 153–156. https://doi.org/10.1145/1297231.1297259.

[82] Chun-Hua Tsai and Peter Brusilovsky. Beyond the Ranked List: User-Driven Exploration and Diversification of Social Recommendation. In: *23rd International Conference on Intelligent User Interfaces, IUI'18*. New York, NY: Association for Computing Machinery, 2018, pp. 239–250. https://doi.org/10.1145/3172944.3172959.

[83] Chun-Hua Tsai and Peter Brusilovsky. Explaining Recommendations in an Interactive Hybrid Social Recommender. In: *Proceedings of the 24th International Conference on Intelligent User Interfaces, IUI'19*. New York, NY: Association for Computing Machinery, 2019, pp. 391–396. https://doi.org/10.1145/3301275.3302318.

[84] Michelle M. E. Van Pinxteren, Mark Pluymaekers, and Jos G. A. M. Lemmink. Human-like Communication in Conversational Agents: A Literature Review and Research Agenda. *Journal of Service Management* 31(2) (2020) 203–225. https://doi.org/10.1108/JOSM-06-2019-0175.

[85] Saúl Vargas and Pablo Castells. Rank and Relevance in Novelty and Diversity Metrics for Recommender Systems. In: *Proceedings of the Fifth ACM Conference on Recommender Systems, RecSys'11*. New York, NY: Association for Computing Machinery, 2011, pp. 109–116. https://doi.org/10.1145/2043932.2043955.

[86] Jesse Vig, Shilad Sen, and John Riedl. Tagsplanations: Explaining Recommendations Using Tags. In: *Proceedings of the 14th International Conference on Intelligent User Interfaces, IUI'09*. New York, NY: Association for Computing Machinery, 2009, pp. 47–56. https://doi.org/10.1145/1502650.1502661.

[87] Jesse Vig, Shilad Sen, and John Riedl. The Tag Genome: Encoding Community Knowledge to Support Novel Interaction. *The ACM Transactions on Interactive Intelligent Systems* 2(3) (2012) 13:1–13:44.

[88] Haoran Xie, Debby D. Wang, Yanghui Rao, Tak-Lam Wong, Lau Y. K. Raymond, Li Chen, and Fu Lee Wang. Incorporating User Experience Into Critiquing-Based Recommender Systems: A Collaborative Approach Based on Compound Critiquing. *International Journal of Machine Learning and Cybernetics* 9(5) (2018) 837–852.

[89] Hongyan Xu, Hongtao Liu, Pengfei Jiao, and Wenjun Wang. Transformer Reasoning Network for Personalized Review Summarization. In: *Proceedings of the 44th International ACM SIGIR Conference on Research and Development in Information Retrieval, SIGIR'21*. New York, NY: Association for Computing Machinery, 2021, pp. 1452–1461. https://doi.org/10.1145/3404835.3462854.

[90] Kun Xiong, Wenwen Ye, Xu Chen, Yongfeng Zhang, Wayne Xin Zhao, Binbin Hu, Zhiqiang Zhang, and Jun Zhou. Counterfactual Review-Based Recommendation. In: *Proceedings of the 30th ACM International Conference on Information & Knowledge Management, CIKM'21*, New York, NY, USA: Association for Computing Machinery, 2021, pp. 2231–2240. https://doi.org/10.1145/3459637.3482244.

[91] Ya Xu, Nanyu Chen, Addrian Fernandez, Omar Sinno, and Anmol Bhasin. From Infrastructure to Culture: A/B Testing Challenges in Large Scale Social Networks. In: *Proceedings of the 21st ACM SIGKDD International Conference on Knowledge Discovery and Data Mining, KDD'15*, New York, NY: Association for Computing Machinery, 2015, pp. 2227–2236.

[92] Yisong Yue, Rajan Patel, and Hein Roehrig. Beyond Position Bias: Examining Result Attractiveness as a Source of Presentation Bias in Clickthrough Data. In: *Proceedings of the 19th International Conference on World Wide Web, WWW'10*, New York, NY: Association for Computing Machinery, 2010, pp. 1011–1018. https://doi.org/10.1145/1772690.1772793.

[93] Yongfeng Zhang, and Xu Chen. Explainable Recommendation: A Survey and New Perspectives. *Foundations and Trends in Information Retrieval* 14(1) (2020) 1–101.

[94] Yongfeng Zhang, Guokun Lai, Min Zhang, Yi Zhang, Yiqun Liu, and Shaoping Ma. Explicit Factor Models for Explainable Recommendation Based on Phrase-Level Sentiment Analysis. In: *Proceedings of the 37th International ACM SIGIR Conference on Research & Development in Information Retrieval - SIGIR'14*. New York, NY: Association for Computing Machinery, 2014, pp. 83–92. https://doi.org/10.1145/2600428.2609579.

Markus Schedl and Elisabeth Lex

3 Fairness of information access systems

Detecting and mitigating harmful biases in information retrieval and recommender systems

Abstract: Information access systems, such as search engines and recommender systems, affect many day-to-day decisions in modern societies by preselecting and ranking content users are exposed to on the web (e. g., products, music, movies or job advertisements). While they have undoubtedly improved users' opportunities to find useful and relevant digital content, these systems and their underlying algorithms often exhibit several undesirable characteristics. Among them, harmful biases play a significant role and may even result in unfair or discriminating behavior of such systems.

In this chapter, we give an introduction to the different kinds and sources of biases from various perspectives as well as their relation to algorithmic fairness considerations. We also review common computational metrics that formalize some of these biases. Subsequently, the major strategies to mitigate harmful biases are discussed and each is illustrated by presenting concrete state-of-the-art approaches from scientific literature. Finally, we round off by identifying open challenges in research on fair information access systems.

Keywords: Bias, fairness, discrimination, equality, trustworthiness, metrics, recommender systems, information retrieval, search engines, machine learning, deep learning, adversarial learning, content filtering, ranking, regularization

3.1 Introduction

Our daily lives are affected by decisions made by algorithms. In particular, algorithms powering information access systems, such as search engines, recommender systems or chatbots, impact which content we are exposed to on the web, which news we read, which products we buy, music we listen to, movies we watch, food we eat or jobs we apply for. This substantially narrows our view of the world. Concretely, *information retrieval* (IR) [8] algorithms powering modern web search engines take as input a user-provided query q and matches it with a (commonly huge) collection of documents $d \in D$.

Acknowledgement: We would like to thank the Human-centered Artificial Intelligence group at Linz Institute of Technology and the Multimedia Mining and Search group at Johannes Kepler University Linz, in particular, Navid Rekabsaz, Alessandro B. Melchiorre, Oleg Lesota and David Penz, as well as the Recommender Systems and Social Computing Lab at Graz University of Technology, for conducting the great research that enabled us to write this chapter. In addition, we are grateful for illustrations provided by Christian Ganhör. Some of the icons used in the figures were made by Freepik from www.flaticon.com.

https://doi.org/10.1515/9783110988567-003

The amount of matching is quantified by some scoring function $s(q, d)$ that is applied to create a ranked list of documents, from which the top k documents are returned to the user as response to q. The main notion used to indicate a successful retrieval process is that of *relevance* of a document to a query. A *recommender system* (RS) [61], in contrast, creates for its users a personalized recommendation list of items, again commonly chosen from a very large catalog $i \in I$. Instead of requesting a user-provided query, a RS bases its decision about which items to recommend and which not on a user model that is often created from user-item interactions $r_{u,i}$, e. g., clicking on an image, purchasing a product, starting the playback of a song or providing a rating for a hotel or movie. Recommendations are then commonly created either by selecting content that is similar to what the user liked in the past (content-based filtering, e. g., "You are recommended the movie Terminator because from your previous watch list it seems you like action movies."), or content that other similar users liked in the past (collaborative filtering, e. g., "You are recommended this song by Rammstein because it is popular among other users who like the same artists as you do."). The notion of *utility* of the recommendations for the user is often adopted to measure the quality of items recommended by a RS. State-of-the-art approaches for both IR and RSs adopt deep neural networks, e. g., to create embeddings for queries, documents, users and items, and perform the matching in the resulting embedding space.

Despite the undeniable advantages in helping their users find relevant, useful or enjoyable contents, retrieval and recommendation algorithms suffer from a variety of problems. Some of them are specific to RSs, some affect both retrieval and recommendation systems alike. First, since nowadays also IR systems deliver personalized results, both IR and RSs are prone to the risk of *overpersonalization* (also known as "hyperpersonalization"), which may result in a *lack of content diversity*, or in other words, users getting stuck in their own "filter bubble." Examples for this problem include the inability of a search engine to cover in its results various points of view about a topic, or the limited coverage of music that is beyond the comfort zone of the listener in a music RS. Second, since information access systems collect and process large amounts of user-generated data to create their user profiles needed for personalization, *privacy and security* concerns are often raised. Even if they are not explicitly provided by the user, many of their traits, such as personality, sexual orientation or demographics, can be quite accurately predicted from user-item interaction data, e. g., [24, 58, 69, 70]. On the other hand, a low amount of user-generated data (such as queries in IR systems or interactions in RSs) yields to inferior personalization abilities, and is particularly problematic in RSs since they cannot rely on a query provided as input by the user, unlike search engines. The complete lack of user-item interaction data is referred to as *cold-start problem* in RSs. This problem occurs when new users register to the system or new contents are added to the item catalog. In such cases, the system has to resort to non-personalized means for creating a ranking of items, for instance, recommending a list of most popular items. Furthermore, like many other applications of machine learning, search engines and RSs lack a decent capability of accurately explaining their reasoning behind selecting (or not selecting) certain contents. As such, they are *not transparent* for their end users. This is partly due to the fledgling stage of research in explainable IR and RSs, but even more due to the major companies' unwillingness to integrate decent explanations into their systems because of fears that these could reveal details of their ranking algorithms, which are classified as business secrets. Finally, the last big challenge we would like to mention here—and the core topic of this chapter—is information access systems' proneness to various kinds of *biases*. On the one hand, certain biases are required to create personalized recommendations or search results, in particular, those reflecting the user's preferences. Other biases, however, negatively impact different parts of the system, and in turn yield unbalanced or even discriminating retrieval or recommendation lists, resulting in algorithmic *unfairness*, e. g., [7, 15, 17].

In the following, we first introduce various kinds of biases and their impact on fairness, and provide common definitions and metrics to quantify them (Section 3.2). Subsequently, we discuss strategies and concrete approaches to mitigate harmful biases (Section 3.3). Finally, we draw conclusions and point to current challenges and avenues for future research on this exciting topic (Section 3.4).

3.2 Biases and fairness

Bias can be broadly described as systematic differences between IR and RS outputs and the observable world, i. e., *statistical bias*, as well as in terms of *societal bias*, which is caused by differences between the observable world and an ideal world, where discriminatory behavior is nonexistent [53]. Societal biases are caused by, e. g., historical inequalities, stereotypes, power imbalances and lead to unfair treatment of minorities or particular groups of people. While some level of bias in IR and RSs is necessary for personalization, certain biases affect the performance of IR and RSs and can even be harmful if they result in discrimination against particular users or user groups, thereby undermining fairness. Therefore, identifying and mitigating harmful bias is crucial to ensure fairness of information access systems [7, 17, 27, 37]. In the following, we introduce various kinds of bias in IR and RSs and elaborate in which stages they can occur. Besides, we outline several approaches to measure bias in IR and RSs.

3.2.1 Sources and categories of bias

Commonly, biases are described in terms of the stage at which they occur. Bias can already be introduced in the data IR and RS algorithms are trained on—commonly referred to as *statistical biases*. Algorithms trained on biased data will learn the biases, and as a result, produce biased predictions or rankings. Also, algorithms can even intensify statistical biases prevalent in the data.

In a recent survey, Chen et al. [13] categorize data bias into: (i) selection or observational bias, (ii) conformity bias in explicit user feedback, (iii) exposure bias and (iv) position bias in implicit user feedback to algorithmic outputs. Selection or observational bias refers to the discrepancy between the distribution of observed explicit user feedback and the distribution of all user ratings, including the ratings not explicitly expressed by the users. It is caused by the fact that users choose items to rate in a subjective manner.[1] Therefore, many data sets are biased if they are created from explicit ratings. This bias is sometimes also described as explicit feedback being *missing-not-at-random (MNAR)*, e. g., [62, 68, 75]. Conformity bias denotes that users tend to align their rating behavior to others, hence collected user feedback can deviate from the true user preferences [36]. Exposure bias results from users being only exposed to a subset of items by the system, e. g., [44, 47, 80]. Correspondingly, unobserved user-item interactions may not necessarily reflect lack of interest in the item, but also lack of awareness of the item; hence, collected user feedback may not be representative of a user's preferences [13]. Finally, position bias in implicit user feedback as a response to the algorithmic outputs refers to the fact that users—if presented a list of items—are more likely to pay attention (and interact with) items at certain positions in the list; see the discussion of *serial positioning effect* below.

Bias can also be described along user or item characteristics that IR and RSs leverage for personalization [74]. Such biases lead to a lower utility for certain user groups characterized by *demographics* such as gender, country of origin or age [18, 26, 49, 55], as well as psychological traits, such as personality [41, 51, 52, 74] or curiosity [74]. On the item level, perhaps the most frequently studied bias is *popularity bias*, which corresponds to already popular items being overrepresented in search and recommendation outputs, e. g., [2, 18, 19, 32, 34, 35, 39, 40, 43, 45].

Algorithmic bias, e. g., [10, 46] occurs in the model itself and results from how it is learned, the design of optimization functions, regularization mechanisms and the use of statistically biased estimators in the algorithms. Applying biased algorithms in real-world scenarios influences users' behavior, which, in turn, leads to more biased training data [48]. Also, IR and RS algorithms can propagate and intensify existing bias over time.

Finally, bias can occur in the *presentation* of results [78]. For instance, users tend to more likely interact with items at the top of a search or recommendation results list, due to the *serial positioning effect*, a cognitive bias that influences users' selection behavior [20, 29, 41]. Collected implicit feedback will be distorted toward these items, even when they are not the most relevant ones. Also other decision biases [57] can affect users' interaction with IR and RS outputs, and hence, data collection of implicit user feedback, including *decoy effects* [31], i. e., inferior items are intentionally added to a set of options

---

1 For instance, users might be more likely to rate a movie they especially love or detest rather than a movie they do not care about.

to increase the selection probability of a particular item, or *framing*, i. e., items are described in a more positive way even when they are not the best fit for a user's need [73].

3.2.2 Measurement of bias

Perhaps the most frequent strategy to measure bias in IR and RSs is to leverage fairness evaluation techniques such as, e. g., investigating if equal utility is achieved for specific types of users, or users belonging to different groups, to understand the impact of bias on the system's fairness [78]. In this vein, Ekstrand et al. [18] find inconsistencies with respect to recommendation accuracy among different demographic groups (i. e., characterized by age and gender) across multiple data sets. Melchiorre et al. [50] propose the *RecGap* metric to identify performance disparities of RSs for different groups (e. g., with regard to users' gender). According to RecGap, an RS is unbiased if it performs the same for different user groups in terms of any arbitrary evaluation metric (e. g., precision, recall, coverage, diversity). It is computed as

$$
\text{RecGap}^{\mu} = \frac{\sum_{\langle g,g' \rangle \in G^{\text{pair}}} \left| \frac{\sum_{u \in U_g} \mu(u)}{|U_g|} - \frac{\sum_{u' \in U_{g'}} \mu(u')}{|U_{g'}|} \right|}{|G^{\text{pair}}|}
\tag{3.1}
$$

where G^{pair} denotes the set of pairs of user groups, U_g the set of users in group g and $\mu(u)$ the evaluation results of the metric μ for a user u. Melchiorre et al. [50] show that female users of a music recommendation platform receive, on average, recommendations of lower utility than male users.

Abdollahpouri et al. [3] show that popularity bias is propagated differently for different user groups and algorithms. They introduce the *group average popularity* (GAP) metric to study popularity bias of recommendation algorithms for different user groups, which quantifies the average popularity of items in the user profiles of a user group:

$$
\text{GAP}(g) = \frac{\sum_{u \in g} \frac{\sum_{i \in p_u} \phi(i)}{|p_u|}}{|g|}
\tag{3.2}
$$

$$
\Delta\text{GAP} = \frac{\text{GAP}_r(g) - \text{GAP}_p(g)}{\text{GAP}_p(g)}.
\tag{3.3}
$$

where $\phi(i)$ corresponds to the popularity score for item i, $\text{GAP}_p(g)$ denotes the average popularity of the items in the user profiles p of a specific user group g and $\text{GAP}_r(g)$ quantifies the average popularity of the items recommended by an algorithm r to the users of group g. Then ΔGAP corresponds to the change in GAP, which determines how the popularity of the recommended item deviates from the popularity of items in the user profiles. Positive values of ΔGAP therefore indicate that the algorithm, on average, recommends more popular items than those users in group g commonly consume.

In follow-up work, Abdollahpouri et al. [4] propose an additional metric called *popularity lift* (PL) that quantifies the extent to which a user is affected by popularity bias using the aforementioned GAP metric:

$$PL(g) = \frac{GAP_q(g) - GAP_p(g)}{GAP_p(g)} \tag{3.4}$$

Also, they leverage a *miscalibration metric* to measure popularity bias. Calibration is a general machine learning concept that denotes the extent to which predictions made by a machine learning model match the true outcomes; in the context of IR and RSs, calibrated search results or recommendations reflect the various user preferences in the results list [72]. Assuming that each item i is described by a set of categories c and user u has rated one or more items i and is interested in the categories c associated with items i, the miscalibration metric is given as

$$MC(P_u, Q_u) = H(P_u, Q_u) = \frac{\|\sqrt{P_u} - \sqrt{Q_u}\|_2}{\sqrt{2}}, \tag{3.5}$$

where H denotes the Hellinger distance between two distributions P_u and Q_u. P_u corresponds to the distribution of categories $c \in C$ rated by user u and Q_u are the categories $c \in C$ that are recommended to user u. Hence, the metric compares the distribution of item characteristics in a user's profile with the results the user receives by the IR or RS.

Another strategy is to investigate the representation of certain properties in the training data and compare it to their representation in the algorithmic output. Here, Lesota et al. [39] compare the item popularity distribution in the user's history with the popularity distribution in a recommendation list using statistical measures, including median and various statistical moments. Besides, they investigate how popularity bias affects users of different demographics (i. e., characterized by gender). Finally, a more recent research strand to measure bias in IR and RSs conducts user-centered bias evaluations to understand how bias affects the perceptions and user experiences of different user groups, typically in the form of interview studies, e. g., [5, 71].

3.3 Methods to mitigate harmful bias

Depending on the stage in the retrieval or recommendation pipeline at which the mitigation of harmful biases happens, it is common to distinguish between *pre-processing*, *in-processing* and *post-processing* debiasing techniques. Figure 3.1 illustrates these three strategies in a recommendation setting. In the following, we present the characteristics of each of these techniques and selected recent research works in more detail.

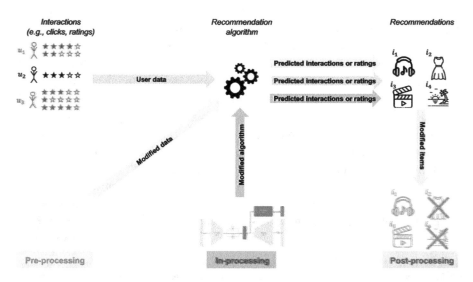

Figure 3.1: Illustrated categories of debiasing approaches. The gray part depicts the standard pipeline of a recommender system: The algorithm is trained on interaction data created by users, and predicts which items the target user might like. The blue part illustrates the pre-processing strategy, which modifies the input data the algorithm is trained on, to achieve a better balance of training data with respect to some user or item characteristic. The red part visualizes the functioning of in-processing techniques, which directly alter the recommendation algorithm to make unbiased predictions. The green part delineates post-processing approaches, which keep input and algorithm untouched, but adapt the recommendation list by removing or reordering its items.

3.3.1 Pre-processing methods

These methods, which are illustrated in blue in Figure 3.1, rely on the idea that biases should be alleviated already before data is fed into the retrieval or recommendation algorithm. This commonly entails modifying the input data the algorithm uses to train a model, to achieve a better balance in the training data with respect to some user or item characteristics. A common approach is *data rebalancing*, e. g., [33, 50]. For instance, from a user perspective, this can be achieved by upsampling training data of a RS (i. e., user-item interactions) created by the minority group or subsampling data created by the majority group, where these groups are defined with respect to the user attribute for which we want to debias. Upsampling is often realized by duplicating existing user-item interactions of the minority group; subsampling by randomly dropping interactions of the majority group. Focusing, in contrast, on the item (creator's) perspective, we can remove parts of the interactions with items that are in the "short-head" of the item popularity distribution, i. e., items that are already among the most popular ones, in order to mitigate popularity bias, i. e., an overexposure of such highly popular items.

To exemplify fairness-aware sampling, we take a closer look at [50]. Melchiorre et al. [50] investigate the effect of upsampling to obtain a balanced representation of different genders[2] in the training data of various recommendation algorithms, on the utility of recommendations for the different gender groups. More precisely, leveraging a popular music recommendation data set from Last.fm,[3] the authors duplicate the user-item interaction data by users of the minority group (female) in the training set until they match the number of training instances of the majority group (male). This idea is adapted from [25], where Geyik et al. argue that a balanced representation of male and female users during training should ideally result in equally good recommendations at inference time. Table 3.1 shows the performance of different recommendation algorithms in terms of normalized discounted cumulative gain (NDCG) computed for the 10 top-ranked recommendations. NDCG@10 is a rank-aware utility metric that takes values in the range $[0, 1]$ and reflects how close the ranking created by an algorithm is to an optimal ranking, where all relevant items occupy the top ranks.

Table 3.1: Utility in terms of NDCG@10 of various recommendation algorithms on the LFM-2b music data set. Results are shown for no pre-processing and for upsampling user-item interactions of the minority group to obtain a balanced training set in terms of genders. Results are provided for all user groups (All), for male (M) users and female users (F) and expressed as absolute difference between genders (Δ) and as relative difference with respect to the better performing group (%Δ). A favorable treatment toward (m)ales or (f)emales is indicated in parentheses. Results where upsampling narrows the utility gap between genders are indicated in boldface. The table is adapted from [50].

Algorithm	Pre-processing	NDCG@10 (All)	NDCG@10 (M/F)	Δ	%Δ
POP	–	.046	.045/.049	.004 (f)	8.2
	Upsampling	.045	.044/.051	.007 (f)	13.7
ItemKNN	–	.301	.313/.259	.054 (m)	17.3
	Upsampling	.292	.304/.250	.054 (m)	17.8
BPR	–	.127	.129/.117	.012 (m)	9.3
	Upsampling	.123	.124/.116	**.008 (m)**	**6.5**
ALS	–	.241	.251/.205	.046 (m)	18.3
	Upsampling	.238	.248/.204	**.044 (m)**	**17.7**
SLIM	–	.364	.378/.315	.063 (m)	16.7
	Upsampling	.359	.372/.312	**.060 (m)**	**16.1**
MultiVAE	–	.192	.197/.173	.024 (m)	12.2
	Upsampling	.183	.188/.166	**.023 (m)**	**12.2**

Briefly introducing the algorithms investigated in [50], POP is a simple non-personalized baseline, which ranks all songs in decreasing order of popularity (listening fre-

---

2 Because of the availability of information in the data sets, the authors only consider binary genders (male and female users).

3 The data set is a variant of LFM-2b [50, 66], which contains more than two billion user-song interactions released by more than 120,000 users of the Last.fm platform.

quency by all users) and recommends the top n items of this list to every user. ItemKNN (item-based k-nearest neighbors) [63] is a basic collaborative filtering approach that considers an item i as relevant for the target user u if it is similar to the items interacted with by u, where this item similarity is computed based on the items' interaction history over users. Alternating least squares (ALS) [30] is a matrix factorization approach, which adopts an alternating training procedure to obtain user and item embeddings in the same joint vector space, in such a way that the dot product of the embeddings approximates the original user-item matrix. BPR (Bayesian personalized ranking) [60] is a learning to rank an algorithm that adapts matrix factorization, but considers pairs of items for each user u instead of single user-item interactions. It aims to maximize the difference between the rating predictions of items that have interactions from the user and those with no interactions. Sparse linear method (SLIM) [56] factorizes the item-item cooccurrence matrix and uses the learned item coefficients to sparsely aggregate past user interactions and recommend the top n items to the target user. MultiVAE (variational autoencoders) [42] adopt a neural network architecture that encodes the item interactions of each user u as a latent representation, in a way that the original interaction vector of u can be reconstructed, and additional items can be recommended based on the generated probability distribution over all items.

Turning to the analysis of algorithmic recommendation fairness between user groups, from Table 3.1, we see that (almost) all algorithms perform worse for female users. Column **NDCG@10 (M/F)** directly confronts the utility for males and females. Column Δ shows the absolute difference between genders, for easier comparison. The gender that receives the better recommendation results is indicated in parentheses. Column %Δ shows the same information, but relative to the performance of the user group with higher performance. To investigate the performance difference when using upsampling, we compare the first row (denoted — in column **Pre-processing**) with the second row (denoted **Upsampling**) for each algorithm. The results show that all personalized recommendation algorithms favor male users.[4] This gender disparity can reach up to 18.3 %, for ALS, meaning that recommendations for female users are on average 18.3 % less useful than those for their male counterparts, according to the NDCG@10 metric. However, by adopting a simple upsampling strategy, this disparity can be narrowed. For instance, considering the case of BPR with no pre-processing applied, we observe that the performance of the RS is on average 9.3 % worse for female users compared to male users. With upsampling, this performance disparity decreases to 6.5 %. While these results provide some evidence that a simple pre-processing method, such as resampling, can already make a RS fairer, one important observation is that the over-

---

4 The better performance of the nonpersonalized POP recommender for female users can be explained by the general more mainstream music taste of female users. Due to the classical offline setup of the evaluation, which divides all data into training, validation and test data, it is therefore more likely to make a correct prediction for female users than males.

all utility of recommendations drops when performing pre-processing (cf. **NDCG@10** between rows – and **Upsampling**).

3.3.2 In-processing methods

The concept of in-processing is illustrated in the red part of Figure 3.1. Corresponding approaches directly integrate a debiasing objective or component into the model training or optimization procedure. This can be done, for instance, by adapting the loss function to include a bias regularization term or by using adversarial training, as proposed for retrieval in [59] and for recommendation in [24, 76]. In the following, we exemplify how adversarial training can be leveraged for gender bias mitigation.

The basic idea of *adversarial training* for this task is to add an additional classifier (called adversary) to the main supervised learning component of the algorithm that predicts whether a document is relevant to a query (retrieval) or whether a user will interact with an item (recommendation). The goal of this adversary is to predict the sensitive attribute that should not be considered by the main algorithm when creating lists of recommendations or retrieved documents. Both components (main and adversary) act as opponents. While the model solving the main task tries to maximize its performance in terms of relevance or utility, the adversary tries to optimize its predictive accuracy on the sensitive attribute (e. g., gender of the RS user [24] or gender neutrality/balance of query and document [59]). During (adversarial) training, latent representations depending on the task at hand are learned (e. g., representations of queries, documents or user-item interactions). The main component uses them to predict the relevance of documents or the utility of items, whereas the adversary uses them to predict the sensitive attribute. The training procedure adopts an approach that tries to optimize for both objectives: maximize the performance in the main task and minimize the performance of the adversary, by unlearning from the latent representation any information about the sensitive attribute. Accordingly, this principle is referred to as "fairness through unawareness" or "fairness through blindness."

While integrating such an adversarial mechanism is, in principle, not bound to a particular type of retrieval or recommendation algorithm, it has predominantly been used in neural network architectures. For instance, Rekabsaz et al. propose an extension of the popular BERT language models [14], which adds to the main component that predicts a relevance score for document-item pairs an adversarial two-layer feed-forward network that predicts the protected attribute [59]. The goal of this AdvBERT architecture is to unlearn gender-biased information from embeddings of query-document interactions. The authors show that AdvBERT models can achieve significant improvements in fairness without significantly sacrificing accuracy. The fairness of a search result, in this case, is measured as the balance between male and female words appearing in the documents returned in response to a gender-neutral query.

Adversarial training has also been used for debiasing latent user representations in RSs. In particular, Ganhör et al. propose an architecture that integrates an adversarial component into a *variational autoencoder* (VAE) network [24]. The proposed Adv-MultVAE architecture is illustrated in Figure 3.2. The main idea of an autoencoder is to learn a latent representation z of its input x in a way that z can be used to optimally reconstruct x at its output x'. The embedding z is created through an encoder network while x is reconstructed from z as x' through a decoder network.[5] Such a VAE architecture has been shown to perform well for recommendation tasks [21, 42]. In this setting, the vector x represents the user-item interactions of one user. Its dimensionality is, therefore, equal to the number of items in the catalog. After the model has been training, presenting a user u's current interaction vector to the network, the items corresponding to the dimensions in x' can be sorted in decreasing order of their probability to create a personalized recommendation list.[6] To enable bias mitigation in VAEs by unlearning a protected attribute y, the network is extended by the blue components in Figure 3.2. Concretely, an adversary component, implemented as a simple feed-forward network, is added to predict y' from z. The loss function that is optimized during training is composed of the recommendation loss (main task) and the loss of the auxiliary task (predicting the protected attribute). Training is performed in a way that both components try to optimize the performance in their respective task by adjusting the model parameters. The interested reader is referred to [24] for details.

Adv-MultVAE has been evaluated by Ganhör et al. on two data sets, one for movie (MovieLens-1M [28]) and one for music recommendation (LFM2b-DB [50]). The authors show that the amount of protected user information (in their case study, gender) that is recoverable from the latent user representation z can be significantly reduced: Balanced accuracy of gender prediction drops from more than 70 % without the adversary (MultVAE) to about 57 % (ML-1M) and 61 % (LFM2b-DB) when including the adversarial network (Adv-MultVAE). The proposed recommendation architecture, therefore, yields more gender-agnostic results. At the same time, only a marginal decrease in NDCG is observed. This slightly lower utility for Adv-MultVAE is partly due to the challenge of selecting a comparable model and in turn understates the recommendation performance of Adv-MultVAE compared to its biased counterpart MultVAE.[7]

All in all, adversarial training, in particular in combination with neural network architectures, has proven a powerful technique to debias retrieval and recommendation algorithms. As a positive side effect, the resulting reduced information leakage from the debiased embeddings improves users' privacy.

---

5 In fact, in a *variational* autoencoder architecture the encoder is not directly used to infer z, but z's are sampled from a Gaussian distribution whose mean μ and standard deviation σ are learned during training.

6 Items already interacted with by u are typically removed.

7 The model selection for Adv-MultVAE is based on lowest performance of the adversary while that for MultVAE on the highest NDCG in the main recommendation task.

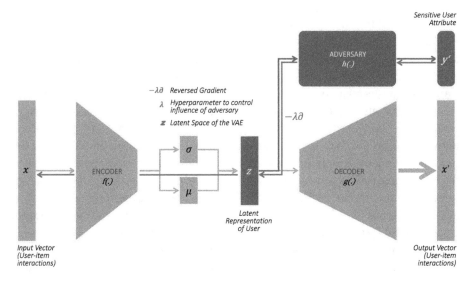

Figure 3.2: Architecture of adversarial multinomial variational autoencoders (Adv-MultVAE), according to [24].

3.3.3 Post-processing methods

Bias mitigation methods that adopt a post-processing scheme are illustrated in green in Figure 3.1. They adjust the scores or ranks of contents in the result list (recommended items or retrieved documents) to enforce a certain bias-reducing objective, without modifying the core ranking algorithm [11, 54, 79]. Therefore, such methods can be applied irrespective of the main search or recommendation engine.

For instance, a simple *reranking* approach is presented by Ferraro et al. who target demographic bias, more precisely, creators' gender bias in music recommendations [22]. The authors first investigate the artist demographics of music recommendations created by the popular ALS algorithm for collaborative filtering [30], which is trained on two music recommendation data sets from Last.fm (LFM-1b [64] and Last.fm 360 K [12]). They find that the average position of the top-ranked track by a female artist is between 8 and 9 while the top-ranked song by a male artist on average occupies position 1 or 2 in the recommendation list.[8] Based on this observation, Ferraro et al. propose a simple reranking approach that moves down all male contents by λ positions in the ranking, to obtain a more balanced gender distribution of music artists in recommendation lists. The authors also conduct a simulation study that iteratively retrains the recommendation model, assuming that a user will listen to all recommended tracks in each iteration.

---

8 Theses statistics have to be considered in the context of an overall underrepresentation of female artists in the data sets, and more generally in the music business. The share of female artists in both investigated data sets is around 23 % versus 77 % for male artists.

The study results suggest that the adopted reranking strategy has a positive long-term effect on gender balance in music RSs, by yielding a more balanced exposure of tracks by male and female artists. On the downside, the proposed reranking approach reduces NDCG@10 by 5 % for $\lambda = 7$, which is the value of λ that yields the most gender-balanced results. This evidences a trade-off between utility of recommendations for the RS users and fairness in terms of balanced exposure for content creators (music artists, in this case) of different genders.

Addressing this trade-off between fairness and accuracy of recommendations, Naghiaei et al. propose a content reranking framework that considers the goals of both consumers and producers alike [54]. The introduced CPFair algorithm uses linear programming/optimization to maximize utility of recommendations for users while minimizing the deviation from a fairness notion on the producer (content creator or provider) side and the end user (content consumer) side. From the creators' perspective, the aim is to achieve exposure parity (e. g., each creator should be recommended to the same number of users) irrespective of their contents' overall popularity. The fairness notion on the consumer side is given by parity in terms of recommendation utility (e. g., with respect to the NDCG metric) regardless of the user's activity level, i. e., number of the user's interactions with items. In short, each user should receive recommendations of the same quality and each content producer should have equal chances of being recommended to users. Note that these notions of fairness relate to popularity bias because they assume that the recommendation frequency of an item should not depend on the number of its historical interactions (creator side), and the utility of recommendations for a user should not depend on the user's level of activity, which is, again, measured as the number of historical interactions with items (consumer side). Naghiaei et al. show for 4 recommendation algorithms on 8 data sets, covering different recommendation domains (movies, music, products), that CPFair can reduce the unfairness for consumers and creators alike, while maintaining or even improving the overall recommendation quality.

3.4 Conclusions and open challenges

In this chapter, we discussed different biases and their relation to fairness in information access systems, with a particular focus on ranking systems such as search engines and recommender systems. While identifying, measuring, and mitigating harmful biases in such systems is still an evolving research direction, significant advances have been made in recent years, some of which we have reviewed here. In particular, we surveyed various sources of bias (e. g., training data, algorithm or presentation of results) and ways to quantify harmful biases that lead to unfair system behavior. As for bias mitigation, we introduced and exemplified pre-processing, in-processing and post-processing methods, and discussed their merits and shortcomings, in particular, their trade-off between fairness and accuracy of results.

Given the young age of the area, research on fairness and debiasing of information access systems is still facing some major challenges. We outline below some of the most important ones, in our opinion.

- Studying the fairness of machine learning technology, in particular, that used in information access systems, calls for a *multidisciplinary research approach* [9, 67]. Unfortunately, the corresponding research landscape is still characterized by a gap between the more technical computer science perspective and the more human-centric perspectives from psychology, social science or law. Bridging this gap is important to acquire a decent understanding of harmful biases from multiple perspectives, and to elaborate holistic solutions for fair information retrieval and recommendation technology. This also entails understanding the societal, ethical and legal implications of (un)fair ranking algorithms.

- Related to the fact that most research conducted in the area of fair information access systems takes a technical/computational perspective, a fundamental and unsolved question is whether the many bias and fairness metrics proposed in the literature do actually reflect human perception of fairness. In other words, the *ecological validity of bias and fairness metrics* is still unknown. However, uncovering and analyzing (likely) discrepancies between computational metrics and human perception of bias and fairness is vital to understand the influence of biased results on individuals and user groups. First steps to address this question have been made in [23], where Ferwerda et al. present a user study to assess whether popularity bias metrics are able to model human perception of popularity bias in recommendation lists of music songs. Also related to the above question, it is barely known to which extent different groups of users are affected by harmful biases. This has been exemplified by Abdollahpouri et al. [6], who investigate to which extent recommendations for users with different levels of interest in popular content are prone to popularity bias.

- Another important challenge revolves around the question to which extent the goals of different stakeholders of information access systems should be considered in the design of the ranking algorithm. Beyond the end user of the system, other stakeholders include the content creators (e. g., music artists or book writers), platform providers (e. g., Amazon or Spotify) and policymakers (e. g., politicians) [67]. Taking a *multistakeholder perspective* that aims at meeting the stakeholders' different goals (e. g., maximizing the relevance/utility of recommendation/retrieval results for the end users, maximizing the exposure of their content by creators, or maximizing the profit for platform providers) is a nontrivial challenge [1]. First steps in this direction have been taken by jointly optimizing fairness for content creators and consumers, e. g., [16, 54, 77].

- To some extent related to the previous point, understanding and algorithmically addressing the sensitive *trade-off between desirable and harmful bias*—the former being needed for personalization, the latter resulting in unfair system behavior—is a challenging endeavor [38]. This can be exemplified, for instance, by the in-processing bias mitigation approaches that adopt adversarial training (see Section 3.3.2). In a recommendation scenario, it was shown in [24] that adversarial training can reduce accuracy of predicting the correct user gender to 57 %. However, this raises the question of what an optimal or desirable accuracy value is. Looking at the interaction data, it is easy to see that men and women actually do differ in their general preferences toward certain contents; so do users from different countries, as evidenced for music in [65]. Do we want to make the recommendation algorithm fully agnostic to any consumption preferences that male, female or other groups of users may naturally have? This can even be considered a philosophical question that does not have a simple answer.

We are looking forward to seeing a lot of exciting research in the next few years in this vibrant research area of fair information access systems.

References

[1] Himan Abdollahpouri, Gediminas Adomavicius, Robin Burke, Ido Guy, Dietmar Jannach, Toshihiro Kamishima, Jan Krasnodebski, and Luiz Augusto Pizzato. Multistakeholder recommendation: Survey and research directions. *User Modeling and User-Adapted Interaction* 30(1) (2020) 127–158.

[2] Himan Abdollahpouri, Masoud Mansoury, Robin Burke, and Bamshad Mobasher. The unfairness of popularity bias in recommendation. In: Robin Burke, Himan Abdollahpouri, Edward C. Malthouse, K. P. Thai, and Yongfeng Zhang, editors. *Proceedings of the Workshop on Recommendation in Multi-stakeholder Environments co-located with the 13th ACM Conference on Recommender Systems (RecSys 2019), Copenhagen, Denmark, September 20, 2019*. CEUR Workshop Proceedings, volume 2440. CEUR-WS.org, 2019.

[3] Himan Abdollahpouri, Masoud Mansoury, Robin Burke, and Bamshad Mobasher. The unfairness of popularity bias in recommendation. In: *RecSys Workshop on Recommendation in Multistakeholder Environments (RMSE)*, 2019.

[4] Himan Abdollahpouri, Masoud Mansoury, Robin Burke, and Bamshad Mobasher. The connection between popularity bias, calibration, and fairness in recommendation. In: *Fourteenth ACM Conference on Recommender Systems*, 2020, pp. 726–731.

[5] Himan Abdollahpouri, Masoud Mansoury, Robin Burke, Bamshad Mobasher, and Edward Malthouse. User-centered evaluation of popularity bias in recommender systems. In: *Proceedings of the 29th ACM Conference on User Modeling, Adaptation and Personalization*, 2021, pp. 119–129.

[6] Himan Abdollahpouri, Masoud Mansoury, Robin Burke, Bamshad Mobasher, and Edward C. Malthouse. User-centered evaluation of popularity bias in recommender systems. In: Judith Masthoff, Eelco Herder, Nava Tintarev, and Marko Tkalcic, editors. *Proceedings of the 29th ACM Conference on User Modeling, Adaptation and Personalization, UMAP 2021, Utrecht, The Netherlands, June, 21–25, 2021*. ACM, 2021, pp. 119–129.

[7] Ricardo Baeza-Yates. Bias on the web. *Communications of the ACM* 61(6) (2018) 54–61.

[8] Ricardo Baeza-Yates and Berthier A. Ribeiro-Neto *Modern Information Retrieval - the concepts and technology behind search*, 2nd edition. Harlow, England: Pearson Education Ltd. 2011.

[9] Solon Barocas, Moritz Hardt, and Arvind Narayanan. *Fairness and Machine Learning: Limitations and Opportunities*. fairmlbook.org, 2019. http://www.fairmlbook.org.

[10] Ludovico Boratto, Gianni Fenu, and Mirko Marras. The effect of algorithmic bias on recommender systems for massive open online courses. In: *Advances in Information Retrieval: 41st European Conference on IR Research, ECIR 2019, Cologne, Germany, April 14–18, 2019, Proceedings, Part I 41*. Springer, 2019, pp. 457–472.

[11] L. Elisa Celis, Damian Straszak, and Nisheeth K. Vishnoi. Ranking with fairness constraints. In: Ioannis Chatzigiannakis, Christos Kaklamanis, Dániel Marx, and Donald Sannella, editors. *45th International Colloquium on Automata, Languages, and Programming, ICALP 2018, July 9–13, 2018, Prague, Czech Republic*. LIPIcs, volume 107. Schloss Dagstuhl - Leibniz-Zentrum für Informatik, 2018, pp. 28:1–28:15.

[12] Òscar Celma. *Music Recommendation and Discovery - The Long Tail, Long Fail, and Long Play in the Digital Music Space*. Springer, 2010.

[13] Jiawei Chen, Hande Dong, Xiang Wang, Fuli Feng, Meng Wang, and Xiangnan He. Bias and debias in recommender system: A survey and future directions. *ACM Transactions on Information Systems* (2020).

[14] Jacob Devlin, Ming-Wei Chang, Kenton Lee, and Kristina Toutanova. BERT: pre-training of deep bidirectional transformers for language understanding. In: Jill Burstein, Christy Doran, and Thamar Solorio, editors. *Proceedings of the 2019 Conference of the North American Chapter of the Association for Computational Linguistics: Human Language Technologies, NAACL-HLT 2019, Minneapolis, MN, USA, June 2–7, 2019, Volume 1 (Long and Short Papers)*. Association for Computational Linguistics, 2019, pp. 4171–4186.

[15] Tommaso Di Noia, Nava Tintarev, Panagiota Fatourou, and Markus Schedl. Recommender systems under european ai regulations. *Communications of the ACM* 65(4) (2022) 69–73.

[16] Virginie Do, Sam Corbett-Davies, Jamal Atif, and Nicolas Usunier. Two-sided fairness in rankings via lorenz dominance. In: Marc'Aurelio Ranzato, Alina Beygelzimer, Yann N. Dauphin, Percy Liang, and Jennifer Wortman Vaughan, editors. *Advances in Neural Information Processing Systems 34: Annual Conference on Neural Information Processing Systems 2021, NeurIPS 2021, December 6–14, 2021, virtual*, 2021, pp. 8596–8608.

[17] Michael D. Ekstrand, Anubrata Das, Robin Burke, Fernando Diaz, et al. Fairness in information access systems. *Foundations and Trends® in Information Retrieval* 16(1–2) (2022) 1–177.

[18] Michael D. Ekstrand, Mucun Tian, Ion Madrazo Azpiazu, Jennifer D. Ekstrand, Oghenemaro Anuyah, David, McNeill, and Maria Soledad Pera. All the cool kids, how do they fit in?: Popularity and demographic biases in recommender evaluation and effectiveness. In: Sorelle A. Friedler and Christo Wilson, editors. *Conference on Fairness, Accountability and Transparency, FAT 2018, 23-24 February 2018, New York, NY, USA*. Proceedings of Machine Learning Research, PMLR, volume 81, 2018, pp. 172–186.

[19] Mehdi Elahi, Danial Khosh Kholgh, Mohammad Sina Kiarostami, Sorush Saghari, Shiva Parsa Rad, and Marko Tkalčič. Investigating the impact of recommender systems on user-based and item-based popularity bias. *Information Processing & Management* 58(5) (2021) 102655.

[20] Alexander Felfernig, Gerhard Friedrich, Bartosz Gula, Martin Hitz, Thomas Kruggel, Gerhard Leitner, Rudolf Melcher, D. Riepan, S. Strauss, Erich Teppan, and Oliver Vitouch. Persuasive recommendation: Serial position effects in knowledge-based recommender systems. In: Yvonne de Kort, Wijnand A. IJsselsteijn, Cees J. H. Midden, Berry Eggen, and B. J. Fogg, editors. *Persuasive Technology, Second International Conference on Persuasive Technology, PERSUASIVE 2007, Palo Alto, CA, USA, April 26–27, 2007, Revised Selected Papers*. Lecture Notes in Computer Science, volume 4744. Springer, 2007, pp. 283–294.

[21] Maurizio Ferrari Dacrema, Paolo Cremonesi, and Dietmar Jannach. Are we really making much progress? a worrying analysis of recent neural recommendation approaches. In: *Proceedings of the 13th ACM Conference on Recommender Systems, RecSys '19*. New York, NY, USA: Association for Computing Machinery, 2019, pp. 101–109.

[22] Andres Ferraro, Xavier Serra, and Christine Bauer. Break the loop: Gender imbalance in music recommenders. In: Falk Scholer, Paul Thomas, David Elsweiler, Hideo Joho, Noriko Kando, and Catherine Smith, editors. *CHIIR '21: ACM SIGIR Conference on Human Information Interaction and Retrieval, Canberra, ACT, Australia, March 14–19, 2021*. ACM, 2021, pp. 249–254.

[23] Bruce Ferwerda, Eveline Ingesson, Michaela Berndl, and Markus Schedl. I Don't Care How Popular You Are! Investigating Popularity Bias From a User's Perspective. In: *Proceedings of the 8th ACM SIGIR Conference on Human Information Interaction and Retrieval (CHIIR 2023)*. ACM, 2023.

[24] Christian Ganhör, David Penz, Navid Rekabsaz, Oleg Lesota, and Markus Schedl. Unlearning protected user attributes in recommendations with adversarial training. In: Enrique Amigó, Pablo Castells, Julio Gonzalo, Ben Carterette, J. Shane Culpepper, and Gabriella Kazai, editors. *SIGIR '22: The 45th International ACM SIGIR Conference on Research and Development in Information Retrieval, Madrid, Spain, July 11–15, 2022*. ACM, 2022, pp. 2142–2147.

[25] Sahin Cem Geyik, Stuart Ambler, and Krishnaram Kenthapadi. Fairness-aware ranking in search & recommendation systems with application to linkedin talent search. In: Ankur Teredesai, Vipin Kumar, Ying Li, Rómer Rosales, Evimaria Terzi, and George Karypis, editors. *Proceedings of the 25th ACM SIGKDD International Conference on Knowledge Discovery & Data Mining, KDD 2019, Anchorage, AK, USA, August 4–8, 2019*. ACM, 2019, pp. 2221–2231.

[26] Elizabeth Gómez, Carlos Shui Zhang, Ludovico Boratto, Maria Salamó, and Mirko Marras. The winner takes it all: geographic imbalance and provider (un) fairness in educational recommender systems. In: *Proceedings of the 44th International ACM SIGIR Conference on Research and Development in Information Retrieval*, 2021, pp. 1808–1812.

[27] Sara Hajian, Francesco Bonchi, and Carlos Castillo. Algorithmic bias: From discrimination discovery to fairness-aware data mining. In: *Proceedings of the 22nd ACM SIGKDD international conference on knowledge discovery and data mining*, 2016, pp. 2125–2126.

[28] F. Maxwell Harper and Joseph A. Konstan. The movielens datasets: History and context. *The ACM Transactions on Interactive Intelligent Systems* 5(4) (2016) 19:1–19:19.

[29] Katja Hofmann, Anne Schuth, Alejandro Bellogin, and Maarten De Rijke. Effects of position bias on click-based recommender evaluation. In: *ECIR*, volume 14. Springer, 2014, pp. 624–630.

[30] Yifan Hu, Yehuda Koren, and Chris Volinsky. Collaborative filtering for implicit feedback datasets. In: *Proceedings of the 8th IEEE International Conference on Data Mining (ICDM 2008), December 15–19, 2008, Pisa, Italy*. IEEE Computer Society, 2008, pp. 263–272.

[31] Joel Huber, John W. Payne, and Christopher Puto. Adding asymmetrically dominated alternatives: Violations of regularity and the similarity hypothesis. *Journal of Consumer Research* 9(1) (1982) 90–98.

[32] Dietmar Jannach, Lukas Lerche, Iman Kamehkhosh, and Michael Jugovac. What recommenders recommend: an analysis of recommendation biases and possible countermeasures. *User Modeling and User-Adapted Interaction* 25 (2015) 427–491.

[33] Ömer Kirnap, Fernando Diaz, Asia Biega, Michael D. Ekstrand, Ben Carterette, and Emine Yilmaz. Estimation of fair ranking metrics with incomplete judgments. In: Jure Leskovec, Marko Grobelnik, Marc Najork, Jie Tang, and Leila Zia, editors. *WWW '21: The Web Conference 2021, Virtual Event/Ljubljana, Slovenia, April 19–23, 2021*. ACM/IW3C2, 2021, pp. 1065–1075.

[34] Dominik Kowald, Peter Muellner, Eva Zangerle, Christine Bauer, Markus Schedl, and Elisabeth Lex. Support the underground: characteristics of beyond-mainstream music listeners. *EPJ Data Science* 10(1) (2021) 1–26.

[35] Dominik Kowald, Markus Schedl, and Elisabeth Lex. The unfairness of popularity bias in music recommendation: A reproducibility study. In: *European Conference on Information Retrieval*. Springer, 2020, pp. 35–42.

[36] Sanjay Krishnan, Jay Patel, Michael J. Franklin, and Ken Goldberg. A methodology for learning, analyzing, and mitigating social influence bias in recommender systems. In: *Proceedings of the 8th ACM Conference on Recommender systems*, 2014, pp. 137–144.

[37] Nicol Turner Lee, Paul Resnick, and Genie Barton. *Algorithmic bias detection and mitigation: Best practices and policies to reduce consumer harms*. Washington, DC, USA: Brookings Institute, 2019, pp. 2.

[38] Oleg Lesota, Stefan Brandl, Matthias Wenzel, Alessandro B. Melchiorre, Elisabeth Lex, Navid Rekabsaz, and Markus Schedl. Exploring cross-group discrepancies in calibrated popularity for accuracy/fairness trade-off optimization. In: Himan Abdollahpouri, Shaghayegh Sahebi, Mehdi Elahi, Masoud Mansoury, Babak Loni, Zahra Nazari, and Maria Dimakopoulou, editors. *Proceedings of the 2nd Workshop on Multi-Objective Recommender Systems co-located with 16th ACM Conference on Recommender Systems (RecSys 2022), Seattle, WA, USA, 18th–23rd September 2022, CEUR Workshop Proceedings*, volume 3268. CEUR-WS.org, 2022.

[39] Oleg Lesota, Alessandro B. Melchiorre, Navid Rekabsaz, Stefan Brandl, Dominik Kowald, Elisabeth Lex, and Markus Schedl. Analyzing Item Popularity Bias of Music Recommender Systems: Are Different Genders Equally Affected? In: *Proceedings of the 15th ACM Conference on Recommender Systems (Late-Breaking Results), Amsterdam, the Netherlands, October–November 2021*, 2021.

[40] Elisabeth Lex, Dominik Kowald, and Markus Schedl. Modeling popularity and temporal drift of music genre preferences. *Transactions of the International Society for Music Information Retrieval* 3(1) (2020).

[41] Elisabeth Lex, Dominik Kowald, Paul Seitlinger, Thi Ngoc Trang Tran, Alexander Felfernig, and Markus Schedl. Psychology-informed Recommender Systems. *Foundations and Trends® in Information Retrieval* 15(2) (2021) 134–242.

[42] Dawen Liang, Rahul G. Krishnan, Matthew D. Hoffman, and Tony Jebara. Variational autoencoders for collaborative filtering. In: Pierre-Antoine Champin, Fabien L. Gandon, Mounia Lalmas, and Panagiotis G. Ipeirotis, editors. *Proceedings of the 2018 World Wide Web Conference on World Wide Web, WWW 2018, Lyon, France*. ACM, 2018, pp. 689–698.

[43] Allen Lin, Jianling Wang, Ziwei Zhu, and James Caverlee. Quantifying and mitigating popularity bias in conversational recommender systems. In: *Proceedings of the 31st ACM International Conference on Information & Knowledge Management*, 2022, pp. 1238–1247.

[44] Masoud Mansoury. Understanding and mitigating multi-sided exposure bias in recommender systems. *ACM SIGWEB Newsletter* (2022, Autumn) 1–4.

[45] Masoud Mansoury, Himan Abdollahpouri, Mykola Pechenizkiy, Bamshad Mobasher, and Robin Burke. *FairMatch: A Graph-Based Approach for Improving Aggregate Diversity in Recommender Systems*. New York, NY, USA: Association for Computing Machinery, 2020, pp. 154–162.

[46] Masoud Mansoury, Himan Abdollahpouri, Mykola Pechenizkiy, Bamshad Mobasher, and Robin Burke. Feedback loop and bias amplification in recommender systems. In: *Proceedings of the 29th ACM international conference on information & knowledge management*, 2020, pp. 2145–2148.

[47] Masoud Mansoury, Himan Abdollahpouri, Mykola Pechenizkiy, Bamshad Mobasher, and Robin Burke. A graph-based approach for mitigating multi-sided exposure bias in recommender systems. *ACM Transactions on Information Systems (TOIS)* 40(2) (2021) 1–31.

[48] Ninareh Mehrabi, Fred Morstatter, Nripsuta Saxena, Kristina Lerman, and Aram Galstyan. A survey on bias and fairness in machine learning. *ACM Computing Surveys (CSUR)* 54(6) (2021) 1–35.

[49] Alessandro B. Melchiorre, Navid Rekabsaz, Emilia Parada-Cabaleiro, Stefan Brandl, Oleg Lesota, and Markus Schedl. Investigating Gender Fairness of Recommendation Algorithms in the Music Domain. *Information Processing & Management* 58(5) (2021) 102666.

[50] Alessandro B. Melchiorre, Navid Rekabsaz, Emilia Parada-Cabaleiro, Stefan Brandl, Oleg Lesota, and Markus Schedl. Investigating gender fairness of recommendation algorithms in the music domain. *Information Processing & Management* 58(5) (2021) 102666.

[51] Alessandro B. Melchiorre and Markus Schedl. Personality correlates of music audio preferences for modelling music listeners. In: Tsvi Kuflik, Ilaria Torre, Robin Burke, and Cristina Gena, editors. *Proceedings of the 28th ACM Conference on User Modeling, Adaptation and Personalization, UMAP 2020, Genoa, Italy, July 12–18, 2020*. ACM, 2020, pp. 313–317.

[52] Alessandro B. Melchiorre, Eva Zangerle, and Markus Schedl. Personality bias of music recommendation algorithms. In: *Fourteenth ACM Conference on Recommender Systems, RecSys '20*, New York, NY, USA: Association for Computing Machinery, 2020, pp. 533–538.

[53] Shira Mitchell, Eric Potash, Solon Barocas, Alexander D'Amour, and Kristian Lum. Algorithmic fairness: Choices, assumptions, and definitions. *Annual Review of Statistics and Its Application* 8 (2021) 141–163.

[54] Mohammadmehdi Naghiaei, Hossein A. Rahmani, and Yashar Deldjoo. Cpfair: Personalized consumer and producer fairness re-ranking for recommender systems. In: Enrique Amigó, Pablo Castells, Julio Gonzalo, Ben Carterette, J. Shane Culpepper, and Gabriella Kazai, editors. *SIGIR '22: The 45th International ACM SIGIR Conference on Research and Development in Information Retrieval, Madrid, Spain, July 11–15, 2022*. ACM, 2022, pp. 770–779.

[55] Nicola Neophytou, Bhaskar Mitra, and Catherine Stinson. Revisiting popularity and demographic biases in recommender evaluation and effectiveness. *CoRR*, abs/2110.08353 (2021).

[56] Xia Ning and George Karypis. SLIM: sparse linear methods for top-n recommender systems. In: Diane J. Cook, Jian Pei, Wei Wang, Osmar R. Zaïane, and Xindong Wu, editors. *Proceedings of the 11th IEEE International Conference on Data Mining, ICDM 2011, Vancouver, BC, Canada*. IEEE Computer Society, 2011, pp. 497–506.

[57] J. Payne, J. Bettman, and E. Johnson. *The Adaptive Decision Maker*. Cambridge University Press, 1993.

[58] Daniele Quercia, Diego B. Las Casas, João Paulo Pesce, David Stillwell, Michal Kosinski, Virgílio A. F. Almeida, and Jon Crowcroft. Facebook and privacy: The balancing act of personality, gender, and relationship currency. In: John G. Breslin, Nicole B. Ellison, James G. Shanahan, and Zeynep Tufekci, editors. *Proceedings of the Sixth International Conference on Weblogs and Social Media, Dublin, Ireland, June 4–7, 2012*. The AAAI Press, 2012.

[59] Navid Rekabsaz, Simone Kopeinik, and Markus Schedl. Societal biases in retrieved contents: Measurement framework and adversarial mitigation of BERT rankers. In: Fernando Diaz, Chirag Shah, Torsten Suel, Pablo Castells, Rosie Jones, and Tetsuya Sakai, editors. *SIGIR '21: The 44th International ACM SIGIR Conference on Research and Development in Information Retrieval, Virtual Event, Canada, July 11–15, 2021*. ACM, 2021, pp. 306–316.

[60] Steffen Rendle, Christoph Freudenthaler, Zeno Gantner, and Lars Schmidt-Thieme. BPR: bayesian personalized ranking from implicit feedback. In: Jeff A. Bilmes and Andrew Y. Ng, editors. *UAI 2009, Proceedings of the Twenty-Fifth Conference on Uncertainty in Artificial Intelligence, Montreal, QC, Canada, June 18–21, 2009*. AUAI Press, 2009, pp. 452–461.

[61] Francesco Ricci, Lior Rokach, and Bracha Shapira. *Recommender Systems Handbook*. Springer US, 2022.

[62] Yuta Saito. Asymmetric tri-training for debiasing missing-not-at-random explicit feedback. In: *Proceedings of the 43rd International ACM SIGIR Conference on Research and Development in Information Retrieval, 2020*, pp. 309–318.

[63] Badrul Sarwar, George Karypis, Joseph Konstan, and John Riedl. Item-based collaborative filtering recommendation algorithms. In: *Proceedings of the 10th International Conference on World Wide Web, WWW '01*. New York, NY, USA: Association for Computing Machinery, 2001, pp. 285–295.

[64] Markus Schedl. The LFM-1b Dataset for Music Retrieval and Recommendation. In: John R. Kender, John R. Smith, Jiebo Luo, Susanne Boll, and Winston H. Hsu, editors. *Proceedings of the 2016 ACM on International Conference on Multimedia Retrieval, ICMR 2016, New York, New York, USA, June 6–9, 2016*. ACM, 2016, pp. 103–110.

[65] Markus Schedl. Investigating country-specific music preferences and music recommendation algorithms with the lfm-1b dataset. *International Journal of Multimedia Information Retrieval* 6(1) (2017) 71–84.

[66] Markus Schedl, Stefan Brandl, Oleg Lesota, Emilia Parada-Cabaleiro, David Penz, and Navid Rekabsaz. Lfm-2b: A data set of enriched music listening events for recommender systems research and fairness analysis. In: David Elsweiler, editor, *CHIIR '22: ACM SIGIR Conference on Human Information Interaction and Retrieval, Regensburg, Germany, March 14–18, 2022*. ACM, 2022, pp. 337–341.

[67] Markus Schedl, Navid Rekabsaz, Elisabeth Lex, Tessa Grosz, and Elisabeth Greif. Multiperspective and multidisciplinary treatment of fairness in recommender systems research. In: *UMAP '22: 30th ACM Conference on User Modeling, Adaptation and Personalization, Barcelona, Spain, July 4–7, 2022, Adjunct Proceedings*. ACM, 2022, pp. 90–94.

[68] Tobias Schnabel, Adith Swaminathan, Ashudeep Singh, Navin Chandak, and Thorsten Joachims. Recommendations as treatments: Debiasing learning and evaluation. In: *International conference on machine learning, PMLR*, 2016, pp. 1670–1679.

[69] Cristina Segalin, Fabio Celli, Luca Polonio, Michal Kosinski, David Stillwell, Nicu Sebe, Marco Cristani, and Bruno Lepri. What your facebook profile picture reveals about your personality. In: Qiong Liu, Rainer Lienhart, Haohong Wang, Sheng-Wei "Kuan-Ta" Chen, Susanne Boll, Yi-Ping Phoebe Chen, Gerald Friedland, Jia Li, and Shuicheng Yan, editors. *Proceedings of the 2017 ACM on Multimedia Conference, MM 2017, Mountain View, CA, USA, October 23–27, 2017*. ACM, 2017, pp. 460–468.

[70] Marcin Skowron, Marko Tkalcic, Bruce Ferwerda, and Markus Schedl. Fusing social media cues: Personality prediction from twitter and instagram. In: Jacqueline Bourdeau, Jim Hendler, Roger Nkambou, Ian Horrocks, and Ben Y. Zhao, editors. *Proceedings of the 25th International Conference on World Wide Web, WWW 2016, Montreal, Canada, April 11–15, 2016, Companion Volume*. ACM, 2016, pp. 107–108.

[71] Nasim Sonboli, Jessie J. Smith, Florencia Cabral Berenfus, Robin Burke, and Casey Fiesler. Fairness and transparency in recommendation: The users' perspective. In: *Proceedings of the 29th ACM Conference on User Modeling, Adaptation and Personalization*, 2021, pp. 274–279.

[72] Harald Steck. Calibrated recommendations. In: *Proceedings of the 12th ACM conference on recommender systems*, 2018, pp. 154–162.

[73] Erich Christian Teppan and Markus Zanker. Decision biases in recommender systems. *Journal of Internet Commerce* 14(2) (2015) 255–275.

[74] Ningxia Wang and Li Chen. User bias in beyond-accuracy measurement of recommendation algorithms. In: *Proceedings of the 15th ACM Conference on Recommender Systems*, 2021, pp. 133–142.

[75] Xiaojie Wang, Rui Zhang, Yu Sun, and Jianzhong Qi. Doubly robust joint learning for recommendation on data missing not at random. In: *International Conference on Machine Learning, PMLR*, 2019, pp. 6638–6647.

[76] Chuhan Wu, Fangzhao Wu, Xiting Wang, Yongfeng Huang, and Xing Xie. Fairness-aware news recommendation with decomposed adversarial learning. In: *Thirty-Fifth AAAI Conference on Artificial Intelligence, AAAI 2021, Thirty-Third Conference on Innovative Applications of Artificial Intelligence, IAAI 2021, The Eleventh Symposium on Educational Advances in Artificial Intelligence, EAAI 2021, Virtual Event, February 2–9, 2021*. AAAI Press, 2021, pp. 4462–4469.

[77] Yao Wu, Jian Cao, Guandong Xu, and Yudong Tan. TFROM: A two-sided fairness-aware recommendation model for both customers and providers. In: Fernando Diaz, Chirag Shah, Torsten Suel, Pablo Castells, Rosie Jones, and Tetsuya Sakai, editors. *SIGIR '21: The 44th International ACM SIGIR Conference on Research and Development in Information Retrieval, Virtual Event, Canada, July 11–15, 2021*. ACM, 2021, pp. 1013–1022.

[78] Eva Zangerle and Christine Bauer. Evaluating recommender systems: Survey and framework. *ACM Computing Surveys* 55(8) (2022) 1–38.

[79] Meike Zehlike, Francesco Bonchi, Carlos Castillo, Sara Hajian, Mohamed Megahed, and Ricardo Baeza-Yates. Fa*ir: A fair top-k ranking algorithm. In: Ee-Peng Lim, Marianne Winslett, Mark Sanderson, Ada Wai-Chee Fu, Jimeng Sun, J. Shane Culpepper, Eric Lo, Joyce C. Ho, Debora Donato, Rakesh Agrawal, Yu Zheng, Carlos Castillo, Aixin Sun, Vincent S. Tseng, and Chenliang Li, editors. *Proceedings of the 2017 ACM on Conference on Information and Knowledge Management, CIKM 2017, Singapore, November 06–10, 2017*. ACM, 2017, pp. 1569–1578.

[80] Chang Zhou, Jianxin Ma, Jianwei Zhang, Jingren Zhou, and Hongxia Yang. Contrastive learning for debiased candidate generation in large-scale recommender systems. In: *Proceedings of the 27th ACM SIGKDD Conference on Knowledge Discovery & Data Mining*, 2021, pp. 3985–3995.

Part II: **User input and feedback**

Mirjam Augstein and Thomas Neumayr

4 Personalization and user modeling for interaction processes

Abstract: Personalization in computer-based systems aims at supporting users individually, by tailoring various system characteristics and components according to their respective needs and prerequisites. Traditionally, the emphasis hereby has most often been on either the content provided by the system, the way it is presented to the users or the way how users navigate through the system. However, additionally, the interaction process itself can be in the focus of a personalization approach. By personalized interaction processes, we subsume activities related to either efforts to personalize input on the user's side (e. g., through an individually tailored choice of input devices or their configuration), or a system's personalized output to a user (e. g., output modalities tailored to a user's abilities or preferences). In this chapter, we provide a concise overview of literature on personalized interaction processes and underlying user modeling activities and domains that have been in the focus of related research, and discuss the evolvement of this field throughout the past decades.

Keywords: Personalized interaction, interaction modeling, user modeling, personalized input, personalized output

4.1 Introduction

Personalization aims to better support individual users, by allowing them to configure the system themselves, or by means of automated adaptation to the user's needs. The initiative underlying a personalization approach can thus be described as either user-driven or system-driven. In this context, Opperman et al. [47] introduced a continuum between the extremes of *adaptivity* (no user initiative, fully system-driven) and *adaptability* (full user initiative).

Throughout the past decades, research on personalized systems has thoroughly focused on *personalization of content, navigation* and *presentation* to the user's needs in different domains such as adaptive hypermedia [35, 36, 56], learning [16, 22, 41, 46], e-commerce [1, 49, 53], music [3, 14, 54] and movie recommendation [23, 26, 42]. This is also underpinned by the popularity of Brusilovsky's early taxonomy of methods and techniques of adaptive hypermedia [15], which has been updated by Knutov et al. 12 years later [36].

However, there is also research on personalization and user modeling focusing on the interaction process itself which is why, in [5], we already suggested an extension of the traditional taxonomy of personalization methods and techniques, adding *interaction* as a distinct category.

https://doi.org/10.1515/9783110988567-004

In this context, personalization can play a crucial role, particularly when users' interaction abilities vary due to individual preferences but also due to impairments affecting interaction processes. Especially because of the latter, for many users it is not possible to use common input devices (such as keyboard, mouse or touchscreen), at least not in their default configuration, or to perceive common system output on certain channels (e. g., auditory or visual). Further, even if users are physically and cognitively capable of using a system's default input and output devices, modalities and activities, their interaction-related preferences might be highly diverse. Thus, *Personalized Interaction (PI)* is an approach bearing high potential to contribute to the reduction of barriers, increase of accessibility but also, more generally, an improvement of User Experience (UX).

By *PI processes* in the context of this chapter, we understand (1) personalized selection, configuration and adaptation of *input* devices, modalities and activities, and (2) personalized selection, configuration and adaptation of *output* devices, modalities and activities. The output-related processes inherently include personalization of content or UI elements as part of the system's feedback in response to user input.

In this chapter, we aim at providing a concise overview of related work on PI and its evolvement over the past decades, based on a targeted literature review. In Sections 4.1.1 and 4.1.2, we further describe the scientific background and early roots of our approach to PI. In Section 4.2, we discuss our methodology and the procedure behind out targeted literature review, including a brief overview of research considered in our review. In Section 4.3, we then present an overview of PI-related research in different domains before we summarize our findings and conclude in Section 4.4.

4.1.1 Foundations of personalized interaction

Representative foundations behind PI without specific focus on any of the adaptive interaction techniques mentioned before can be seen in the elaboration on *user modeling in HCI* by Fischer [25] and the discussion of ability-based design by Wobbrock et al. [61].

Fischer [25] describes the challenges for designers of human-computer systems and states that they "face the formidable task of writing software for millions of users (at design time) while making it work as if it were designed for each individual user (only known at use time)." He further explains that at design time, developers create systems and have to make decisions for users for situational contexts and tasks that they can only anticipate. This is also emphasized by Bauer and Dey [11], who state that context has to be anticipated before run time and argue that user modeling helps to deliver at run time the optimal version of the anticipated features. This again is in line with Fischer's explanation that an important point about user modeling is related to use time and design time getting blurred, so if a system constantly adapts to its users, use time becomes a different kind of design time [30]. This consideration applies also for what we understand by PI.

The discussion of Wobbrock et al. [61] is rooted in the motivation to make technology accessible for people with disabilities, but applies to personalized systems in general. They identify seven principles in three categories: *stance* (ability, accountability), *interface* (adaptation, transparency) and *system* (performance, context, commodity). The *stance* category involves (and notes as a requirement) that designers should respond to user performance by changing systems, not users. From our point of view, this should be the premise behind all PI approaches. The *interface* category subsumes *adaptation* and *transparency*, suggesting that interfaces might be self-adaptive or user-adaptable to provide the best possible match to users' abilities and that interfaces should give users awareness of adaptations, which strongly relates to the *output* branch of PI as defined above. The *system* category involves that systems may monitor, measure and model user performance and encourages usage of low-cost, readily available hardware and software. This is again in line with our understanding of PI as it involves the selection and configuration of interaction methods and devices based on user models.

4.1.2 Personalization of input and output methods

Within recent years, the available number of different input and output methods for a broad spectrum of users has expanded massively (voice UIs, or more generally, dialog-based systems, just to name one example). Thus, the demand for systems that can handle a multitude of input and output methods and techniques have increased. This again has implications on the underlying user modeling approaches in case these systems should provide personalization. Related to this, Kaklanis et al. [32] introduce a complex taxonomy of user model variables that also involve many related to user input and system output, e. g., *motor parameters* (such as gait parameters [step length and step width] or upper body parameters), *strength parameters* (such as maximum gripping force of one hand), *hearing parameters*, *visual parameters* or *equilibrium* (parameters concerning sense of balance). Although originally published as a recommendation for standardized user models without particular focus on PI, the taxonomy of [32] can be seen as a solid basis for personalization of input and output methods.

A notable early example of a system that takes into consideration the personalization of input and output methods is the AVANTI framework introduced by Stephanidis et al. [58]. The framework facilitates the construction of systems supporting adaptability and adaptivity and comprises the following main components: (i) a multimedia database interface, (ii) a user modeling server, (iii) a content model, (iv) a hyperstructure adaptor and (v) the UI. The AVANTI framework puts a clear focus on hypermedia content (using static elements and alternative hypermedia objects as a basis for the construction of individual views of this content). Furthermore, the AVANTI framework suggests an incorporation of support for multiple interaction modalities based on the user profile.

A more recent example of a system that is capable of judging individual input performance in connection with different input methods was described by Biswas and

Langdon [13]. They discuss a multimodal adaptation algorithm for mobility-impaired users based on evaluation of their hand strength. They point out that there is little reported work on quantitative analysis of the effects of different impairments on pointing performance and there is also a lack of work on the objective evaluation of human factors, relating them with interaction parameters. They measured different variables for hand strength (e. g., grip strength, radial or ulnar deviation or static tremor) and performed a user study with mobility-impaired and able-bodied participants. Within the study, Biswas and Langdon analyzed pointing tasks and predicted average velocity (with different input devices) and the so-called index of performance, which is based on movement time and index of difficulty for each participant.

Another discussion of user modeling related to interaction that suggests the introduction of a specific *input model* is provided by Kurschl et al. [39]. Their approach involves fine-grained modeling of users' abilities related to input, focusing on touch-based and touchless input devices. For example, they measure swipe ability, pan ability, hold time, and preferred input device for touch-based input and precision or hand coordination for touchless input. They further suggest the automated selection of input devices (e. g., a touchscreen instead of hardware switches) and the personalized configuration of device and input method (e. g., the system's hold and lock time after a touch was detected). Based on this approach, we introduced a more complex analysis and modeling framework for personalized interaction as described in [5, 7, 9]. This framework facilitates a fine-grained analysis of users' input and output abilities and preferences in order to allow for automated personalization (i. e., selection and configuration) of input and output devices, modalities and methods. Several different show cases including alternative interaction devices (see [6, 10]) have been developed to demonstrate how the framework can be applied to implement personalized interaction for users with and without motor impairments.

4.2 Approach and methodology

In order to provide a concise yet systematic overview on PI research, we conducted a targeted literature review, querying the SCOPUS database on February 7, 2023. The search query leading to a result set of 41 (including 28 relevant) publications was:

```
(
      TITLE-ABS-KEY ( personaliz*  W/5  output )  OR
      TITLE-ABS-KEY ( personaliz*  W/5  input )  OR
      TITLE-ABS-KEY ( adapt*  W/5  output )  OR
      TITLE-ABS-KEY ( adapt*  W/5  input )  OR
      TITLE-ABS-KEY ( "personalized interaction" )
  )   AND  TITLE-ABS-KEY ( "user model*" )
```

The query was designed to include all combinations of personalization and adaptation with both input and output, considering all plural and singular as well as verbal or substantive forms of the left-positioned terms. Additionally, terms did not have to be exactly consecutive, but it was enough that the terms were within a range of five words from each other to trigger the query. Furthermore, the term "personalized interaction" was added as an umbrella term. To narrow down the result set and prevent selection of publications that only apply ad hoc short term adaptations (which is outside the scope of this chapter), we additionally added the restriction that some form of user modeling should be part of the title, abstract or keywords. The general approach and the query as well are designed to be rather exclusive. This means that we explicitly did not aim at presenting an exhaustive collection of related literature (with potentially a large number of false positives, and additionally, a large number of approaches only marginally relevant). Rather, we aimed at retrieving a rather modest number of well representative publications. Such a result set was expected to help us comprehend and trace the evolvement of directly PI-focused work in the literature throughout the past decades, without the potential "noise" created by work on the edge of our target focus. The 41 results we retrieved were then reviewed in detail by one of the two researchers involved in this chapter who judged them as (1) of sufficient quality, and (2) as relevant or not relevant (aiming to identify and exclude false positives in the result set). Following this, the results were jointly discussed (focusing particularly on borderline cases). After this discussion, we ended up with 28 related publications covering the years 1994 up until 2022. In total, six publications were excluded (mostly proceedings introductions or workshop descriptions not containing original research), and further six publications were regarded as thematically unrelated (i. e., false positives in the result set). Those publications that we regard as unrelated did not describe personalized interaction according to our descriptions in section 4.1. For instance, two publications by Bures and Jelinek [17, 18] discuss a theorem for deciding at which point it is favorable to introduce a fully adaptive system [18], or deal with the automated generation of a user model [17]; however, both do not report descriptions related to PI. In a similar fashion, the other four publications were thematically false positives as well and not included in our final list, accordingly.

Tables 4.1 to 4.3 provide an overview of the related publications. Table 4.1 assigns the publications to the respective domain in the context of which the research has been conducted (e. g., entertainment or education). Assignment of publications to more than one is possible. Publications not related to one or more specific domains are categorized as "general" (this is, e. g., the case for general user modeling approaches). Table 4.2 then shows the type of research reported in the publications (i. e., concept, method, system or evaluation). Again, some publications appear more than once since they describe, for instance, a system and its evaluation. Table 4.3 finally provides a concise overview of all selected publications, their domain (multiple possible) and type (multiple possible). Further, in the last column we indicate whether the respective approach can be subsumed under *(1) personalized selection, configuration and adaptation of input devices, modalities and activities, (2) personalized selection, configuration and adaptation of output devices, modalities and activities* according to the definition introduced in Section 4.1, or neither (yet still viewable as PI process). For the latter, we introduced a third, more general category in the table, i. e., *interaction*. As can be seen in the table, related work is spread over several domains, however, with the majority of publications being categorized as rather domain-independent. Also, the types of contributions are all represented in an almost equal way (however, with conceptual work being most prominently present). Regarding input, output and general interaction, there is a clear focus on output, as can be seen in the table.

Table 4.1: Related publications categorized according to domain the research has been conducted in, sorted in order of number of publications (ascending).

Domain	Publications
Education	[60]
Robots	[57]
Search	[38]
Accessible & Assistive Systems	[24, 40]
Personalized UI	[28, 33, 55]
Dialog Systems	[12, 20, 34, 50]
Culture & Entertainment	[2, 19, 21, 48, 52]
General	[4, 5, 8, 27, 27, 37, 43, 44, 51, 59, 62]

Table 4.2: Related publications categorized according to type of research.

Type	Publications
Concept	[2, 8, 19, 24, 33, 34, 37, 40, 44, 45, 48, 52, 59]
Method	[5, 20, 28, 38, 51, 57, 62]
System	[4, 5, 8, 12, 21, 43, 50, 55, 60]
Evaluation	[5, 12, 21, 34, 43, 45, 51, 57]

While Table 4.3 conveys the impression that work on PI has been conducted regularly since 1994 (with some years with more than one publication and some years without any), it should be noted that for earlier work it was much harder to classify it as PI-related according to our definition than for more recent work. This might be due to establishment of vocabulary in certain periods of time but also due to the evolving research focus in the user modeling community (e. g., interaction processes have gained much importance in recent years while they were not so often explicitly discussed in earlier years although they were sometimes implicitly present).

Table 4.3: An overview of personalized interaction approaches' publication years, domains, types and foci. The domains are **ED**ucation, **RO**bots, **SE**arch, **A**ccessible & **A**ssistive Systems, Personalized **UI**, **DI**alog Systems, **C**ulture & **E**ntertainment and **G**eneral. Types include **C**oncepts, **M**ethods, **S**ystems and **E**valuations. The focus of the publications is either on **I**nput or **O**utput.

Year	Ref.	ED	RO	SE	AA	UI	DI	CE	G	C	M	S	E	I	O
2022	[12]					x				x	x				x
2021	[34]					x			x	x			x		x
2021	[57]		x						x	x			x		x
2020	[48]						x			x					x
2019	[2]						x			x				x	x
2019	[5]								x	x	x	x	x	x	
2019	[60]	x									x				x
2017	[8]								x	x	x			x	x
2017	[20]					x					x				x
2016	[28]				x						x				x
2016	[43]								x			x	x	x	x
2015	[27]								x		x				x
2015	[51]								x	x			x	x	
2014	[38]			x							x				x
2012	[40]				x					x				x	x
2011	[24]				x					x				x	x
2011	[45]								x	x			x	x	x
2010	[59]						x			x					x
2009	[44]								x	x				x	x
2009	[52]						x			x				x	x
2007	[62]								x		x				x
2006	[21]						x					x	x		x
2005	[19]						x			x					x
2004	[55]				x						x				x
2003	[37]								x	x				x	x
2002	[33]				x					x					x
1999	[4]								x			x		x	x
1994	[50]					x						x			x

4.3 Application areas of personalized interaction

In this section, we describe notable prior work in the form of related literature (as previously listed in Table 4.3), categorizing it according to the areas where PI was applied. Within the related Sections 4.3.1 to 4.3.5, we organize our descriptions based on publication date, starting with the earliest publications. We discuss if personalizing input or output was in the focus of these publications and provide background information on the underlying data and where the initiative of personalization mechanisms lies (based on Opperman et al.'s continuum [47] introduced in Section 4.1).

4.3.1 Personalized interaction in culture and entertainment

Callaway and Kuflik [19] describe an adaptive application in a museum, where based on a user model and domain ontology, a personalized report of a museum visit is generated for visitors. For this, an interest model is used, which is fed by visitors' movement through the museum and choices made on a mobile device's interface. The focus is on personalized output of the report as well as additional suggestions for interesting exhibits based on the interest model. The adaptation can be regarded as adaptivity (no user initiative).

In [21], Cena et al. describe a personalized mobile tourist guide, which provides information about the city of Turin and adapts it to the employed input device (e. g., laptop or smartphone), to users' features and preferences, and contextual information (such as time and location). The underlying data consist of user interests, special needs, device characteristics and context conditions (in addition to the aforementioned time and location, movement is captured). While there is a focus on personalizing output, the free selection of input devices can be regarded a simple form of personalization of input. With exception of the just-mentioned selection of input devices, the system can be regarded as adaptive because all personalization is done without user initiative.

Roes et al. [52] present a personalized tour guide through a museum, including recommendations of artworks and paths. The semantic relations of artworks (e. g., their "styles, artists, themes or locations") as well as user interest is considered for recommendations. Interestingly, the art recommender and tour guide can be used by both online (e. g., to plan a personalized tour) and onsite users. The process is to first remove less interesting artworks, then add interesting artworks, and finally plan an optimal path through the site. Both explicit (e. g., ratings) and implicit (e. g., location or dwell time) data is used to fuel the user model. On the scale between adaptability and adaptivity, there are aspects near to both poles: user initiative is needed for planning and configuring the visit, system initiative is given for recommendations and route planning.

Finally, the remaining two publications in this category can be regarded as important groundwork for later personalization approaches in the museum/cultural heritage domain. Almeshari et al. [2] recently pointed out that in the museum domain in the year 2019 still most museums did not provide a personalized interaction approach. They state a common problem for personalization in museum visitors: data sparsity due to most visitors being first timers and visits being rather short. Consequently, they carried out a questionnaire-based study to find out if visitors could be connected to certain predefined stereotypes whose characteristics could be utilized to come to better conclusions. In a similar fashion, Pandolfo et al. [48] also conducted a questionnaire study in order to come up with relevant user characteristics for "personalizing access to cultural heritage collections" with the aim of creating a user model ontology based on them.

To summarize the personalization approaches in this domain, most use multiple data sources (both explicit and implicit), are focused more on the output side of personalization, and lean more toward adaptivity without the need of user initiative (although there are examples that include configurability). This tendency can be explained through the ad hoc and short-term nature of interaction with these systems, which typically do not afford elaborate configurations on the user side.

4.3.2 Personalized dialog systems

Peter and Rösner [50] present a system,, which includes generating explanations as well as implicit and explicit knowledge acquisition for a user model to generate instructions for car maintenance. The system is an early example of personalizing output, in this case, instructions and explanations in the form of generated natural language, according to users' knowledge. While there is a feedback loop with explicit user interaction, the system generally is adaptive (mainly system initiative for adaptations).

Callejas and Griol [20] propose a model for personal counseling dialog systems (e. g., to achieve a healthy lifestyle) that consider users' actual motivations instead of the mere results, which is what contemporary systems usually did. Several psychological theories about utility and attribution are incorporated into the model. The authors concluded that this more elaborate model makes it possible to keep track of fluctuations in user motivation which, in turn, can be used to fuel personalization. The publication presents groundwork for later targeted PI approaches.

Kim et al. [34] present further groundwork, this time in the domain of intelligent agents. They make the case for incorporating users' preferences regarding utilitarian (seeing agents as a tool) or relational (expecting more sociality in agents) orientation into user models. In their study, they found that there are differences regarding three aspects: "tolerance to unpredictability, sensitivity to privacy, and sensitivity to an agent's autonomy" [34, p. 448] and they conclude that these dimensions should be considered in future user models for personalized intelligent agents.

Finally, Benedictis et al. [12] suggest—among other contributions—using information about users according to the "classification of functioning, disability and health (ICF)" (a classification scheme proposed by the World Health Organization including both stable and dynamic user parameters) in their user model with a specialized two-layer architecture for socially assistive robots. The presented robot system is envisioned to guide cognitive training sessions for older adults and included personalized verbal interaction in dialog form. First evaluations around usability, attitude and personality capturing capabilities of the system showed positive results. Furthermore, it is a vivid example of a system that incorporates both personalized input (i. e., deciding which type of input is most suitable for a user, e. g., text-based or voice-based dialog) and personalized output (e. g., adapting the current communication strategy). While many of the descriptions hint at a high system initiative during deployment, an expert user is still needed for configuration during the programming stage.

Overall, the approaches in this domain partly deal with suggestions of architectures and groundwork for future user modeling endeavors. Due to the longer-term usage perspective, a higher degree of configurability can be advantageous for users and there are indications that both personalized output and personalized input are considered.

4.3.3 Personalized user interfaces

In the domain of UI personalization, Kelly and Belkin [33] propose a fully adaptive approach to user modeling for personalized information retrieval. This important groundwork suggests several considerations for PI in information retrieval systems, such as the tracking and representation of short- and long-term information needs, or the reliance on implicit data for "acquir[ing] and updat[ing] the user model automatically, without explicit assistance from the user."

In another application example, Schwarzkopf and Jameson [55] propose the concept and present a partial implementation of a personalized academic document retrieval and management system including a recommender component. They propose modeling users' interests based on implicit user interactions with the documents but plan to incorporate controllability (in addition to transparency of adaptations) in their pursuit of a system that will be accepted.

Lastly, Gullà et al. [28] describe their approach of basing a user model on a Bayesian Belief Network. Users' "skills, expertise and disabilities" as well as contextual information influence a smart user interface. The method covered in this publication can be seen as groundwork for personalized interaction, mainly for personalizing output of smart user interfaces.

To summarize, the publications in this domain present groundwork for how user modeling can keep track of the profound intricacies inherent to users' characteristics according to which personalization can be applied. Adaptability (high user initiative) plays a lesser but still important role in these approaches as compared to adaptivity. Lastly, the focus of personalization clearly lies on output (i. e., the UIs).

4.3.4 Generalizable applications of personalized interaction

In this section, we present those publications, which describe generalizable approaches to personalized interaction.

Ardissono et al. [4] present the architecture and implementation of a personalized web store that relies on a user model containing explicit information about the user (e. g., age, education) as well as implicit ("predictive") information, such as preferences. Overall, PI is fueled by users' "domain expertise, preferences and needs." This information is further used to dynamically generate the product catalog, individually rendering product detail pages and recommending items within product categories. As a consequence, we regard this system as personalized output with a high level of system initiative (few initiative by the user is necessary for the adaptations). We expect these descriptions to hold true in other commercial applications and beyond.

Kobsa and Schreck [37] in their seminal article suggest achieving privacy through anonymity through an architectural approach to combat the intrinsic danger of privacy violations by user-adaptive systems, whereas personalized interaction approaches can be counted toward them. Such systems usually rely on user and usage data providing information about users' preferences, interests or abilities through implicit and explicit user interactions, as the other examples in this section show. The descriptions in the article can be seen as an important groundwork but also afterthought for designers of PI approaches in general.

Yang et al. [62] propose a semantic user model including both static and dynamic user information to predict features, such as familiarity, interest or preferences. While the authors rightfully claim generalizability, the end goal is to "provide semantically-enriched, added-value tourism services tailored to the user." The stage of the endeavor is preimplementation meaning that actual applied PI is part of their future work.

Octavia et al. [44] present important groundwork for general personalizing input (e. g., showing only "a subset of all possible interaction techniques to the user") and output in virtual environments. Their envisioned user model captures "interaction patterns, preferences, interests and characteristics."

In a subsequent publication, Octavia et al. [45] proceed with their endeavors by conducting experiments to build a user model template as well as individual user models for personalizing interaction in virtual environments. As interaction techniques in the experiments, a bubble cursor and a depth ray were provided to select items in a virtual 3D space. User feedback was positive in regards to the suggested interaction techniques.

Stoica and Avouris [59] propose an architecture for PI in "digitally augmented spaces," such as libraries, museums or retail shops. A combination of physical onsite interaction and interaction via personal mobile devices (smartphones and PDAs are mentioned) is envisioned to take place in these spaces. Among the information stored for each user, there are explicit (e. g., personal data, settings, stated preferences) and implicit ones (e. g., interaction data, inferred interests). Concerning initiative, the authors envision both adaptability (e. g., "choose [...] preferred language for content or policy for personal and identity data") as well as adaptivity (e. g., recommendations based on inferred interests) to play a role when following the proposed architecture. The main focus of the architecture is on personalizing output but several descriptions hint at a possibility to incorporate input personalization, e. g., to support individually preferred input devices or their configuration in future implementations.

Gong et al. [27] present an approach that allows for the creation of an individual 3D avatar resembling physical user features by using a depth-sensing device. As a borderline case according to our definitions, we still decided to briefly discuss this publication because it can be regarded as a lightweight example of ad hoc (in the sense that no historical data or inferences about users is done) personalization of output.

Pisani et al. [51] present a method and experiments in the field of biometrics that can be applied, e. g., to user authentication by inferring identity from keystroke dynamics. The authors hold that biometric features can vary over time and, therefore, suggest keeping track of these changes in a user model. Their experiments showed a good prediction accuracy and we regard this as groundwork for later personalized output (with keystroke dynamics as the underlying data as decision criteria).

In previous publications [5, 8, 43], as outlined in Section 4.1.2 already, we presented an analysis and modeling framework for personalization of interaction processes, a full implementation and several evaluations. The user model stores interaction data and the system recommends best-fitting interaction devices and configures them according to users' capabilities. The system leans more toward the adaptivity side although some user initiative is required, e. g., to freely choose a device from the recommendation list. Because some aspects of UIs are also adapted to information in the user model, the system is an example of both personalized input and personalized output.

Summing up, the publications which presented generalizable approaches in this section range from important groundwork and ethical considerations to full implementations of systems covering many different shades of initiative handling (i. e., adaptability, adaptivity and everything in between) as well as personalized input and output.

4.3.5 Miscellaneous domains

Duarte et al. [24] describe an accessibility framework, which lays the foundation for multimodal interaction and "adaptation to individual needs" among other aspects. The application area is a TV application for the elderly, which relies on a user model comprising individual impairment information (i. e., interaction abilities). Both input and output personalization are part of the framework, and at run time, applications can be regarded as adaptive (no user initiative) because they "self-adapt[...] according to [users'] interaction."

Margetis et al. [40] present a landscape for future personalized assistive technologies solutions for ambient assisted living. The descriptions in an envisioned scenario of a blind user in a smart home environment hint at which type of information about users and context is necessary to provide personalized output, namely location, information about a users interaction capabilities and about the current interaction. Also, the authors state that it is necessary to provide alternative inputs for assisted living scenarios.

Kumar and Sharan [38] present an approach to personalize web search by keeping track of individuals' browsing history and domain knowledge. This information is used in a user model to recommend pages that are especially relevant to a user. Their adaptive approach with full system initiative can be regarded as an example of personalized output, because search results tailored to user model information are presented.

Wang et al. [60] present a gaze-based e-learning tool for students with learning difficulties. In prior work, they established a model of how learners' motivation can be captured, and showed that features captured by an eye-tracking device (e. g., pupil dilation, fixations) can predict motivation with an accuracy of "up to 81.3 %" while providing the advantage of nonreliance on self-reports, which are prone to bias. Their e-learning system uses gaze-inferred motivation as well as input data to personalize the learning experience. Furthermore, it has a learner and an expert view. Experts can prepare the learning materials but are not configuring adaptive components, which work under a full system initiative. The system can be regarded as an example of personalized output, adapting motivational feedback according to the user model.

Spaulding et al. [57] propose the concept of "life-long personalization," which means that models and algorithms should account for different tasks at different times, which is in contrast to traditional views of inferring knowledge or "mastery" of a certain task. For evaluation purposes, the authors developed two literacy game systems that can be played against a robot tutor and the student model captures the underlying knowledge. The game applications are clearly on the personalized-output side, as they adapt both content and tutoring actions to the student model.

In conclusion, the publications in these miscellaneous domains consist of a multifaceted bouquet regarding their orientation toward user or system initiative as well as input or output personalization.

4.4 Discussion and conclusions

In this chapter, we have discussed PI as a means of individually tailoring interaction processes, which include input and output modalities, to users' distinct prerequisites related to interaction. In order to uncover application domains in which PI has been discussed throughout the past decades up until now, we conducted a targeted literature review. The review methodology as described in Section 4.2 followed an approach of narrowing down the result set to representative examples actually focusing on PI on one hand and including a wide range of research domains on the other. Based on our query, we identified various areas of application of PI, ranging from culture and entertainment to robots or health (see Section 4.3). We discussed the concrete examples resulting from our query, regarding their focus on either input or output, and related to the level of user- or system initiative according to Opperman et al.'s scale [47].

However, one particularly illustrative application field that has not been so prominently represented in our query results, is related to assistive technology (also see the description of PI roots in Section 4.1.2). The reason why only a few related examples have been retrieved through the literature review might lie in the fact that such approaches have oftentimes not been designated as "personalization" in combination with "user modeling." We nevertheless consider it an important foundation for the field of PI, because for the target group of people with impairments, interaction abilities vary particularly drastically. In many cases, e. g., motor impairments might lead to the complete exclusion of people regarding the usage of certain interaction devices and methods by nonpersonalized systems. The exclusion from certain interaction methods and devices is further often accompanied by the exclusion from usage of certain pieces of software (e. g., smartphone or tablet apps if a user cannot operate a common touchscreen). This kind of inequity and exclusiveness for certain user groups can be alleviated via means of PI, thus constituting a good use case for personalization in general. Nevertheless, in the broader field of personalized and adaptive systems research, interaction, as a direct target area of personalization, has played a minor role in past research, compared to content, presentation or navigation adaptation.

During the coming years, we expect the importance of PI to increase for a broader spectrum of users. First, the product range in the area of input devices grows rapidly. Furthermore, the era of post-WIMP user interfaces, which we are in, postulates making use of all bodily capabilities when interacting with technology [31]. Thus, users' preferences among these input devices can be expected to vary even more drastically. Second, a more general trend toward individualization can be observed that we expect to affect also the selection of input devices and their configuration. The ubiquity era, as predicted already in 2008 by [29], also involves that "more people than ever will be using computing devices of one form or other" and that "computers can now be interwoven with almost every aspect of our lives." This again emphasizes the need for personalization regarding interaction with these devices, in order not to exclude certain people or groups of people from these developments—that influence not only small parts of humans' lives, but might be fully interwoven with them in the future.

References

[1]   Pegah Malekpour Alamdari, Nima Jafari Navimipour, Mehdi Hosseinzadeh, Ali Asghar Safaei, and Aso Darwesh. A systematic study on the recommender systems in the e-commerce. *IEEE Access* 8 (2020) 115694–115716.

[2]   Moneerah Almeshari, John Dowell, and Julianne Nyhan. Using personas to model museum visitors. In: *ACM UMAP 2019 Adjunct – Adjunct Publication of the 27th Conference on User Modeling, Adaptation and Personalization*, 2019, pp. 401–405.

[3]   Ivana Andjelkovic, Denis Parra, and John O'Donovan. Moodplay: Interactive music recommendation based on artists' mood similarity. *Interactive Journal of Human-Computer Studies* 121 (2019) 142–159.

[4]   L. Ardissono, C. Barbero, A. Goy, and G. Petrone. Agent architecture for personalized Web stores. In: *Proceedings of the International Conference on Autonomous Agents*, 1999, pp. 182–189.

[5]   Mirjam Augstein and Thomas Neumayr. Automated personalization of input methods and processes. In: Mirjam Augstein, Eelco Herder, and Wolfgang Wörndl, editors. *Personalized Human-Computer Interaction*. DeGruyter, 2019.

[6]   Mirjam Augstein, Thomas Neumayr, and Thomas Burger. The role of haptics in user input for people with motor and impairments. *Studies in Health Technology and Informatics* 242 (2017) 183–194.

[7]   Mirjam Augstein, Thomas Neumayr, Daniel Kern, Werner Kurschl, Josef Altmann, and Thomas Burger. An analysis and modeling framework for personalized interaction. In: *IUI17 Companion: Proceedings of the 22nd International Conference on Intelligent User Interfaces Companion, Limassol, Cyprus*, 2017.

[8]   Mirjam Augstein, Thomas Neumayr, Daniel Kern, Werner Kurschl, Josef Altmann, and Thomas Burger. An analysis and modeling framework for personalized interaction. In: *International Conference on Intelligent User Interfaces, Proceedings IUI*, 2017, pp. 57–60.

[9]   Mirjam Augstein, Thomas Neumayr, Werner Kurschl, Daniel Kern, Thomas Burger, and Josef Altmann. A personalized interaction approach: Motivation and use case. In: *Adjunct Publication of the 25th Conference on User Modeling, Adaptation and Personalization*. ACM, 2017, pp. 221–226.

[10] Mirjam Augstein, Thomas Neumayr, Stephan Vrecer, Werner Kurschl, and Josef Altmann. The role of haptics in user input for simple 3d interaction tasks – an analysis of interaction performance and user experience. In: *Proceedings of the 13th International Joint Conference on Computer Vision, Imaging and Computer Graphics Theory and Applications – Volume 2: HUCAPP, INSTICC*. SciTePress, 2018, pp. 26–37.

[11] Christine Bauer and Anind K. Dey. Considering context in the design of intelligent systems: Current practices and suggestions for improvement. *The Journal of Systems and Software* 112(2016) (2016) 26–47.

[12] Riccardo De Benedictis, Alessandro Umbrico, Francesca Fracasso, Gabriella Cortellessa, Andrea Orlandini, and Amedeo Cesta. A dichotomic approach to adaptive interaction for socially assistive robots. *User Modeling and User-Adapted Interaction* (2022).

[13] Pradipta Biswas and Patrick Langdon. Developing multimodal adaptation algorithm for mobility impaired users by evaluating their hand strength. *International Journal of Human-Computer Interaction* 28(9) (2012) 576–596.

[14] Dmitry Bogdanov. *From Music Similarity to Music Recommendation: Computational Approaches Based in Audio Features and Metadata*. PhD thesis. Universitat Pompeu Fabra, Barcelona, Spain, 2013.

[15] Peter Brusilovsky. Methods and techniques of adaptive hypermedia. *User Modeling and User-Adapted Interaction* 6(2–3) (1996) 87–129.

[16] Peter Brusilovsky and Nicola Hence. Open corpus adaptive educational hypermedia. In: Peter Prusilovsky, Alfred Kobsa, and Wolfgang Nejdl, editors. *The Adaptive Web*, 2007.

[17] Miroslav Bures and Ivan Jelinek. Automatic generation of user model from non-trivial hypermedia in adaptive E-learning hypermedia system. In: *Proceedings of the Fifth IASTED International Conference on Web-based Education*, volume 2006, 2006, pp. 112–115.

[18] Miroslav Bures and Ivan Jelinek. Decision theorem for construction of adaptive hypermedia system. In: *Proceedings of the Second IASTED International Conference on Web Technologies, Applications, and Services, WTAS 2006*, 2006, pp. 84–89.

[19] Charles Callaway and Tsvi Kuflik. Using a domain ontology to mediate between a user model and domain applications. In: *PIA 2005 - Workshop on New Technologies for Personalized Information Access, Proceedings of the 1st International Workshop - Held in Conjunction with: 10th Int. Conference on User Modeling, UM 2005*, 2005, pp. 13–22.

[20] Zoraida Callejas and David Griol. An affective utility model of user motivation for counselling dialogue systems. In: *Lecture Notes in Computer Science (including subseries Lecture Notes in Artificial Intelligence and Lecture Notes in Bioinformatics)*. LNAI, volume 10341, 2017, pp. 86–97.

[21] Federica Cena, Luca Console, Cristina Gena, Anna Goy, Guido Levi, Sonia Modeo, and Ilaria Torre. Integrating heterogeneous adaptation techniques to build a flexible and usable mobile tourist guide. *AI Communications* 19(4) (2006) 369–384.

[22] Paul De Bra, David Smits, Kees Van der Sluijs, Alexandra Cristea, Jonathan Foss, Christian Glahn, and Christina Steiner. Grapple: Learning management systems meet adaptive learning environments. In: *Intelligent and Adaptive Educational Learning Systems*. Springer, 2013.

[23] Yashar Deldjoo, Maurizio Ferrari Dacrema, Constantin Mihai Gabriel, Hamid Fghbal-zadeh, Stefano Cereda, Markus Schedl, Bogdan Ionescu, and Paolo Cremonesi. Movie genome: Alleviating new item cold start in movie recommendation. *User Modeling and User-Adapted Interaction* 29 (2019) 291–343.

[24] Carlos Duarte, Pat Langdon, Christoph Jung, Jose Coelho, Pradipta Biswas, and Pascal Hamisu. GUIDE: Creating accessible TV applications. *Assistive Technology Research Series* 29 (2011) 905–912.

[25] Gerhard Fischer. User modeling in human-computer interaction. *User Modeling and User-Adapted Interaction* 11 (2001) 65–86.

[26] Carlos Gomez-Uribe and Neil Hunt. The netflix recommender system: Algorithms, business value, and innovation. *ACM Transactions on Management Information Systems* 6(4), 2016.

[27] Wenjuan Gong, Zhichao Wang, and Weishan Zhang. Creating personal 3d avatar from a single depth sensor. In: *Proceedings of the 2015 IEEE 12th International Conference on Ubiquitous Intelligence and Computing*, 2015, pp. 1193–1198.

[28] Francesca Gullà, Lorenzo Cavalieri, Silvia Ceccacci, and Michele Germani. A BBN-based Method to Manage Adaptive Behavior of a Smart User Interface. In: *Procedia CIRP*, volume 50, 2016, pp. 535–540.

[29] Richard Harper, Tom Rodden, Yvonne Rogers, and Abigail Sellen. Being human: Human-computer interaction in the year 2020. Technical report, 2008.

[30] Austin Henderson and Morten Kyng. There's no place like home: Continuing design in use. In: Joan Greenbaum and Morten Kyng, editors. *Design at Work: Cooperative Design of Computer Systems*. Lawrence Erlbaum Associates, Inc., 1992, pp. 219–240.

[31] Robert J. K. Jacob, Audrey Girouard, Leanne M. Hirshfield, Michael S. Horn, Orit Shaer, Erin Treacy Solovey, and Jamie Zigelbaum. Reality-based interaction: a framework for post-wimp interfaces. In: *Proceedings of the SIGCHI conference on Human factors in computing systems*, 2008, pp. 201–210.

[32] N. Kaklanis, P. Biswas, Y. Mohamad, M. F. Gonzalez, M. Peissner, P. Langdon, D. Tzovaras, and C. Jung. Towards standardisation of user models for simulation and adaptation purposes. *Universal Access in the Information Society* (2014) 1–28.

[33] Diane Kelly and Nicholas J. Belkin. A User Modeling System for Personalized Interaction and Tailored Retrieval in Interactive IR. *Proceedings of the ASIST Annual Meeting* 39 (2002) 316–325.

[34] Hankyung Kim, Hoyeon Nam, Uichin Lee, and Youn-kyung Lim. Utilitarian or relational? exploring indicators of user orientation towards intelligent agents. *Communications in Computer and Information Science* 1419 (2021) 448–455.

[35] Ana Carolina T. Klock, Isabela Gasparini, Marcelo Soares Pimenta, and José Palazzo M. Oliveira. Adaptive hypermedia systems. In: Mehdi Khosrow-Pour, editor, *Advanced Methodologies and Technologies in Media and Communications*. IGI Global, 2019.

[36] Evgeny Knutov, Paul De Bra, and Mykola Pechenizkiy. Ah 12 years later: A comprehensive survey of adaptive hypermedia methods and techniques. *New Review of Hypermedia and Multimedia* 15(1) (2009) 5–38.

[37] Alfred Kobsa and Jörg Schreck. Privacy through Pseudonymity in User-Adaptive Systems. *ACM Transactions on Internet Technology* 3(2) (2003) 149–183.

[38] Rakesh Kumar and Aditi Sharan. Personalized web search using browsing history and domain knowledge. In: *Proceedings of the 2014 International Conference on Issues and Challenges in Intelligent Computing Techniques, ICICT 2014*, 2014, pp. 493–497.

[39] Werner Kurschl, Mirjam Augstein, Thomas Burger, and Claudia Pointner. User modeling for people with special needs. *International Journal of Pervasive Computing and Communications* 10(3) (2014) 313–336.

[40] George Margetis, Margherita Antona, Stavroula Ntoa, and Constantine Stephanidis. Towards accessibility in ambient intelligence environments. In: *Lecture Notes in Computer Science (including subseries Lecture Notes in Artificial Intelligence and Lecture Notes in Bioinformatics)*. LNCS, volume 7683, 2012, pp. 328–337.

[41] Vladimir Mikić, Miloš Ilić, Lazar Kopanja, and Boban Vesin. Personalisation methods in e-learning a literature review. *Computer Applications in Engineering Education* 30(6), 2022.

[42] Bradley N. Miller, Istvan Albert, Shyong K. Lam, Joseph A. Konstan, and John Riedl. Movielens unplugged: experiences with an occasionally connected recommender system. In: *IUI '03: Proceedings of the 8th international conference on Intelligent user interfaces*. New York, NY, USA: ACM, 2003, pp. 263–266.

[43] Thomas Neumayr, Mirjam Augstein, Stephan Vrecer, Werner Kurschl, and Josef Altmann. Learning special input methods with personalized game applications. In: *Proceedings ABIS 2016 – 22nd International Workshop on Intelligent and Personalized Human-Computer Interaction*, 2016.

[44] Johanna Renny Octavia, Chris Raymaekers, and Karin Coninx. A conceptual framework for adaptation and personalization in virtual environments. In: *Proceedings - International Workshop on Database and Expert Systems Applications, DEXA*, 2009, pp. 284–288.

[45] Johanna Renny Octavia, Chris Raymaekers, and Karin Coninx. Adaptation in virtual environments: Conceptual framework and user models. *Multimedia Tools and Applications* 54(1) (2011) 121–142.

[46] Eileen O'Donnell, Séamus Lawless, Mary Sharp, and Vincent P. Wade. A review of personalised e-learning: Towards supporting learner diversity. *International Journal of Distance Education Technologies* 13(1), 2015.

[47] Reinhard Oppermann, Rossen Rashev, and Kinshuk. Adaptability and Adaptivity in Learning Systems. *Knowledge Transfer* 2 (1997) 173–179.

[48] Laura Pandolfo, Sara Spanu, Luca Pulina, and Enrico Grosso. Understanding and modeling visitor behaviours for enhancing personalized cultural experiences. *International Journal of Technology and Human Interaction* 16(3) (2020) 24–38.

[49] Dimitris Paraschakis, Bengt Nilsson, and John Holländer. Comparative evaluation of top-n recommenders on e-commerce: an industrial perspective. In: *Proceedings of the 14th International Conference on Machine Learning and Applications*, 2015.

[50] Gerhard Peter and Dietmar Rösner. User-model-driven generation of instructions. *User Modeling and User-Adapted Interaction* 3(4) (1994) 289–319.

[51] Paulo Henrique Pisani, Ana Carolina Lorena, and Andre C. P. L. F. De Carvalho. Ensemble of adaptive algorithms for keystroke dynamics. In: *Proceedings – 2015 Brazilian Conference on Intelligent Systems, BRACIS 2015*, 2015, pp. 310–315.

[52] Ivo Roes, Natalia Stash, Yiwen Wang, and Lora Aroyo. A personalized walk through the museum: The CHIP interactive tour guide. In: *Conference on Human Factors in Computing Systems – Proceedings*, 2009, pp. 3317–3322.

[53] Ben Schafer, Joseph Konstan, and John Riedl. E-commerce recommendation applications. In: Ron Kohavi and Foster Provost, editors. *Applications of Data Mining to Electronic Commerce*, Springer, 2001, pp. 115–153.

[54] Markus Schedl, Peter Knees, Brian McFee, Dmitry Bogdanov, and Marius Kaminskas. Music Recommender Systems. In: Francesco Ricci, Lior Rokach, Bracha Shapira, and Paul B. Kantor, editors. *Recommender Systems Handbook*, 2nd edition. Springer, 2015, pp. 453–492. Chapter 13.

[55] Eric Schwarzkopf and Anthony Jameson. Personalized Support for Interaction with Scientific Information Portals. In: *Lecture Notes in Computer Science (including subseries Lecture Notes in Artificial Intelligence and Lecture Notes in Bioinformatics)*, volume 3094, 2004, pp. 58–71.

[56] David Smits and Paul De Bra. Gale: A highly extensible adaptive hypermedia engine. In: *Proceedings of the 22nd ACM Conference on Hypertext and Hypermedia*. The Netherlands: Eindhoven, 2011.

[57] Samuel Spaulding, Jocelyn Shen, Hae Won Park, and Cynthia Breazeal. Lifelong Personalization via Gaussian Process Modeling for Long-Term HRI. *Frontiers in Robotics and AI* 8 (2021).

[58] Constantine Stephanidis, Alexandros Paramythis, Demosthenes Akoumianakis, and Michael Sfyrakis. Self-adapting web-based systems: Towards universal accessibility. In: *Proceedings of the 4th Workshop on User Interface For All, Stockholm, Sweden*, 1998.

[59] Adrian Stoica and Nikolaos Avouris. An architecture to support personalized interaction across multiple digitally augmented spaces. *International Journal on Artificial Intelligence Tools* 19(2) (2010) 137–158.

[60] Ruijie Wang, Yuanchen Xu, and Liming Chen. GazeMotive: A Gaze-Based Motivation-Aware E-Learning Tool for Students with Learning Difficulties. In: *Lecture Notes in Computer Science (including subseries Lecture Notes in Artificial Intelligence and Lecture Notes in Bioinformatics)*. LNCS, volume 11749, 2019, pp. 544–548.

[61] Jacob O. Wobbrock, Shaun K. Kane, Krysztof Z. Gajos, Susumu Harada, and Jon Froehlich. Ability-based design: Concept, principles and examples. *ACM Transactions on Accessible Computing* 3(3) (2011).

[62] Yang Yanwu, Christophe Claramunt, and Marie-Aude Aufaure. Towards a DL-based semantic user model for web personalization. In: *3rd International Conference on Autonomic and Autonomous Systems, ICAS'07*, 2007.

Tobias Moebert, Jan N. Schneider, Dietmar Zoerner, Anna Tscherejkina, and Ulrike Lucke

5 How to use socio-emotional signals for adaptive training

Abstract: A closer alignment of mutual expectations between technical systems and their users regarding functionality and interactions is supposed to improve their overall performance. In general, such an alignment is realized by automatically adapting the appearance and the behavior of a system. Adaptation may be based on parameters regarding the task to be fulfilled, the surrounding context or the user himself. Among the latter, the current emphasis of research is shifting from a user's traces in the system (for instance, to derive his level of expertise) toward transient aspects (like his current mental or emotional state). For educational technology, in particular, adapting the presented information and the tasks to be solved to the current personal needs of a learner promises a higher motivation, and thus a better learning outcome. Tasks which are equally challenging and motivating the users can keep them in a state of flow, and thus foster enduring engagement. This is of certain importance for difficult topics and/or learners with disabilities. The chapter explains the complex cause-and-effect models behind adaptive training systems, the mechanisms that can be facilitated to implement them, as well as empirical results from a clinical study. We exemplify this for the training of emotion recognition by people with autism, but not limited to this user group. For this purpose, we present two approaches. One is to extend the Elo algorithm regarding dimensions of difficulty in social cognition. This allows not only to judge the difficulty of tasks and the skills of users, but also to freely generate well-suited tasks. The second approach is to make use of socio-emotional signals of the learners in order to further adapt the training system. We discuss current possibilities and remaining challenges for these approaches.

Keywords: Educational technology, social cognition, emotion, task difficulty, adaptivity

5.1 Introduction

Most skills can be improved through practice. A human trainer or tutor can provide motivation during training. However, IT-based training systems are often used without the presence of a caregiver. In the design of such a system, therefore, the challenge arises to compensate for the lack of support by the human trainer and to sufficiently support

Acknowledgement: This work was partly funded by the German Federal Ministry of Education and Research in the joint project Emotisk under contract number 16SV7241. Moreover, we would like to thank our project partners from HU Berlin, namely I. Dziobek, A. Weigand and L. Enk, for providing the data from the usability study conducted with the EVA system.

https://doi.org/10.1515/9783110988567-005

the self-motivation of the trainee. Depending on the specific training goals, a defined period of continuous training should be aimed for as well as promoting training over a certain period of time. This can be achieved by adjusting the system's behavior to the current emotional state and mental ability of the users.

5.1.1 Challenges of personalization

Adjusting the behavior of a system is not a radically new approach. For instance, a feedback control circuit as known from climate control provides the same functionality: First, parameters of the environment are measured (e. g., using a thermometer). Then an assessment of the situation is derived from that (e. g., it is slightly too cold). Comparing this to a targeted state leads to a regulation strategy (e. g., to moderately increase temperature). This is carried out by certain actuators (e. g., open heating one more grade). The same cycle of adaptivity can be applied to education, as depicted in Figure 5.1, where learning outcomes are the overall goal and teaching provides the methods to achieve that.

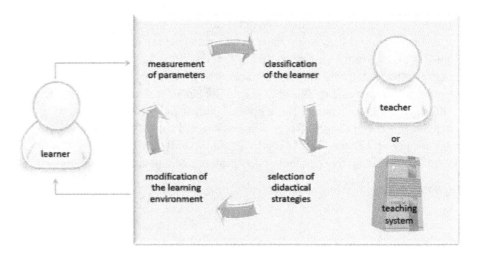

Figure 5.1: The adaptivity cycle applied to an educational scenario.

This is independent from the nature of the training: A training system carries out the same steps as a human teacher. However, teachers do not always decide explicitly or consciously, which makes it hard to model and implement such behavior in a technical system. While some parameters for adaptation in educational settings are well understood, like defined learning goals or characteristics of the environment, others are still subject of research. Here, the challenge is three-fold:
–   the classification of the learner based on measured parameters

- the deduction of appropriate didactical strategies
- the corresponding modification of the learning environment

In this article, we present our findings in these fields regarding a certain example, namely the training of socio-emotional cognition. Deriving emotions from faces or voices help to understand the intentions and needs of others. Along with recognizing one's own emotions this is a prerequisite to successfully interact and participate in society. This is of special importance, yet difficult for people with autism. However, other users can also benefit from such training, like certain age groups or professions. This variety underlines the need for a personalized, adaptive approach. Our basic assumptions for this are that (a) learning outcome may increase with motivation, (b) a condition of flow may preserve motivation and (c) too simple or too complex tasks may hamper flow. From this perspective, we analyze how the difficulty of tasks and the skill of users can be modeled, how suitable tasks for recognizing emotions can be generated, and how such training can evolve over time.

5.1.2 Related work

Research on adaptive educational technology is looking for sophisticated models beyond heuristics [45]. A challenge is that existing models from pedagogy and cognitive psychology are dealing with a rather high level of abstraction, like Adaptive Control of Thought (Anderson [1] or Motivational Design [37]. Since internal mechanisms of human cognition and learning cannot be directly measured, these models are rather constructs of thought than descriptions of processes within the brain. This makes it hard to operationalize them in algorithms of a technical system [39].

Nevertheless, based on such models a variety of adaptive educational systems have been developed, for instance, to select proper learning contents [9] or to provide helpful feedback to the learner [2]. Later, hypermedia technology and the eXtensible markup language (XML) provided the basis for dynamically adjusting a given learning arrangement to certain needs [7]. While selecting and adapting content was sufficiently described [43], new challenges arise from the complex authoring process for such content (Moebert et al. [51], Moebert [50]). However, this is independent from education but applies to digital publishing in general. With the rise of mobile technologies, the field of adaptivity is now also labeled as context aware [66] or pervasive education [44]. Here, sufficient means to analyze the learning process, to model didactical strategies and to react to changing conditions of the learner itself as well as of his environment are targeted. However, the challenges still can be seen in the translation between pedagogical, psychological and technological approaches.

To provide an example, the field of game-based learning shall be sketched. Games are supposed to promote the motivation of learners (Garris et al. [27], Zoerner et al. [77]). This includes both mini-games that offer short-term entertainment when performing a learning task (so-called gamification) as well as mid- or long-term games that embed the educational content into a consistent story (so-called serious games). Besides an intriguing narrative, games may provide explicit rewards for frequent training and can thus (re)activate passive learners. This may not only help to sustain motivation during a longer period of training, but in the short term may also foster a feeling of flow within the learner. However, flow is a very individual mechanism. Shaping it requires insights of the current mindset of the learner as well as general regulative models of the learning process. Besides the achieved learning progress, additional parameters can indicate if the learner is in a productive state, e. g., the displayed emotion: While a bored learner tends to be underchallenged, a frustrated learner may be overstrained. As a consequence, recognizing the emotional state of the learner and adjusting the difficulty of the task accordingly may help to maintain a condition of flow, which in turn may foster the learning progress. We will explain this mechanism (and others) in more detail throughout this chapter by using the example of an adaptive training system for social cognition.

Regarding the targeted application field of social cognition, there is a well-grounded state of research in psychology. It is known that certain populations, such as the elderly [61] and individuals with autism [70], struggle with the intuitive recognition of facial expressions. Previous research has already shown that computer-based training of the ability to recognize emotions is possible [6]. Existing training tools often rely on concepts of gamification. However, these systems follow strict rules and assumptions about the levels of difficulty to be passed and do not adapt to the individual progress of the learner [40], which is even more harmful facing an extremely diverse and sensitive target group. A special challenge is that autistic people usually have no great interest in looking at faces [72] and additionally suffer from a dysfunction of the reward system of the brain [41]. The latter presents as a lack of attendance to social but also nonsocial stimuli, e. g., money in autistic individuals. Therefore, autistic individuals might not be motivated by the same things and as easily as neurotypical individuals. They can be seen as a population that, on one hand, have a substantial need for emotion recognition training, but on the other hand, might not benefit from traditional tutoring approaches. In the worst case, human tutoring could cause them substantial discomfort. Conversely, an adaptive training system could provide a safe environment, which fosters self-motivated learning. We will use this as an example throughout this article.

In general, various lab experiments provided clues that the success of learning depends on various personal factors. For game-based learning, these include different levels of gaming experience and gamer types [55]. For education in general, different learning styles and habits have been studied [10], which have to be addressed by a proper educational or game design. In a broader sense, age and gender may also have an influence. We will analyze these influencing factors in more detail for the field of social cognition. However, several findings and principles can be transferred to adaptivity for other subjects of training or learning.

5.1.3 Relevance of socio-emotional signals for adaptive systems

For our targeted field of application, emotions are relevant in two perspectives. First, they are the core subject of training, which means that it may be useful to reflect the ability of the learner not only to recognize, but also to display a certain emotion (mainly basic emotions like joy, fear or anger) within the training system. Second, the current emotional state of the learner (mainly complex emotions like boredom or frustration) may influence his degree of flow or motivation. This is another reason why detecting the emotional state of the user and processing it within the training system may be useful. We will demonstrate that with current technological means this is feasible for basic emotions, but not trivial (if possible at all) for complex emotions.

This chapter is grounded on an elaboration of previously identified relationships between the characteristics of emotions and personal aspects of people displaying or recognizing this emotion, which is presented in Section 5.2. Knowing what is difficult in recognizing emotions can help to adapt a system to train this ability. Afterwards, we will discuss how adaptive learning arrangements with respect to emotions can be realized. Section 5.3 is focused on emotions as the subject of the learning process, where we present a novel approach for modeling the difficulty of tasks and the skills of learners. Section 5.4 is devoted to emotions as a parameter for adaptation. This includes feedback on emotions imitated by the learner as well as adaptation regarding the mental state of the learner. Though at first sight it might look contradictory to have emotions as a subject and as a parameter of learning, we will show that both approaches are based on similar mechanisms, and thus can be realized using similar technological means. In Section 5.5, we will present findings from a study with a clinical sample using our system and a discussion of these results. The chapter concludes with a summary and outlook to further work in Section 5.6.

5.2 The concept of emotions and human emotion recognition

Emotions will reappear as a topic throughout the entire chapter, either as a content of teaching or as a parameter for adaptation. The following section will therefore describe the basic concept of emotions and introduce important findings from the literature.

5.2.1 Emotions and emotion representation systems

While there is no consensus in the scientific literature on a definition of the term "emotion," most authors agree that emotions are psychological and physiological affective states, which are triggered as a reaction to events or situations, which are coupled with bodily processes and sensations and which affect behavior, decision-making and inter-action with the environment [5, 8, 12, 19]. The relationship between the subjective emo-tional experience of these affective states and their expression is still debated [20, 36] and there is disagreement on the optimal representation system for emotions, e. g., in the context of human computer interfaces [57].

Two of the most applied theories of emotion are Ekman's basic emotion theory [19] and Russel's core affect [62, 63] model. Basic emotion theory describes six discrete emo-tional states (happiness, sadness, anger, fear, surprise and disgust) that are universal, and thus recognized and expressed across cultures. According to Ekman, these states were shaped throughout evolution to provide mammalian organisms with effective and survival promoting responses to the demands of the environment.

While there is evidence for the universality of these emotions, this emotion model is very limited in representing the multitude of emotions outside of the six basic emotions or the degree of emotional activation. However, research has shown that observers read-ily attribute a mixture of emotional states of varying intensity to emotional expressions [30, 58, 60].

The core affect model is an equally simple yet less restrictive model of emotions that allows for the representation of virtually any emotion in a dimensional sense. Emotions are described on the dimensions, valence and arousal. Valence is the level of pleasant-ness or pleasure of an emotion and typically measured on a scale ranging from "very positive" to "very negative." Arousal captures the level of activation or excitement of an emotion and is typically measured on a scale ranging from "very calm" to "very aroused." These dimensions are empirically validated in that they frequently appear as the underlying variables in dimension reduction analyses (such as factor analysis or multidimensional scaling) on self-reported or ascribed affect and ordered emotional words [25, 62, 63].

The advantage of this representation lies in the continuous character of the two constructs, valence and arousal, which also includes a representation of intensity of an emotion. Every point in the space spanned by the two dimensions represents an emo-tional state of a certain intensity. An emotional state is characterized by the relative proportion of valence and arousal, while the intensity is the absolute distance from the neutral middle ground on both dimensions. This representation allows for meaningful distance calculations between emotions, which can be used for adjusting difficulty of emotion recognition tasks (see Section 5.3.5). The bigger the distance between two emo-tions in valence-arousal space, the more different, and consequently, the easier to tell apart they should be.

5.2.2 The difficulty of emotion recognition from faces

Facial expressions (FE) have been a research topic for more than a century [13]. FE are an essential channel for emotional expression and facilitate human interaction. The accurate recognition of FE is dependent on the individual displaying the expression (called actor in the following) and the individual perceiving the expression (called observer in the following). For FE to function as a communication channel, the actor has to produce expressions that will be readily understood by the majority of observers. On the other hand, a potential observer has to possess recognition abilities to understand the majority of expressed FE. Some FE seem to be generally easier to recognize than others. For example, happiness shows a higher recognition accuracy across cultures than disgust or fear [21]. A variety of variables are known to influence the perception accuracy of emotional FE. These are age and sex of the actor and observer on the one hand and valence and arousal properties of the displayed emotion itself on the other hand. For the design of appropriate tasks of a training system, it is important to know how these variables contribute to the difficulty of an emotional stimulus. Understanding the size of these contributions will determine which variables are most useful for task generation. Variables that strongly influence the difficulty of an emotional expression will have to be manipulated carefully to ensure the generation of tasks that cover a great range of difficulty, whereas variables with lower influence could be neglected with little consequences. The following sums up the scientific literature about these variables and discusses their usefulness for task generation.

5.2.2.1 Age and sex of actor

A review by Fölster et al. [24] concluded that emotional expressions were harder to read from old faces than from young ones. This difference might stem from morphological changes of the face, such as folds and wrinkles, interfering with the emotional display, worse intentional muscle control in the elderly affecting posed emotions and/or negative implicit attitudes toward old faces [26].

Women are more expressive in their facial expressions [23], e. g., women smile more than men [33]. A recent study by McDuff et al. [49] on over 2,000 participants from five countries also found that women displayed most investigated facial actions more frequently than men. However, they also found that men show a greater frequency of brow furrowing compared to women, meaning that while women show a higher frequency of displayed expressions overall, there are certain facial actions that are more often displayed by men. However, it is unclear how differences in expressivity between the sexes relate to emotional decoding difficulty of the observers.

5.2.2.2 Age and sex of observer

Emotional decoding abilities are not stable across the lifespan. There is evidence that decoding abilities decline with increasing age in adulthood [61]. By contrast, developmental effects of emotion recognition capabilities can also be observed until the end of adolescence [53].

Previous studies have found a sex difference in recognition abilities only when employing subtle emotional stimuli [35, 52]. A recent meta-analysis concluded that women have a small advantage over men in the recognition of non-verbal displays of emotion (mean Cohen's $d = 0.19$) [68].

5.2.2.3 Peer group effects

Peer group effects are based on the attribution of group membership of individuals. Although there seems to be evidence for a "like-me" bias in the attention toward and memory of faces from the same age group, little evidence exists for a noteworthy peer-group effect in facial emotion recognition [24]. Interactions of observer and actor sex seem to be restricted to specific emotional expressions. For example, male observers react with higher skin conductance responses [48] to angry male faces, although this does not seem to translate into a perceptual advantage.

5.2.2.4 Valence and arousal effects

Of the six basic emotions, happiness is recognized with the highest accuracy [21]. Extending this line of research, we found evidence for a strong correlation of participants' happiness and valence judgments ($r = 0.88$) and could furthermore show that a moderate quadratic relationship between valence and the perceived difficulty of emotional facial expressions exists. In practice, this means that expressions that are judged as being of particularly high or low valence will be easy to decode for observers whereas expressions that are of neutral valence will be the most difficult for observers to decode. The valence of a FE is twice as important as a predictor for the perceived difficulty of the FE than the age of the observer or the arousal of the FE. It is three times as important as the age of the actor and more than ten times as important as the sex of the actor or the sex of the observer.

Arousal is as important as a predictor for perceived difficulty of an FE as the age of the observer and twice as important as the actor age and more than five times as important as the sex of the actor or observer. To sum up, the valence and arousal characteristics of a FE are at least as or more important than all the person specific characteristics of observer and actor. Following this line of thought, adaptivity mechanisms of a learning system should focus on the valence and arousal of emotional FE stimuli to adjust difficulty because these variables have a greater influence on the perceived difficulty of the learner. Furthermore, the dimensional nature of valence and arousal allows a much finer grained manipulation than the person-specific characteristics. This is because person-specific characteristics are either unchangeable (user age and sex), allow only a binary choice (actor sex) or a choice among a limited range of values (actor age). The combination of valence and arousal, on the other hand, allows for a wide range of possible values.

5.2.3 Recognizing emotions from other cues

Emotions can not only be found in the face of people but are also present in their voices and their body language—in every social interaction. In fact, the system we will introduce in the next sections is targeting several aspects of emotion display and recognition. However, this chapter is limited to facial emotion for the sake of simplicity.

5.3 Adaptivity on the example of the training of emotion recognition

This section describes the general principles of an adaptive training system, which is built on the Elo rating system [22]. We will discuss potential mechanisms, which enable an adaptive training system to align with the learner's momentary ability. We illustrate the described concepts on the example of our implementation of an adaptive training system for emotion recognition. This mechanism can be easily transferred to other subjects of training or learning.

5.3.1 Possible adaptation mechanisms

When designing the difficulty level of tasks in a game-based learning environment, two things are central. First, a way has to be found to measure and map the learner's skills. Second, training tasks must be designed so that their level of difficulty increases and decreases to match the skills of the learner.

Training systems often follow the idea of gradual learning progress. In this case, exercises are often created in advance in different degrees of difficulty and are then processed consecutively with increasing difficulty. In contrast to traditional curriculum design [67], where knowledge and skills are gradually accumulated, training (especially of socio-emotional skills) is also about form-related performance, which must be reflected in the difficulty of the tasks. In fact, it is the case that the exerciser can move faster or slower than anticipated by the training system. If he is faster, he has to spend a lot of time with tasks that will not challenge him, and if he is slower the tasks will sooner or later exceed his abilities. This can sometimes lead to frustration because the sense of one's own abilities is no longer consistent with the assessment given by the system.

Another often chosen way to increase the level of difficulty is to implicitly introduce new concepts and game elements to make tasks more difficult. However, if this change in the game is not explicitly communicated, the lack of transparency in the parameterization of the level of difficulty can make the trainee feel that his skills are inadequate, even though he lacks only the understanding of the structure of the task. Moreover, additional game elements may result in primarily training other skills than desired, e. g., the training of the memory or the concentration on irrelevant subtleties in those elements. In addition, introducing more game elements as distractors may result in training primarily other skills than desired, e. g., the training of the memory or the concentration on irrelevant subtleties in the distractors.

A third variant is the use of algorithms for estimating a gradual degree of difficulty for certain compilations of task components. This estimation can then be used again to construct tasks that correspond to the skill level of the trainee. The challenge here is to find a simple and comparable mapping of both the skill level of the trainee and the requirement of the task to be generated. In the following, we want to present how we used the Elo rating system as the basis for such a comparison, and how we developed an adaptation mechanism for our game-based training system based on it.

5.3.2 The Elo rating system

The Elo rating system was initially invented by Arpad Elo to improve the rating of chess players [22]. It was developed with the idea to have an easy-to-use comparison tool, which is why the mathematics used is quite simple. Its calculation method allows estimating the relative skill levels of two chess players. The system assumes that the chess performance of each player in each game is a normally distributed variable, and that the mean value of the performances of any given player changes only slowly over time. In most implementations, the score of a player equals a number between 0 and about 2500 (although the rating theoretically has no upper limit). The difference in player rating serves as a predictor of the outcome of the match (equation (5.1)).

$$\text{Estimate}_A = \frac{1}{1 + 10^{(\text{Elo}_B - \text{Elo}_A)/400}} \tag{5.1}$$

with: Estimate_A = estimated probability of winning for player A; Elo_A = elo score of player A; Elo_B = elo score of player B; the 400 was chosen by Arpad Elo for compatibility reasons

Figure 5.2 depicts the probability of winning a match for one player (Player A) in relation to the difference of his opponent's Elo score and his own Elo score (Elo Score Player B – Elo Score Player A). It is obvious that the probability of Player A winning a match is proportional to the number of points he is ahead of his opponent Player B. For example, a player whose rating is 200 points higher than their opponent's score has a 76 % win expectation; a player with more than 400 points is expected to win 91 % of the

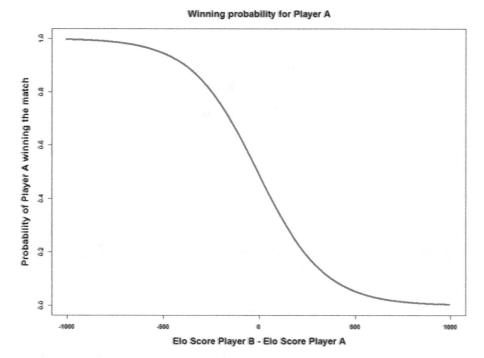

Figure 5.2: Winning probability of Player A as a function of the difference in Elo scores of Player B and Player A. The probability follows a sigmoid function centered at a difference of 0 between the scores of the two players, which equals a probability of 50 % for winning and losing. The larger the difference between the player's scores, the higher the probability for winning or losing, depending on whose score is larger.

matches. The score increases or decreases, depending on whether the player wins or loses the match and whether this result corresponds to the prediction. Thus, in a game with a high chance of victory, winning only scores a few points, whereas defeat in such a game means losing several points. The system therefore adapts if the prediction does not correspond to reality. The lost points are deducted from the loser and credited to the winner (equation (5.2)).

$$\text{Elo}'_A = \text{Elo}_A + k * (\text{Result}_A - \text{Estimate}_A) \qquad (5.2)$$

with: Elo'_A = change of elo score for player A; k = adjusts how many points the player will gain or lose; Result_A = actual result of the match (1 for a win, 0.5 for a draw, 0 for a defeat)

New players are rated with an initial estimated value. In order for such a player not to have to play a large number of matches against too strong or too weak opponents in order to be assessed correctly at some point, there is the k-value, which adjusts how many points a player wins or loses. Typically, this value is high at the start of the career

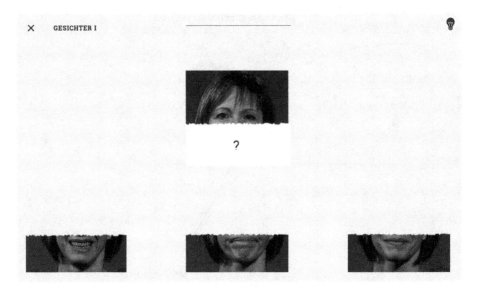

Figure 5.3: The Face Puzzle requires the player to arrange film snippets of emotions. Only the eyes of the target emotion and the mouths of three different emotions are visible.

and decreases with the number of games played, but the k-value adjustment varies from implementation to implementation.

However, the Elo rating system is not only applicable to chess games. In fact, it can be used to rate the contestants in any zero-sum game. Because of that the Elo system or variations of it are often used to rate the players in competitive video games, e. g., Dota 2, League of Legends or Overwatch.

5.3.3 Modeling of learner's skills

Adaptivity requires user modeling, in this case learner modeling. In principle, this can be achieved with qualitative means, e. g., learner style, or with quantitative means, e. g., level of expertise [56]. We use a quantitative approach based on the Elo score but differentiated by task and skill categories. Since our training system focuses on the training of emotion recognition in three areas, namely facial expression, voice and social situations, the skills of the player were also modeled so that these three areas can be found there. For each of these skills, there are several training modules. The various training modules differ, e. g., in that the emotion to be recognized must be identified implicitly, i. e., by intuition, or explicitly, i. e., by naming. Figure 5.3 shows one of the modules.

The Elo rating system has previously been used in competitive video games as well as in IT-based teaching systems. Our contribution to this is the scientifically-based transfer of multidimensional aspects of emotion recognition (as explained in Section 5.2) to the one-dimensional Elo rating system. Also new is the prediction of Elo scores, representing the expected difficulty of a previously unplayed task, based on psychological models. This allows the generation of new training tasks that adequately fit the user's current level of skills, even though these tasks have never been played or rated before (which will be explained in the next section). Inspired by the Elo rating system, each player has an Elo value for each training module: the EVA score. This represents the presumed skill level for emotion recognition within this specific training module. The EVA score ranges from 0 to 2500, and each player has separate scores for the different training modules. Originally, there was an EVA score for each skill. However, since multiple modules train the same skill, this would have meant that points would be passed between different point pools (see detailed description in Section 5.3.5). This is not intended in the Elo rating system and would have distorted the rating. Whenever a new module is unlocked, the player starts with an EVA score of 1200. In an assessment session, the player is then confronted only with tasks from the currently unlocked module. The level of difficulty of the tasks within this session varies greatly, so that an initial assessment of the skill level can be given. This is achieved by using a high k value to calculate the degree of change of the scores. Since different training modules can train the same area of emotion recognition, e. g., recognizing emotions in faces, voices and so on, the player will only see the average EVA score of all modules that train the same skill.

5.3.4 Generation of tasks with predicted level of difficulty

Similar to the players, the training tasks also have an EVA score, which is initially estimated. In order to always provide the player with a fair challenge, tasks should have an EVA score that does not deviate too much from the players. Training tasks usually consist of a target, the emotion to be recognized and distractors that are meant to distract from the correct solution. Based on the number of trainable emotions and available actors, in a task consisting of a single target emotion and two distractors, about 3 million possible combinations of training tasks are possible. Storing all task combinations in advance would be impractical. Instead, tasks are generated on-the-fly using estimates to meet the needs of the current player. In terms of content, the individual tasks are structured as simply as possible. For this purpose, tasks are presented in such a way that exercises of higher difficulty are not generated by a higher number or more complex representation of the emotions to be recognized, but by the use of different parameters, e. g.:

- Similarity of emotions: According to the core affect model [62], emotions with high similarity in valence and arousal should be more difficult to distinguish. Incorrect answer choices, i. e., distractors, with low similarity to the target are easier to rule out as a potential answer. Consequently, distractors located close to the target emotion in valence arousal space make the overall task harder.
- Variability in the expressivity of the actors: Different actors present the same emotion to different degrees, which in turn can complicate or facilitate recognition.

– Complexity of emotions: One property of basic emotions (such as joy, sadness, fear or anger) is that they are recognized reliably across cultures [19], which is due to the innateness of these emotions. In contrast, nonbasic emotions or so-called complex emotions do not have this property and, therefore, depend much more on learned cultural conventions and can thus be expected to be more difficult to recognize.

In the following, the estimation of the task difficulty will be demonstrated using the Face Puzzle Implicit Module (see Figure 5.3). The tasks in this module consist of a target emotion, which should be recognized, and two distractors, which represent wrong answer possibilities. For implicit face puzzle tasks, differentiating emotions is more important than naming. This is because in these tasks, no emotion labels are used, but different emotions are only to be distinguished by valence and arousal, e. g., an actor playing the emotion "anger" looks more negative and excited than an actor playing the emotion "relieved." To determine the difficulty to distinguish two emotions, we calculate the distance in space between the corresponding valence and arousal vectors, normalized by the size of this space (see equation (5.3)). Emotions, which are easy to differentiate, are further apart, while emotions difficult to distinguish, are closer together. Our research suggests that valence has a greater influence on the difficulty of emotion recognition. We expect this effect to also play a role in emotion differentiation, which is why we weigh valence more heavily in the distance calculation. Note that these factors are specific to our scales of difficulty and do not reflect a generalized relation between valence and arousal:

$$\text{dist}(e1, e2) = \frac{1}{18} * \sqrt{4 * ((e1_{\text{valence}} - e2_{\text{valence}}) - 2)^2 - ((e1_{\text{arousal}} - e2_{\text{arousal}}) - 2)^2} \quad (5.3)$$

with: $\text{dist}(e1, e2)$ = distance between the two emotions $e1$ and $e2$; $e1_{\text{valence}}, e2_{\text{valence}}$ = valence value for both emotions; $e1_{\text{arousal}}, e2_{\text{arousal}}$ = arousal value for both emotions.

This results in a distance value (dist) between 0 and 1, with 0 being closest together and 1 being furthest away. Reference values for valence and arousal ($e1_{\text{valence}}, e2_{\text{valence}}, e1_{\text{arousal}}, e2_{\text{arousal}}$) are a combination of previous studies [32] and our own investigations. The estimated EVA score for differentiating both distractors (EVA$_{\text{diff}}$) from the target emotion (formula 5.3) is then calculated from these distance values:

$$\text{EVA}_{\text{diff}}(\text{dist 1}, \text{dist 2}) = 2500 * (1 - \sqrt{\text{dist 1} * \text{dist 2}}) \quad (5.4)$$

with: EVA$_{\text{diff}}$ = eva score for differentiating both distractors from the target emotion; dist1, dist2 = the distance from the target emotion for both distractor emotions.

In several studies, we have determined for all 40 emotions covered by the training system how difficult they are to recognize on average. From these degrees of difficulty, we have derived corresponding EVA scores between 0 and 2500, where the maximum corresponds to the level of a grand master in the original Elo algorithm for chess rating. For instance, considering the task category of Implicit Face Puzzle presented above, the overall recognition difficulty (EVA_{ident}) of a certain task (equation (5.4)) is calculated from the average EVA scores of the target (EVA_{target}) and the two distractors ($EVA_{distractor1}$, $EVA_{distractor2}$):

$$EVA_{ident}(EVA_{target}, EVA_{distractor1}, EVA_{distractor2}) = \frac{EVA_{target} + EVA_{distractor1} + EVA_{distractor2}}{3}$$

(5.5)

with: EVA_{ident} = eva score for identifying all the emotions that are part of the task; EVA_{target}, $EVA_{distractor1}$, $EVA_{distractor2}$ = the eva score for recognizing the emotions represented in the target and the distractors.

As mentioned earlier, identifying emotions plays a minor role in this task type. Therefore, in the final calculation of the task difficulty (equation (5.6)), the EVA score for differentiation is amplified:

$$EVA_{task}(EVA_{ident}, EVA_{diff}) = (EVA_{ident} * EVA_{diff}^{2})^{\frac{1}{3}}$$

(5.6)

with: EVA_{task} = final eva score for the task; EVA_{ident} = eva score for identifying all the emotions that are part of the task; EVA_{diff} = eva score for differentiating both distractors from the target emotion.

This estimation formula can now be used to generate a wide variety of such tasks with different difficulty. However, as this is only an initial estimate, the difficulty levels of the tasks have to be constantly adjusted, similar to the player's skill assessment. This will be explained in the next subchapter.

5.3.5 Dynamic classification of learner skills and task difficulty

Since both player and task have an EVA score, both can compete against each other, much like two chess players. Any attempt to solve a task is considered a match. The task is treated like a player and, therefore, when a task "wins" or "loses" against a player, its score improves or worsens as well. As a result, the assessment of already generated tasks becomes more and more accurate over time. As an example, if a player with an EVA score of 1425 would take on a task with a score of 1480, he would have a 42% chance of winning—similar to the Elo principle of rating player versus player. It is therefore expected that it is statistically more likely that in this case the user cannot solve the task. The following results are possible (with a k value of 20):

- Task solved (unlikely result): The player wins 12 points EVA score. The EVA score of the task drops by 12 points. Although it was less likely that the player could have solved the task, he still solved it. The player is probably better than expected and / or the task is easier than expected.
- Task not solved (more likely result): The task was finished as expected. The player loses 8 points on the EVA score; after all, it would have been possible to solve the

task, and the EVA score of the task increases by 8 points. Nevertheless, the player loses fewer points than he could have won as winning the match was less likely.

In our training concept, the player plays a session of several tasks from different modules in one piece. The tasks within a session are selected or generated based on the player's current EVA score. While playing the session, in the background, his EVA score is constantly changing. Only at the end of the session, the new score and its change will be presented, averaged over all abilities and modules (see Figure 5.4).

Figure 5.4: The feedback screen reflects the user's performance (in German language). left: EVA score, center: experience level, right: library of emotions, bottom: user feedback.

The EVA score is divided into different groups, similar to titles in chess. The naming of the groups was chosen to avoid degrading users with a stigmatizing label like beginner or amateur. We defined a group hierarchy consisting of Bronze, Silver, Gold, Platinum and Diamond.

The updated EVA score of the player will be used again when creating the next session to generate or select new tasks. The pool of generated tasks is shared between all players. A player can therefore be given a task in a session that was generated or played by another player. In this way, both the players and the training tasks, over the course of the training sessions are increasingly estimated and the generated training sessions are tailored more and more to the skills of the players.

An additional measure is the experience level (see Figure 5.4). It expresses nothing about the training progress but is merely a measure of the invested training time. Unlike the EVA score, it is not intended to communicate training success but to reward the endurance invested in the training.

5.4 The emotional state of the learner as a supporting parameter for adaptivity

Section 5.3 showed how theoretical knowledge about emotions was used for the adaptation of training tasks in the context of an emotion recognition training system. Conversely, Section 5.4 will describe how the emotions of the trainee himself can be leveraged to improve the training outcome. The basic assumption is that it should be possible to automatically assess the emotional state of the learner, e. g., from their facial expressions during the training, since humans have that capability, too. However, this poses several technical and conceptual challenges, as the next sections will describe. In brief, it has to be considered which physiological signals can be captured easily and without substantial discomfort for the user to assess their emotions. Furthermore, not all emotional states that can potentially be automatically assessed are of equal importance for determining learning success and the adequacy of the training situation. Finally, if learning relevant states can be detected, the question is how this information can be used to maintain a positive engagement of the user with the training system. The following section will discuss these aspects in detail and provide an overview of the current knowledge and state of the art. Furthermore, we will provide an example on how automatic emotion recognition technology can be used successfully despite its shortcomings.

5.4.1 Automatic emotion recognition from facial expressions

Automatic emotion recognition is the classification of a subjects' emotional state by computational methods. In the context of adaptive learning systems, the aim of automatic emotion recognition is to assess the current motivation and ability of a user in order to foster further engagement and learning gain.

Automatic emotion recognition is conventionally achieved by applying machine learning algorithms to labeled emotional expression data. In the training phase, such an algorithm computationally extracts the underlying patterns that separate the classes given by the labels of the data. The set of complex rules found through this behavior is called a classifier and can be applied to unseen data.

Physiological signals, such as skin conductance response or heart rate [38] can be used for emotion classification, however, these methods usually require scientific equipment not available outside of the laboratory. FE, on the other hand, provide emotional information and can be recorded with conventional webcams which are widely available. FE therefore can be used to build emotion classifiers.

Available FE data sets typically consist of static pictures of a number of actors displaying each or some of the six basic emotions, e. g., [42]. Most data sets only feature actors facing the camera, although there are exceptions, e. g., the Amsterdam Dynamic Facial Expression Set (ADFES) [71], which contains the additional emotions contempt, pride and embarrassment and which also contains videos with head movement during the display of facial expressions.

An issue that also lies within the limitations of available data sets is the use of acted expressions instead of spontaneous displays of emotion. Classifiers built on posed facial expressions can be expected to suffer from a loss of accuracy when applied to spontaneous emotional expressions.

Traditionally, FE classifiers were built with established machine learning techniques such as support vector machines or random forests and the combination of various feature extraction methods. Depending on the data sets used for evaluation accuracy rates greater than 90 % (e. g., [74]) could be reached, which is comparable to human emotion recognition skills. An extensive overview over classification approaches, common data sets of the field and respective results can be found in [64].

With the recent advent of deep learning classification techniques accuracy rates could be further improved. For example, [46] showed deep learning approaches that beat many of the existing state-of-the-art methods across a variety of typically used data sets.

5.4.2 Relevant emotions for learning environments

While the automatic recognition of basic emotions under ideal conditions could be considered a solved problem, the sensible integration of these methods into learning environments proves to be difficult. This might be because Ekman's basic emotions are rarely triggered during learning and their relationship with learning outcomes remains unclear. More relevant to learning might be emotions such as engagement, confusion, boredom or frustration. Engagement but also confusion have been shown to be positively correlated with learning gain while boredom and frustration have been found to have a negative correlation with learning gain [3, 11, 28].

D'Mello and Graesser [15] synthesize these findings in a framework that describes confusion as an indicator of cognitive disequilibrium, which can either be resolved in which case the learner will return to a state of equilibrium and engagement or turn into a state of frustration and later boredom if unresolved. They reason that cognitive disequilibrium is essential for deep learning. In that sense, a fruitful learning experience should entail frequent obstacles that are overcome by the learner by additional causal reasoning that will lead to a deeper conceptual understanding. Prolonged periods of confusion and frustration should however be avoided because they will lead to boredom and disengagement.

5.4.3 Challenges of automatic emotion recognition

Outside of the laboratory automatic FE emotion recognition systems are faced with additional disturbances such as users' head and body movements, varying illumination conditions and camera angles and partial or full obstruction of the face. This is reflected in drastically reduced accuracy rates in naturalistic test sets compared to what is known from standardized test data. For example, a competition called "Emotions in the Wild" contained a challenge on classifying facial expressions cropped out of movies and TV series into basic emotion categories. The winner of this competition could only achieve 62 % accuracy on the test set [14]. These results illustrate that the major challenge of automatic emotion recognition systems might not lie in the classification task itself anymore but in dealing with the circumstances of natural environments in which they are to be employed.

Another noninvasive way to measure emotions, apart from FE recognition, is to analyze mouse movements and keyboard input. In the laboratory, it was shown that both forms of input are suitable for capturing the emotional state of the user [29, 34, 47, 75, 76]. In addition, current research focuses on the detection of psychological states, such as psychosocial stress, outside of a laboratory setting [54]. The presented methods show that it is possible, e. g., while surfing the internet, to detect the user's emotional state unnoticed via the browser. In the case of negative emotions, the system behavior can then be adapted by means of assistance or explanations.

Another challenge is to translate readings of emotional state into changes in the learning experience. This poses questions on how to best transfer users from undesired emotional states into learning-facilitating states. Even though theoretical models exist, which describe the transitions between emotional states during learning (see Section 5.4.2), little research has been conducted to validate these models. Hence, even less is known on how transitions from one emotional state into another can be successfully guided by adaptive changes of the training system.

5.4.4 Training of facial expression

The technical prerequisites exist for reading out the basic emotions, such as anger or happiness, with the use of automatic emotion recognition software, called face reading in the following. However, using them outside of the laboratory usually proves difficult (see Section 5.4.4). Fortunately, in a game-based training context, a player can be motivated to provide appropriate conditions for face reading. This is partly because the face reading can be made explicit for the player. This means that the player can see himself on the display as part of the task during face reading. As a result, he or she can detect faults, such as overshooting light, and correct them if necessary. In addition, the player has a self-interest that the face reading works well, since he wants to shine in the game. For the training system presented here, this led to a mimicry module. There are several variants of the module. As an example, in one variant, the player has to imitate an actor-played base emotion to a certain extent (see Figure 5.5).

The training success in performing mimicry tasks can only be used for the EVA score algorithm if this success is quantifiable. The challenge is to automatically calculate the

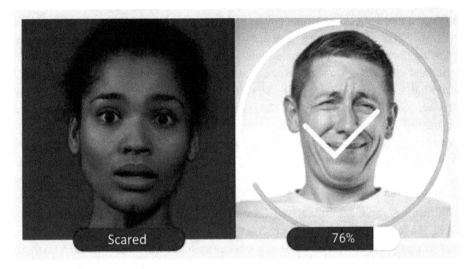

Figure 5.5: The automated rating of similarity in facial mimicry: An actor displays an emotion (left). The player is requested to imitate it (right).

similarity between a given expression and the user's imitation in such a way that the value is both meaningful to estimate training success and to provide transparent feedback to the user.

5.5 Discussion

The Elo rating provides a straightforward mechanism which, as shown, can also be used to assess trainers and training tasks in a game-based training context. However, there are limits. For what constitutes its simplicity, namely that only the victories and defeats are evaluated, there is also a weakness for adaptation. Only the outcome is considered for the calculation, but not the cause. For the player, it remains unclear why he was successful or not. Was it just his abilities or was he unfocused, distracted or simply in a bad mood? A possible intervention is to ask simple questions to the player after training, such as: "Was the session instructive for you?" However, a less invasive method of detecting frustration or motivation, such as emotion recognition through face-reading, would be a rewarding alternative to better assess player and task performance. Moreover, a player could perform better for some emotions than for others, or for some actors better than for others. An open question is whether the actual task difficulty depends only on the selection of the emotions as target and distractor, or whether other factors (such as the acting performance, gender or age of the actors) play a role. Although these factors affect the assessment of the tasks, this happens only implicitly over time. Further research and more precise models are needed to integrate this into calculations.

Clinical studies of previous (nonadaptive) versions of such training have proven effective in terms of learning outcome, i. e., sustainable improvement of social cognition and social behavior [40]. A study examining the usability and flow of our software was conducted by our project partners. In addition, we performed an investigation into the progress of users and the accuracy of EVA score predictions for newly generated tasks.

As previously noted, we have used a science-based algorithm to predict the EVA score (difficulty level) of newly generated tasks (see Section 5.3). From a computer science point of view, one of our core research interests was to find out how this estimate fits in with reality. For this purpose, we have saved the generated EVA score for each generated task. After the study, we then measured the real difference between the generated EVA score and the actual EVA score after several runs. The average relative difference in relation to the number of task occurrences is shown in Figure 5.6 as an example for the Face Puzzle.

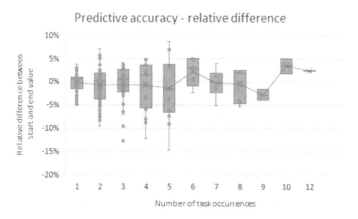

Figure 5.6: The estimated EVA scores do not differ much from the actual measurement even after several runs.

Our measurements have shown that, even after several runs of a single task, their EVA score averages no more than 5 % relative difference between estimation and measurement. This suggests that, while there is still scope for improvement, our estimate is already very accurate.

Figure 5.7 shows the development of EVA scores for multiple users across their training sessions. EVA scores increase continuously for most users, which reflects an increase in the users' emotion recognition abilities. Different learning rates of the users, as represented by the slopes of the lines, are also evident: While some users' scores increase rapidly, others display rather slow increases. Only a few users show stagnating scores and, therefore, little or no increase of their measured emotion recognition abilities over the course of their training sessions. Overall, this exemplifies that the EVA scoring sys-

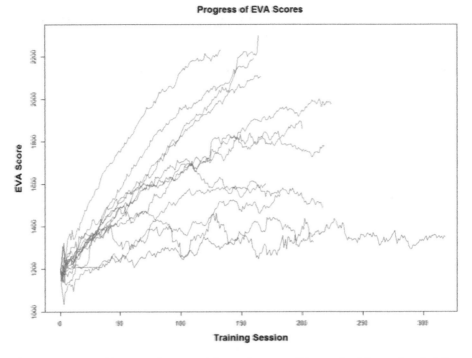

Figure 5.7: Progress of EVA scores for one module over the course of the users' training sessions. Each line represents a user's EVA score. All users start with a score of 1200. Most users' scores increase over time.

tem is able to measure the training success of the users accurately and, furthermore, that most users benefit from the training sessions.

Figure 5.8 shows the flow state measured using the Flow Short Scale questionnaire [59], which separates Flow in the two subfactors fluency of performance (FI), absorption by activity (FII) and the additional factor concern (FIII). The highlighted bars show training tools that train socio-emotional skills (see also Tscherejkina, Morgiel and Moebert [69]). The other bars are comparative values from the work of Rheinberg et al. The NT-group has a relatively high level of absorption and fluency and relatively little concern. Overall, the EVA system shows high values for flow experience. In the other studies, the highest values for flow and concern were found in a sample of graffiti sprayers.

High values for concern correlate with findings from [73], where autistic users as compared to neurotypical users reported significantly higher levels of effort (67 ± 20 versus 39 ± 26) when performing the training with EVA, measured with NASA Task Load Index [31].

The usability of the EVA app was measured with the system usability scale (SUS). Two groups with different characteristics were studied: people with autism spectrum condition (ASC) and neurotypical people (NT). Each group was again divided into a laboratory and a longitudinal testing group. A laboratory session lasts 90 min. and a longi-

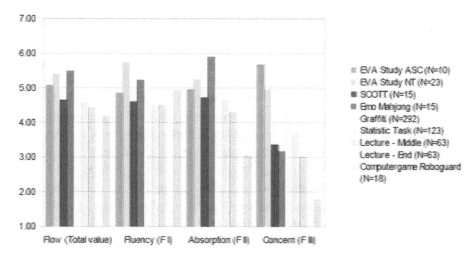

Figure 5.8: Flow data. Studies on socio-emotional skills and ASC are highlighted in color.

tudinal session contains a 2-week home-based training with the EVA app. The values for the laboratory NT-group (M = 81.9; SD = 11) and the longitudinal ASC-group (M = 82.5; SD = 6.6) are almost excellent (see Figure 5.9).

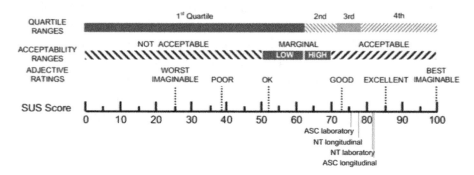

Figure 5.9: SUS Scores from our EVA study and original ranking [4].

Previous research could provide evidence for the effectiveness of adaptive training only for low-prior knowledge students and in some conditions [17]. Further research is required to assess which adaptive features (like task difficulty, duration and composition or the display of additional information) are efficient in general, and which only for specific training setups. This could be measured in terms of impact on learning gain, training time or user satisfaction. Another option is to assess the smoothness of changes in task difficulty, for instance, by determining the user's motivation or intensity of flow throughout the training (either explicitly by using a questionnaire, or implicitly by monitoring his behavior). Unfortunately, explicit assessment will most likely disturb the flow effect and the gaming experience in general, while methods for an implicit and unobtrusive measurement still have to be designed.

A general challenge for such research is to shift emotion recognition from clinical labs to real-life conditions. This is not only a technical issue, since there are plenty of mechanisms less prone to disturbances than facial expression detection, as discussed in Section 5.4.4, and multimodal solutions can provide an additional increase in accuracy [16]. In situ research becomes even more important since emotions are a very personal affair, and thus expressing and recognizing complex emotions, in particular, may benefit from a familiar environment. Also, socio-emotional training will preferably take place in informal settings. If robustness of automatic emotion recognition can be improved under real-life conditions, user satisfaction, flow states and engagement could be dynamically assessed, which provides additional cues to assess and to adjust difficulty of individual exercises.

5.6 Conclusion

In this chapter, we presented the scientific principles and the results of developing adaptive training systems based on emotions. First, emotions as a subject of training were discussed. We showed that the training can be improved by adapting the difficulty of tasks based on the difference of emotions, which was derived from empirical findings on human emotion recognition. Our evaluation of the adaptivity algorithm in EVA demonstrated that (a) our initial rating of the difficulty of previously unplayed tasks was appropriate, (b) the adaptation of task difficulty converged with more than five sessions this task was played and (c) the skill level of users (both autistic and neurotypical) continuously increased over time. Previous studies could prove that social cognition as well as social behavior in general can be sustainably enhanced by such training. This has still to be proven for EVA in a clinical intervention study. Moreover, it has to be proven if adapting the difficulty of tasks in EVA helps to keep users in a state of flow or to maintain the motivation for training, respectively.

On that basis, we presented mechanisms to facilitate emotions as an additional parameter for adaptivity. However, facial emotion detection is still a challenge, especially when it comes to real-life conditions outside a lab. Adapting the behavior of a system to the emotions of a user, so-called affective computing, is on the rise. A typical field of application is education. However, this brings up several additional issues. From a technical point of view, the demand for affect detection by different applications leads to offering this as a basic service across a computer system (instead of integrating a separate library into every single app, as is common). This requires standardized interfaces for such services, maybe as a part of the operating system or close to it, which can be invoked by various apps.

From a societal point of view, training systems that react to the emotions of the learner are of interest in a much broader scope than considered today. Regarding the target group, there is a current focus on people with autism, while different user groups (in terms of profession or psychological disposition) could also benefit from training their social cognition. Regarding the setting, there is high potential for emotion-sensitive training on various educational levels, from school to university and vocational training. However, supposing that automated emotion recognition will work properly under real-life conditions still leaves open the question of how a training system should translate this into changes in learning experience. Currently, there is little experience and empirical studies available, since interdisciplinary understanding of actually executable models from didactics and psychology is not yet pronounced.

As a final remark, there are several ethical questions associated with the use (and potential misuse) of such technology. The consequences for individuals and for society as a whole of having emotion recognition and emotion-sensitive systems fully operational are still to be understood [18]. For instance, using a training system for social cognition as an invisible assessment tool is not intended, but possible, e. g., by employers. Moreover, the mere availability of such training may shift societal norms toward a mainstreamed understanding of how people should behave in order to be accepted (in terms of tolerance) and legally allowed (e. g., for granting public aid). Ethical guidelines have to be developed for this.

References

[1] J. R. Anderson. *The Architecture of Cognition*. Cambridge, MA: Harvard University Press, 1983.
[2] J. R. Anderson, A. T. Corbett, K. Koedinger, and R. Pelletier. Cognitive tutors: Lessons learned. *The Journal of the Learning Sciences* 4 (1995) 167–207.
[3] R. S. Baker, S. K. D'Mello, M. M. T. Rodrigo, and A. C. Graesser. Better to be frustrated than bored: The incidence, persistence, and impact of learners' cognitive–affective states during interactions with three different computer-based learning environments. *International Journal of Human-Computer Studies* 68(4) (2010) 223–241.
[4] A. Bangor, P. Kortum, and J. Miller. Determining what individual SUS scores mean: adding an adjective rating scale. *Journal of Usability Studies* 4 (2009) 114–123.
[5] L. F. Barrett, B. Mesquita, K. N. Ochsner, and J. J. Gross. The experience of emotion. *Annual Review of Psychology* 58 (2007) 373–403.
[6] S. Bölte, S. Feineis-Matthews, S. Leber, T. Dierks, D. Hubl, and F. Poustka. The Development and Evaluation of a Computer-Based Program to Test and to Teach the Recognition of Facial Affect. *International Journal of Circumpolar Health* 61(02) (2002) 61–68.
[7] P. Brusilovsky. *Methods and techniques of adaptive hypermedia. Adaptive hypertext and hypermedia*. Dordrecht: Springer, 1998, pp. 1–43.
[8] M. Cabanac. What is emotion? *Behavioural Processes* 60(2) (2002) 69–83.
[9] J. Chambers and J. Sprecher. *Computer-Assisted Instruction: Its Use in the Classroom*. Englewood Cliffs, New Jersey: Prentice-Hall, 1983.

[10] F. Coffield. Learning styles: unreliable, invalid and impractical and yet still widely used. In: P. Adey and J. Dillon, editors. *Bad education: debunking myths in education*. Maidenhead, UK: Open University Press, 2012, pp. 215–230.

[11] S. Craig, A. Graesser, J. Sullins, and B. Gholson. Affect and learning: an exploratory look into the role of affect in learning with AutoTutor. *Journal of Educational Media* 29(3) (2004) 241–250.

[12] A. R. Damasio. Emotion in the perspective of an integrated nervous system. *Brain Research Reviews* 26(2–3) (1998) 83–86.

[13] C. Darwin. *The expression of emotion in animals and man*. London: Murray, 1872.

[14] A. Dhall, R. Goecke, J. Joshi, J. Hoey, and T. Gedeon. Emotiw 2016: Video and group-level emotion recognition challenges. In: *Proc. International Conference on Multimodal Interaction*. ACM, 2016, pp. 427–432.

[15] S. D'Mello and A. Graesser. Dynamics of affective states during complex learning. *Learning and Instruction* 22(2) (2012) 145–157.

[16] S. D'Mello and J. Kory. A review and meta-analysis of multimodal affect detection systems. *ACM Computing Surveys* 47(3) (2015) 43.

[17] S. D'Mello, B. Lehman, J. Sullins, R. Daigle, R. Combs, K. Vogt, L. Perkins, and A. Graesser. A time for emoting: When affect-sensitivity is and isn't effective at promoting deep learning. In: *Proc. International Conference on Intelligent Tutoring Systems*. Berlin: Springer, 2010, pp. 245–254.

[18] I. Dziobek, U. Lucke, and A. Manzeschke. Emotions-sensitive Trainingssysteme für Menschen mit Autismus: Ethische Leitlinien. In: *Proc. Informatik 2017, LNI P-275*. Bonn: Köllen, 2017, pp. 369–380.

[19] P. Ekman. An argument for basic emotions. *Cognition and Emotion* 6(3–4) (1992) 169–200.

[20] P. Ekman, R. J. Davidson, and W. V. Friesen. The Duchenne smile: Emotional expression and brain physiology: II. *Journal of Personality and Social Psychology* 58(2) (1990) 342.

[21] H. A. Elfenbein and N. Ambady. On the universality and cultural specificity of emotion recognition: a meta-analysis. *Psychological Bulletin* 128(2) (2002) 203.

[22] A. E. Elo. The rating of chess players. Past and present. Ishi Press, Mountain View (CA), 2008.

[23] A. Fischer and M. LaFrance. What drives the smile and the tear: Why women are more emotionally expressive than men. *Emotion Review* 7(1) (2015) 22–29.

[24] M. Fölster, U. Hess, and K. Werheid. Facial age affects emotional expression decoding. *Frontiers in Psychology* 5 (2014) 30.

[25] J. R. Fontaine, K. R. Scherer, E. B. Roesch, and P. C. Ellsworth. The world of emotions is not two-dimensional. *Psychological Science* 18(12) (2007) 1050–1057.

[26] M. Freudenberg, R. B. Adams Jr., R. E. Kleck, and U. Hess. Through a glass darkly: facial wrinkles affect our processing of emotion in the elderly. *Frontiers in Psychology* 6 (2015) 1476.

[27] R. Garris, R. Ahlers, and J. Driskell. Games, motivation, and learning: A research and practice modell. *Simulation & Gaming* 33(4) (2002) 441–467.

[28] J. F. Grafsgaard, J. B. Wiggins, K. E. Boyer, E. N. Wiebe, and J. C. Lester. Automatically recognizing facial indicators of frustration: a learning-centric analysis. In: *Affective Computing and Intelligent Interaction (ACII)*. IEEE, 2013, pp. 159–165.

[29] M. Grimes, J. L. Jenkins, and J. S. Valacich. Exploring the Effect of Arousal and Valence on Mouse Interaction. In: *Proc. International Conference on Information Systems*, 2013.

[30] J. A. Hall, and D. Matsumoto. Gender differences in judgments of multiple emotions from facial expressions. *Emotion* 4(2) (2004) 201.

[31] S. G. Hart, and L. E. Staveland. Development of NASA-TLX (Task Load Index): Results of Empirical and Theoretical Research. *Advances in Psychology* 52 (1988) 139–183.

[32] R. Hepach, D. Kliemann, S. Grüneisen, H. R. Heekeren, and I. Dziobek. Conceptualizing emotions along the dimensions of valence, arousal, and communicative frequency - implications for social-cognitive tests and training tools. *Frontiers in Psychology* 2 (2011) 266.

[33] U. Hess and P. Bourgeois. You smile–I smile: Emotion expression in social interaction. *Biological Psychology* 84(3) (2010) 514–520.

[34] M. Hibbeln, J. L. Jenkins, C. Schneider, J. S. Valacich, and M. Weinmann. How Is Your User Feeling?: Inferring Emotion Through Human-Computer interaction Devices. *MIS Quarterly* 41(1) (2017) 1–21.

[35] H. Hoffmann, H. Kessler, T. Eppel, S. Rukavina, and H. C. Traue. Expression intensity, gender and facial emotion recognition: Women recognize only subtle facial emotions better than men. *Acta Psychologica* 135(3) (2010) 278–283.

[36] C. E. Izard. Facial expressions and the regulation of emotions. *Journal of Personality and Social Psychology* 58(3) (1990) 487.

[37] J. Keller. Motivational design of instruction. In: C. Reigeluth, editor. *Instructional design theories and models. An overview of their current studies*. Hillsdale, NJ: Erlbaum, 1983.

[38] K. H. Kim, S. W. Bang, and S. R. Kim. Emotion recognition system using short-term monitoring of physiological signals. *Medical & Biological Engineering & Computing* 42(3) (2004) 419–427.

[39] Kinshuk and A. Patel. A Conceptual Framework for Internet Based Intelligent Tutoring Systems. *Knowledge Transfer* II (1997) 117–124.

[40] S. Kirst, R. Diehm, S. Wilde-Etzold, M. Ziegler, M. Noterdaeme, L. Poustka, and I. Dziobek. Fostering socio-emotional competencies in children with autism spectrum condition: Results of a randomized controlled trial using the interactive training app "Zirkus Empathico". In: *Proc. International Meeting for Autism Research (IMFAR)*, 2017, pp. 743–744.

[41] G. Kohls, et al.. 2018. Altered reward system reactivity for personalized circumscribed interests in autism. In Mol Autism, 9.

[42] P. Lucey, J. F. Cohn, T. Kanade, J. Saragih, Z. Ambadar, and I. Matthews. The extended cohn-kanade dataset (ck+): A complete dataset for action unit and emotion-specified expression. In: *Proc. Computer Vision and Pattern Recognition Workshops (CVPRW)*. IEEE CS Press, 2010, pp. 94–101.

[43] U. Lucke. An Algebra for Multidimensional Documents as Abstraction Mechanism for Cross Media Publishing. In: *Proc. Automated Production of Cross Media Content for Multi-Channel Distribution (AXMEDIS)* IEEE CS Press, 2006, pp. 165–172.

[44] U. Lucke and C. Rensing. A survey on pervasive education. *Pervasive and Mobile Computing* 14 (2014) 3–16.

[45] U. Lucke and M. Specht. Mobility, Adaptivity and context awareness in e-learning. *I-Com* 11(01) (2012) 26–29.

[46] A. T. Lopes, E. de Aguiar, A. F. De Souza, and T. Oliveira-Santos. Facial expression recognition with convolutional neural networks: coping with few data and the training sample order. *Pattern Recognition* 61 (2017) 610–628.

[47] W. Maehr. *eMotion: Estimation of User's Emotional State by Mouse Motions*. Saarbrücken: VDM, 2008.

[48] E. J. Mazurski, N. W. Bond, D. A. Siddle, and P. F. Lovibond. Conditioning with facial expressions of emotion: effects of CS sex and age. *Psychophysiology* 33(4) (1996) 416–425.

[49] D. McDuff, E. Kodra, R. el Kaliouby, and M. LaFrance. A large-scale analysis of sex differences in facial expressions. *PLoS ONE* 12(4) (2017) e0173942.

[50] T. Moebert. Zum Einfluss von Adaptivität auf die Interaktion mit Bildungstechnologien. In: P. A. Henning, M. Striewe, and M. Wölfel, editors. *DELFI 2022, Die 20. Fachtagung Bildungstechnologien der Gesellschaft für Informatik e. V., 12.*–*14.Karlsruhe 2022*. Gesellschaft für Informatik e. V., 2022, pp. 51–62.

[51] T. Moebert, H. Jank, R. Zender, and U. Lucke. A Generalized Approach for context-Aware Adaption in Mobile E-Learning Settings. In: *Proc. Advanced Learning Technologies (ICALT)*. IEEE CS Press, 2014, pp. 143–145.

[52] B. Montagne, R. P. Kessels, E. Frigerio, E. H. de Haan, and D. I. Perrett. Sex differences in the perception of affective facial expressions: Do men really lack emotional sensitivity? *Cognitive Processing* 6(2) (2005) 136–141.

[53] R. Montirosso, M. Peverelli, E. Frigerio, M. Crespi, and R. Borgatti. The Development of Dynamic Facial Expression Recognition at Different Intensities in 4-to 18-Year-Olds. *Social Development* 19(1) (2010) 71–92.

[54] M. Norden, A. G. Hofmann, M. Meier, F. Balzer, O. T. Wolf, E. Böttinger, and H. Drimalla. Inducing and Recording Acute Stress Responses on a Large Scale With the Digital Stress Test (DST): Development and Evaluation Study. *Journal of Medical Internet Research* 24(7) (2022) e32280. https://doi.org/10.2196/32280.

[55] R. Orji, R. L. Mandryk, and J. Vassileva. Improving the Efficacy of Games for Change Using Personalization Models. *ACM Transactions on Computer-Human Interaction* 24(5) (2017) 32.

[56] R. Pelanek. Applications of the Elo Rating System in Adaptive Educational Systems. *Computers and Education* 98(C) (2016) 169–179.

[57] C. Peter and A. Herbon. Emotion representation and physiology assignments in digital systems. *Interacting with Computers* 18(2) (2006) 139–170.

[58] L. H. Phillips and R. Allen. Adult aging and the perceived intensity of emotions in faces and stories. *Aging Clinical and Experimental Research* 16(3) (2004) 190–199.

[59] F. Rheinberg, R. Vollmeyer, and S. Engeser. Die Erfassung des Flow-Erlebens. In: J. Stiensmeier-Pelster and F. Rheinberg, editors. *Diagnostik von Selbstkonzept, Lernmotivation und Selbstregulation*. Tests und Trends, volume 16. Göttingen: Hogrefe, 2003, pp. 261–279.

[60] M. Riediger, M. C. Voelkle, N. C. Ebner, and U. Lindenberger. Beyond "happy, angry, or sad?": Age-of-poser and age-of-rater effects on multi-dimensional emotion perception. *Cognition and Emotion* 25(6) (2011) 968–982.

[61] T. Ruffman, J. D. Henry, V. Livingstone, and L. H. Phillips. A meta-analytic review of emotion recognition and aging: Implications for neuropsychological models of aging. *Neuroscience and Biobehavioral Reviews* 32(4) (2008) 863–881.

[62] J. A. Russell. Core affect and the psychological construction of emotion. *Psychological Review* 110(1) (2003) 145.

[63] J. A. Russell and L. F. Barrett. Core affect, prototypical emotional episodes, and other things called emotion: dissecting the elephant. *Journal of Personality and Social Psychology* 76(5) (1999) 805.

[64] E. Sariyanidi, H. Gunes, and A. Cavallaro. Automatic analysis of facial affect: A survey of registration, representation, and recognition. *IEEE Transactions on Pattern Analysis and Machine Intelligence* 37(6) (2015) 1113–1133.

[65] R. Schultz, I. Gauthier, A. Klin, R. Fulbright, A. Anderson, F. Volkmar, P. Skudlarski, C. Lacadie, D. Cohen, and J. Gore. Abnormal Ventral Temporal Cortical Activity During Face Discrimination Among Individuals with Autism and Asperger Syndrome. *Archives of General Psychiatry* 57(4) (2000) 331–340.

[66] M. Sharples, I. Arnedillo Sanchez, M. Milrad, and G. Vavoula. Mobile learning: small devices, big issues. In: *Technology Enhanced Learning: Principles and Products*. Heidelberg: Springer, 2009, pp. 233–249.

[67] E. Soare. Perspectives on Designing the Competence Based Curriculum. *Procedia – Social and Behavioral Sciences* 180 (2015) 972–977.

[68] A. E. Thompson and D. Voyer. Sex differences in the ability to recognise non-verbal displays of emotion: A meta-analysis. *Cognition and Emotion* 28(7) (2014) 1164–1195.

[69] A. Tscherejkina, A. Morgiel, and T. Moebert. *Computergestütztes Training von sozio-emotionalen Kompetenzen durch Minispiele. Evaluation von User Experience. E-Learning Symposium 2018*. Lecture Notes in Informatics (LNI), volume 1. Bonn: Gesellschaft für Informatik, 2018.

[70] M. Uljarevic and A. Hamilton. Recognition of Emotions in Autism: A Formal Meta-Analysis. *Journal of Autism and Developmental Disorders* 43(7) (2012) 1517–1526.

[71] J. Van Der Schalk, S. T. Hawk, A. H. Fischer, and B. Doosje. Moving faces, looking places: Validation of the Amsterdam Dynamic Facial Expression Set (ADFES). *Emotion* 11(4) (2011) 907.

[72] C. Wang, E. Shimojo, and S. Shimojo. Don't look at the eyes: Live interaction reveals strong eye avoidance behavior in autism. *Journal of Vision* 15(12) (2015) 648.

[73] A. Weigand, L. Enk, T. Moebert, D. Zoerner, J. Schneider, U. Lucke, and I. Dziobek. 2019. Introducing E.V.A. – A New Training App for Social Cognition: Design, Development, and First Acceptance and Usability Evaluation for Autistic Users. In: *12th Scientific Meeting for Autism Spectrum Conditions*, Augsburg, Februar 2019.

[74] G. Zhao and M. Pietikainen. Dynamic texture recognition using local binary patterns with an application to facial expressions. *IEEE Transactions on Pattern Analysis and Machine Intelligence* 29(6) (2007) 915–928.

[75] P. Zimmermann, S. Guttormsen, B. Danuser, and P. Gomez. Affective computing - a rationale for measuring mood with mouse and keyboard. *International Journal of Occupational Safety and Ergonomics* 9(4) (2003) 539–551.

[76] P. Zimmermann, P. Gomez, B. Danuser, and S. G. Schär. Extending usability: Putting affect into the user-experience. In: *Proc. NordiCHI'06*, 2006, pp. 27–32.

[77] D. Zoerner, T. Moebert, A. Morgiel, S. Strickroth, and U. Lucke. Spielbasierte Förderung von Motivation und Aufmerksamkeit für sozioemotionales Training bei Autismus: Durch Minecraft und eine mobile App die Geheimnisse der Mimik erlernen. In: D. Krömker and U. Schroeder, editors. *DeLFI 2018. Die 16. E-Learning Fachtagung Informatik der Gesellschaft für Informatik e. V., 10.-12., Frankfurt am Main, Deutschland*. Bonn: Köllen, 2018.

Dietmar Jannach, Michael Jugovac, and Ingrid Nunes

6 Explanations and user control in recommender systems

Beyond black-box personalization systems

Abstract: Adaptive, personalized recommendations have become a common feature of today's web and mobile app user interfaces. In most of modern applications, however, the underlying recommender systems are black boxes for the users, and no detailed information is provided about why certain items were selected for recommendation. Users also often have very limited means to influence (e. g., correct) the provided suggestions and to apply information filters. This can potentially lead to a limited acceptance of the recommendation system. In this chapter, we review explanations and feedback mechanisms as a means of building trustworthy recommender and advice-giving systems that put their users in control of the personalization process, and outline existing challenges in the area.

Keywords: Recommender systems, personalization, explanations, feedback user control

ACM CCS: Human-centered computing, collaborative and social computing

6.1 Introduction

Many of today's user interfaces of web and mobile application feature system-generated, often personalized and context-adaptive recommendations for their users regarding, for example, things to buy, music to discover or people to connect with. To be able to automatically generate such tailored suggestions, the underlying recommender systems maintain a *user profile*, which serves as a basis to (i) infer individual user's preferences, needs and current contextual situation and to (ii) correspondingly select suitable items for recommendation. Given the huge potential value of such systems for both consumers and providers [32], a variety of algorithmic approaches has been proposed over the past two decades to generate suitable item recommendations for a given user profile. A prominent class of such systems is based on the principle of *collaborative filtering*, where the user profile consists of a set of recorded explicit or implicit preference statements of individual users, and recommendations are generated by also considering preference or behavioral patterns of a larger user community.

Collaborative filtering approaches based on often complex machine learning models have shown to lead to increased business value in practice in various application domains [15, 34, 35, 41]. However, a potential limitation of these systems is that, from the perspective of the end user, the factors and mechanisms that determine the pro-

https://doi.org/10.1515/9783110988567-006

vided recommendations usually remain as a *black box*. This is in particular the case for popular technical approaches based on matrix factorization and, more recently, complex neural network architectures. In some applications, users may be given an intuition about the underlying recommendation logic, e. g., through a descriptive label like "Customers who bought ... also bought." Often, however, recommendation lists are only labeled with "Recommended for you" or "Based on your profile," and no in-depth explanation is given about how the recommendations were selected. In case no such information is provided, users may have doubts that the recommendations are truly the best choice for them and suspect that the recommendations are mostly designed to optimize the profit of the seller or the platform.

A potentially even more severe problem with such black-box approaches can arise when the system's assumptions about the user's preferences are wrong or outdated. A typical example is when users purchase a gift for someone else but the system considers the gift to be part of the users' own interests. Many of today's systems provide no mechanisms for users to give feedback on the recommendations or to correct the system's assumptions [38]. In some cases, users might not even be aware of the fact that the content provided by the system is personalized according to some assumed preferences, as it is probably the case in the news feeds of major social networks. In either case, when recommendations are of limited relevance for the users, they will eventually stop to rely on the system's suggestions or, in the worst case, abandon the platform as a whole.

In the academic literature, different proposals have been made to deal with the described problems. One main stream of research is devoted to the topic of *explanations* for recommender systems [26, 57, 70], e. g., with the goal to make recommender systems more transparent and trustworthy. Explanations for decision support systems have, in fact, been explored for decades. We can, however, observe an increased interest in the field of explanations in the recent past, as more and more decisions are transferred to machine learning algorithms and, in many cases, these decisions must be open to scrutiny, e. g., to be able to assess the system's fairness [9, 11].[1]

Providing explanations can also serve as a starting point to address the second type of problem, i. e., how to better put users in control of their recommendations. Some e-commerce platforms, like Amazon.com, present explanations in the form "Because you bought," and let their users give feedback if this recommendation reasoning should be applied by the system in the future. Providing user control mechanisms in the context of explanations is, however, only one of several approaches proposed in the literature, which we review various of these in this chapter.

---

1 This aspect is of increasing importance also due to the European Union's recent General Data Protection Regulation (https://eur-lex.europa.eu/eli/reg/2016/679/oj), which aims to provide more transparency and additional rights for individuals in cases where decision-making is done on a solely algorithmic basis.

Generally, both explanations and user control mechanisms represent a potential means to increase the user's trust in a system and to increase the adoption of recommendations and advices it makes. In this chapter, we overview approaches from both areas and highlight the particular potential of explanation-based user control mechanisms.

6.2 Explanations in recommender systems

6.2.1 Purposes of explanations

There are a number of possible ways in which one can explain the recommendations of a system to a user. When designing an explanation facility for a recommender system, one has therefore to consider *what should be achieved* by adding an explanation component to an application, i. e., what its *purpose(s)* should be. For example, in an e-commerce system, a seller might be interested in *persuading* customers to buy particular products or increasing their *trust* in order to promote loyalty.

In early medical expert systems, explanations were, e. g., often provided in terms of the system's internal inference rules, which allowed users to understand or check the plausibility of the provided diagnosis or advice. But *understanding* the system's decision was soon recognized not to be the only reason for including explanations. Buchanan and Shortliffe [6] list *debugging, education, acceptance* and *persuasion* as additional potential goals in the context of expert systems. This list was later extended with additional perspectives in [68] and [57], leading to a more comprehensive list as shown in Table 6.1.

Table 6.1: Explanation purposes (based on [6, 57, 68]).

Purpose	Description	Example works
Transparency	Explain how the system works	[23, 26, 73]
Effectiveness	Help users make good decisions	[3, 19, 22]
Trust	Increase users' confidence in the system	[5, 28, 61]
Persuasiveness	Convince users to try or buy	[1, 26, 75]
Satisfaction	Increase the ease of use or enjoyment	[3, 22, 61]
Education	Allow users to learn something from the system	[21, 25, 46]
Scrutability	Allow users to tell the system it is wrong	[20, 30, 40]
Efficiency	Help users make decisions faster	[2, 50, 61]
Debugging	Help users identify defects in the system	[14, 29, 44]

The entries in the table are organized by their importance in the research literature according to the survey presented in [57]. In the majority of the cases, research papers focused mostly on one single purpose, like in the seminal work by Herlocker et al. [26].

There are, however, also works that investigate multiple dimensions in parallel [17, 29]. In a number of research works on explanations, in particular earlier ones, the authors did not explicitly state for which purpose their explanation facility was designed [13]. In several cases, the purpose can also not be indirectly inferred due to a surprisingly large fraction of works that lack a systematic evaluation of the explanation component [57].

Explanations are in general one of the natural "entry points" for giving the user control of recommendations, e. g., by displaying the assumptions about the user's preferences for inspection and correction. However, in a review of over 200 papers on the topic of explanations, Nunes and Jannach [57] could identify only seven works that focused on scrutability, i. e., allowing the user to correct the system, which indicates a major research gap in this area.

6.2.2 Explanation approaches

We can find a variety of different ways of explaining the suggestions made by a recommender or, more generally, advice-giving system in the literature. The choice of the type of information that is used for explaining the recommendation and how the explanation is presented to the user depends on different factors. These can, e.g., include the availability of certain types of information (e. g., an explicit inference chain) or the specific application domain.

With respect to the *explanation content*, four main content categories—summarized as follows—were identified in [57]. Table 6.2 exemplifies how a system can present these different types of content in the context of an interactive recommender system for mobile phones.

Table 6.2: Examples of explanation content categories.

Content	Explanation example
Preferences and user inputs	*"We recommend this phone because you specified that you prefer light-weight models."*
Inference process	*"We consider light phones those that weigh less than 150 g."*
Background knowledge	*"We recommend this phone because it is currently popular in our shop."*
Alternatives and their features	*"This camera has a removable battery, which other similar models do not have."*

- *Preferences and user inputs*: Explanations in this category refer to the specific user inputs or inferred preferences that led to the given recommendation. For example, the explanation details to what extent a recommended alternative matches the user's assumed preferences, or presents the predicted user rating.
- *Inference process*: Historically, *inference traces* were popular in classical expert systems. With today's complex machine learning algorithms, such inference chains are

not available. Instead, one approach can be to explain the system's *general* reasoning strategy, e. g., that it recommends objects that similar users liked.

– *Background knowledge and complementary information*: Explanation approaches of this type use additional information, for example the popularity of a recommended alternative in the entire community or among users with similar profiles, to generate explanations.

– *Alternatives and their features*. This type of explanation focuses on certain attributes of the recommended alternative. They, e. g., point out the decisive features of an item, show pros and cons of different alternatives, or highlight when one alternative dominates another.

With respect to how the explanations are *presented to the user*, natural language representations (text-based explanations) are dominating the research landscape. In some works, more structured representations, e. g., in the form of lists of relevant features, other users, or past cases, are provided. Finally, different forms of graph-based and alternative visual approaches can be found in the literature as well, e. g., in the form of rating distributions for an item [26] or in the form of tag clouds [16, 17].

Generally, when explanations are used as an entry point for *user control*, not all forms of explanations seem equally helpful. Presenting the general inference strategy, for example, might be of limited use. Providing information about relevant inputs and features of the recommended items, in contrast, opens more opportunities for control mechanisms for users. When provided such input-output oriented explanations, users can interactively adapt or correct their preference information as in [5] or give feedback on the recommendations, e. g., in the form of attribute-level *critiques* [53].

6.2.3 Challenges of explaining complex models

In traditional expert systems, which in many cases had an explanation component, the content that was presented to the user was often determined by collecting information about how the underlying inference algorithm ended up with its suggestion. In a rule-based system, e. g., one could record which of the rules fired, given the user's specific input. Parts or all of this internal reasoning process is then presented in a user-friendly way. As a result, the process of computing the explanations as well as the explanations themselves are tightly related to the underlying recommendation process.

In the field of recommender systems, rule-based or knowledge-based approaches are nowadays only used for certain types of products, e. g., high-involvement goods. In most of the cases, content-based filtering and collaborative filtering, which often rely on various types of machine learning models, dominate the research landscape. However, these models cause the extraction of the rationale underlying the recommendation to be less straightforward. This led to two groups of approaches to generate explanations: (1) *white-box* approaches, which extract particular kinds of information from the algorithm and model that were used to produce recommendations; (2) *black-box* approaches, which do not take into account how recommendations are made, but explain them using different sources of information.

Early approaches focused mostly on white-box explanation generation. Consequently, collaborative filtering mostly rely on nearest-neighbor techniques, and, correspondingly, a number of approaches were proposed, which use information about user neighborhoods to derive appropriate explanations for the users [17, 26]. Herlocker et al. investigated the persuasiveness of visualizing such neighborhoods through a user study [26]. Even more complex visualization approaches, based on three-dimensional or interactive representations, were proposed in [43] or [48]. However, it remains somewhat unclear how such approaches would be perceived by an average user of a recommender system.

Today, with modern collaborative filtering techniques based on matrix factorization and deep learning, explaining recommendations that are computed based on such machine learning models is much more difficult. Matrix factorization models consist of vectors of uninterpreted latent factor weights for users and items; deep neural networks train a large number of weights for nodes that have no obvious attached meaning. Such complex models make it very difficult to provide users with information about how the set of recommendations was *exactly* determined for them, let alone allow them to influence the system's strategy of selecting items.[2] In general, because more and more decisions are nowadays made by algorithms, the topics of transparency, fairness and accountability become increasingly important in machine learning research. A recent survey on approaches to interpreting the outcomes of deep neural networks can, e. g., be found in [54].

Given the complexity of this problem, an alternative is to rely on other ways of computing the explanations, leading to black-box explanation generation. In such a case, one goal could be to provide *plausible* justifications to users, which, e. g., describe why a certain recommended item matches their preferences. One could, e. g., mine association rules ("Customers who bought ...") and then use these rules to explain a given item recommendation, even though the recommended item was selected in a different way [60]. Alternatively, customer reviews can be mined to extract explanations that are in accordance with recommendations made using complex models, such as in [55].

6.2.4 A case study of the effects of different explanations

Gedikli et al. [17] reported the results of a laboratory study in which they analyzed the impact of different explanation types on users in several dimensions. The specific targets of investigation were efficiency, effectiveness, direction of persuasiveness, trans-

---

2 There is work in the context of matrix factorization techniques to find interpretations of at least the most important latent factors [10, 51, 62].

parency and trust. We summarize their experiment and insights here as a case study of the evaluation of different types of explanations. The study also represents an example of a common research methodology that is applied in this context.

6.2.4.1 Study design

Ten different forms of explaining recommendations from the literature were considered in the study. Some of them were personalized and, e. g., showed the ratings of the user's peers for a recommended item. Other explanation types were nonpersonalized and, e. g., simply presented the items' average community ratings as an explanation. The second main differentiating factor was whether the explanation referred to the "content" of the recommended items (e. g., by displaying certain item features). Figures 6.1 and 6.2 show examples of two explanation types.

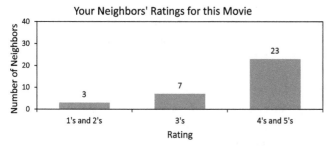

Figure 6.1: Histogram explanation type adapted from [26], showing the rating distribution of the neighbors of the current user. The explanation type was considered particularly effective in terms of persuasion in [26].

Figure 6.2: Tag Cloud explanation type adapted from [16], which shows the item features that are assumed to be particularly desired and undesired for the user in different colors.

Procedure

The experimental procedure in the study followed the multistep protocol from [4].[3] In a first step, the study participants were asked to provide ratings for a number of movies,

---

3 The protocol is referred to as "explanation exposure delta" in [57], expressing the difference of the users' evaluation of an item when provided with detailed item information in comparison to their explanation-based evaluation of the same item.

which was the domain of the study. Then the participants were provided matching recommendations based on some underlying algorithm. Instead of showing the movie details to the participants, they were only shown the system-generated explanations. Each participant received only one treatment, i. e., was shown one form of explanation. The participants were then asked to rate the recommended items, expressing the probability that they would like to watch the movie. In the next step, the same recommendations were presented to the user again (in randomized order), now showing all the details of the movie and a trailer. The participants were asked to also rate these movies. However, they did not know that these were the exact same movies from the previous step. After the participants had completed the procedure, they were asked to fill out a questionnaire where they could rate their satisfaction with the explanations and could also express how transparent they found the explanations.

Dependent variables and measurement method

Perceived transparency and satisfaction were, as said, measured through a questionnaire, where satisfaction was determined based on *ease of use* and *enjoyment*. The *efficiency* of an explanation type was determined by measuring the time needed by the participants to rate a movie based on the explanations. The *effectiveness* was approximated by comparing the participant's rating for a movie when only provided the explanation with the rating when full information was available [4]. A small difference means high effectiveness; large differences, in contrast, indicate that the explanations are persuasive. The effectiveness measure was therefore also used to measure the *direction of persuasiveness*, i. e., if the explanation have the effect that the participant over or underestimates the true suitability of a recommendation based on the explanations.

6.2.4.2 Observations and implications

The following observations were made based on the responses of 105 participants. In terms of *efficiency*, it turned out that the participants needed significantly more time when they were provided with *content-based* explanations, i. e., those based on tag clouds as shown in Figure 6.2. The tag clouds were, in contrast, among the explanation types with the highest *effectiveness*. The difference between the explanation-based rating and the "informed" rating were close to zero, with a high positive correlation between the values. By definition, the *persuasiveness* of highly effective explanations is low. There were, however, a number of explanation types that led to a strong overestimation of the preference match of the shown movies. In particular, nonpersonalized explanations that simply indicated how many other users gave the movie a rating of four or higher led to the highest level of positively-oriented persuasion. Overall, the main conclusion resulting from this part of the analysis is that *the provision of information related to the features of an item can be key to effectiveness*, i. e., to help users making good decisions.

Looking at the participants' answers regarding the *perceived transparency*, the different explanation types fell into two groups for which statistically significant differences could be observed. The provision of a rating prediction and a confidence value is an example of an explanation form that led to low perceived transparency. In general, however, the obtained results were not fully conclusive. A personalized version of the tag clouds, e. g., led to the highest level of transparency, whereas its nonpersonalized counterpart was in the group with the lowest transparency.

The personalized tag clouds also led to the highest levels of user *satisfaction*. However, the difference to several other forms of explanations, including in particular very simple ones, was in most cases not statistically significant. The lowest satisfaction level (based on ease of use and enjoyment) were observed for explanations that involved information about the rating behavior of the peers. Overall, the authors concluded that *explanations should be presented in a form that users are already familiar with* and require limited cognitive effort.

By analyzing the correlations between the variables, two more guidelines were proposed in [17]. The first guideline is to use explanations with *high transparency to increase user satisfaction*, as was also found in [56]. Second, *explanations should not be primarily optimized for efficiency*, but rather for, e. g., effectiveness, as users seem to be willing to invest more time to understand the explanations. The resulting set of guidelines obtained in this particular study is summarized in Table 6.3. A summary of outcomes and insights of other studies about different aspects of explanations can be found in [57].

Table 6.3: Guidelines for explanation design [17].

Nr.	Guideline
1	Use domain specific content data to boost effectiveness
2	Use explanation concepts the user is already familiar with, as they require less cognitive effort and are preferred by the users
3	Increase transparency through explanations for higher user satisfaction
4	Explanation types should not primarily be optimized for efficiency. Users take their time for making good decisions and are willing to spend the time on analyzing the explanations

6.2.4.3 Open issues

While the presented study led to a number of insights and design guidelines, some aspects require further research. First, a deeper understanding is needed regarding which factors of an explanation lead to higher transparency. Second, the study also led to inconclusive results about the value of personalization of explanations. Two types of tag clouds were used in the study. In some cases, the personalized method worked best, while in other dimensions it made no difference if the explanations were personalized. Finally, some of the explanations were based on providing details of the inner workings of the algorithm, e. g., by presenting statistics of the ratings provided by similar users. Given today's more complex machine learning based recommendation algorithms, alternative approaches for explaining the outcomes of such black-box algorithms are needed. One can for example rely on approaches that disconnect the explanation process from the algorithmic process of determining suitable recommendations and mainly use the features of the recommended items (and possibly the user profile) as a basis to generate the explanations ex post [58, 66, 69].

6.3 Putting the user into control

One of the least explored purposes of explanations, as mentioned above, is *scrutability*. While the word "scrutable" can be defined as "capable of being deciphered,"[4] Tintarev and Masthoff extend the interpretation of the word in the context of explanations and consider scrutability as allowing "[...] the user to tell the system it is wrong" [68]. The explanations provided by the system should therefore be a part of an iterative process, where the system explains and users can give feedback and correct the system's assumptions if necessary. In that context, explanations can be part of a mechanism that is provided to put users into control of the system, a functionality that is considered a key aspect or effective user interface design [65].

In the case of a recommender application, the system could, e. g., explain to a user that a movie is recommended because she or he liked action movies in the past. If provided with an opportunity to give feedback, the user could then correct the system's assumption in case this interest in action movies no longer exists.

In the literature, there are a number of different ways in which users can give feedback and exert control over the system's recommendations. The literature is, however, still scattered. In this section, we provide a review of these mechanisms based on [37] and [39]. Our review covers user control mechanisms in the context of explanations, but also considers other situations in the recommendation process where users can take control. Additionally, we present the results of a survey from [37], which investigates the reasons why the explanation-based control features of Amazon are not widely used.

6.3.1 Review framework

We base our review of user control mechanisms on the conceptual framework presented in [37], as illustrated in Figure 6.3.

---

4 https://www.merriam-webster.com/dictionary/scrutable

Figure 6.3: Research framework for user control in recommender systems (adapted from [37]).

The mechanisms for user control can be classified in the following two categories:

– Users can be put into control during the *preference elicitation* phase, e. g., when the system is collecting initial information about their individual preferences. We describe these approaches in Section 6.3.2.
– Another option for recommendation providers is to allow users to control their recommendations in the *presentation* phase. We review examples of such approaches in Section 6.3.3.

6.3.2 User control during preference elicitation

Many online services, including in particular e-commerce shops or media sites, allow users to rate individual items, either in the context of a purchase or independent from any business transaction. These feedback signals, e. g., thumbs up/down ratings, can be used by an underlying recommendation system to build long-term user models and to adapt the recommendations accordingly. In some sense, the provision of additional feedback opportunities can therefore be seen as a mechanism for user control, as the user feedback influences which items a user will see. However, such user inputs are typically not taken into account immediately by the system and the provision of such feedback might not have a recognizable effect for the user. Furthermore, which effects individual preference statements have on the recommendations is usually not transparent for users, who might not even be aware that this feedback is taken into account at all.

In the following sections, we focus on three *explicit* forms of user control during the preference-building phase, namely preference forms/dialogs, conversational recommender systems and critiquing.

6.3.2.1 Preference forms and static dialogs

Static *forms* are a common approach to let users specify and update their explicit taste profiles. The general idea, in most cases, is to let users choose their favorite category of items, e. g., musical genres or news topics, or to let them express their level of interest on a numerical scale. Such approaches are easy to understand and, consequently, used in a number of web applications, such as music and movies streaming sites (e. g., Netflix) or news websites (e. g., Google News). The user model can, in most cases, be updated immediately or filters can be applied to the recommendations so that they reflect the updated preferences instantly.

Another way to collect explicit preferences from the user is to use static preference *dialogs* instead of forms. These dialogs guide users through a series of questions to identify their taste profile. One example is the website of TOPSHOP, where users can take a "quiz" to determine their fashion style profile step by step (see Figure 6.4). The advantage of such dialogs over a single form is that more information can be gathered without overwhelming the user with too many options at once. In the recommender systems literature, we find static preference forms and dialogs in domains such as music recommendation [27], in-restaurant menu suggestion [72] or the recommendation of energy-saving measures [42].

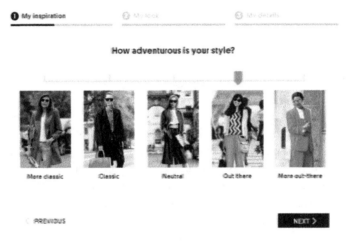

Figure 6.4: Static preference elicitation dialog on the fashion shopping website TOPSHOP.com.

However, even though these specific user control modalities are frequently used in the literature and practical applications, some open questions remain regarding their user-friendliness. For example, it is unclear how such systems should deal with user interests drifts, since a major fraction of users will most likely *not* edit their taste profiles manually and keep them up-to-date on a regular basis. Furthermore, as the name suggests, these forms and dialogs are static, i. e., the same set of questions is presented to all users, which might reduce their usefulness for users with more specific needs.

6.3.2.2 Conversational recommender systems

A possible solution to the described problems of static dialogs are *conversational* recommender systems [33]. Such systems typically elicit the preferences by asking users about their preferences step by step, but they usually dynamically adapt the dialogs, e. g., based on previous answers of the user. The preference dialogs can, for example, be varied in terms of the number of questions, their details or even with respect to the type of interaction itself. For example, if the user is a novice, a natural language-based avatar could be used to interact with the user. Experts, in contrast, might feel more comfortable when they can specify their preferences using a set of detailed forms.

A variety of conversational recommender system approaches were presented in the literature. For example, in the Adaptive Place Advisor system [18], users can construct travel plans in a conversational manner where the degree of presentational detail is adapted based on the users' previous answers. Other systems, such as the Advisor Suite [12, 36], offer additional features such as personalized explanations of the recommendations or recovery suggestions in case the user requirements cannot be fulfilled. Examples of practical applications of such systems exist as well (see, e. g., [31, 36]). A main challenge in such systems is to find ways to stimulate users to go through a multistep preference elicitation process at least once. Personalizing the dialog according to the user's estimated willingness to answer more questions can be one possible approach in that direction.

Generally, conversational systems, also in the more modern form of chatbots, can lead to a more engaging user experience than the provision of static series of fill-out forms. A main hindrance to the large-scale usage of such systems lies in the fact that they can require substantial efforts for the creation and maintenance of the explicit knowledge that is needed to conduct such dialogs. Differently from recommendation approaches based on collaborative filtering, such knowledge-based approaches have no built-in learning capacity, i. e., the recommendation models have to be continuously maintained. In addition, conversational systems are usually only designed for one-shot recommendations and do not consider long-term user models. In most recent years, a number of "end-to-end learning" approaches were proposed. In such systems, deep learning models are trained on large corpora of human-to-human recommendation dialogs, e. g., [47, 76]. These however do not come without limitations; see [49].

6.3.2.3 Critiquing

Similar to some of the user control methods discussed so far, *critiquing* techniques [8] also allow users to explicitly state their preferences regarding certain item features. However, in contrast to conversational recommender systems or static forms, preferences are expressed in the context of a reference item. For example, if the user is searching for a restaurant to eat at, a critiquing system will typically offer one selected recommendation at the beginning of the process. Users can then study the features of the recommended restaurant and critique it, e. g., using statements like "cheaper" or "closer to my location." Based on the critiques, the recommender system will come up with better suggestions until the user is satisfied.[5]

Critique-based systems are easy to understand in terms of their interaction scheme and have the advantage of giving users immediate feedback by updating the recommended (reference) item after every critique. Consequently, a number of these systems have been proposed in the recommender systems literature (see, e. g., [7, 71, 72]). However, depending on the user's requirements and the domain, critiquing approaches can result in a higher number of interaction steps than other preference acquisition methods. One solution proposed in the literature to tackle this problem are compound critiques (see, e. g., [52, 74]), which allow users to critique items in more than one dimension at once, which might, however, also increase the cognitive load of the users.

6.3.3 User control in the recommendation presentation phase

Letting users state their preferences in a more explicit or interactive manner is not the only way in which users can be put into control of their recommendations. Once the initial user preferences are collected, recommender systems can also offer a range of user control mechanisms when the recommendations are presented to users. Such control mechanisms can allow users to either (a) manipulate the recommendation lists, in the simplest form by trying different sort orders, or (b) inspect and eventually correct the presented recommendations based, e. g., on the provided explanations.

6.3.3.1 Filtering or adjusting the provided recommendations

One simple form of user control in the context of result presentation can be achieved by giving users the option to filter, sort and manipulate the contents of the given recommendation list, e. g., by removing individual items. For example, when given a list of movie recommendations, a filter feature can be provided to enable users to exclude movies of certain genres from the recommendations, as done, e. g., in [63]. Another example is the microblog recommender system presented in [67], where users can sort the tweets in some ways or vary the importance of different filters. Considering real-world applications, such filters can also be defined by users for Facebook's automated news feed to make sure that posts of favorite users always appear at the top.

More sophisticated approaches allow the user to manipulate the recommendations in a more interactive way based, e. g., on the exposure of the algorithm's inner logic.

---

5 Considering our research framework in Figure 6.3, critiquing falls into both main categories and is a technique that has both a preference elicitation facet and at the same time implements a feedback mechanism during result presentation.

For example, in [5] and [64], recommendations are presented within graph structures that show the relations of the recommended items to those that were previously rated by the user, friends or similar users. Users can then take control of the recommendation outcomes by adjusting their item ratings or by assigning custom weights for the influencing friends. These inputs are then taken into account to create an updated list of recommendations.

Generally, the provision of additional interaction and feedback instruments can make users more satisfied with the recommendations, as was shown in the study of [5], and many of the more simple forms of user control, such as sorting or filtering, are easy to implement for providers. However, some of the more complex methods assume that users are (a) willing to spend a significant amount of time to improve their recommendations and (b) can understand the system's logic, such as the relations between recommendations and similar users. This might, however, not always be the case for average users.

6.3.3.2 Choosing or influencing the recommendation strategy

A quite different form proposed in the literature to put users into control of their recommendations is to allow them to choose or influence the recommendation strategy or algorithm parameters. Such mechanisms in principle offer the maximum amount of user control in some sense, but also the highest risk that the user interfaces and the complexity of the task might overwhelm users. Consequently, these user control measures can primarily be found in the academic literature.

For example, in a study in the context of the MovieLens movie recommendation system [24], a widget was added to the user interface for users to change the recommendation algorithm to be used. Selecting one of the four available strategies led to an immediate change of the displayed recommendations. However, the mechanics of the algorithms were not explained to the users, which might make the presented system somewhat less transparent and users dissatisfied if their choices do not lead to the expected effects. A different approach was implemented in the system presented in [59]. The system allows users to fine-tune the weights of different recommendation strategies in a hybrid recommender system. In addition, a Venn diagram was used to illustrate which of the substrategies was responsible for the inclusion of individual items.

The mentioned works show through user studies that such forms of in-depth user control can have a positive effect on the user experience. However, how such a mechanism can be successfully integrated into real-world systems without overwhelming everyday users, remains to some extent unclear.

6.3.3.3 Interactive explanations and user control

As mentioned earlier, explanations represent one possible entry point for users to *scrutinize* the provided recommendations and to interactively improve them or correct the system's assumptions. Both in the literature and in real-world systems, there are only a handful of examples of recommender systems that provide such interactive explanations.

The previously-discussed interactive visualization approaches from [5, 64], which show the relation between rated items and recommendation in a graph structure, can be considered as a form of scrutable explanation. They expose the algorithm's reasoning and allow users to exert control by changing their ratings, which leads to updated recommendations. Another example are the conversational recommenders from [12, 36], which generate textual explanations that describe which internal rules were triggered due to the user's stated requirements. Users can then, in case they do not agree with the recommendation rules, change the weights of specific rules, which immediately leads to an updated set of recommendations. Finally, in the mobile shopping recommender system Shopr [45], a critiquing-based approach is taken where users are shown recommendations along with feature-based explanations such as "because you currently like blue." Users can then improve the recommendations by either rating them with a thumbs up/down button or by clicking on the assumedly preferred features to revise their user model. In the latter case, users can, e. g., click on the word "blue." This would lead them to a screen where they can select the colors they are actually interested in at the moment. The additional preference information that is gathered in this way is then used by the underlying active learning algorithm to immediately "refine" the recommendation.

There is also a small number of real-world applications that feature user control mechanisms in the context of explanations. In case of the website of Amazon.com, users are at different occasions provided with explanations as shown in Figure 6.5. In Amazon's case, the system explains the recommendation of a product in terms of other products with which the user has interacted in the past, e. g., clicked on, added the shopping cart, or purchased. Users can then correct the system by indicating that they either already own the recommended product, are not interested in it, or that they do not want the item from their profile to be used for recommendations. The latter case can, e. g., be helpful when a user purchased an item as a gift. On YouTube, a similar explanation mechanism exists that explains individual video recommendations with other videos from the user's viewing history. In this case, the user can also reject the recommendation or tell the system not to consider a particular video from the profile as a source for generating future recommendations.

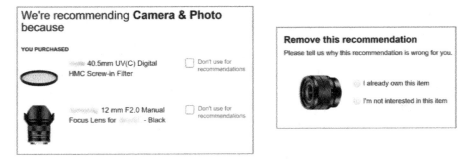

Figure 6.5: The interactive explanations of Amazon.com's recommendation system.

6.3.3.4 Acceptance of Amazon's explanation-based user control Ffeatures

While the more complex explanation and control mechanisms as proposed in [12, 36] are part of real-world applications, their usefulness was not systematically evaluated. To obtain a deeper understanding of the usability and adoption of the much simpler explanation-based user control mechanism of Amazon.com (Figure 6.5), a questionnaire-based survey was conducted in [37].

In the first part of the study, participants were shown a screen shot of the explanation feature, and they were asked 15 questions, e. g., about whether they knew about the existence of the functionality, if the provided functionality is clear to them, or if they think it is useful. In the second phase, which was conducted at a later time with a different group of participants, the same screen shot was shown, but the emphasis of the questions was on why participants would or would not use the feature, including the opportunity to give free-text answers.

The results from the first phase of the study showed that more than 90 % of the participants said they were aware that they could influence their recommendations in some way, but to some surprise, only 20 % knew about the special page where the explanation and feedback feature can be found. Only about 8 % had actively used the feature before. However, when asked if the feedback feature ("Don't use for recommendation," see Figure 6.5) is clear, about 75 % of the participants said that it was either very clear or that the meaning could be guessed, indicating that understandability was not the reason why the feature was scarcely used. Interestingly, although participants stated on average that the functionality seemed useful, the average answer as to whether they intended to use the feature in the future was rather low.

To find possible reasons as to why participants seemed to think the feature was useful, but in the end did not use it, the second part of the study collected free-text feedback, which was then analyzed manually. As a result, four main reasons were identified for why participants do not use the explanation-based control mechanism, listed as follows:

- About a third of the participants were not interested in recommendations in general.
- About a fourth said that it would be too much effort to use the feature.
- Again, about a fourth mentioned a fear of bad consequences, such as irreversible changes to their user preference profile, if they tried to use the feature to improve the recommendations.
- Finally, 19 % of the participants did not want use the feature because of privacy concerns.

Overall, even though the functionality is rather simple, it seems that providers need to communicate the effects and benefits of their control features in a more understandable way. Also, adding an "undo" functionality, which is proposed as a functionality for highly-usable interfaces in general [65], could help to increase the acceptance of the provided functionality.

6.4 Summary and future directions

Overall, a number of works exist in the literature on recommender systems that show that providing explanations can have positive effects, e. g., in terms of the adoption of the recommendations or the development of long-term trust. In real-world applications, the use of elaborate explanation mechanisms, as provided on Amazon.com, is however still very limited. In many cases, recommendation providers only add informative labels like "Similar items" to give the users an intuition of the underlying recommendation logic.

In terms of user control, we can observe that major sites such as Google News or Facebook nowadays provide their users with features to fine-tune their profile and to personalize what they will see, e. g., in their news feed. A small number of sites such as Amazon.com or Yahoo! also allow users to give finer-grained feedback on the recommendations. Academic approaches, as discussed in the previous section, usually propose much richer types of visualizations and user interactions as can be found on real-world sites.

A main challenge that is shared both by explanation approaches and user control mechanisms is that their usage can easily become too complex for average users. In fact, for many academic approaches, it is not fully clear if they would not overwhelm the majority of users. One possible approach in that context is to *personalize* the provided explanations and user control mechanisms according to the assumed expertise or IT-literacy level of the individual user. Such a personalization process can either be implemented by dynamically selecting from a predefined set of explanation types or by adapting individual explanations, e. g., by leaving out technical details for nonexpert users.

But even when the provided mechanisms are intuitive and easy to use, users might be reluctant to manually fine-tune their recommendations for different reasons, e. g., because it requires additional effort. Therefore, in addition to the development of appropriate user interface mechanisms, better ways are needed to incentivize users and to convince them of the *value* of investing these additional efforts to receive better-matching recommendations. In this way, providers can make sure that their recommender does not filter out things that are actually relevant to their users.

References

[1]   Nicola Barbieri, Francesco Bonchi, and Giuseppe Manco. Who to follow and why: Link prediction with explanations. In: *Proceedings of the 20th ACM SIGKDD International Conference on Knowledge Discovery and Data Mining, KDD '14*, 2014, pp. 1266–1275.

[2]   Punam Bedi, Sumit Kumar Agarwal, Samarth Sharma, and Harshita Joshi. SAPRS: Situation-Aware Proactive Recommender system with explanations. In: *Proceedings of the 2014 International Conference on Advances in Computing, Communications and Informatics, ICACCI '14*, 2014, pp. 277–283.

[3]   Punam Bedi and Ravish Sharma. Trust based recommender system using ant colony for trust computation. *Expert Systems with Applications* 39(1) (2012) 1183–1190.

[4]   Mustafa Bilgic and Raymond J. Mooney. Explaining recommendations: Satisfaction vs. promotion. In: *Proceedings of Beyond Personalization 2005: A Workshop on the Next Stage of Recommender Systems Research in Conjunction with the 2005 International Conference on Intelligent User Interfaces, IUI '05*, 2005.

[5]   Svetlin Bostandjiev, John O'Donovan, and Tobias Höllerer. Tasteweights: A visual interactive hybrid recommender system. In: *Proceedings of the Sixth ACM Conference on Recommender Systems, RecSys '12*, 2012, pp. 35–42.

[6]   B. G. Buchanan and E. H. Shortliffe. Explanations as a Topic of AI Research. In: *Rule-based Systems*. Reading, MA, USA: Addison-Wesley, 1984, pp. 331–337.

[7]   Robin D. Burke, Kristian J. Hammond, and Benjamin C. Young. Knowledge-based navigation of complex information spaces. In: *Proceedings of the 13th National Conference on Artificial Intelligence and 8th Innovative Applications of Artificial Intelligence, AAAI '96*, 1996, pp. 462–468.

[8]   Li Chen and Pearl Pu. Critiquing-based recommenders: survey and emerging trends. *User Modeling and User-Adapted Interaction* 22 (2012) 125–150.

[9]   Yashar Deldjoo, Dietmar Jannach, Alejandro Bellogin, Alessandro Difonzo, and Dario Zanzonelli. A survey of research on fair recommender systems, 2022. https://arxiv.org/abs/2205.11127.

[10] Tim Donkers, Benedikt Loepp, and Jürgen Ziegler. Towards understanding latent factors and user profiles by enhancing matrix factorization with tags. In: *ACM RecSys 2016 Posters*, 2016.

[11] Michael D. Ekstrand, Anubrata Das, Robin Burke, and Fernando Diaz. Fairness in Information Access Systems. *Foundations and Trends® in Information Retrieval* 16(1–2) (2022) 1–177.

[12] Alexander Felfernig, Gerhard Friedrich, Dietmar Jannach, and Markus Zanker. An integrated environment for the development of knowledge-based recommender applications. *International Journal of Electronic Commerce* 11(2) (2006) 11–34.

[13] Gerhard Friedrich and Markus Zanker. A taxonomy for generating explanations in recommender systems. *AI Magazine* 32(3) (2011) 90–98.

[14] Alejandro J. García, Carlos I. Chesñevar, Nicolás D. Rotstein, and Guillermo R. Simari. Formalizing dialectical explanation support for argument-based reasoning in knowledge-based systems. *Expert Systems with Applications* 40(8) (2013) 3233–3247.

[15] Florent Garcin, Boi Faltings, Olivier Donatsch, Ayar Alazzawi, Christophe Bruttin, and Amr Huber. Offline and online evaluation of news recommender systems at swissinfo.ch. In: *Proceedings of the Eighth ACM Conference on Recommender Systems, RecSys '14*, 2014, pp. 169–176.

[16] Fatih Gedikli, Mouzhi Ge, and Dietmar Jannach. Understanding recommendations by reading the clouds. In: *Proceedings of the 12th International Conference on E-Commerce and Web Technologies, EC-Web '11*, 2011, pp. 196–208.

[17] Fatih Gedikli, Dietmar Jannach, and Mouzhi Ge. How Should I Explain? A Comparison of Different Explanation Types for Recommender Systems. *International Journal of Human-Computer Studies* 72(4) (2014) 367–382.

[18] Mehmet H. Göker and Cynthia A. Thompson. The Adaptive Place Advisor: A conversational recommendation system. In: *Proceedings of the 8th German Workshop on Case Based Reasoning, GWCBR '00*, 2000, pp. 187–198.

[19] M. Sinan Gönül, Dilek Önkal, and Michael Lawrence. The Effects of Structural Characteristics of Explanations on Use of a DSS. *Decision Support Systems* 42(3) (2006) 1481–1493.

[20] K. Gowri, C. Marsh, C. Bedard, and P. Fazio. Knowledge-based assistant for aluminum component design. *Computers & Structures* 38(1) (1991) 9–20.

[21] H. A. Güvenir and N. Emeksiz. An expert system for the differential diagnosis of erythemato-squamous diseases. *Expert Systems with Applications* 18(1) (2000) 43–49.

[22] Ido Guy, Naama Zwerdling, David Carmel, Inbal Ronen, Erel Uziel, Sivan Yogev, and Shila Ofek-Koifman. Personalized recommendation of social software items based on social relations. In: *Proceedings of the Third ACM Conference on Recommender Systems, RecSys '09*, 2009, pp. 53–60.

[23] Ido Guy, Naama Zwerdling, Inbal Ronen, David Carmel, and Erel Uziel. Social media recommendation based on people and tags. In: *Proceedings of the 33rd International ACM SIGIR Conference on Research and Development in Information Retrieval, SIGIR '10*, 2010, pp. 194–201.

[24] F. Maxwell Harper, Funing Xu, Harmanpreet Kaur, Kyle Condiff, Shuo Chang, and Loren G. Terveen. Putting users in control of their recommendations. In: *Proceedings of the Ninth Conference on Recommender Systems, RecSys '15*, 2015, pp. 3–10.

[25] Diane Warner Hasling, William J. Clancey, and Glenn Rennels. Strategic explanations for a diagnostic consultation system. *International Journal of Man-Machine Studies* 20(1) (1984) 3–19.

[26] Jonathan L. Herlocker, Joseph A. Konstan, and John Riedl. Explaining collaborative filtering recommendations. In: *Proceedings of the 2000 ACM Conference on Computer Supported Cooperative Work, CSCW '00*, 2000, pp. 241–250.

[27] Yoshinori Hijikata, Yuki Kai, and Shogo Nishida. The relation between user intervention and user satisfaction for information recommendation. In: *Proceedings of the 27th Annual ACM Symposium on Applied Computing, SAC '12*, 2012, pp. 2002–2007.

[28] Yifan Hu, Yehuda Koren, and Chris Volinsky. Collaborative filtering for implicit feedback datasets. In: *Proceedings of the Eighth IEEE International Conference on Data Mining, ICDM '08*, 2008, pp. 263–272.

[29] J. E. Hunt and C. J. Price. Explaining qualitative diagnosis. *Engineering Applications of Artificial Intelligence* 1(3) (1988) 161–169.

[30] Tim Hussein and Sebastian Neuhaus. Explanation of spreading activation based recommendations. In: *Proceedings of the First International Workshop on Semantic Models for Adaptive Interactive Systems, SEMAIS '10*, 2010, pp. 24–28.

[31] Dietmar Jannach. ADVISOR SUITE – A knowledge-based sales advisory-system. In: *Proceedings of the 16th Eureopean Conference on Artificial Intelligence, ECAI '04*, 2004, pp. 720–724.

[32] Dietmar Jannach and Gedas Adomavicius. Recommendations with a purpose. In: *Proceedings of the 10th ACM Conference on Recommender Systems, RecSys '16*, 2016, pp. 7–10.

[33] Dietmar Jannach and Li Chen. Conversational Recommendation: A Grand AI Challenge. *AI Magazine* 43(2), 2022.

[34] Dietmar Jannach and Kolja Hegelich. A case study on the effectiveness of recommendations in the mobile internet. In: *Proceedings of the Third ACM Conference on Recommender Systems, RecSys '09*, 2009, pp. 205–208.

[35] Dietmar Jannach and Michael Jugovac. Measuring the business value of recommender systems. *ACM Transactions on Management Information Systems* 10(4), 2019.

[36] Dietmar Jannach and Gerold Kreutler. Personalized user preference elicitation for e-services. In: *Proceedings of the 2005 IEEE International Conference on e-Technology, e-Commerce, and e-Services, EEE '05*, 2005, pp. 604–611.

[37] Dietmar Jannach, Sidra Naveed, and Michael Jugovac. User control in recommender systems: Overview and interaction challenges. In: *Proceedings of the 17th International Conference on Electronic Commerce and Web Technologies, EC-Web '16*, 2016, pp. 21–33.

[38] Dietmar Jannach, Paul Resnick, Alexander Tuzhilin, and Markus Zanker. Recommender systems — beyond matrix completion. *Communications of the ACM* 59(11) (2016) 94–102.

[39] Michael Jugovac and Dietmar Jannach. Interacting with Recommenders — Overview and Research Directions. *Transactions on Interactive Intelligent Systems* 7(3) (2017) 10:1–10:46.

[40] Lalana Kagal and Joe Pato. Preserving privacy based on semantic policy tools. *IEEE Security Privacy* 8(4) (2010) 25–30.

[41] Evan Kirshenbaum, George Forman, and Michael Dugan. A live comparison of methods for personalized article recommendation at Forbes.com. In: *Proceedings of the 2012 European Conference on Machine Learning and Knowledge Discovery in Databases, ECML/PKDD '12*, 2012, pp. 51–66.

[42] Bart P. Knijnenburg, Niels J. M. Reijmer, and Martijn C. Willemsen. Each to his own: how different users call for different interaction methods in recommender systems. In: *Proceedings of the Fifth ACM Conference on Recommender Systems, RecSys '11*, 2011, pp. 141–148.

[43] Johannes Kunkel, Benedikt Loepp, and Jürgen Ziegler. A 3d item space visualization for presenting and manipulating user preferences in collaborative filtering. In: *Proceedings of the 22nd International Conference on Intelligent User Interfaces, IUI '17*, 2017, pp. 3–15.

[44] Carmen Lacave, Agnieszka Oniśko, and Francisco J. Díez. Use of Elvira's explanation facility for debugging probabilistic expert systems. *Knowledge-Based Systems* 19(8) (2006) 730–738.

[45] Béatrice Lamche, Ugur Adıgüzel, and Wolfgang Wörndl. Interactive explanations in mobile shopping recommender systems. In: *Proceedings of the Joint Workshop on Interfaces and Human Decision Making in Recommender Systems, IntRS '14*, 2014.

[46] M. Levy, P. Ferrand, and V. Chirat. SESAM-DIABETE, an expert system for insulin-requiring diabetic patient education. *Computers and Biomedical Research* 22(5) (1989) 442–453.

[47] Raymond Li, Samira Ebrahimi Kahou, Hannes Schulz, Vincent Michalski, Laurent Charlin, and Chris Pal. Towards deep conversational recommendations. In: *NIPS '18*, 2018, pp. 9725–9735.

[48] Benedikt Loepp, Katja Herrmanny, and Jürgen Ziegler. Blended recommending: Integrating interactive information filtering and algorithmic recommender techniques. In: *Proceedings of the 33rd Annual ACM Conference on Human Factors in Computing Systems, CHI '15*, 2015, pp. 975–984.

[49] Ahtsham Manzoor and Dietmar Jannach. Towards retrieval-based conversational recommendation. *Information Systems* (2022) 102083.

[50] Paul Marx, Thorsten Hennig-Thurau, and André Marchand. Increasing consumers' understanding of recommender results: A preference-based hybrid algorithm with strong explanatory power. In: *Proceedings of the Fourth ACM Conference on Recommender Systems, RecSys '10*, 2010, pp. 297–300.

[51] Julian McAuley and Jure Leskovec. Hidden factors and hidden topics: Understanding rating dimensions with review text. In: *Proceedings of the 7th ACM Conference on Recommender Systems, RecSys '13*, 2013, pp. 165–172.

[52] Kevin McCarthy, James Reilly, Lorraine McGinty, and Barry Smyth. On the dynamic generation of compound critiques in conversational recommender systems. In: *Proceedings of the 3rd International Conference on Adaptive Hypermedia and Adaptive Web-Based Systems, AH '04*, 2004, pp. 176–184.

[53] Kevin McCarthy, James Reilly, Lorraine McGinty, and Barry Smyth. Experiments in dynamic critiquing. In: *Proceedings of the 10th International Conference on Intelligent User Interfaces, IUI '05*, 2005, pp. 175–182.

[54] Grégoire Montavon, Wojciech Samek, and Klaus-Robert Müller. Methods for interpreting and understanding deep neural networks. *Digital Signal Processing* 73 (2018) 1–15.

[55] Khalil Muhammad, Aonghus Lawlor, Rachael Rafter, and Barry Smyth. Great explanations: Opinionated explanations for recommendations. In: Eyke Hüllermeier and Mirjam Minor, editors. *Case-Based Reasoning Research and Development*. Cham: Springer International Publishing, 2015, pp. 244–258.

[56] Mehrbakhsh Nilashi, Dietmar Jannach, Othman bin Ibrahim, Mohammad Dalvi Esfahani, and Hossein Ahmadi. Recommendation quality, transparency, and website quality for trust-building in recommendation agents. *Electronic Commerce Research and Applications* 19(C) (2016) 70–84.

[57] Ingrid Nunes and Dietmar Jannach. A systematic review and taxonomy of explanations in decision support and recommender systems. *User Modeling and User-Adapted Interaction* 27(3–5) (2017) 393–444.

[58] Sergio Oramas, Luis Espinosa-Anke, Mohamed Sordo, Horacio Saggion, and Xavier Serra. Information extraction for knowledge base construction in the music domain. *Data & Knowledge Engineering* 106 (2016) 70–83.

[59] Denis Parra, Peter Brusilovsky, and Christoph Trattner. See what you want to see: visual user-driven approach for hybrid recommendation. In: *Proceedings of the 19th International Conference on Intelligent User Interfaces, IUI '14*, 2014, pp. 235–240.

[60] Georgina Peake and Jun Wang. Explanation mining: Post hoc interpretability of latent factor models for recommendation systems. In: *Proceedings of the 24th ACM SIGKDD International Conference on Knowledge Discovery & Data Mining, KDD '18*, 2018, pp. 2060–2069.

[61] Pearl Pu and Li Chen. Trust-inspiring explanation interfaces for recommender systems. *Knowledge-Based Systems* 20(6) (2007) 542–556.

[62] Marco Rossetti, Fabio Stella, and Markus Zanker. Towards explaining latent factors with topic models in collaborative recommender systems. In: *24th International Workshop on Database and Expert Systems Applications, DEXA 2013*, 2013, pp. 162–167.

[63] J. Ben Schafer, Joseph A. Konstan, and John Riedl. Meta-recommendation systems: user-controlled integration of diverse recommendations. In: *Proceedings of the 11th International Conference on Information and Knowledge Management, CIKM '02*, 2002, pp. 43–51.

[64] James Schaffer, Tobias Höllerer, and John O'Donovan. Hypothetical recommendation: A study of interactive profile manipulation behavior for recommender systems. In: *Proceedings of the 28th International Florida Artificial Intelligence Research Society, FLAIRS '15*, 2015, pp. 507–512.

[65] Ben Shneiderman. *Designing the User Interface: Strategies for Effective Human-Computer Interaction*. Boston, MA, USA: Addison-Wesley Longman Publishing Co., Inc., 3rd edition, 1997.

[66] Wee-Kek Tan, Chuan-Hoo Tan, and Hock-Hai Teo. Consumer-based decision aid that explains which to buy: Decision confirmation or overconfidence bias? *Decision Support Systems* 53(1) (2012) 127–141.

[67] Nava Tintarev, Byungkyu Kang, Tobias Höllerer, and John O'Donovan. Inspection mechanisms for community-based content discovery in microblogs. In: *Proceedings of the 2015 Joint Workshop on Interfaces and Human Decision Making for Recommender Systems, IntRS '15*, 2015, pp. 21–28.

[68] Nava Tintarev and Judith Masthoff. A survey of explanations in recommender systems. In: *Proceedings of the 23rd IEEE International Conference on Data Engineering Workshop, ICDE '07*, 2007, pp. 801–810.

[69] Nava Tintarev and Judith Masthoff. Evaluating the effectiveness of explanations for recommender systems. *User Modeling and User-Adapted Interaction* 22(4–5) (2012) 399–439.

[70] Nava Tintarev and Judith Masthoff. *Explaining Recommendations: Design and Evaluation*, 2nd edition, Springer US, 2015, pp. 353–382.

[71] Shari Trewin. Knowledge-based recommender systems. *Encyclopedia of Library and Information Science* 69 (2000) 180–200.

[72] Rainer Wasinger, James Wallbank, Luiz Pizzato, Judy Kay, Bob Kummerfeld, Matthias Böhmer, and Antonio Krüger. Scrutable user models and personalised item recommendation in mobile lifestyle applications. In: *Proceedings of the 21th International Conference on User Modeling, Adaptation, and Personalization, UMAP '13*, 2013, pp. 77–88.

[73] Youngohc Yoon, Tor Guimaraes, and George Swales. Integrating artificial neural networks with rule-based expert systems. *Decision Support Systems* 11(5) (1994) 497–507.

[74] Jiyong Zhang and Pearl Pu. A comparative study of compound critique generation in conversational recommender systems. In: *Proceedings of the 4th International Conference on Adaptive Hypermedia and Adaptive Web-Based Systems (AH '06)*, 2006, pp. 234–243.

[75] Yongfeng Zhang, Guokun Lai, Min Zhang, Yi Zhang, Yiqun Liu, and Shaoping Ma. Explicit factor models for explainable recommendation based on phrase-level sentiment analysis. In: *Proceedings of the 37th International ACM SIGIR Conference on Research & Development in Information Retrieval, SIGIR '14*, 2014, pp. 83–92.

[76] Jie Zou, Evangelos Kanoulas, Pengjie Ren, Zhaochun Ren, Aixin Sun, and Cheng Long. Improving conversational recommender systems via transformer-based sequential modelling. In: *SIGIR '22*, 2022, pp. 2319–2324.

Eelco Herder and Claus Atzenbeck

7 Feedback loops and mutual reinforcement in personalized interaction

Abstract: In personalized interaction between humans and computers, not only computers and personalization algorithms learn about the users: the users also learn about the system's behavior and adapt their expectations accordingly. Particularly, as users expect systems to support their daily activities, this feedback loop may result in long-term changes in these daily activities and user decisions themselves. This can be observed in activities as different as autonomous driving and social media consumption. In this chapter, we investigate these effects by reviewing and analyzing a wide range of relevant literature.

Keywords: Personalization, mutual reinforcement, bounded rationality, choice, cognitive friction

7.1 Introduction

Everyday computer devices—including laptops, smartphones, smartwatches and other wearables and smart devices—are commonly used to *support* us in our daily activities. Many of these devices and corresponding apps aim to help us in decision-making and selecting between available choices. The currently dominating interface paradigm is that available choices—such as news articles, books, movies or food—are provided in a list or feed, ordered by their relevance, as deemed by the system.

The most common technique for creating ordered lists or feeds is by using recommender systems, such as collaborative filtering [28]. A widely recognized inherent limitation of this approach is that the recommendations are bound to be safe choices that are in line with our daily routines. This may sound attractive at first sight, but there is wide evidence that in the longer term, these safe recommendations actually *transform* our daily routines into safe routines that may end up boring, such as binge-watching [32] or, worse, *unlearn* us to make conscious, arguably better or more satisfying, choices or even make us *unaware* of different opinions, options or perspectives, because we are comfortably stuck in our filter bubbles [44].

In this chapter, we explore how personalized systems support us in human decision-making and which—potentially undesirable—effects may happen, in the short term, but particularly in the long term. In Section 7.2, we discuss human decision models and how this process is supported by computer systems. We then continue, in Section 7.3, with current insights on how computer-generated lists of choices and user responses to these (often safe) choices reinforce one another and how this eventually

https://doi.org/10.1515/9783110988567-007

may lead to fundamentally different systems and types of interaction than anticipated. In Section 7.4, we provide and discuss examples on how this affects our current interaction with recommendations, as given by—among others—streaming providers and social media networks. Finally, in Section 7.5 we provide insight in current, earlier and prospective approaches and strategies for stimulating users to make conscious choices, should they want to. We end the chapter with a summary, discussion and future perspectives.

7.2 Computer-supported human decision-making

In this section, we explore computer-supported decision-making. First, we briefly introduce the concept of bounded rationality and discuss how this concept plays a role in computer-supported decisions. Then, in Section 7.2.2, we have a look at persuasive recommendations in the wild; we argue that all recommendations have a persuasive aspect. Finally, we look at the interaction between recommendations, user acceptance and user expectations.

7.2.1 Bounded rationality and personalized decision support

A commonly accepted model of human decision-making is Kahneman's concept of *bounded rationality* [33]. According to this theory, spontaneous human decisions are often reflexive and intuitive—in terms of Kahneman, this is *system-1 behavior*. In many situations, this type of "fast thinking" allows us to make quick decisions, which are surprisingly often correct. However, when one feels or suspects that there is reason for doubt, we resort to logical reasoning and conscious decision-making, so-called *system-2 behavior*.

As an example, when you drive on the highway while talking with the front-seat passenger and see the exit to your hometown that you always take, you probably would leave the highway without deeply thinking about it. Only when this routine is interrupted, you start thinking about this activity consciously; for instance, when there are construction works just before the exit, or when you actually planned to take one exit further, in order to bring your passenger home.

Arguably, (personalized) computer decision support aims to simplify or even (further) automatize our decision processes—to reduce our cognitive load or to let us make better choices by showing appropriate options [6]. In terms of bounded rationality, one could say that personalized support keeps users comfortably in their low-effort system-1 mode of behavior.

To illustrative this further, we go back to our car-driving example. Most drivers commonly use voice navigation support apps, even on routine rides, and they have gotten used to automatically following prompts to stay on the road or to take the exit. Suppose that you erroneously would have taken your usual exit and then realize your mistake: most likely, your navigation support system would have noticed it even before you have realized it yourself, so that you can comfortably follow its prompts in order to get back to the highway.

Building upon the car-driving example, it should be noted that there are several levels of support that can be provided [9]. Many cars have built-in tools that mainly *support* our actions, such as antilock braking, cruise control or warning systems that, e. g., alert the driver when a speed limit is exceeded. On a higher level, navigation systems provide *proactive advice* which direction to take or which route to follow, but they still leave the driver in charge. Even more automated, highway pilot and traffic jam pilot systems, *partially take over decision-making* from the driver, while still leaving the driver in control. Arguably, in all above-mentioned usage contexts, users and computers work together, but with clear differences in how decisions are initiated, evaluated and executed.

7.2.2 Persuasive recommendations in the wild

A further effect of our bounded rationality is that many of our choices are largely driven by our fast system-1 thinking. This does not only yield for activities such as driving, as discussed in the previous section, but also for consumer choices, which have been observed to be choices that look attractive in the short term or that satisfy our (hedonistic) needs [42].

Persuasive recommender systems are a particular category of recommender systems that attempt to persuade users to adopt particular behavior or to make particular choices by using one or more cues [19]. Traditionally, cues considered in persuasive systems are *social*, such as a particular type of wording, or emphasizing certain desirable or undesirable social dynamics associated with particular choices. Since 2008, so-called *nudges* form a particularly popular category of cues [55]. Nudges are small interventions in a choice environment that make certain—arguably better—choices more attractive, in order to steer user behavior in a gentle way.

Increasingly, it has been recognized, though, that *any* recommender system is persuasive in some sort of way. Following Netflix, commercial recommender algorithms have been mainly designed to optimize click-through rates, and they have been evaluated based on choices that users have already made—"some of the worst possible real-world recommendations", as observed by [36]. In terms of bounded rationality, these recommendations reinforce—and do not challenge—users' system-1 behavior, the natural preference for attractive, easy choices [42].

Our natural preference for easy, intuitive choices is clearly visible in *user interaction* on the web as well. Users have consistently been observed to click on only a few of the highest ranked search results or recommended items; items that require additional scrolling or navigating to a next page receive considerably less attention [4, 41]. Arguably, the combination of optimized recommendations that are presented in a feed-based paradigm results in a choice environment with very persuasive arguments to indulge in system-1 behavior.

It should be noted that this phenomenon is far from new. For example, it is commonly known and accepted that supermarkets design their stores in such a way that maximizes visual attention for the most profitable products [22]. On the other hand, in-store shopping strategies for reducing time and money costs in the supermarket—in other words, strategies for avoiding any "traps" set up by the supermarket—are well known and counterbalance this effect [58].

7.2.3 Recommendations, recommendation take-up and user expectations

In principle, one can see commercial recommender systems—including those used by streaming services, personalized stores and social networks—as technology that simply provides what the users expect. Given the success of these platforms, this may be a valid point of view.

Another perspective is that user expectations are largely driven by the options that are provided or promoted by these platforms. Theoretically, this would lead to a balance between supply and demand, in which platforms adjust their offerings to the users' expectations [47]. However, as discussed in the previous section, user expectations are shaped by the available choices—not just in the short-term, but also by long-term effects, as will be elaborated in the upcoming Section 7.3.2. A particular effect that we will discuss is that the combination of feed-based interfaces and recommender algorithms has conditioned us, the users, to conveniently consume what "the feed" provides, and that these feeds are aligned with our (system-1) expectations. As a result, these systems are said to create what is popularly called *filter bubbles* [44].

However, as previously discussed in Section 7.2.1, users often feel comfortable themselves with fast, routine choices, and only engage in more active (system-2) decision-making activities when prompted that they might want or need to do so. Persuasive recommender systems and nudging techniques aim to provide such prompts for making "prudent" or generally more informed choices [19].

Persuasive literature often concentrates on systems that aim to motivate users to make choices that society considers better—e. g., in terms of health or environmental impact, but in this chapter we mainly concentrate on mechanisms that aim to support users in making active decisions that they feel more comfortable with in the long term, but not necessarily in the short term. This type of self-optimization or self-control is not limited to ambitious lifestyle changes, but also for more mundane decisions, such as actively choosing a documentary or music album, instead of just consuming what happens to be offered [51].

As we will discuss in Section 7.5, it is difficult to design nudges or other mechanisms that support users to be "their better self": a related and perhaps more fundamental problem is that users themselves have difficulty to become their more effortful (system-2) better self [33]—the proverbial "I will start my diet tomorrow" trap. Being reminded of goals—even if set or planned by yourself—by an external system quickly feels patronizing [60]. Even more difficult perhaps than influencing a single choice is *changing* a users' attitude and behavior in such a way that—at some point—this changed behavior becomes natural, even without (strong) support [45].

7.2.4 Summary and outlook

In this section, we have discussed the mutual interaction between users and (recommender) systems in decision-making. Depending on its design, a recommender system may automate this choice process to a smaller or to a larger extent. Current commercial, often feed-based, recommender systems appear to take more control in this process than we—as users or society—consider desirable.

Persuasive systems are designed to stimulate users to adopt a particular kind of behavior. In academic contexts, this usually implies helping the user to be their better, healthier (system-2) self. Commercial recommender systems are by design persuasive as well, but largely serving system-1 goals, which may result in systems behaving as "friends with a bad influence" [57]. However, poor decisions or decisions that are regretted at a later point are (almost) never (entirely) the system's fault: it is ultimately the users' decision, reflecting their own desires, ambitions and self-control [27]. That is to say, unless users have come in the habit of lending too much responsibility to the system. This is what will be explored in the next section.

7.3 Mutual reinforcement in classical user modeling and HCI

A basic premise in human-computer interaction is that users aim to accomplish a goal, aided by an interactive system [17]. For this purpose, the user plans and executes several actions—such as clicking on an icon or a link, typing a search query or following a link—and then evaluates whether the system state matches the expectations, e. g., whether the click on the link indeed leads to the loading of a new page. This is a classic human-system feedback loop that we experience on a daily basis.

Personalized systems—including recommender systems—create even tighter feedback loops, as they "build a model of the goals, preferences and knowledge of each individual user, and use this model throughout the interaction with the user, in order to adapt to the needs of that user" [6].

7.3.1 Short-term mutual reinforcement

Web search is a classic example in which the user and the system work together to reach a certain outcome, and respond to each others responses. Users start with an initial query, inspect the results and then, if needed, reformulate the query; for example, they may decide to add or remove some keywords or to replace a term by a synonym [49]. It has been recognized that this iterative process helps the user to build a context in which to interpret and understand the results [54].

In user modeling, particularly in the earlier days, *concept drift* was seen as potentially problematic. Users' interests were recognized as being dynamic and likely to change. In [59], a special case of concept drift was described in which a news recommender presents news stories to the user. These stories "are assumed to directly affect the user's information needs," which raised the need for the system to anticipate and respond to this expected effect. This effect—described as early as in 2001—is still quite short-term, but can already be seen as a forebode for current longer-term effects of misinformation and fake news in social media [52].

Short-term tensions in feedback loops between users and personalized systems have been recognized by commercial providers. Among others, it is considered problematic that systems may have different goals—such as optimizing click-through rates—than the user may have. However, longer-term effects of interventions in the algorithm or in the interface are underinvestigated and hardly documented [13].

7.3.2 Long-term mutual reinforcement

In Section 7.2.1, we have discussed how car automation has made decision-making a collaborative activity between human drivers and the driving support tools, such as navigation systems and cruise control. Short-term implications of human-car feedback loops in terms of driver attention and division of responsibility in case of accidents and emergency situations have been discussed in the literature [9, 24, 35]. It appears that only recently it has been recognized or acknowledged that (partial) automation reshapes the driving task and, therefore, the driver's behavior. As expected, it has been observed that most drivers prefer to use high levels of automation, when available [21]. For instance, car navigation systems have made us accustomed to passively following turn-by-turn instructions, which has been observed to have a negative impact on our sense of direction or our inclination to comprehend the environment in which we are driving [29].

In a similar manner, automation and personalization have changed our media consumption behavior—and consequently our expectations of what media outlets should offer and the goals these offerings should fulfill. During the first decades after the introduction of the television in households, television watching was observed to be a mix of active and passive choices: consumers had particular expectations on what programs to expect at particular times, but program choices were often an active family decision and viewers, with the possibility to select another channel—or to turn the television off—if a program turned out not to be satisfying enough [2, 38]. In the early 2000s, streaming services such as Netflix or Amazon Prime dramatically changed watching behavior from weekly "watching appointments" with one or more series to *binge-watching*: watching two episodes or more of the same series in a row [48]. This behavior has arguably been reinforced by optimizing the recommender algorithm based on the click-through rate, which was exactly the goal of the Netflix Prize challenge [36]. As will be discussed in Section 7.4, this click-rate optimization largely was achieved by creating feeds largely consisting of safe choices that reinforce routine "system-1" behavior.

Largely, the changes as described above are designed and anticipated, but often there are also unexpected effects and (user) responses that need to be repaired or addressed. Moreover, in the long term, this can lead to systems—and associated user behavior—that are fundamentally different from their predecessors. Researchers in the field of *second-order cybernetics* fundamentally regard this as a long-term feedback loop between the system, its designers, its users and other stakeholders—and all parties involved, including stakeholders who may consider themselves as mere "observers," play an active role in this process [37]. In other words, they treat this human-system feedback loop as a *self-organizing system*.

A particular aspect of the systems discussed above is that they are used on a regular basis in order to achieve something in our daily lives. Moreover, we have observed that these systems actually have an impact on our lives, e. g., by simplifying or automating tasks or decisions. In terms of cybernetics, there is an ongoing process or regulation and feedback—in both directions—in order to maintain a state of relative stability [43]. This does not only imply that the algorithms and interfaces of a (personalized) system do not dramatically change, but also that the user contexts and the way users interact with the system remain fairly stable. Any disturbance of this equilibrium may lead to the need or desire for "reparation."

As we have observed earlier, users have a natural tendency toward easy, convenient system-1 choices. Therefore, it is tempting for (commercial) system designers to cater for these decisions. Voluntarily or involuntarily, this may lead to increased system-1 behavior—such as active television program selection that has gradually largely been replaced by a habit of picking a series that happens to be in the feed and appears acceptable enough. This is not a bad choice on itself, it may save precious time and prevent choice overload, but it may create a choice environment that users themselves—or society as a whole—may perceive as not healthy or not optimal.

Social media is a particularly problematic example, in which several iterations of design changes—responding to and anticipating user responses—have led to social media platforms being prone to polarization, misinformation and fake news [52]. As discussed earlier in Section 7.2.3, the feed-based design of social media may lead to filter bubbles of safe choices; however, users usually feel quite comfortable as well in a choice environment that does not challenge their current views or expectations—the so-called *echo chamber effect* [10]. Even though both the filter bubble and the echo chamber effects appear limited for individual users in a high-choice environment [18], the polarizing effects on the platform as a whole are undeniable. The long-term effect of user responses to seemingly small interface design decisions can best be illustrated by Facebook's introduction of Reactions ("Love," "Care," "Haha," "Wow," "Sad," and "Angry") in 2016, which has been shown to lead to more emotional user responses, with increased polarization on the platform and in society in general as a result [53].

7.3.3 Summary and outlook

In this section, we have explored the mutual reinforcement between users and the systems that they use. In human-computer interaction research, short-term reinforcement is a well-researched and quite well-understood process: users and systems interact with one another in order to reach a state of relative stability that allows users to achieve what they aim to achieve in a satisfactory manner. This state of relative stability does allow for minor changes in system design or usage patterns, but these changes may lead to the need of slight adjustments on either side—in the field of cybernetics, it is not uncommon to use the term *thermodynamics* for this [43].

The process of long-term mutual reinforcement is far less understood [13]. This does not come as a surprise, as these long-term effects are usually the result of a chain of planned and unplanned short-term effects. As we have seen in this chapter, users have a natural tendency toward convenience and automation. Personalized systems—and commercial recommender systems in particular—are often designed to support and encourage convenient, routine behavior and routine choices [5], either or not with clickthrough optimization as an explicit system goal [13].

Naturally, these longer-term effects are often easily observed in hindsight, as we have seen in the fields of recommender systems in general as well as in social media [36, 53]. Particularly when it comes to negative effects, it would be desirable to better anticipate them or to recognize them in an early stage, before "the damage is done." For personalized systems, it appears imperative to have a deeper understanding of these chains of feedback loops. For this purpose, in the next section we will further explore the history of academic and commercial recommender systems.

7.4 Everyday recommendations from commercial providers

Originally, adaptive or personalized systems were thought to help users with activities such as online learning, finding relevant information, or managing personal information spaces; still, already in an early stage, opportunities for e-commerce were recognized [6]. With the advent of commercial recommender systems, the importance of metrics increased, in order to quantify sales, click-through rates or conversion rates [36]. As discussed before in Section 7.3.2, this is best exemplified by the data-driven Netflix Prize challenge. More fundamentally, recommender systems designed for such purposes might be considered *sales instruments* that may—or may not—act in line with the users' interests.

In this section, we explore the expectations and roles of users and recommender systems in terms of expected outcomes. We first briefly discuss how users may evaluate a situation differently in hindsight than while experiencing a situation.

7.4.1 Conflicting short-term and long-term user goals

Traditional user goals for online recommender systems include exploring information spaces, finding good items—such as movies that received good reviews, or simply browsing for entertainment; other, more purposeful goals include improving oneself in one way or another, expressing oneself or helping other people [28]. It is common and natural for humans to evaluate particularly the latter activities in terms of increased satisfaction or happiness. Kahneman argues that a person might evaluate an outcome differently while *experiencing* a situation than when *remembering* a situation [34]. Arguably, the experiencing self is mainly interested in an enjoyable experience, whereas the remembering self also reflects on the purposefulness of the outcomes.

As discussed in Section 7.3.2, users have a natural preference for automation and convenience, which is one of the reasons for the popularity of streaming services and activities such as binge-watching. However, in hindsight, the remembering self might reflect upon some lost time that could have been used for more purposeful or urgent activities, which arguably would have been the more rational choice.

7.4.2 Recommender systems acting as salespersons

Algorithmic recommender systems that are trained with (user) data are essentially an application of machine learning. In a review of deep learning—a currently popular strand of research in machine learning—it is argued that machine learning is particularly good at *system-1* tasks that involve recognizing previously learned situations and common, expected responses; tasks that "require a deliberate sequence of steps" is observed to be still in its infancy [5].

Moreover, as many recommender systems have been deliberately designed to optimize click-through rates [36], this inherent limitation of machine learning is not countered but rather increased. In terms of Kahneman, recommender systems mainly serve the goals of our experiencing selves, not the remembering selves. Typical commercial evaluation measures—such as the cost per click or the click through rate [25]—can be considered as indications how well the "recommender system as a salesperson" served the needs as perceived by the user at that very moment.

As discussed in Section 7.2.2, visual attention plays an important role in advertisements and sales. Visual cues may lead to *unplanned behavior*, largely driven by availability; for instance, common advice for preventing unintended supermarket purchases is to make use of a shopping list and to not deviate from it [1]. Building upon this perspective, it is not surprising that users who have been trained that they only need to scroll further in a feed to find new posts, stories, movies or songs, increasingly engage in such unplanned behavior—as observed by Derakshan.[1]

Of course, these differences in interest between parties do not (necessarily) imply that recommender systems are a user's adversaries: one of the premises of multistakeholder recommendation is that *reciprocal recommendations* are acceptable for both parties—and that ideally both parties benefit. This mutual benefit can theoretically be calculated as a multistakeholder evaluation measure—and attempts to do so have been made [8].

However, most—if not all—of these efforts focus on the utility from the perspective of the *experiencing users*, not of the *remembering users*—who in hindsight might wish to have spent their time in a more purposeful manner. As we have seen in Section 7.2.3, making "prudent" or generally more informed choices—directed at the "remembering user"—are the field of persuasive systems [19].

7.5 Integrating conscious decision-making into the interface

In Section 7.3.2, we discussed how drivers have been accustomed—and how they accustomed themselves—to following turn-by-turn instructions from their navigation support system instead of consciously choosing directions themselves. Arguably, for this purpose, the benefits of automation outweigh drawbacks such as a drivers' reduced sense of orientation [29].

A fundamental difference with driving—an activity that is usually carried out to bring a person from a start point to a planned end point—is that online activities, such as web search or social media use, often are meant to further shape a user's goals and expectations (as discussed in Section 7.3.1) or that these online activities actually are meaningful by themselves—such as keeping up with the news or politics, or interacting with family, friends and colleagues.

Already in Section 7.2.1, we have discussed that there are several levels of automation that systems can provide and in Section 7.3.2, we observed a user's natural prefer-

---

1 https://www.theguardian.com/technology/2015/dec/29/irans-blogfather-facebook-instagram-and-twitter-are-killing-the-web

ence for automation. Without imposing any moral views, we believe that—at least in hindsight—users often would prefer some more initiative and conscious decision making and a bit less turn-by-turn following of system recommendations [27, 44]. Sometimes we want or should want to be challenged, in order to review our current behavior or to consciously look for better—tastier, more interesting, more challenging, environment-friendlier—options.

In this section, we discuss several strands of techniques that aim to activate and support a user's conscious *system-2* behavior. Several of these approaches fall in the field of persuasive systems, but we think it is important to keep in mind that personalized systems and recommender systems are inherently persuasive by themselves—as discussed in Section 7.2.2.

7.5.1 Traditional recommender system approaches: Explanations and cognitive forcing

Explanations play an important role in recommender systems. Common goals of these explanations include helping users understand how a system works, allowing users to tell the system when it is wrong, increase users' confidence in a system and convincing users to make a certain decision [56]. Explanations and user control increase user trust and satisfaction, and make personalized systems more transparent—in the chapter "Explanations and user control in recommender systems," elsewhere in this book, Jannach and colleagues discuss several techniques for doing so.

A fundamental issue with explanations in recommender system is that users need to *engage* with them in order to experience the benefits of them. Early attempts on explainable recommender systems—then called *scrutable adaptive hypertext*—already found that it is challenging to provide an effective interface that encourage users to actively explore the rationale behind certain recommendations [14].

Moreover, explainable recommender systems usually focus on explaining why certain items are being recommended—and not on which items have *not* been recommended and which alternative directions or solutions a user may want to consider. As discussed by Baeza-Yates [4], recommender systems on the web generally suffer from activity bias and data bias, which leads to lists of search results or recommendations that only represent a very small part of a solution space. Unfortunately, this issue is aggravated by *user interaction bias*, the already observed effect that users naturally prefer convenience and automation. According to a recent study, even if users do interact with recommendations and their explanations, this usually does not have long-term effects [20].

An alternative technique is *cognitive forcing* [7], which appears to be an extension of *cognitive friction* [12]. Cognitive forcing involves designers consciously building hurdles in the UX experiences, in order to force the user to make conscious decisions, e. g., by asking users to make an initial choice before showing any recommendation. The problem with such approaches is that users typically experience these interventions as unpleasant and cumbersome [7].

7.5.2 Mixed-initiative or conversational interfaces

Rather than considering requesting or requiring user involvement as a hurdle, one could consider user involvement as a *conversation* with a personalized system. Recommender systems that involve one or more steps of interaction are called *mixed-initiative* interfaces.

Explicit user involvement may take place already before the recommendation process starts, e. g., by asking users to provide some initial ratings of selected items [39]. Another approach for soliciting user responses is to allow them to give explicit feedback on recommended items, e. g., by rating or reordering them. Similar to explainable recommenders systems—as discussed in the previous subsection—it was found that putting users into control can be challenging [31].

A problem with many mixed-initiative recommender systems is that the conversation between user and system does not flow naturally: often it still is the system that asks or requires user input, not the user who naturally reacts to a certain proposition. A promising development for conversational recommender systems is the growing popularity of voice assistants that users can talk with and that are already commercially exploited by various big tech companies [46]. However, it is still considered a challenge to initiate or stimulate natural dialogues between users and conversational (voice) assistants that go beyond simple requests and responses [30].

It should be noted that voice interaction is not mandatory for mixed-initiative interfaces. For instance, as discussed in Section 7.3.1, many users feel comfortable refining their queries in several iterations, in response to the list of results of their previous query [49]. In terms of second-order cybernetics (see Section 7.3.2), this—arguably trained—user interaction with search engines by means of queries and query results appears to be a fairly unstable equilibrium, though. Already, longer-term reinforcement effects between search engines and their users can be observed: current search engines increasingly provide direct answers and information snippets in response to user queries, which has led to a reduction in user interaction with the result sets [61]. In a sense, this development may gradually turn a search engine into an "answer engine," with users considering the results to their initial query as an answer to their question, without further exploring the solution space [54].

7.5.3 Hypertext-inspired choice models

In the previous sections, we discussed the role of explanations, cognitive forcing, mixed-initiative and conversational interfaces on conscious decision-making. Despite the differences, all approaches have in common that the initial initiative lies on the computer side: all user considerations start with one or more items proposed by the system, with an explicit prompt to make a choice.

By contrast, the original ambitions of hypertext—the concept that lies at the core of web interfaces and personalized systems—was to *support* human thinking by means of rich interfaces with typed and bidirectional links and visualizations, which would allow users to read, think and reason in a nonsequential manner [40]. A hypertext system was envisioned to function as a personal assistant, or a secretary that would follow a user's instructions, therewith *augmenting human intellect* [11].

Hypertext systems were explicitly designed to facilitate interaction and conscious deliberations, exploiting visual metaphors and connections, such as fixed-sized cards, landmarks, footprints or birds' eye overviews [26, 41]. A particular approach for representing and support human thinking and decision-making is the concept of *spatial hypertext*, which visualizes associations between items (or nodes) by their position on a (hyper)space and the relative distances from one another—further enhanced by visual cues, such as color, shape and size. Hypertext systems encourage users to directly manipulate these positions to better reflect their current line of thinking, their preferences or their priorities.

Indeed, a premise of hypertext is that it supports associative thinking and conscious decision-making, an activity that Kahneman coined as *system-2* thinking. In contrast to linear feeds, which suggest or implicate an order, spatial hypertext structures provide a choice landscape that may trigger users to explore information or solutions that they might not have considered first [16].

Particularly in the early days of the web, it was lamented that the lack of rich links, visual metaphors and cues for direct manipulation made web navigation only a far cry from the original intentions of hypertext researchers and designers [15]. In contrast to the associative nature of hypertext, navigation on the web is largely hierarchical, guided by menu structures and particularly in the domain of recommender systems by linear feeds.

7.5.4 Interventions and nudges versus interface paradigms

As discussed in more detail in [3], the popularity of linear feeds and hierarchical menus can be explained by the users' natural tendency toward routines and safe choices [23], ideally supported by a system that confirms and reinforces these choices.

Despite the benefits, convenience and commercial success of recommender systems, the limitations in terms of supporting conscious decision-making and its narrowing effects on user choices has been recognized [36]. In response, several research efforts are carried out in order to build cognitive friction as discussed in Section 7.5.1 into recommender interfaces: elements that stop or slow down interaction flows and that are expected to encourage users to reconsider initial impressions or decisions.

Accepting the perspective of feed-based recommender systems as decision support that largely reinforces those choices that we routinely would make, *nudges* are defined as a "*de facto* influence on choices that is 'easy and cheap to avoid'" [55]. Nudging theory builds upon psychological theory that separates the "experiencing self" from the "remembering self," a notion that we briefly discussed in Section 7.4.1. In leisure science, for instance, it has been recognized that there is a difference between what a user experiences in the moment and how the same user remembers this experience at the end of the day [62].

In the context of this chapter, we mainly focus on nudges or interventions that help users making decisions that they feel satisfied about afterwards, a goal that arguably is in the best interest of the user. However, if we consider the combination of feed-based recommenders that largely reinforce a user's system-1 behavior together with interventions that aim to reinforce system-2 choices—such as nudges, explanations or cognitive friction—then it can be argued that every single choice is managed by the system [50]. In other words, this type of choice architecture may still seduce the user to make easy, convenient, attractive choices—such as watching the next episode of a series—and at the same time remind the user that making a different, at first sight perhaps less attractive choice, such as reading a book instead, may be more prudent and make the user more satisfied by the end of the day. Such an ambivalent choice architecture that simultaneously seduces and patronizes the user is likely to cause frustrating user experiences.

7.5.5 Summary and considerations

In this section, we have discussed several approaches for integrating conscious decision-making into the interface of recommender systems, as we know them now. In a sense, all these approaches aim to "repair" a situation in which users have learned to appreciate the convenience of feed-based suggestions. Efforts to address this issue—including explanations, cognitive forcing and mixed-initiative interfaces—have an impact on the choice architecture, but still leaves the initiative for generating the options largely on the system-side.

Building upon the notions on the balance in levels of support in decision-making, which we discussed in Section 7.2.1, interfaces that allow and encourage users to actively consider several options and to develop their own choice architecture would bring the users more in control. Theoretically, this would lead to more satisfactory outcomes, but unfortunately interfaces that attempt to do so are often considered as cumbersome.

This leads us to a somewhat paradoxical situation: as a long-term effect of mutual reinforcement, users have learned to appreciate personalized interfaces that make it easy to make safe, convenient choices that look attractive to the experiencing self—and recommender systems have been optimized for exactly this purpose; but now, we need to find mechanisms to convince users that at the end of the day they would be happier with decision support that helps them with choices that their remembering self would be happier with at the end of the day.

7.6 Discussion and future perspectives

In this chapter, we have explored and discussed feedback loops and mutual reinforcement in personalized interaction between users and systems, with a focus on systems that help users in making decisions and choices. We have observed that users appreciate the convenience of personalized decision support, including recommendations that reduce the need for making active decisions.

In the past decades, the ecosystem of personalized systems and their users has largely been shaped by commercial recommender systems, which responded to and shaped user expectations and user appreciation. A particular long-term effect of this coevolution is that users have become accustomed to rather passively following suggestions rather than actively shaping and investigating their choice architecture.

This natural preference for automation and convenience, with recommender systems that support convenient system-1 decisions, works perfectly fine if these decisions do not have negative consequences at the end of the day; in other words, when the reflecting user would still be happy with, or at worst indifferent about, these choices. However, there are quite some situations where users—or society as a whole—realize too late that active decisions at an earlier stage would have led to leisure activities, social interactions or choices that in hindsight would have been more purposeful, prudent or productive.

Several approaches have been explored to combat this effect, to make recommender systems "more fair" by means of explanations, conversations or nudges. However, it is still an open question how the short-term effects of such interventions translate to long-term effects—and how this will shape our daily activities, our social interactions and the way we approach decisions and choices.

In order to move recommender systems as a technology forward, Konstan and Terveen plead for a more holistic approach, taking user perceptions, choice overload and differences in user objectives into account. They also argue that recommender systems should learn from situations in which recommended items are *not* selected by the user [36]. While helpful, the proposed approaches still leave the initiative for decisions at the system.

As argued by Bengio et al. [5], machine learning—and therewith also recommender systems—are not (yet) able to carry out tasks that "require a deliberate sequence of steps." By contrast, humans are quite good in tasks that require reasoning and active decision-making, but they may only engage in such tasks when prompted to do so. As discussed in Section 7.5.2 and Section 7.5.3, designers find it hard to create interfaces that stimulate user to do so.

Throughout this chapter, we have observed that system designers as well as the users prefer recommendations and results to be presented as a list of options to choose from, already prioritized by the system. We believe it would be productive if result sets would contain elements that prompt users to treat such lists as a selection of possible choices that can be accepted, deliberated, challenged or discarded. Building in such choice moments may involve simple interventions such as breaking an "infinite feed" into separate pages: even the single activity of clicking on a "next" button may create a (very) brief moment for reflection. More elaborate strategies may be adopted by voice-based conversational recommender systems [30], with dialogue strategies that specifically encourage users to engage in deliberation.

To conclude, a general and arguably unforeseen long-term effect in user interaction with personalized systems is the user's inherent preference for convenience and automation, a preference that personalized systems may need to challenge more often. Particularly, it seems very useful and productive to explicitly engage users in a process of active decision-making, ensuring that at the end of the day the remembering user will be satisfied with the choices made by the experiencing user, supported—and not driven—by a personalized system.

References

[1]   Russell Abratt and Stephen Donald Goodey. Unplanned buying and in-store stimuli in supermarkets. *Managerial and Decision Economics* 11(2) (1990) 111–121.

[2]   William J. Adams. How people watch television as investigated using focus group techniques. *Journal of Broadcasting & Electronic Media* 44(1) (2000) 78–93.

[3]   Claus Atzenbeck, Eelco Herder, and Daniel Roßner. Breaking the routine: spatial hypertext concepts for active decision making in recommender systems. *New Review of Hypermedia and Multimedia* (2023) 1–35.

[4]   Ricardo Baeza-Yates. Bias on the web. *Communications of the ACM* 61(6) (2018) 54–61.

[5]   Yoshua Bengio, Yann Lecun, and Geoffrey Hinton. Deep learning for ai. *Communications of the ACM* 64(7) (2021) 58–65.

[6]   Peter Brusilovsky. Adaptive hypermedia. *User Modeling and User-Adapted Interaction* 11(1) (2001) 87–110.

[7]   Zana Buçinca, Maja Barbara Malaya, and Krzysztof Z. Gajos. To trust or to think: cognitive forcing functions can reduce overreliance on ai in ai-assisted decision-making. *Proceedings of the ACM on Human–Computer Interaction* 5(CSCW1) (2021) 1–21.

[8]   Robin D. Burke, Himan Abdollahpouri, Bamshad Mobasher, and Trinadh Gupta. Towards multi-stakeholder utility evaluation of recommender systems. In: *UMAP (Extended Proceedings)*, volume 750, 2016.

[9]   Stephen M. Casner, Edwin L. Hutchins, and Don Norman. The challenges of partially automated driving. *Communications of the ACM* 59(5) (2016) 70–77.

[10] Matteo Cinelli, Gianmarco De Francisci Morales, Alessandro Galeazzi, Walter Quattrociocchi, and Michele Starnini. The echo chamber effect on social media. *Proceedings of the National Academy of Sciences* 118(9) (2021) e2023301118.

[11] Jeff Conklin, Albert Selvin, Simon Buckingham Shum, and Maarten Sierhuis. Facilitated hypertext for collective sensemaking: 15 years on from gibis. In: *Proceedings of the 12th ACM conference on Hypertext and Hypermedia*, 2001, pp. 123–124.

[12] Alan Cooper and Paul Saffo. *The Inmates Are Running the Asylum*. USA: Macmillan Publishing Co., Inc., 1999.

[13] Henriette Cramer and Juho Kim. Confronting the tensions where ux meets ai. *Interactions* 26(6) (2019) 69–71.

[14] Marek Czarkowski and Judy Kay. A scrutable adaptive hypertext. In: *Adaptive Hypermedia and Adaptive Web-Based Systems: Second International Conference, AH 2002 Málaga, Spain, May 29–31, 2002 Proceedings 2*. Springer, 2002, pp. 384–387.

[15] David R. Danielson. Web navigation and the behavioral effects of constantly visible site maps. *Interacting with Computers* 14(5) (2002) 601–618.

[16] Andrew Dillon, John Richardson, and Cliff McKnight. Navigation in hypertext: a critical review of the concept. In: *Proceedings of the 3rd International Conference on Human-Computer Interaction*. North Holland, 1990.

[17] Alan Dix, Janet Finlay, Gregory D. Abowd, and Russell Beale. *Human-computer interaction*. Pearson Education, 2003.

[18] Elizabeth Dubois and Grant Blank. The echo chamber is overstated: the moderating effect of political interest and diverse media. *Information, Communication & Society* 21(5) (2018) 729–745.

[19] Brian J. Fogg. Persuasive technology: using computers to change what we think and do. *Ubiquity* 2 (2002) 2002.

[20] Krzysztof Z. Gajos and Lena Mamykina. Do people engage cognitively with ai? impact of ai assistance on incidental learning. In: *27th International Conference on Intelligent User Interfaces*, 2022, pp. 794–806.

[21] Pnina Gershon, Sean Seaman, Bruce Mehler, Bryan Reimer, and Joseph Coughlin. Driver behavior and the use of automation in real-world driving. *Accident Analysis and Prevention* 158 (2021) 106217.

[22] Kerstin Gidlöf, Andrey Anikin, Martin Lingonblad, and Annika Wallin. Looking is buying. how visual attention and choice are affected by consumer preferences and properties of the supermarket shelf. *Appetite* 116 (2017) 29–38.

[23] Marta C. Gonzalez, Cesar A. Hidalgo, and Albert-Laszlo Barabasi. Understanding individual human mobility patterns. *Nature* 453(7196) (2008) 779–782.

[24] Noah J. Goodall. Can you program ethics into a self-driving car? *IEEE Spectrum* 53(6) (2016) 28–58.

[25] Asela Gunawardana, Guy Shani, and Sivan Yogev. Evaluating recommender systems. In: *Recommender systems handbook*. Springer, 2012, pp. 547–601.

[26] Frank G. Halasz. Reflections on" seven issues" hypertext in the era of the web. *ACM Journal of Computer Documentation* 25(3) (2001) 109–114.

[27] Eelco Herder, Daniel Roßner, and Claus Atzenbeck. Reflecting on social media behavior by structuring and exploring posts and comments. *I-Com* 19(3) (2020) 239–250.

[28] Jonathan L. Herlocker, Joseph A. Konstan, Loren G. Terveen, and John T. Riedl. Evaluating collaborative filtering recommender systems. *ACM Transactions on Information Systems (TOIS)* 22(1) (2004) 5–53.

[29] Toru Ishikawa. Satellite navigation and geospatial awareness: Long-term effects of using navigation tools on wayfinding and spatial orientation. *The Professional Geographer* 71(2) (2019) 197–209.

[30] Dietmar Jannach and Li Chen. Conversational recommendation: A grand ai challenge. *AI Magazine* 43(2) (2022) 151–163.

[31] Dietmar Jannach, Ahtsham Manzoor, Wanling Cai, and Li Chen. A survey on conversational recommender systems. *ACM Computing Surveys (CSUR)* 54(5) (2021) 1–36.

[32] Mareike Jenner. Is this TVIV? on Netflix, TVIII and binge-watching. *New Media & Society* 18(2) (2016) 257–273.

[33] Daniel Kahneman. Maps of bounded rationality: A perspective on intuitive judgment and choice. *Nobel Prize Lecture* 8(1) (2002) 351–401.

[34] Daniel Kahneman. *Thinking, fast and slow*. Macmillan, 2011.

[35] Katja Kircher, Annika Larsson, and Jonas Andersson Hultgren. Tactical driving behavior with different levels of automation. *IEEE Transactions on Intelligent Transportation Systems* 15(1) (2013) 158–167.

[36] Joseph Konstan and Loren Terveen. Human-centered recommender systems: Origins, advances, challenges, and opportunities. *AI Magazine* 42(3) (2021) 31–42.

[37] Klaus Krippendorff. The cybernetics of design and the design of cybernetics. In: *Design Cybernetics*. Springer, 2019, pp. 119–136.

[38] Barbara Lee and Robert S. Lee. How and why people watch tv: Implications for the future of interactive television. *Journal of Advertising Research* 35(6) (1995) 9–19.

[39] Sean M. McNee, Shyong K. Lam, Joseph A. Konstan, and John Riedl. Interfaces for eliciting new user preferences in recommender systems. In: *User Modeling 2003: 9th International Conference, UM 2003 Johnstown, PA, USA, June 22–26, 2003 Proceedings 9*. Springer, 2003, pp. 178–187.

[40] Theodor Holm Nelson. Complex information processing: a file structure for the complex, the changing and the indeterminate. In: *Proceedings of the 1965 20th national conference*, 1965, pp. 84–100.

[41] Jakob Nielsen. User interface directions for the web. *Communications of the ACM* 42(1) (1999) 65–72.

[42] Harri Oinas-Kukkonen. A foundation for the study of behavior change support systems. *Personal and Ubiquitous Computing* 17(6) (2013) 1223–1235.

[43] Michael Paetau. Niklas luhmann and cybernetics. *Journal of Sociocybernetics* 11(1/2), 2013.

[44] Eli Pariser. *The filter bubble: How the new personalized web is changing what we read and how we think*. Penguin, 2011.

[45] Michel Peeters, Carl Megens, Elise Van Den Hoven, Caroline Hummels, and Aarnout Brombacher. Social stairs: taking the piano staircase towards long-term behavioral change. In: *Persuasive Technology: 8th International Conference, PERSUASIVE 2013, Sydney, NSW, Australia, April 3–5, 2013. Proceedings 8*. Springer, 2013, pp. 174–179.

[46] Marta Perez Garcia and Sarita Saffon Lopez. Exploring the uncanny valley theory in the constructs of a virtual assistant personality. In: *Intelligent Systems and Applications: Proceedings of the 2019 Intelligent Systems Conference (IntelliSys) Volume 1*. Springer, 2020, pp. 1017–1033.

[47] Guilherme D. Pires John Stanton, and Paulo Rita. The internet, consumer empowerment and marketing strategies. *European Journal of Marketing* 40(9/10) (2006) 936–949.

[48] Matthew Pittman and Kim Sheehan. Sprinting a media marathon: Uses and gratifications of binge-watching television through netflix. *First Monday* (2015).

[49] Soo Young Rieh et al. Analysis of multiple query reformulations on the web: The interactive information retrieval context. *Information Processing & Management* 42(3) (2006) 751–768.

[50] Andreas T. Schmidt and Bart Engelen. The ethics of nudging: An overview. *Philosophy Compass* 15(4) (2020) e12658.

[51] Christoph Schneider, Markus Weinmann, and Jan Vom Brocke. Digital nudging: guiding online user choices through interface design. *Communications of the ACM* 61(7) (2018) 67–73.

[52] Kai Shu, Amy Sliva, Suhang Wang, Jiliang Tang, and Huan Liu. Fake news detection on social media: A data mining perspective. *ACM SIGKDD Explorations Newsletter* 19(1) (2017) 22–36.

[53] Heloisa Sturm Wilkerson, Martin J. Riedl, and Kelsey N. Whipple. Affective affordances: Exploring facebook reactions as emotional responses to hyperpartisan political news. *Digital Journalism* 9(8) (2021) 1040–1061.

[54] Jaime Teevan, Christine Alvarado, Mark S. Ackerman, and David R. Karger. The perfect search engine is not enough: a study of orienteering behavior in directed search. In: *Proceedings of the SIGCHI conference on Human factors in computing systems*, 2004, pp. 415–422.

[55] Richard H. Thaler and Cass R. Sunstein. *Nudge: Improving decisions about health, wealth, and happiness*. Penguin, 2009.

[56] Nava Tintarev and Judith Masthoff. Designing and evaluating explanations for recommender systems. In: *Recommender systems handbook*. Springer, 2010, pp. 479–510.

[57] Martin K. J. Waiguny, Michelle R. Nelson, and Ralf Terlutter. The relationship of persuasion knowledge, identification of commercial intent and persuasion outcomes in advergames—the role of media context and presence. *Journal of Consumer Policy* 37(2) (2014) 257–277.

[58] Rosemary Walker and Brenda Cude. In-store shopping strategies: Time and money costs in the supermarket. *The Journal of Consumer Affairs* 17(2) (1983) 356–369.

[59] Geoffrey I. Webb, Michael J. Pazzani, and Daniel Billsus. Machine learning for user modeling. *User Modeling and User-Adapted Interaction* 11 (2001) 19–29.

[60] Paul Weiser, Dominik Bucher, Francesca Cellina, and Vanessa De Luca. A taxonomy of motivational affordances for meaningful gamified and persuasive technologies. In: *EnviroInfo and ICT for Sustainability 2015*. Atlantis Press, 2015, pp. 271–280.

[61] Zhijing Wu, Mark Sanderson, B. Barla Cambazoglu, W. Bruce Croft, and Falk Scholer. Providing direct answers in search results: A study of user behavior. In: *Proceedings of the 29th acm international conference on information & knowledge management*, 2020, pp. 1635–1644.

[62] Chris A. B. Zajchowski, Keri A. Schwab, and Daniel L. Dustin. The experiencing self and the remembering self: Implications for leisure science. *Leisure Sciences* 39(6) (2017) 561–568.

Part III: **Personalization purposes and goals**

Julio Abascal, Olatz Arbelaitz, Xabier Gardeazabal, Javier Muguerza, and Ainhoa Yera

8 Personalizing the user interface for people with disabilities

Abstract: Computer applications and internet access provide many people with disabilities with unique opportunities for interpersonal communication, social interaction and active participation (including access to labor and entertainment). Nevertheless, rigid user interfaces often present accessibility barriers to people with physical, sensory or cognitive impairments. Accordingly, user interface personalization is crucial to overcome these barriers, allowing a considerable part of the population with disabilities to have computer access. Adapting the user interface to people with disabilities requires considering their physical, sensory or cognitive abilities and restrictions and providing alternative access procedures according to their capacities. This chapter presents a number of methods and techniques that are applied to research and practice on user interface personalization for people with disabilities and discusses possible approaches for diverse application fields where personalization is required: accessibility to the web using transcoding, web mining for eGovernment and human–robot interaction for people with severe motor restrictions.

Keywords: Digital accessibility, modeling users with disabilities, data mining and machine learning for user modeling, assistive user-adapted interaction

8.1 Introduction

A significant number of everyday human activities can currently be carried out using computers and networks. People with disabilities, who were previously unable to perform these activities physically, can now carry them out through digital applications, which provide ways to overcome specific motor, sensory or intellectual barriers. Nevertheless, most common interfaces present accessibility barriers that hinder access for numerous users with disabilities. Users with restrictions would especially benefit from personalized applications, which adapt access procedures to the specific characteristics of each person. In this way, personalization would help to overcome accessibility barriers, enabling access to computers for a large population with restrictions.

The need to adapt specific functions and characteristics of the human interface to be used by people with particular restrictions arose from the appearance of the first com-

Acknowledgement: The authors are members of the ADIAN research team, supported by the Basque Government, Department of Education, Universities and Research under grant (IT-1437-22). The authors are grateful for the contributions Juan Eduardo Pérez and Xabier Valencia, former members of ADIAN.

https://doi.org/10.1515/9783110988567-008

mercial computers. Initially, these accommodations were done manually by friends and colleagues for each user with a disability. Later, many applications provided ways to adjust the interface parameters to the user's wishes. Due to the variability of user needs, and the difficulty of making these manual adjustments, they were often insufficient [1]. Therefore, automatic personalization—or adaptation—emerged as an exciting possibility. Recognizing that manual adjustments are a necessary starting point for adaptation, this chapter will focus on automatically adapted systems.

Automatically user-adapted interaction is a discipline with a long tradition of interface personalization in which adaptation is primarily supported by user modeling. User models contain abstract representations of user properties that are *relevant* to the interaction. These properties include user needs, preferences, knowledge, etc. Physical, cognitive and behavioral characteristics can also be included. Current values of static and dynamic characteristics, *observable* through the interaction, can be used to personalize the interface.

There are two essential requisites for applying these techniques to personalize the interfaces used by people with disabilities . On the one hand, the main characteristics of the initial interface (such as content, presentation, navigation or behavior) must be adjustable to be able to match user restrictions and needs. On the other hand, the user model must contain information about the specific abilities and restrictions of the user.

Merely adjusting general-purpose personalization systems (extending the user model with fields that record potential disabilities) is not usually enough. Personalized user interfaces for accessibility have to meet the specific characteristics of specific users, taking advantage of the abilities they do have and overcoming their physical, sensory or cognitive restrictions.

Personalization requires a thoroughly considering the interface parameters and features that can be adapted. Areas of possible interface adaptation to enhance accessibility include *presentation* (e. g., "place important areas of content near the top of the page"), *content* (e. g., "incorporate specific scrolling icons on each page"), *navigation* (e. g., "create a table of contents for the website") and *behavior* (e. g., "avoid automatic page updating"), as set out by several seminal works [17, 47, 49].

The wide range of disabilities and the significant variability of user characteristics, even within users with similar disabilities, hinder the application of approaches focused on specific restrictions. For this reason, advanced personalized interaction systems are preferably oriented to the abilities of the user, which can be similar across diverse types of disabilities. Data mining and machine learning methods can be used to find common interaction barriers and shared interaction patterns not limited to specific disabilities. These methods help to detect the most convenient interaction procedures for each user, avoiding preconceived schemes.

Many people with disabilities use specific devices and applications (known as assistive technology) to gain access to computers, whether these are commercialized or custom-made [23]. The huge diversity of these devices can strongly condition the adaptation of the interface. They include (i) special switches, keyboards and pointing devices,

(ii) software such as screen readers and communication programs and (iii) devices for eye gaze and head trackers. Therefore, user interface personalization methods have to devote specific consideration to the assistive technology, as pointed out by Koutkias et al. [52] and empirically proved by Wobbrock and Gajos [83] and Valencia et al. [77].

In addition to analyzing the technical and human requisites for valid and efficient modeling and adaptation, specific areas of interaction are introduced in this chapter to discuss how diverse needs can be collected and included in the design to create interfaces that enable users with disabilities to overcome interaction barriers. As illustrative application cases, we focus on three diverse areas of interaction:

1. *Transcoding* to personalize access to the web. Starting from the specific characteristics of a particular user (obtained from its user model), inaccessible web pages are automatically recoded, applying a number of *accessibility techniques*.
2. Accessing *eGovernment* sites, which are crucial for helping people with disabilities to exercise their right to interact with the administration. Since access to administration sites is usually anonymous, web-mining techniques are applied to extract patterns that allow for some degree of personalization.
3. Interfaces for *Augmented and Alternative Manipulation*. Based on human–robot interaction techniques, these interfaces require very distinctive interaction modes that will be essential in the near future to provide autonomy to people with severe motor restrictions. Personalization in augmented and alternative manipulation is essential because users cannot produce all the detailed parameters of the complex orders required to control a robot. Therefore, a significant part of the interaction must be deduced from the user, the task and the context models.

Even if personalization provides excellent opportunities to users with physical, sensory or cognitive impairments, it also raises additional challenges relating to privacy, data acquisition and modeling, which are briefly discussed at the end of the chapter.

8.2 User modeling and personalized interaction for people with disabilities

Personalization of user interfaces for people with disabilities usually involves both customization and adaptation. According to Norman and Draper [60], a system is *adaptable* when the user manually changes several parameters to customize its appearance, behavior or functionality. *Adaptive* systems, however, automatically perform adaptations without direct user intervention. Customization is the first step in adapting the interface to the needs and preferences of people with disabilities, although this task is not always easy and may sometimes require expert support.

In addition to permanent impairments, people with disabilities may experience significant variations in their capabilities over short periods of time. For this reason, digital systems which are able to dynamically adapt themselves to the users' changing conditions without inconveniencing them are especially appealing. These systems decrease the burden on the users by reducing customization demands and are prepared for short-term changes in the users' conditions.

Adaptive systems employ user models that gather and process information about user characteristics, interests, restrictions, abilities, etc., to perform dynamic adaptations in a transparent way for the users. User models can collect information both manually, from the users' answers to specific questions in a registration process, and implicitly, by observing and interpreting their interaction with the system. User modeling has been frequently used in web design to support people through personalized access. These techniques are reported to be very successful in commercial websites [36] for customers who receive personalized treatment which better satisfies their interests, and for online retailers that can recognize, understand and ultimately serve their customers more efficiently.

Concerning people with disabilities, user modeling requires advanced data structures to enable the management of diverse (and sometimes incoherent) personalization parameters. This is because the individual capabilities of people with special needs are highly heterogeneous [82], as are their preferences and behaviors when interacting with technology [79]. Quite simple data structures have been used successfully for the data management of user models. In recent years, ontologies have been extensively used to build user models due to their notable advantages in this domain. These include advanced automated reasoning with complex data structures and better suitability to deal with expandable fields of knowledge.

Consequently, understanding human diversity when interacting with technology is crucial to improve the methods of interaction, and thus facilitate access to computers for people with disabilities. However, the most widely used interaction models to describe human behavior focus on people without disabilities and are, therefore, not always suitable for modeling people with special needs.

8.3 Evolution and types of interface personalization for people with disabilities

The idea of personalization was present in the early intelligent user interfaces [48]. But, according to Stephanidis [73], the first attempts to bring closer the adaptivity and accessibility concepts were only initiated in the 1990s, with the European project ACCESS[1] being one of the pioneers in focusing on user interface adaptations to support the require-

---

1 ACCESS European project (1994–1996) "Development platform for unified ACCESS to enabling environments." https://cordis.europa.eu/project/id/1001 (Accessed: February 1, 2023).

ments of people with disabilities and older adults. Subsequently, the AVANTI project continued this line of work.

The AVANTI[2] project applied adaptability and adaptivity techniques to tailor the interface to the characteristics of people with disabilities to provide accessibility in web-based multimedia applications. It took into account the different contexts of use and the changing characteristics of the interaction between the user and the system. In the first phase, AVANTI considered static user characteristics (abilities, skills, requirements and preferences) stored in the user model. During the interaction, the system collected users' procedures to deduce their dynamic characteristics (such as idle time and error rate). Adaptation was performed by applying rule-based system reasoning [74].

8.3.1 Modeling users with disabilities

Several user models have been created to address the particular needs of specific types of users. For instance, the PIUMA project (Personalized Interactive Urban Maps for Autism), focused on personalized support to people within autism spectrum disorder, employs a holistic user representation to capture different aspects of cognition, affects and habits, stressing the exploitation of data from the real world to build a broad representation of the user. The main goal is to provide support instructions to autism-affected users according to their preferences and interests and consider their current level of stress and anxiety in specific locations. The model is structured on cognitive status and skills, spatial activities and habits, likes and interests and aversions. This representation is used to recommend points of interest according to the current physical context, personalized on the basis of the user's preferences, habits and current emotional status [68].

A different application of user modeling is presented by Biswas et al. [15] in their simulator devoted to reflecting problems faced by older and disabled users while they use a computer, a television or similar electronic devices. The simulator embodies both the internal state of an application and its user's perceptual, cognitive and motor processes. Its purpose is to help interface designers understand, visualize and measure the effect of the impairment on the interaction with an interface.

At the same time, personalization has also been used in other fields related to disability, such as healthcare. Health-oriented user models are very descriptive and accurate in providing details about the diverse disabilities, their combinations and their practical effects [82]. Information systems devoted to generating personalized instructions for medical personnel and informing patients with disabilities about their condition require detailed user models that can explain the peculiarities of the many existing

---

2 AVANTI European project (1995–1998) "Adaptive and adaptable interactions for multimedia telecommunications applications." https://cordis.europa.eu/result/rcn/21761_en.html (Accessed: February 1, 2023).

disabilities. Identifying and modeling all the impairments of each patient with disability to personalize health service operations is a challenging task because patients with disability can be affected by numerous different and unrelated conditions that are not taken into account by generic disability stereotypes [21].

In this sense, the International classification of functioning, disability and health [82] is a source for several user models in the accessibility field. This is a World Health Organization (WHO) international standard focused specifically on disabilities. The ICF is organized into two parts: the first one, devoted to functioning and disability, is structured in two areas: body functions and structures and activities and participation. The second part covers contextual factors, structured in environmental factors and personal factors. Despite its evident value, the 1400 categories contained in the ICF may be excessive for user modeling applied to user interface personalization. Nevertheless, this model has influenced several accessibility-oriented user interface personalization projects because it is instrumental as a source of relations between disabilities and restrictions for activities and participation related to environmental and personal factors.

8.3.2 Adaptation techniques and resources

A crucial point is how inaccessible interface elements can be modified to suit each user better. To do this, *adaptation techniques* are frequently applied. Adaptation techniques are models or templates that describe how to convert specific non-accessible features into accessible ones. They often come from reliable guidelines proposed by experts in each type of disability. Adaptation techniques are especially useful when they can be specified as code snippets that automated user interface adapters can use. Typically, when a specific accessibility barrier is found, the adapter looks in its repository for a suitable adaptation technique and inserts it [76].

Adaptation techniques can be integrated into the user interface as annotations. For instance, the WAI-Adapt Task Force of the Accessible Platform Architectures Working Group, belonging to the WAI[3] has released various draft documents on their work in progress on personalization to improve web accessibility for people with disabilities. A recent document[4] proposes various module specifications to allow authors to selectively add semantic information about content to enable content and interface personalization for individual users. This draft provides a collection of new attributes and values, with a list of fixed tokens (taxonomies) that content authors can utilize to add additional semantic information that personalization tools can later use.

---

3 The Web Accessibility Initiative, WAI, https://www.w3.org/WAI/ is part of the World Wide Web Consortium, W3C, https://www.w3.org/Consortium/ (Accessed: February 1, 2023).

4 Group Draft Note 03 January 2023. https://www.w3.org/TR/adapt/ (Accessed: February 1, 2023).

8.3.3 Automatic generation of personalized interfaces

Among the various applications and tools developed to automatically personalize the human interface for people with disabilities,[5] the Egoki system can be taken as a representative of the "classical" personalization approach.

Egoki is an automatic generator of accessible user interfaces designed to allow people with disabilities to access ubiquitous supportive services. Egoki follows a model-based approach to select appropriate interaction resources and modalities depending on users' capabilities. It uses three modules: *knowledge base, resource selector* and *adaptation engine*. The knowledge base, mainly supported by the Egonto ontology, stores, updates and maintains the models regarding user abilities, access to device features and interface adaptations. Automated generation of user-tailored interfaces is based on transforming a logical specification of the user interface described in UIML into a final functional user interface using the information specified in the models [33].

On the other hand, the Supple system takes a very distinctive approach to personalization [32]. Supple automatically generates interfaces for people with motor impairments adapted to their devices, tasks, preferences, and abilities. To this end, the authors formally defined the interface generation as an optimization problem and demonstrated that, despite a large solution space, the problem is computationally feasible for a particular class of cost functions. Several different design criteria can be expressed in the cost function, allowing different kinds of personalization. This approach enables extensive user- and system-initiated runtime adaptations to the interfaces once they have been generated. Supple relies on an *interface specification,* an *explicit device model* and a *usage model* for the automatic user interface generation system. The last of these is represented in user traces corresponding to actual or anticipated usage. They provide interaction frequencies for primitive widgets and frequencies of transitions between different interface elements.

8.3.4 Control of the adaptation by the user

Adaptations can cause usability problems, including disorientation and a feeling of losing control. To tackle this problem, the MyUI[6] system contains different adaptation patterns or techniques developed to increase the transparency and controllability of runtime adaptations [64]. These patterns help users to optimize the subjective utility of the system's adaptation behavior. A design pattern repository created for MyUI includes different types of techniques that serve distinct functions in the adaptation process. There

---

5 Firmenich et al. [29] present a comprehensive description and discussion of methods and tools applied to adapt user interfaces to make them more accessible.

6 MyUI European project (2010–2012) "Mainstreaming Accessibility through Synergistic User Modelling and Adaptability." https://cordis.europa.eu/project/id/248606 Accessed February 2023.

are patterns for creating and updating a user interface profile, which includes global variables to define general settings throughout the entire user interface (e. g., font size). Other adaptation techniques provide alternative user interface components and elements for current interaction situations. Finally, adaptation dialogue patterns describe the transition from one instance of the user interface to another. Four adaptation patterns to provide the user control over the adaptation are available: *Automatic Adaptation without Adaptation Dialogue* (the baseline condition), *Automatic Adaptation with Implicit Confirmation, Explicit Confirmation before Adaptation* and *Explicit Confirmation after Adaptation* [63].

8.3.5 Use of ontologies for user modeling

Most current personalization systems for people with disabilities use ontologies to maintain their user models,[7] which are more or less based on the structure and content of the WHO's International Classification of Functioning, Disability and Health (ICF) [82].

For instance, the ACCESSIBLE project[8] created an ontology, which was an extension of two previous ones developed for mobility-impaired users in the ASK-IT project, and for older adults in the OASIS[9] project. The ACCESSIBLE ontology included characteristics of users with disabilities, devices, applications and other aspects to be considered to develop personalized applications. In addition, it contained accessibility guidelines as checkpoints. It also included rules for semantic verification describing the requirements and constraints of users with disabilities, associating them with the accessibility checkpoints. ACCESSIBLE had an engine that answered basic rules coded in SWRL (a Semantic Web Rule Language Combining OWL and RuleML). The form of the rules was: *"For user X, interacting on device Z, is application Y accessible?"*

On the other hand, the AEGIS project[10] developed the AEGIS ontology to perform the mapping between accessibility concepts and their application in accessibility scenarios. This ontology shared the definition of personal aspects with the ACCESSIBLE ontology. The AEGIS ontology aimed at unambiguously defining accessibility domains, as well as the possible semantic interactions between them. To this end, conceptual information about (i) the characteristics of users with disabilities, functional limitations and impairments, (ii) technical characteristics of I/O devices, (iii) general and functional character-

---

7 Sosnovsky and Dicheva (2010) [72] present a broad review of the use of ontological technologies for user modeling in combination with the semantic web.

8 ACCESSIBLE European Project (2008–2010) "Applications Design and Development." https://cordis.europa.eu/project/id/224145 (Accessed: February 1, 2023).

9 OASIS European project (2008–2011) "Open architecture for Accessible Services Integration and Standardisation." https://cordis.europa.eu/project/id/215754 (Accessed: February 1, 2023).

10 AEGIS European project (2008–2012) "Open Accessibility Everywhere: Groundwork, Infrastructure, Standards." https://cordis.europa.eu/project/id/224348 (Accessed: February 1, 2023).

istics of web, desktop and mobile applications, and (iv) other assistive technology was formalized. The AEGIS ontology was provided with a Wikipedia-like interface to allow access to nonontological users [51].

More recently, the Egoki system (see Section 8.3.3) uses an ontology called Egonto to select appropriate accessible resources for each user, mobile device and service [33]. Egonto stores, updates and maintains the following models: *User Model* (including cognitive, physical, sensory and affective abilities); *Device model* (hardware and software components); *Adaptation Model* (including content, navigation, and presentation adaptations); *Reasoning Rules* (for initial profiling, detailed adaptation, multiple impairments); *User Interface Model* (UIML description of the UI and functionality of the ubiquitous services). In addition, Egonto can learn: when a specific user requires a missing profile or adaptation, Egonto includes new rules covering a profile with these characteristics.

Other user-modeling tools have advanced toward frameworks that are not focused on a particular application-specific context to be more inclusive than application-oriented solutions. For instance, the Global Public Inclusive Infrastructure[11] has proposed an ontological framework for addressing universal accessibility in the domain of user interaction with Information and Communication Technologies (ICT). This framework builds its knowledge by reflecting the linkage between user characteristics, interaction requirements (including assistive technologies), personal needs and preferences, and the context of the use of ICT [52].

8.3.6 Learning ontologies

Mechanisms to populate user models are very diverse and depend on the application. When ontologies are used to maintain the user model, automatic and semi-automatic methods exist for ontology acquisition from structured, semistructured and unstructured sources [72]. In particular, the outcomes from Data Mining processes can be used to learn ontologies. In this case, methods range from the manual introduction of the types or stereotypes obtained to the application of reasoning methods provided by the ontological framework to create new items in the ontology or to connect existing ones. In addition, other sources can be used. For instance, in the Semantic Matching Framework Project, the population of the model exploited crowdsourcing mechanisms to enrich the representation, allowing people to provide ratings, comments and reviews about places [68].

8.3.7 Sharing user models

An essential challenge in current user modeling development is the fragmentation of user model definitions. New definitions of user models for disability are often produced

---

11 Global Public Inclusive Infrastructure (GPII). https://gpii.net/ (Accessed: February 1, 2023).

based on each research project's specific focus and objectives. As a result, reusing or sharing user models across different projects turns out to be complicated. Nevertheless, the advantages of reusing existing models compensate for the difficulties arising from the differences in research objectives and the diversity among user groups.

Different R&D fields would benefit from user model sharing. For instance, Ambient-Assisted Living (AAL) provides technological support for the daily life of people with disabilities, primarily based on ubiquitous computing. In-home support can be extended to public spaces, where ubiquitous accessible applications allow people with disabilities to access location-dependent services. The objective is to transfer existing knowledge about the users, their ordinary activities and their environment to be used in ubiquitous applications outside the home. However, sharing models between in-home and out-of-home supportive applications requires model interoperability [4].

Two main approaches to achieving syntactic and semantic interoperability can be outlined, *shared format* and *conversion*. The shared format approach requires a unified user profile that can be based on various standards or semantic web languages. The conversion approach uses algorithms to convert the syntax and semantics of user model data utilized in one system to be used in another system. A third approach is possible, combining the benefits of both approaches to allow flexibility in representing user models and to provide a emantic mapping of user data from one system to another. To ensure interoperability, embracing a standard, such as RDF,[12] allows the exchange of semantically rich data. Ontology definition languages (e. g., RDF, OWL) can achieve interoperability between models under both centralized and decentralized architectures [18, 19].

The semantic matching approach addresses the problem of semantic interoperability by transforming data structures into lightweight ontologies and establishing semantic correspondences between them. For example, the Semantic Matching Framework (SMF) handles daily routines at home for people with special needs. SMF uses ontologies to describe the semantics of the user model to represent devices (e. g., doors, windows, sensors, etc.). The adaptation of the environment to people with special needs is based on the detection of disability-related situations that limit the capabilities of users, and it provides adapted processes to personalize the provision of services [44].

The Virtual User Modelling and Simulation Standardisation (VUMS) cluster of European projects[13] proposed an interoperable user model able to describe both nondisabled people and people with various kinds of disabilities. The unified user model is used by all the participant projects and aims to be the basis of a new user model standard based

---

12 Resource Description Framework (RDF) is a Semantic Web Standard. https://www.w3.org/RDF/ (Accessed: February 1, 2023).

13 The European VUMS Cluster was a joint initiative of the European Commission and the research projects VERITAS, GUIDE, VICON and MyUI with the objective of aligning user development research in the projects and to foster common standardization activities.

on the VUMS exchange format. As a first step toward the standardization of user models, the VUMS cluster defined a Glossary of Terms supporting a common language and the VUMS user model. A VUMS exchange format was defined to store user characteristics in a machine-readable form. This format contains a superset of user variables allowing any user model expressed in any project-specific format to be transformed into a model, which follows the VUMS exchange format. To this end, a set of converters able to transform a user profile following the VUMS exchange format into specific user models and vice versa would be developed [45].

8.4 Data collection and analysis for user modeling

User modeling implies the definition of *observable* parameters that are *relevant* for the interaction. The current values of these parameters must be collected to model each user.[14] Static models hold fixed user data, while dynamic models can update the user's profile with data collected during the interaction.

Usually, there is a phase prior to the personalization process in which it is necessary to collect preliminary data from the users. This allows for establishing an initial user model or assigning the user a previously designed stereotype. Users are sometimes asked to answer questionnaires (which can be time consuming) or adjust system parameters (which can require advanced knowledge or experience). People with disabilities are often motivated to enter this phase only if they expect long-term use, but not if the intended access is sporadic (as is the case with access to most eGovernment services). To lessen this nuisance, some of these data may also be collected implicitly from external sources (databases, previous interactions, social networks, etc.), which is less intrusive to users with disabilities than explicit data collection, although it may have an impact on the privacy of users.

Dynamic modeling systems include an additional phase in which *implicit data acquisition* methods are applied to update user parameters at the time of use. This acquisition technique is especially convenient for certain people with disabilities who experience significant changes in their performance during the interaction process (due to fatigue, motivation, learning, etc.). Several systems use machine learning for this because it is an appropriate technique for acquiring dynamic models.

New knowledge derived from data directly collected from the user or indirectly acquired from the interaction process may contain errors or contradictions. Tools for reasoning and making inferences concerning the data collected, e. g., by means of inference rules, may contribute to enhancing the coherence of the model.

---

14 According to Chin [20], the most challenging aspect of user modeling is the acquisition of the models: after an initial model is built, the acquisition process often continues throughout the life of the modeling system, making the acquisition of models a type of machine learning.

Therefore, when users have disabilities, it is useful to collect information automatically while they are using the interface (browsing, making cursor movements, scrolling or targeting, etc.). In addition to using these data to update the model, it can also be used to accurately assign specific stereotypes based on similarities to previously modeled users.

8.4.1 Tools for remote and local data collection

Direct observation of the users in the laboratory provides valuable information about how each participant uses the system. Still, according to Webb et al. [81], substantial labeled data sets are necessary to apply machine learning for user modeling. However, it can be challenging to recruit the appropriate number of participants (due to the lack of users with suitable characteristics, scheduling difficulties, etc.) to obtain such a quantity of information. Though, remote user testing can provide vast amounts of data with less effort than direct collection.

Remote data collection-based methods are frequently used for user modeling, even though they are not well accepted for formal accessibility or usability evaluations because of the lack of control in the experimental sessions, the impossibility of direct observation of the users, etc. Nevertheless, their evident advantages have increased their use for informal evaluations.

Among these advantages, remote data collection allows experimentation "in the wild" with a broader range of participants. Unobtrusive data collection can take place while the users perform the evaluated tasks at home, using their own equipment, whenever they want. These advantages are even more convenient when people with disabilities are part of the study. Remote data collection saves them from having to travel to a specific testing site. In addition, they can use their usual equipment and applications. We cannot forget that the assistive technology (hardware and software) used by several users with disabilities is tuned and adapted to their specific needs. It is not easy to replicate all these facilities in the laboratory.

Even though remotely collected data can provide valuable knowledge, no reliable information can be obtained about the cognitive processes followed by users to perform specific actions or how users utilize their assistive technology unless they are explicitly asked.

As shown in the following examples, remote data logging has been widely applied to collect data about screen cursor movements to detect user restrictions. Claypool et al. [22] used remote observation of a set of events to learn about the users' interests on a page. At the same time, other authors [31, 38, 39] collected various user characteristics, such as users' dexterity, from the movements they performed with the on-screen cursor. MacKenzie et al. [57] analyzed cursor trajectories on pointing and clicking tasks and classified them into seven accuracy measurements: target reentry, task axis crossing, movement direction change, orthogonal changes, movement variability, movement error and movement offset, which served to determine differences among devices in precision pointing tasks. While Keates et al. [46] extended these categories with six new cursor characteristics to capture a variety of features of cursor movement performed by motor-impaired users. Hwang et al. [39] discovered that several measurements from the submovement structure of cursor trajectories can help to identify difficulties found by people with motor impairments. Perez et al. [67] studied the benefits of two types of cursor adaptation for assisting web navigation in a longitudinal experiment with eight participants with motor impairments over several weeks. Seven metrics for cursor path evaluation were calculated from the collected data: movement time, pointing time, clicking time, distance traveled, curvature index, number of pauses and target reentry. The results showed significant improvements over the original for both virtual cursors tested in six of the seven features studied. These measurements, among others, are used to characterize people with physical impairments in pointing and clicking tasks [83].

Concerning the apparatus used to gather data from web navigation, early tools [71] could only log data generated by servers.[15] Later technologies, such as JavaScript or Java Applets, enabled the monitoring and recording of events generated by the cursor or keyboard, among others,[16] providing more valuable information than server logs [27, 62]. These systems were first located on the server side, adding the required code to the web pages to gather the generated data. However, interaction data can only be obtained from the pages located on the server in which the tracking tools are deployed using server-side tools. On the other hand, proxy tools [11, 13] and client tools [22, 38, 77] allow data to be gathered from any existing page.

As far as user modeling is concerned, some of these tools were used to observe the behavior of people with disabilities [13, 38, 77]. Even if they were not strictly used to create or update models [77], they allowed accessibility barrier detection and interaction methods and adaptations' evaluation [76]. For example, Hurst et al. [38] used these data to classify users with respect to their input events. While Bigham et al. [13] applied these data to analyze the strategies used by blind people during web navigation. Gajos et al. [32] provided an interesting example of the application of data collection for user modeling. They created an ability model that elicits the user needs using a test composed of four tasks (pointing, dragging, list selecting and multiple clicking). Thus, with this system, each user's most adequate user interface configuration can be determined and stored in the model.

8.4.2 Data mining and machine learning for user modeling

The data collected through the systems described in the previous section can be automatically processed using machine learning techniques. The application of these tech-

---

15 Extended Log File Format (2018). https://www.w3.org/TR/WD-logfile (Accessed: February 1, 2023).
16 UI Events. https://www.w3.org/TR/uievents/ (Accessed: February 1, 2023).

niques to user modeling aims to find sets of users with common interaction characteristics by detecting similar behavior patterns or profiles. Machine learning techniques are mainly applied to interaction data that are collected while users are using the system. Ideally, this information should be collected in a noninvasive way, without disturbing the users. This makes server-side weblog collection the simplest source of in-use data applicable to the broadest range of users. By contrast, client-side data collection tools such as those described by [11, 77] capture low-level interaction unobtrusively but require explicit hardware or software installation on the user side. Therefore, they limit the data sample size that can be monitored in the modeling process. Gathering additional information, such as the interface's content or the platform's structure, is often helpful for the profiling process [6, 55]. In web environments specifically, natural language processing or information retrieval techniques allow information concerning the website's content to be extracted. In addition, part of the information structure can be extracted from the network of links contained in the accessed web pages.

Machine learning techniques can be used to build or enrich user models following different approaches [16]. Content-based filtering approaches use the history of each specific user to build a profile that describes their characteristics (e. g., needs and preferences). In this way, the resulting profiles, combined with the information about the web pages, can be used to obtain predefined personalization schemes for each user or to enrich other data structures, such as ontology-based models. This approach can only be applied when the data contain user identification information. If the user is not identified, user and session identification heuristics can be used in a collaborative filtering approach that enables the estimation of the needs and preferences of a user based on the experience acquired from other users with similar characteristics.

The treatment of this information requires a complete data mining process: data acquisition, data preprocessing, selecting the most adequate machine learning techniques, and application of these techniques to obtain the user profiles [30, 61]. Finally, this methodology requires the validation of the achieved results and some feedback that allows the process to be enhanced and repeated when required.

Machine learning algorithms cannot handle raw data in their original format. They require removing nonuseful information, generating aggregate and derived features, etc. Weblog analytic tools, such as Piwik (renamed Matomo[17]) [24], can be used to generate preprocessed data with a higher semantic level, which is directly usable by machine learning algorithms. This is only possible if the platform was previously designed to include the collection of all the types of required data, which is not a common practice.

There are two main groups of machine learning algorithms: supervised and unsupervised learning algorithms. *Supervised learning* (also known as classification) [25] is the task of inferring a mapping function from labeled training data allowing the identification of new unlabeled data. These techniques can be applied in user modeling in

---

17 Matomo. https://matomo.org/ (Accessed: February 1, 2023).

controlled contexts where explicit user information is known. Input data are labeled as belonging to different types of users in the database used to build the supervised model. Models built by means of supervised techniques can distinguish the diverse existing profiles. *Unsupervised learning* techniques are designed to work with unlabeled data. Clustering is an unsupervised pattern classification method that partitions the input space into groups or clusters [42]. Its goal is to perform a partition where objects within a cluster are similar and objects in different clusters are dissimilar. Therefore, the purpose of clustering would be to identify natural structures among the users of a system.

The following sections include examples of interaction data modeling in the context of users with disabilities working with client-side data and server-side data.

8.4.2.1 Using client-side interaction data

When machine learning techniques are applied to user interaction data, selecting features extracted from the interaction is critical. Depending on the extracted features, machine learning algorithms will be able to solve the problem or not. Almanji et al. [5] present a revision of features extracted using pointing devices from client-side interaction data of users with upper limb impairments due to cerebral palsy. They propose a model that measures the influence of each user's Manual Ability Classification System (MACS) level and the characteristics of the analyzed features. Among the analyzed features, time for movement, acceleration–deceleration cycles and average speed are the most significant.

Some systems automatically detect cursor-pointing performance to learn how to deploy adaptations at the correct time without prior knowledge of the participant's ability. They use client-side interaction data to build several systems to (i) discriminate pointing behaviors of individuals without problems from individuals with motor impairments, (ii) discriminate pointing behaviors of young people from people with Parkinson's disease or older adults and (iii) detect the need for adaptations (such as "Steady Click") designed to minimize pointer slips during a click. All these systems are built over labeled databases, including features related to the click action, the movement, pauses and task-specific features. They use wrapper methods to select the features and C4.5 classifiers [38].

WELFIT is a remote evaluation tool for identifying web usage patterns through client-side interaction data (event streams). It provides insights into differences in the composition of event streams generated by people with and without disabilities. This tool uses the Sequence Alignment Method (SAM) for measuring the distances between event streams and uses a previously proposed heuristic to "point out" usage incidents. It labels the groups built in the clustering procedure as AT (users using assistive technologies), or non-AT, according to the corresponding majority. While trying to identify web usage patterns within the discovered groups, the authors found significant differences in the distribution of several features between AT and non-AT users [70].

Supervised techniques can be used to model predefined types of users. They are focused on identifying one of the key interaction characteristics: the (assistive) device being used to interact with the computer, which is critical in selecting the best automatic adaptations [65]. To this end, specifically defined rich web user interaction data are collected by the RemoTest platform in controlled experiments where the device used for interaction is known [77]. A thorough data mining process is carried out to build a system able to identify the device used: keyboard, trackball, joystick or mouse. The classifiers are built with different sets of features: the ones considered most important by the experts, a complete set of features and features selected automatically by wrapper systems. The analysis reveals that not all the features considered to be of the highest priority by accessibility experts are important from the classification point of view. In contrast, some of the features considered less important are, in fact, more relevant with regard to classification. The resulting system is able to efficiently determine the device used with an accuracy of 93 %. In a later work, Yera et al. [86] refined their previous work and adapted it to a two-step strategy to detect the problems the user may be having while interacting with the computer in mechanical tasks or tasks requiring both mechanical and cognitive effort. First, the system automatically detects the device used to interact with the web, and later identifies web navigation problems. Identification of the device being used and the issues being encountered will allow the most adequate adaptation to be deployed, and thus will make the navigation more accessible, ultimately contributing to reducing the digital divide for people with disabilities.

8.4.2.2 Using server-side interaction data

Arbelaitz et al. [7] provide an example of the application of machine learning techniques to server-side interaction data for determining user profiles. These authors model the interaction with Discapnet,[18] a website aimed mainly at visually disabled people. It is a noninvasive system that first uses clustering to group users with similar navigation patterns into the same segment and then extracts the characteristics corresponding to each group of users. The analysis of the extracted features leads to the identification of anomalous behaviors or groups, which are undergoing navigation difficulties. The system allows knowing if the interaction problem comes from the user, the characteristics of the website, the platform used or both. In the former case, systems personalized to this specific type of user are required to make their navigation activities easier. In the latter, the site should be redesigned or transcoded. Using this system in an experiment

---

18 Discapnet: el Portal de las Personas con Discapacidad (The Disability Portal). https://www.discapnet.es/ (Accessed: February 1, 2023).

involving navigation under supervision carried out with mainly disabled people, 82.6 % of users with disabilities were automatically flagged as having experienced problems. Compared with the original logs used to build the system, in which a more diverse range of people were accessing the system, only 33.5 % of the sessions revealed that problems were being experienced.

8.5 User interface personalization for specific applications

In this section, we present and discuss three challenging application areas where user interface personalization is applied with diverse results. The first one addresses the personalization of regularly used web user interfaces. In this case, a registration process may be required, enabling the interface to be personalized from the available information about the user. The second deals with the personalization of sporadically—and often anonymously—used web interfaces, such as those in eGovernment portals. In this case, personalization requires observation of the behavior of the user to match it with a previously built stereotype. The last one deals with an interface where the input from the user is insufficient to specify a task. Therefore, intelligent transformation of the commands, based on the user context and model, is required. In this case, the task is to control an assistive robot for augmented or alternative manipulation.

8.5.1 Transcoding for web accessibility personalization

Several organizations that promote web standards and accessibility legislation, among which the W3C Consortium[19] stands out, have campaigned for equal access to the internet for everyone. Nevertheless, numerous websites do not yet meet the required accessibility levels. In addition, even if the accessibility guidelines and standards are met, full accessibility is not guaranteed. Diverse factors, including people's ability to use assistive technology to access the web, can also influence the existence of accessibility barriers [79]. From the early days of web accessibility research, people have embraced the objective of automatically converting a nonaccessible page into an accessible one by modifying the code. This approach permits the modification of the presentation (e. g., changing colors, sizes, background) and also the addition of new content (e. g., widgets, JS code) to make the site more accessible.

Transcoding is a technique that aims to modify "on the fly" the code of a nonaccessible web page to convert it into an accessible one by adding, changing or tagging

---

19 Web Content Accessibility Guidelines (WCAG) 2.0. Web Accessibility Initiative of the W3C. http://www. w3.org/WAI/intro/wcag.php (Accessed: February 1, 2023).

its content [10]. Compared with CSS settings, transcoding allows more thorough adaptations, adding new code or altering the elements to augment the functionalities of a web page.

This technique has been used to improve the accessibility of web pages, providing more accessible variants of pages for any users that might need them. General transcoding methods that are independent of the specific website require sufficient information about the semantics of each element. The rise of the Semantic Web[20] and the possibility of semantically tagging the elements of web pages made general transcoding methods possible and opened the way to using transcoding as a personalization technique.

First transcoders were devoted to performing adaptations such as web page serialization, inserting missing "alt text" fields (alternative texts) to images, or content re-ordering[21] [35], the main objective of which was to make the navigation easier for low-vision or blind users.

However, to perform more thorough or wide-reaching adaptations, a transcoder needs to know the purpose that the designer gave to each element, such as which features are devoted to providing main content and which provide navigation menus. In addition, it is also essential to know the role of the element itself. For example, a DIV element is intended to be a container of elements, but by adding some JavaScript code, it can act as a button, link or even a text area. These different roles cannot be detected without annotations.

Therefore, annotations add the necessary semantic information, allowing a more accurate transformation of the content to express the "intention" of page elements. Moreover, annotations can provide better access to the web by offering alternative content, personalized presentation and navigation support. Only the website owner can insert annotations in the HTML code, although anyone can annotate a web page when annotations are externally stored.

Humans performing manual annotations are able to assign a role to each element accurately. However, manual annotation is time-consuming. For example, Asakawa et al. [9] use XPATH expressions to identify elements and assign annotations. In this case, the annotator has to annotate the entire website page by page. To ease the annotation task, automatic or semiautomatic tools are employed to help the annotators. For instance, Takagi et al. [75] propose a tool to insert annotations based on previously annotated web pages. In addition, most modern content management systems avoid repeating the same annotation for each page of the entire website. Alternatively, Bigham et al. [14] use crowdsourcing techniques to propose annotations.

---

20 Semantic Web. https://www.w3.org/standards/semanticweb/ (Accessed: February 1, 2023).

21 BBC Education Text to Speech Internet Enhancer (Betsie) is a script written for people using text to speech systems for web browsing used on the BBC website and on several other sites. http://betsie. sourceforge.net/ (Accessed: February 1, 2023).

Transcoding was successfully applied before the advent of the Semantic Web standards and their utilization. Heuristics were applied to this purpose to infer the role of page elements or the knowledge of the "templates" used in particular websites. Nevertheless, the appearance of the Semantic Web boosted its use for web access personalization.

Nowadays, advances in the Semantic Web allow transcoders and assistive technologies to perform adaptations more accurately. Screen readers such as NVDA or JAWS use the WAI-ARIA[22] annotation language to transform the visual content into speech. For instance, a tool presented by Valencia et al. [76] uses the WAI-ARIA annotations to transform the web automatically when the annotation is present without the intervention of an annotator. The tool also enables the WAI-ARIA annotations to be added to the web pages that lack the annotation.

Adaptations made for a specific type of user may negatively affect other types of users due to the diverse characteristics of people with disabilities. Some systems are targeted at only one user group, such as the ones proposed by Asakawa and Takagi [9] or Bigham et al. [14], which are devoted to blind and low-vision people. On the other hand, Gajos et al. [32] present a system for people with motor impairments, and Richards and Hanson [69] for older adults.

In a pioneering work, Lunn et al. [56] included the AxsJAX framework (developed by Google to facilitate the accessibility of dynamic content) to their SADIe system. AxsJAX can dynamically insert Accessible Rich Internet Applications (ARIA) statements into the content. The SADIe transcoder uses semantic annotations of a CSS to drive a transformation process to improve access to web pages for screen-reader blind users. These CSS annotations generate the AxsJAX code and insert it into web pages. Such an approach allows users to access static content using a consistent set of key presses in a manner akin to an online application.

Personalized transcoding systems devoted to a broader range of people require user profiling [59] or user modeling [32, 76] to decide which adaptations should be applied to a given user. In this way, personalization can be carried out by performing the transcoding actions relevant to each user's specific characteristics, considering personal data contained in the user model (an example can be seen in Figure 8.1).

8.5.2 Personalized universally accessible eGovernment

According to Layne and Lee [54], electronic government, or eGovernment, is the use of digital technology, especially web-based applications, to enhance access to—and the efficient delivery of—government information and services. Eurostat[23] stated that in 2021,

---

22 WAI-ARIA. https://www.w3.org/TR/wai-aria/ (Accessed: February 1, 2023).

23 Eurostat: Individuals using the internet for interaction with public authorities. Data set code: TIN00012. http://ec.europa.eu/eurostat/web/products-datasets/-/tin00012 (Accessed: February 1, 2023).

Figure 8.1: Left: an original nonaccessible web page. Right: the same page after applying adaptations for people with motor impairments using tablets. The layout, size of elements, space between links and color contrast were modified in the adapted page to make page sections more visible (split between the navigation menu, banner, main content and footer) to enable comfortable reading and easier target selection. Data mining applied to the logs obtained by the RemoTest tool was used for the transcoding personalization. Taken from [6].

58 % of the individuals in Europe used the internet for interacting with public authorities for tasks such as obtaining information from public websites and downloading or submitting official forms. This represents an increase of 9 % compared to 2017, when the COVID-19 context may have been a key factor. In this regard, a recent study suggests that the educational level and the frequency of buying goods over the internet are also determining factors in the use of eGovernment [85]. On the other hand, eGovernment development generates a rising demand for publicly accessible web services . One of its main benefits is that people can avoid face-to-face interaction with the administration insofar as public services are delivered to citizens at any time (during 24 hours, 7 days a week) and are provided in a personalized way (different languages, adaptations for users with disabilities, etc.) [34].

Web access to eGovernment services avoids the need to go to the administration facilities physically. In this way, it provides alternatives to people with disabilities who have difficulties navigating the physical environment, although it does require the ability to have free access to the internet. Therefore, eGovernment plans may be rendered useless if large segments of the target population, including persons with disabilities, are unable to access the system [26]. Thus, universal access is one of the main challenges of this area, together with privacy, confidentiality and citizen-focused government management [37].

eGovernment services must be accessible and personalized to be fully inclusive. Governmental services provided through the Internet have distinctive characteristics: they are sporadically used, and many of them do not require registration because they are solely devoted to providing information. Therefore, the design of accessible, personalized eGovernment interfaces presents two main difficulties. First, the characteristics of the users are not known in advance. Even if they have registration procedures, governmental portals do not usually require the disclosure of sensitive information (e. g., about disabilities or limitations), making it difficult to personalize the interface to a particular profile. Second, eGovernment users sporadically access electronic services; hence, the available usage information is limited or nonexistent. In any case, eGovernment users are more willing to provide personal information when they have previously performed a customization process [78].

User profiling for the personalization of governmental eServices that do not require registration can be carried out by (i) asking the user to fill in a form prior to the navigation, (ii) importing a user profile shared with other systems [19] or provided in a smart-card by the user themselves or (iii) mining the user interaction to search for navigation patterns that can relate the user to similar previous users displaying the same behavior (and probably exact accessibility needs).

Most approaches to adaptive interfaces for eGovernment use questionnaires and other sources, such as social networks, to obtain information about the preferences and interests of the users [12, 53]. However, questionnaires may be tedious for users, who may therefore try to avoid them. In addition, most social networks do not have enough public information about personal characteristics relevant to accessibility, or this information is unreliable when available. Nevertheless, some user profiling can be done using the information collected while the user is navigating the website. In this scenario, web usage mining techniques can be used for modeling eGovernment users by gathering their interaction data unobtrusively from web server logs [2]. Thus, these techniques avoid the use of personal data, implementing a user segmentation process based on the usage information where participants with similar navigation patterns are grouped together. Profiles extracted in this way provide relevant information about the navigation preferences and the user behavior that can be effective for different tasks. In the eGovernment context, web usage mining has been effective in modeling eServices, enabling the automatic prediction of successful and unsuccessful navigation behaviors based on the user's access patterns exhibited [84].

Although the type of data that is currently collected in most weblogs does not provide enough information to produce reliable and suitable user models, administrations should not lose sight of the vast possibilities that data mining techniques offer to improve accessibility to their electronic services. Even machine learning techniques applied to anonymous user logs (see Section 8.4.2) in *Common Log Format* (CLF) combined with content and structure information can lead to the development of user profiles from different viewpoints, which would provide an opportunity to model and adapt governmental eServices. In this regard, maintaining the navigation logs of eGovernment portals, enabling their exploitation for their usage analysis and undertaking a commitment to take the findings into account is a reasonably cheap and straightforward process when weighed against the sizable benefits that could be obtained.

8.5.3 Personalization of assistive human–robot interaction

Previous examples showed cases of personalization of ordinary human–computer interfaces for accessible web access. Now we will analyze a different personalization environment: human–robot interaction for people with severe physical disabilities. This field requires personalizing not only the user interface (especially the dialogue), but also the behavior of the robot.

From the diverse types of assistive robots, we will focus on a particular case: articulated arms used by people with severe mobility restrictions for *augmented and alternative manipulation*. This is quite a recent research field, favored by the availability of collaborative robots that allow safe working areas to be shared with humans.

Human–robot interfaces provided for industrial articulated arms cannot be used by people with severe motor restrictions. Industrial robots are controlled using special keyboards and joysticks to "teach" them specific movements and other actions. The use of joysticks for commanding robotic actions is beyond the capabilities of most people with severe motor restrictions, as articulated arms possess many degrees of freedom (usually around six), allowing complex spatial movements. Matching the actions of a joystick to the movements of an articulated arm can be difficult and may produce counterintuitive interactions.

Textual programming can still produce low-level commands (such as *move_to, open_gripper, close_gripper*, etc.). Nevertheless, this is not a choice in a domestic environment. For example, it is unlikely that users with motor disabilities would be able to provide commands with precise spatial coordinates.

Therefore, two main issues arise when users with severe physical disabilities attempt to control an articulated arm. The first one is the personalization of the user interface (taking into account that the set of possible interaction modalities is very much reduced; in most cases pointing devices, joysticks, large keyboards and voice commands are excluded). The second is bridging the conceptual gap considering the difference between the user's and robot's goals and procedures.

8.5.3.1 Multimodal interaction

Multimodal interfaces for human–robot interaction (based on diverse combinations of voice, text and gestures) are becoming increasingly popular [66]. For instance, robot control through gesture-based computer vision interfaces [80] may be an alternative when the user can produce several differentiated voluntary gestures. Still, they are hardly accessible to many people with severe movement restrictions.

When the user commands are verbal or textual orders, gestures or signs, they may be incomplete or ambiguous. For instance, saying "give me that book" or pointing to an object by any means (such as eye gaze) requires disambiguation to be interpreted. For this purpose, the robot can consider the user and context model where information about user preferences, restrictions, activities, timetables, etc., are available. In addition, users with severe motor disabilities use assistive technology to access computers, which significantly conditions the mode of interaction.

Finding new means for controlling and interacting with this type of robot is one of the main focus areas of robotics nowadays. For instance, physiological data, such as electromyographic signals [8], or brain–machine interfaces would allow for the design of human–robot interfaces for simple instructions.

8.5.3.2 Personalization and shared control

To simplify the interaction, two research lines are explored: shared control and personalization of the human–robot interface. These lines have in common the need for user models: according to Mason and Lopes [58], higher levels of autonomy required by shared control can be achieved through user adaptation. In the case of assistive robotics, the adaptation can take place at the interface level, in the input and output channels, in dialog management or in the selection of available services [43], while models are usually based on user preferences, user needs and user context.

Assistive robots partially share the activity area with the user, breaking the safety rules set out for industrial installations. Domestic robots must consider the users' proximity and interact with them without causing any damage or harm. To this end, it is desirable that, in addition to following commands from the user, the robot makes autonomous decisions to ensure the safety and performance of the commands. Ideally, an assistive robot adapts to the user's needs and behavior automatically and decides when and how to do so autonomously while providing the user with an easy means to override the decision of the robot directly [41] using the shared control or joint initiative approach [40, 58, 87]. Designing a robot that shares control with a human is more complex than creating a completely autonomous robot because it requires an interaction meta-level at which each party knows the characteristics, limitations and abilities of the other party and takes over control only when necessary.

Shared control robots are adaptable *per se*. They require user models that contain relevant contextual parameters and store past interactions in addition to the user needs and characteristics. The robot should be able to produce assumptions about the user's intentions and to behave in consequence, comparing its knowledge about user habits and likes with the current situation.

Mason and Lopes [58] present how a proactive robot applying the shared control paradigm provides a basis for adaptation through repeated interactions that are rewarded by the user. The robot can anticipate the user's needs by selecting appropriate tasks according to a user profile and a context model, and then plan the execution of these tasks without an explicit user request. Since this robot uses verbal instructions, it does not solve the communication issue. Nevertheless, when the conceptual gap between the two agents (user and robot) is bridged, substituting voice commands with inputs from some assistive technology is more feasible.

8.6 Impact of interface personalization on the privacy of users with disabilities

All users employing personalized services are exposed to risks relating to personal harassment and privacy attacks, including identity theft [3]. While most users can cope with these attacks, specific populations are more vulnerable to them, even reaching situations of helplessness. This is the case for some users with disabilities when using digital services. In this sense, systems collecting data about users for personalization purposes can be considered as being in the category of risky applications.

User modeling for user-adapted interaction has frequently raised concerns about its possible impact on privacy and personal security [50]. These concerns are based on the fact that part of the data collected in user models can be sensitive and might be used to the user's detriment. The danger of misuse increases when models include information about sensory, physical, or cognitive disabilities. For this reason, most people with disabilities are reluctant to provide information about their restrictions.

Privacy issues arise if users access the system by revealing their identity rather than remaining anonymous. Data stored in personalized systems include usage records, data supplied by users, and assumptions inferred from users' data and usage behavior. If users provide information on disabilities and interests, these data are not only person-related but possibly even sensitive [28].

According to Fink et al. [28], confidentiality issues can be found in data transmission and storing (personal information about users is usually contained in the user model server). Encryption and authentication methods proved adequate for protecting data from being stolen. Another issue is the service provider's misuse of data [3]. Most protective applications that collect data about their users state that these data are only used for the personalization of the application and would never be disclosed, sold or lent to any other organizations. However, in general, nondisclosure statements are vague, and some companies are not particularly reluctant to break them.

Therefore, privacy protection requires measures to meet legal regulations regarding systems that process personal information and to increase user acceptance by making the system transparent. In any case, the fact that user data are gathered and processed should be pointed out to the users at the beginning of each session [28]. For instance, in the AVANTI project, the system offered the following options to accommodate the user's privacy expectations:
- If possible, users should be given the option of accessing the system anonymously (e. g., with a pseudonym) if they do not want to reveal their identities.

- In an (optional) initial dialog, the user should be able to choose between no user modeling, short-term user modeling (e. g., for the current session only) and long-term modeling using persistent user models that are augmented with information from the current session.
- At the end of each session, the user should be asked if their model is to be deleted or stored for subsequent sessions.

Sharing user data among diverse applications is even more critical. Data sharing might mean almost public disclosure of personal data, making it barely acceptable if there is no transparent and effective permission policy. Smartcards have been proposed as a safer way to share user models. With these, users can provide their personal data only to the applications they have selected. This approach reduces public exposure of data but again relies on the integrity of the applications.

Aïmeur and Tremblay [3] mention Personal Management Information systems (PMIs) as an active area of research for privacy protection. These would be programs running on personal computers acting as gateways interacting with online content providers. They may use diverse privacy protection techniques such as pseudonyms, user anonymization, cryptography and user data perturbation algorithms. In principle, PMIs would give end users control over their data usage. However, a more detailed description of their functionality would be required to judge the validity of this proposal.

A different approach comes from the data mining field. Unsupervised learning can create user stereotypes from the data collected from anonymous interactions. These models contain data about user stereotypes rather than personal data, thereby ensuring privacy protection. In addition, the use of stereotypes allows the personalization to focus on the users' abilities (which may be shared across disabilities) more than on users' restrictions.

In any case, designers and developers must be aware of the national and international privacy protection regulations to produce safe, personalized interaction systems, especially for the most vulnerable users.

8.7 Conclusions

User interface personalization for people with disabilities has shown a vital capacity to support digital accessibility, and hence to drive social integration and participation. Nevertheless, most efforts in this field focus on research projects rather than commercial products. Interface personalization is currently a well-developed area that can be applied to different domains with sufficiently high levels of security. For example, it can be applied to eGovernment services to ensure equal opportunities for all users. Therefore, academia should increase its efforts to produce practical personalization methods that practitioners can adopt. On the other hand, industry and public administrations should study the possibility of adopting interface personalization to guarantee the accessibility of their applications and services.

Ontologies are currently the favored technology for supporting user models, mainly because they permit the use of reasoning methods in addition to their flexibility and expandability. Ontologies containing models of users with disabilities have proliferated in several diverse research actions. Although research requires diversity and experimentation, there is a consensus concerning the need for user model sharing and reusing. Advances in this line require the definition and adoption of standards for the lexical level and the development of tools for semantic translation. Nevertheless, the most critical barrier to achieving progress in this line is the problem of ensuring user control over their own data when these are shared.

User data collection is vital to populate user models. Nowadays, enormous quantities of data can be mined and processed to extract information valid for user models. Web mining is particularly promising in this sense. Valuable types of data are available, but they need to be collected in the logs of most web server applications. Data mining experts must agree with web server administrators to log specific data helpful in characterizing the interaction.

Data about the users collected by user modeling systems, required for most personalization methods, may impact user privacy. This may be a barrier to accepting personalized interaction systems in the minds of possible users. Therefore, to enhance their accessibility for users, practical personalized systems must guarantee their commitment to user privacy, at least in the following directions: information collection must be limited to data strictly necessary for the application, and user data must be safely kept, anonymized when possible and removed when they are not required. In addition, users must be able to access their data and modify or remove them. They must also be warned about the use of data gathering methods when they are using a personalized system. Finally, users must be able to stop the personalization module without losing the right to use the service.

Bibliography

[1]   J. Abascal. Human-computer interaction in assistive technology: from "Patchwork" to "Universal Design". In: *IEEE Int. Conf. on Systems, Man and Cybernetics 2002*, volume 3. IEEE, 2002, p. 6.

[2]   J. Abascal, O. Arbelaitz, M. Arrue, A. Lojo, J. Muguerza, J. E. Pérez, I. Perona, and X. Valencia. Enhancing Web Accessibility through User Modelling and Adaption Techniques. In: *Assistive Technology: From Research to Practice: AAATE 2013*, volume 33, 2013, pp. 427–432.

[3]   E. Aïmeur, and A. Tremblay. Me, Myself and I are Looking for a Balance between Personalization and Privacy. In: *UMAP'18, Adjunct Publication of the 26th Conference*. ACM, 2018, pp. 115–119.

[4]   A. Aizpurua, I. Cearreta, B. Gamecho, R. Miñón, N. Garay-Vitoria, L. Gardeazabal, and J. Abascal. Extending In-Home User and Context Models to Provide Ubiquitous Adaptive Support Outside the Home. In: Martín et al., editors. *User Modeling and Adaptation for Daily Routines: Providing Assistance to People with Special Needs*. London: Springer-Verlag, 2013, pp. 25–59.

[5]   A. Almanji, T. C. Davies, and N. S. Stott. Using cursor measures to investigate the effects of impairment severity on cursor control for youths with cerebral palsy. *International Journal of Human-Computer Studies* 72(3) (2014) 349–357.

[6]   O. Arbelaitz, I. Gurrutxaga, A. Lojo, J. Muguerza, J. M. Pérez, and I. Perona. Web usage and content mining to extract knowledge for modelling the users of the Bidasoa Turismo website and to adapt it. *Expert Systems with Applications* 40(18) (2013) 7478–7491.

[7]   O. Arbelaitz, A. Lojo, J. Muguerza, and I. Perona. Web mining for navigation problem detection and diagnosis in Discapnet: a website aimed at disabled people. *JASIST* 67(8) (2016) 1916–1927.

[8]   P. K. Artemiadis and K. J. Kyriakopoulos. EMG-Based Control of a Robot Arm Using Low-Dimensional Embeddings. *IEEE Transactions on Robotica* 26(2) (2010) 393–398.

[9]   C. Asakawa and H. Takagi. Annotation-based transcoding for nonvisual web access. In: *Procs. of the fourth Int. ACM Conf. on Assistive technologies*, 2000, pp. 172–179.

[10] C. Asakawa and H. Takagi. Transcoding. In: S. Harper and Y. Yesilada, editors. *Web Accessibility*. London: Springer-Verlag, 2008, pp. 231–260.

[11] R. Atterer, M. Wnuk, and A. Schmidt. Knowing the user's every move: user activity tracking for website usability evaluation and implicit interaction. In: *Procs. of the 15th Int. Conf. on World Wide Web*, 2006, pp. 203–212.

[12] R. Ayachi, I. Boukhris, S. Mellouli, N. B. Amor, and Z. Elouedi. Proactive and reactive e-government services recommendation. *Universal Access in the Information Society* 15(4) (2016) 681–697.

[13] J. P. Bigham, A. C. Cavender, J. T. Brudvik, J. O. Wobbrock, and R. E. Ladner. WebInSitu: a comparative analysis of blind and sighted browsing behavior. In: *Procs. of the 9th Int. ACM SIGACCESS Conf. on Computers and Accessibility*, 2007, pp. 51–58.

[14] J. P. Bigham, R. S. Kaminsky, R. E. Ladner, O. M. Danielsson, and G. L. Hempton. WebInSight: making web images accessible. In: *Procs. of the 8th Int. ACM SIGACCESS Conf. on Computers and accessibility*, 2006, pp. 181–188.

[15] P. Biswas, P. Robinson, and P. Langdon. Designing Inclusive Interfaces Through User Modeling and Simulation. *International Journal of Human-Computer Interaction* 28(1) (2012) 1–33.

[16] P. Brusilovsky, A. Kobsa, and W. Nejdl. *The Adaptive Web: Methods and Strategies of Web Personalization*. Berlin, Heidelberg: Springer-Verlag, 2007.

[17] A. Bunt, G. Carenini, and C. Conati. Adaptive content presentation for the web. In: *The adaptive web*. Berlin, Heidelberg: Springer, 2007, pp. 409–432.

[18] F. Carmagnola. Handling Semantic Heterogeneity in Interoperable Distributed User Models. In: T. Kuflik, S. Berkovsky, F. Carmagnola, D. Heckmann, and A. Krüger, editors. *Advances in Ubiquitous User Modelling*. LNC, volume 5830. Berlin, Heidelberg: Springer, 2009, pp. 20–36.

[19] F. Carmagnola, F. Cena, and C. Gena. User model interoperability: a survey. *User Modeling and User-Adapted Interaction* 21(3) (2011) 285–331.

[20] D. N. Chin. Acquiring user models. *Artificial Intelligence Review* 7 (1993) 185–197.

[21] L. Chittaro, R. Ranon, L. De Marco, and A. Senerchia. User Modeling of Disabled Persons for Generating Instructions to Medical First Responders. In: G. J. Houben, G. McCalla, F. Pianesi, and M. Zancanaro, editors. *User Modeling, Adaptation, and Personalization. UMAP 2009*. LNCS, volume 5535. Berlin: Springer, 2009.

[22] M. Claypool, P. Le, M. Wased, and D. Brown. Implicit interest indicators. In: *Procs. of the 6th Int. Conf. on Intelligent user interfaces*, 2001, pp. 33–40.

[23] A. M. Cook and J. M. Polgar. *Assistive Technologies: Principles and Practice*. Elsevier Health Sciences, 2014.

[24] A. Cooper 2014. *Learning analytics interoperability-the big picture in brief*. Learning Analytics Community Exchange.

[25] P. Cunningham, M. Cord, and S. Delany. Supervised learning. In: *Machine Learning Techniques for Multimedia*. Berlin, Heidelberg: Springer, 2008, pp. 21–49.

[26] J. Esteves and R. C. Joseph. A comprehensive framework for the assessment of eGovernment projects. *Government Information Quarterly* 25 (2008) 118–132.

[27] M. Etgen and J. Cantor. What does getting WET (web event-logging tool) mean for web usability. In: *Procs. of Fifth Human Factors and the Web Conf.*, 1999.

[28] J. Fink, A. Kobsa, and J. Schreck. Personalized Hypermedia Information Provision through Adaptive and Adaptable System Features: User Modeling, Privacy and Security Issues. In: A. Mullery, M. Besson, M. Campolargo, R. Gobbi, and R. Reed, editors. *Intelligence in Services and Networks: Technology for Cooperative Competition*. LNCS, volume 1238. Berlin: Springer, 2005, pp. 459–467.

[29] S. Firmenich, A. Garrido, F. Paternò, and G. Rossi. User Interface Adaptation for Accessibility. In: Y. Yesilada and S. Harper, editors. *Web Accessibility. A foundation for Research*, 2nd edition. Human–Computer Interaction Series. London: Springer, 2019, pp. 547–568.

[30] E. Frank, M. A. Hall, and I. H. Witten. *The WEKA Workbench. Online Appendix for "Data Mining: Practical Machine Learning Tools and Techniques"*. Morgan Kaufmann, 2016.

[31] K. Z. Gajos, K. Reinecke, and C. Herrmann. Accurate measurements of pointing performance from in situ observations. In: *Procs. of the SIGCHI Conf. on Human Factors in Computing Systems*, 2012, pp. 3157–3166.

[32] K. Z. Gajos, D. S. Weld, and J. O. Wobbrock. Automatically generating personalized user interfaces with Supple. *Artificial Intelligence* 174(12) (2010) 910–950.

[33] B. Gamecho, R. Miñón, A. Aizpurua, I. Cearreta, M. Arrue, N. Garay-Vitoria, and J. Abascal. Automatic generation of tailored accessible user interfaces for ubiquitous services. *IEEE Transactions on Human-Machine Systems* 45(5) (2015) 612–623.

[34] R. Gonzalez, J. Gasco, and J. Llopis. e-Government success: some principles from a Spanish case study. *Industrial Management & Data Systems* 107 (2007) 845–861.

[35] S. Goose, M. Wynblatt, and H. Mollenhauer. 1-800-hypertext: browsing hypertext with a telephone. In: *Procs. of the ninth ACM conference on Hypertext and hypermedia: links, objects, time and space—structure in hypermedia systems: links, objects, time and space—structure in hypermedia systems*. ACM, 1998, pp. 287–288.

[36] A. Goy, L. Ardissono, and G. Petrone. Personalization in E-Commerce Applications. In: *The Adaptive Web*, volume 4321. Berlin, Heidelberg: Springer, 2007, pp. 485–520.

[37] D. Griffin, P. Trevorrow, and E. F. Halpin. *Developments in e-government: a critical analysis*. Ios Press, 2007, pp. 13.

[38] A. Hurst, S. E. Hudson, J. Mankoff, and S. Trewin. Automatically detecting pointing performance. In: *Procs. of the 13th international conference on Intelligent user interfaces (IUI '08)*. New York, NY, USA: ACM, 2008, pp. 11–19.

[39] F. Hwang, S. Keates, P. Langdon, and J. Clarkson. Mouse movements of motion-impaired users: a submovement analysis. In: *ACM SIGACCESS Accessibility and Computing*, volume 77–78, 2004, pp. 102–109.

[40] S. Iba, C. J. J. Paredis, and P. K. Khosla. Intention aware interactive multi-modal robot programming. In: *IEEE/RSJ International Conference on Intelligent Robots and Systems (IROS 2003)*, volume 3, 2003, pp. 3479–3484.

[41] T. Inamura, M. Inabe, and H. Inoue. User adaptation of human-robot interaction model based on Bayesian network and introspection of interaction experience. In: *Procs. Int. Conf. on Intelligent Robots and Systems*. IEEE, 2002.

[42] A. K. Jain and R. C. Dubes. *Algorithms for Clustering Data*. USA: Prentice-Hall, 1988.

[43] E. S. John, S. J. Rigo, and J. Barbosa. Assistive Robotics: Adaptive Multimodal Interaction Improving People with Communication Disorders. *International Federation of Automatic Control–Papers* 49(30) (2016) 175–180.

[44] R. Kadouche, B. Abdulrazak, S. Giroux, and M. Mokhtari. Disability centered approach in smart space management. *International Journal of Smart Home* 3(2) (2009) 13–26.

[45] N. Kaklanis, P. Biswas, Y. Mohamad, M. F. Gonzalez, M. Peissner, P. Langdon, D. Tzovaras, and C. Jung. Towards standardisation of user models for simulation and adaptation purposes. In: *Universal Access in the Information Society*. Berlin: Springer-Verlag, 2016, pp. 21–48.

[46] S. Keates, F. Hwang, P. Langdon, P. J. Clarkson, and P. Robinson. Cursor measures for motion-impaired computer users. In: *Procs. of the fifth Int. ACM Conf. on Assistive technologies*, 2002, pp. 135–142.

[47] E. Knutov, P. De Bra, and M. Pechenizkiy. AH 12 years later: a comprehensive survey of adaptive hypermedia methods and techniques. *New Review of Hypermedia and Multimedia* 15(1) (2009) 5–38.

[48] A. Kobsa. User Modeling: Recent Work, Prospects and Hazards. In: M. Schneider-Hufsmidt, T. Küme, and U. Malinowski, editors. *Adaptive User Interfaces: Principles and Practise*. Amsterdam: Elsevier Science, North Holland, 1993.

[49] A. Kobsa. Generic user modeling systems. *User Modeling and User-Adapted Interaction* 11(1–2) (2001) 49–63.

[50] A. Kobsa. Privacy-Enhanced Web Personalization. In: *The Adaptive Web*. Springer-Verlag, 2007, pp. 628–670.

[51] P. Korn, E. Bekiaris, and M. Gemou. Towards Open Access Accessibility Everywhere: The ÆGIS Concept. In: C. Stephanidis, editor. *Universal Access in Human-Computer Interaction. Addressing Diversity*. LNCS, volume 5614. Springer, Berlin, 2009, pp. 535–543.

[52] V. Koutkias, N. Kaklanis, K. Votis, D. Tzovaras, and N. Maglaveras. An integrated semantic framework supporting universal accessibility to ICT. *Universal Access in the Information Society* 15(1) (2016) 49–62.

[53] V. Krishnaraju, S. K. Mathew, and V. Sugumaran. Web personalization for user acceptance of technology: An empirical investigation of E-government services. *Information Systems Frontiers* 18(3) (2016) 579–595.

[54] K. Layne and J. Lee. Developing fully functional E-government: A four stage model. *Government Information Quarterly* 18 (2001) 122–136.

[55] B. Liu. *Web Data Mining: Exploring Hyperlinks, Contents, and Usage Data (Data-Centric Systems and Applications)*. Secaucus, NJ, USA: Springer-Verlag. New York, Inc., 2006.

[56] D. Lunn, S. Harper, and S. Bechhofer. Combining SADIe and AxsJAX to improve the accessibility of web content. *Government Information Quarterly*. In: *Proceedings of the 2009 international cross-disciplinary conference on web accessibililty (W4A)-W4A 2009*. New York: ACMPress, 2009, pp. 75.

[57] I. S. MacKenzie, T. Kauppinen, and M. Silfverberg. Accuracy measures for evaluating computer pointing devices. In: *Procs. of the SIGCHI Conf. on Human factors in computing systems*, 2001, pp. 9–16.

[58] M. Mason and M. C. Lopes. Robot self-initiative and personalization by learning through repeated interactions. In: *Procs. of the 6th int. Conf. on Human-robot interaction*, 2011, pp. 433–440.

[59] S. Mirri, P. Salomoni, C. Prandi, and L. A. Muratori. GAPforAPE: an augmented browsing system to improve Web 2.0 accessibility. *New Review of Hypermedia and Multimedia* 18(3) (2012) 205–229.

[60] D. A. Norman and S. W. Draper. *User Centered System Design; New Perspectives on Human-Computer Interaction*. Hillsdale, US: L. Erlbaum Associates, 1986.

[61] Z. Pabarskaite and A. Raudys. A process of knowledge discovery from web log data: Systematization and critical review. *Journal of Intelligent Information Systems* 28(1) (2007) 79–104.

[62] L. Paganelli and F. Paternò. Intelligent analysis of user interactions with web applications. In: *Procs. of the 7th Int. Conf. on Intelligent user interfaces*, 2002, pp. 111–118.

[63] M. Peissner and R. Edlin-White. User Control in Adaptive User Interfaces for Accessibility. In: Kotzé et al., editors. *Procs. INTERACT 2013, Part I*. LNCS, volume 8117, 2013, pp. 623–640.

[64] M. Peissner, D. Häbe, D. Janssen, and T. Sellner. MyUI. In: *Procs of the 4th ACM SIGCHI symposium on engineering interactive computing systems – EICS 2012*. New York: ACM Press, 2012, pp. 81–90.

[65] I. Perona, A. Year, O. Arbelaitz, J. Muguerza, N. Ragkousis, M. Arrue, J. E. Pérez, and X. Valencia. Automatic device detection in web interaction. In: *Procs. of the XVII Conf. Asociación Española para la Inteligencia Artificial (CAEPIA) – (TAMIDA)*, 2016, pp. 825–834.

[66] D. Perzanowski, A. C. Schultz, W. Adams, E. Marsh, and M. Bugajska. Building a multimodal human-robot interface. *IEEE Intelligent Systems* 16(1) (2001) 16–21.

[67] J. E. Perez, M. Arrue, X. Valencia, and J. Abascal. Longitudinal study of two virtual cursors for people with motor impairments: a performance and satisfaction analysis on web Navigation. *IEEE Access* 8 (2020) 110381–110396.

[68] A. Rapp, F. Cena, C. Mattutino, A. Calafiore, C. Schifanella, E. Grassi, and G. Boella. Holistic User Models for Cognitive Disabilities: Personalized Tools for Supporting People with Autism in the City. In: *UMAP'18 Adjunct: 26th Conf. on User Modeling, Adaptation and Personalization*. NY: ACM, 2018, pp. 109–113.

[69] J. T. Richards and V. L. Hanson. Web accessibility: a broader view. In: *Procs. of the 13th Int. Conf. on World Wide Web*, 2004, pp. 72–79.

[70] V. F. Santana and M. C. Calani. WELFIT: A remote evaluation tool for identifying Web usage patterns through client-side logging. *International Journal of Human-Computer Studies* 76 (2015) 40–49.

[71] J. Scholtz, S. Laskowski, and L. Downey. Developing usability tools and techniques for designing and testing web sites. In: *Procs. of the HFWeb*, volume 98, 1998, pp. 1–10.

[72] S. Sosnovsky and D. Dicheva. Ontological technologies for user modelling. *International Journal of Metadata, Semantics and Ontologies* 5(1) (2010) 32–71.

[73] C. Stephanidis. Adaptive Techniques for Universal Access. *User Modeling and User-Adapted Interaction* 11 (2001) 159–179.

[74] C. Stephanidis, A. Paramythis, M. Sfyrakis, A. Stergiou, N. Maou, A. Leventis, G. Paparoulis, and C. Karagiannidis. Adaptable and adaptive user interfaces for disabled users in the AVANTI project. In: S. Trigila, A. Mullery, M. Campolargo, H. Vanderstraeten, and M. Mampaey, editors. *Intelligence in Services and Networks: Technology for Ubiquitous Telecom Services*. LNCS, volume 1430. Berlin: Springer, 1998.

[75] H. Takagi, C. Asakawa, K. Fukuda, and J. Maeda. Site-wide annotation: reconstructing existing pages to be accessible. In: *Procs. of the fifth Int. ACM Conf. on Assistive technologies*, 2002, pp. 81–88.

[76] X. Valencia, J. E. Pérez, M. Arrue, J. Abascal, C. Duarte, and L. Moreno. Adapting the Web for People With Upper Body Motor Impairments Using Touch Screen Tablets. *Interacting with Computers* 29(6) (2017) 794–812.

[77] X. Valencia, J. E. Pérez, U. Muñoz, M. Arrue, and J. Abascal. Assisted interaction data analysis of web-based user studies. In: *Human-Computer Interaction*. Springer, 2015, pp. 1–19.

[78] L. van Velsen, T. van der Geest, L. van de Wijngaert, S. van den Berg, and M. Steehouder. Personalization has a Price, Controllability is the Currency: Predictors for the Intention to use Personalized eGovernment Websites, *Journal of Organizational Computing and Electronic Commerce* 25(1) (2015) 76–97.

[79] M. Vigo and S. Harper. Coping tactics employed by visually disabled users on the web. *International Journal of Human-Computer Studies* 71(11) (2013) 1013–1025.

[80] S. Waldherr, R. Romero, and S. Thrun. A gesture based interface for human-robot interaction. *Autonomous Robots* 9 (2000) 151–173.

[81] G. I. Webb, M. J. Pazzani, and D. Billsus. Machine Learning for User Modeling. *User Modeling and User-Adapted Interaction* 11 (2001) 19–29.

[82] WHO 2001. World Health Organization. International Classification of Functioning, Disability and Health (ICF) http://www.who.int/classifications/icd/en/index.html. Accessed October 1, 2018.

[83] J. O. Wobbrock and K. Z. Gajos. Goal crossing with mice and trackballs for people with motor impairments: Performance, submovements, and design directions. *ACM Transactions on Accessible Computing (TACCESS)* 1(1) (2008) 1–37.

[84] A. Yera, I. Perona, O. Arbelaitz, and J. Muguerza. Modelling the enrolment eService of a university using machine learning techniques. In: *Procs. of 16th International Conference e-Society 2018, Lisbon, Portugal*, 2018, pp. 83–91.

[85] A. Yera, O. Arbelaitz, O. Jauregui, and J. Muguerza. Characterization of e-Government adoption in Europe. *PLoS ONE* 15(4) (2020) 1–22.

[86] A. Yera, I. Perona, O. Arbelaitz, J. Muguerza, J. E. Pérez, and X. Valencia. Automatic Web Navigation Problem Detection Based on Client-Side Interaction Data. *Human-Centric Computing and Information Sciences* 11 (2021) 1–16.

[87] H. Yu, M. Spenko, and S. Dubowsky. An adaptive shared control system for an intelligent mobility aid for the elderly. *Autonomous Robots* 15(1) (2008) 53–66.

Judith Masthoff and Julita Vassileva

9 Personalized persuasion for behavior change

Abstract: Persuasive technology refers to technology designed to influence or change people's attitudes or behaviors. This chapter provides an overview of personalized persuasive technology interventions that aim to support and motivate people to initiate, maintain, engage in, or discontinue specific behaviors. It presents some of the key theories that inform the design of persuasive technology interventions. Additionally, it outlines four models of behavior change used in persuasive technology design, developed by Cialdini, Fogg, Oinas-Kukkonen and Harummaa, and Michie, that involve persuasive techniques such as goal-setting, feedback and emotional support, rewards, (self-) monitoring, social comparison, and persuasive messages.

Personalization is critical for effective persuasive technology. The chapter discusses the adaptation of (1) the *choice* of behavior change techniques, and (2) the *instantiation* of commonly used behavior change techniques. It also discusses application domains in which personalized persuasive technology has been used, such as healthy living, sustainability and user participation and engagement.

Evaluating the effectiveness of personalized persuasive technology is not easy, and the chapter provides an overview of the main issues to consider: perceived versus actual persuasiveness, layered evaluation, direct versus indirect studies, short-term versus longitudinal studies, domain effects and metrics and scales. Finally, the paper highlights the ethical considerations in designing and deploying personalized persuasive technology.

Overall, this chapter provides a comprehensive overview of the field of persuasive technology, emphasizing the importance of personalization in designing effective interventions for behavior change. It discusses different theories, techniques and approaches to personalization and provide an overview of different application domains and evaluation methods. By highlighting the ethical considerations of designing and deploying persuasive technology interventions, the chapter underscores the importance of responsible design and emphasizes the potential of persuasive technology to bring about positive change in people's lives.

Keywords: Persuasive technology, behavior change interventions, personalization

9.1 Introduction

"Persuasive Technology" (PT) is a term coined by B. J. Fogg [50, 51] referring to interactive systems intentionally designed to change attitudes and behaviors through persuasion and social influence without deception or coercion. In other words, persuasive

https://doi.org/10.1515/9783110988567-009

technology is meant to help people make choices that are in their best interest, and to do so in a way that is transparent, ethical and effective. Fogg coined also the term "captology" from an acronym of "computers as persuasive technology" [51] referring to the science and art of designing and building such persuasive technology and noted that it applies to desk-top, web-based and mobile systems, generally, to any systems interacting with humans. Over the past 20 years, we have seen many application areas of PT emerging, from ecommerce to health, education, cyber-security, for engaging users in social networking and social media, in sustainability projects and in social causes. What is common for all these PT systems is that they aim to change or optimize the behavior of their users for some purpose that benefits some or all of the stakeholders: the platform and its owners, the users, the user community, the society or environment. For example, e-commerce systems aim to motivate users to buy more products on the site, to engage them in rating and reviewing their purchases and the sellers. Health mobile applications aim to motivate users to exercise, eat healthy, fight addictions and develop healthy habits. Persuasive e-learning applications aim to engage students in learning activities and maintain their motivation and self-efficacy during the learning process. Persuasive technologies may aim to motivate and enable users to perform a new behavior, to help them maintain a behavior (habit building), or to discontinue an undesirable behavior (e. g., stop procrastination).

Persuasive technologies deploy different approaches and strategies to achieve behavior change. Yet, human behavior depends on environmental, social and cognitive factors and the same approach or strategy is not equally effective for different people and circumstances. Therefore, personalization is needed to amplify the effect of the PT. Personalization may be based on the user's psychological type, level of ability or knowledge, individual goals, social or environmental context. This chapter presents the main theories and behavior determinants underlying personalized PPT, the main personalization design approaches (adaptive versus tailored), the persuasive techniques used and some of the main application areas. It concludes with a discussion of the ethical issues surrounding PPT currently and in the future when new technologies such as the metaverse, ubiquitous sensing and user modeling and generative AI enable the creation of tools for "mind-control" [136].

9.2 Theories

PT has been inspired by an eclectic set of theories from behavioral economics, psychology (social psychology and psychology of motivation), education and health sciences (regarding learning and behavior change), as well as some theoretical constructs proposed specifically for the practical needs of advertisement and persuasive technologies. The personalization of persuasive technologies has been explored along various dimensions, some defined by personality traits based on different psychological models of personality (general or contextualized to a particular application domain) and others defined by demographic features (age, gender, culture, educational level), as well as pretheoretical models derived from lab and empirical studies.

9.2.1 Behavioral economics

Much of the persuasion literature has origins in ancient writings on rhetorics (logos, ethos and pathos) [10] but it has burgeoned more recently, in the area of marketing [31]. The science of marketing has roots in economics and social psychology, and evolved into behavioral economics, an area that has gained a lot of popular attention [68]. Behavioral economics studies empirically how humans make decisions, contrasting the findings with standard economic theory of rational decision-making, which presumes that humans are utility optimizers. Explaining the observed "irrational behaviors" [9] needs insights from both cognitive and social psychology and has lead to the discovery of a number of cognitive biases, or "blind spots," which predicate poor decisions [82]. Examples of cognitive biases are loss aversion, and the effect of "free" (zero-risk bias), placebo (believing something is better makes one perceive it physically as being better), anchoring (judging based on the first piece of information) and stereotyping, the Dunning–Kruger effect (the less knowledge one has, the more confidence they display), sunken cost (continuing to invest effort or money in something that one has invested heavily before). Some of these biases can be observed in human behavior not only in the real world, but also online in social networks, in online shopping and other online activities, e. g., group deliberation and decision-making. For example, confirmation bias, or the tendency of people to prefer interacting with people who share similar views, or to discard information that disagrees with their views, can explain the propagation of conspiracy theories on social media and the formation of filter bubbles on social network sites. Many of these cognitive biases are being exploited in marketing, both off-line and online, to make people purchase more expensive products, e. g., by placing products in a particular way, manipulating prices, and applying user interface design aiming to trick the user into doing things that are not beneficial for them. Exploiting cognitive biases is clearly manipulative, so these techniques have been called "dark patterns" (a term originating from the User Experience (UX) design literature [102].

Unfortunately, the terms "persuasive technology" and "dark patterns" have been used together or even interchangeably in the popular media when discussing the attention economy of targeted advertising. This is not always fair, since the variable rewards causing dopamine boosts and resulting in addictiveness of the application are often due to the nature of the application and not necessarily caused by deliberate exploitative design. Behavioral economics can provide explanations for the effectiveness of some successful strategies and techniques for persuasion, which do not depend on cognitive biases. Following B. J. Fogg's [50] definition of persuasive technology, which excludes manipulation or coercion, in this chapter, we do not discuss persuasive strategies that exploit cognitive biases.

9.2.2 Psychology

Many theories of motivation exsit; we will briefly cover only a few. Operant conditioning, also known as Skinnerian conditioning, is one of the oldest and most fundamental theories in behavioral psychology, behaviorism. According to the theory people learn new behaviors by connecting their actions to the results or rewards they get [8]. External rewards, which can be positive or negative (punishments), according to this theory, can be used to drive and control learning and behavior change. Also, according to classical economics theories rewards provide motivation to engage in a specific behavior or make specific decisions. Persuasive technology strategies based on conditioning utilize rewards when the user performs the target behaviors. More details about rewards-based techniques can be found in Section 9.3.3.

Ryan and Deci [139] introduced a distinction between extrinsic (coming from a different entity or the environment) and intrinsic (from within the individual) rewards. When people are motivated to do an activity for their own enjoyment and satisfaction, the motivation that drives this activity is called intrinsic motivation. The self-determination theory (SDT) was developed to differentiate task engagement between extrinsic and intrinsic motivation. According to SDT, intrinsic motivation is directly related to the satisfaction of fundamental psychological requirements of autonomy, competence and relatedness. When people feel independent and in control of their action choices, their demand for autonomy is satisfied. When a person has the chance to advance, perform effectively and become an expert in a task, their demand for competence is satisfied [66]. The relatedness needs of an individual are satisfied when they can meaningfully relate to the learning environment. Persuasive technologies can support user autonomy by providing means to set behavior goals and control the way of achieving them, competence–by providing users with means to learn and practice their behavior skills and monitor their progress, relatedness–by providing means to communicate and share their experience with other users.

Proposed by Albert Bandura [16], the Social Cognitive Theory (SCT) holds that human behaviors are influenced by environmental factors and mediated by cognitive processes. It extends Bandura's social learning theory, which holds that people learn not only through their own experiences but also by observing the behaviors of others and their consequences. The SCT is centered around the conceptual triad of reciprocal determinism [13]. The triad holds that three main factors (personal, environmental and the target behavior) reciprocally influence one another in a dynamic fashion to shape human behaviors [6]. The personal factors are cognitive factors such as self-efficacy [15], outcome expectation and self-regulation, while the environmental factors are external, socio-structural factors, which could be physical, social or technological [14]. Persuasive technology is an example of a technological system that can influence human behaviors via cognitive processes.

Two other theoretical models for behavior change, originating from the area of Health Science have been used widely in designing persuasive applications: the Trans-Theoretical Model (TTM) [126] and the Theory of Planned Behavior (TPB). The TTM posits that health behavior change involves progress through six stages of change: precontemplation, contemplation, preparation, action, maintenance and termination. It also outlines ten processes of change for producing progress in each stage. The TPB originates from the theory of reasoned action and posits that behavior originates from beliefs. It has three core components: attitude, subjective norms and perceived behavioral control, that predict an individual's intention to engage in a specific behavior.

As different people are motivated by different things, a logical approach is to look at personality models to explain and possibly predict motivation and behavior change. There are many general personality models developed in Psychology, with Meyers–Briggs [94] and The Big 5 (OCEAN) [87] models the most prominent ones. There are many other, specialized models or personality developed to explain and predict human behavior in specific domains, e. g., in games (Bartle's model [17], BrainHex [95], Hexad [163]), learning styles (e. g., the VARK model [80], and shopper types [75, 135]). These personality models have been developed empirically and there exist validated survey tools to measure individuals on their dimensions.

9.2.3 Behavioral determinants

Based on the many behavior theories available, there have been several attempts to identify common behavioral determinants. First, Fishbein et al. [49] analyzed theories to change people from engaging in risky to healthy HIV preventive behaviors, and identified eight factors that determine the adoption or avoidance of a given behavior (see Table 9.1). Intention, environmental constraints and skills were considered necessary and sufficient factors for carrying out a behavior. The remaining five factors are described as influencing the strength and direction of intention. Consider the example of injected drug use and needle sharing: if a *"user is committed to using bleach every time he shares injection equipment, has bleach available, and has the necessary skills to use the bleach, the probability is close to 1.0 that he will use the bleach..."* [49, p. 16]. Second, Michie et al. [88] analyzed thirty-three theories with 128 constructs (including the five theories used by Fishbein et al. [49]) from a wide variety of fields and identified twelve factors that are most likely to determine behavior (see Table 9.1). Third, within the field of persuasive technology, Fogg [52] proposed an integrated model which is deliberately simple: it states that three elements, namely motivation, ability, and trigger must occur at the same time for a behavior to happen. The lack of any of these will cause noncompliance. According to this model, if the motivators are right, the behavior is made easy to do and triggered, then the behavior is more likely to occur. Table 9.1 shows the common

Table 9.1: Common key behavioral determinants.

Fishbein et al. [49]	Michie et al. [88]	Fogg [52]
Self-standards	Social/professional role and identity	
	Knowledge	
Skills	Skills	Ability
Self-efficacy	Beliefs about capabilities	
Anticipated outcomes/ Attitude	Beliefs about consequences	
Intention	Motivation and goals	Motivation
	Memory, attention and decision processes	
Environmental constraints	Environmental context and resources	
Norms	Social influences	
Emotion	Emotion	
	Behavioral regulation	Trigger
	Nature of the behaviors	

behavioral determinants as suggested by Fishbein et al. [49], Michie et al. [88] and Fogg [52].

9.3 Behavior change frameworks and techniques and personalization

A wide palette of techniques for changing human behavior has been developed in the area of PT. There are several categorizations, known by the names of their creators. The most widely used categorization is Cialdini's [31] principles of persuasion, which consist of six techniques: authority, consensus, commitment, liking, reciprocity and scarcity. Cialdini [32] recently added one more technique, unity. These principles or techniques are widely used in marketing and in PT because they are easy to implement with messages (nudges) as will be shown in Section 9.3.5. Fogg's behavior model [52] shows that three elements must converge at the same moment for a behavior to occur: motivation, ability, and a trigger (also called prompt, signal or nudge). He proposed persuasive techniques aimed at each of these three elements.[1]

The Persuasive Systems Design (PSD) model by Oinas-Kukkonen and Harumaa [104] categorizes persuasive techniques into 4 groups: Primary Task Support, Dialogue Support, Credibility Support and Social Support. Each group contains 7 persuasive strategies that could be applied effectively to change behavior depending on the persuasion con-

---

1 Fogg's techniques for motivation (pleasure, hope, social acceptance) are related to the Rewards and Incentives technique discussed below. Prompts will be discussed under Persuasive Messages. Ability is related to Goal Setting.

text.[2] The PSD approach consists of four stages: (1) *analysis*: understanding the behavior that needs to be changed and its behavioral determinants (e. g., users' motivations, beliefs, attitudes, values and their social and cultural context), (2) *design*: tailoring the persuasive technology design and behavior change strategy selection to users' needs and preferences, (3) *development*: creating the technology and iteratively testing it with users, (4) *evaluation*: testing the effectiveness through, for example, user testing.

Michie et al. [89] identified 137 behavior change techniques,[3] and mapped these to the behavioral determinants. Behavior-change theories predict effective combinations of techniques. For example, control theory advocates goal setting, specifying action plans, self-monitoring, feedback and reviewing goals. In this section, some of the most common techniques will be discussed, focusing in particular on the need and opportunities for personalization. Based on 19 frameworks of behavior change interventions, Michie et al. [90] developed a new framework called the behavior change wheel to help intervention designers. It has three layers: (1) behavioral determinants (capability, opportunity and motivation), (2) nine broad categories of behavior change techniques and (3) seven policy categories that can be used to support the intervention (e. g., marketing, regulation, legislation, etc.).

In addition to personalizing the application of individual techniques (as discussed in the sections below), there is also a need to personalize the choice of techniques as a technique that works well for one user may be counterproductive for another. The mappings between persuasive techniques and user features are usually created through statistical analysis of data from lab- or crowd-sourced studies that suggest that users with particular features are more responsive to specific techniques or strategies. Many studies have investigated the mappings of persuasive techniques to user Personality, e. g., using the Big 5 model, e. g., [4], player personality typologies, e. g., Brainhex [113], and shopper personality typologies, e. g., [1]. Other studies have investigated the influence of user features such as Motivation [171], Gender and Culture [76, 114, 118, 120], and other user characteristics, such as the user's stage according to the TTM [119].

9.3.1 Goal setting

Goal setting involves determining what the user should or wants to achieve both in the long term and in a shorter period (e. g., a week or day). It also involves deciding on activities or challenges for the user to do.[4] For example, a user may want to become more physically active, walking 10,000 steps a day in the long term. In a particular week, they

---

2 They regard personalization (and tailoring) as techniques for primary task support. In this paper, personalization is not a technique, but something that can be applied to any of the techniques.

3 Some authors use the term "strategies"; in this paper, the term "techniques" will be used.

4 Some may argue that this is part of another technique called action planning.

may have a goal of 5,000 steps a day, which may be, e. g., 10 % more than they walked on average in the preceding week. On a particular day, they may be challenged to park their car further away and walk the last two kilometers to work.

According to goal-setting theory [81], behavior change is more likely the higher the specificity and (achievable) difficulty of a goal. To obtain so-called flow (a state of utter motivation), there needs to be a good balance between skills and difficulty, with challenges being neither too hard nor too easy: *"When goals are clear, when above-average challenges are matched to skills, and when accurate feedback is forthcoming, a person becomes...so involved in an activity that nothing else seems to matter; the experience is so enjoyable that people will do it even at great cost, for the sheer sake of doing it"* [38].

Nguyen and Masthoff [101] adapted goals in a physical activity PPT, in consultation with the user, to the user's past performance and how they were feeling. Qualitative research by Ciocarlan et al. [33] showed the wish to adapt challenges to personality. Okpo et al. [108] adapted activity selection to performance, effort and personality (self-esteem). Adapting difficulty levels is also frequently done in games[5] [124].

9.3.2 Feedback and emotional support

Persuasive technology often provides feedback on how well a user performs, e. g., compared to their goals, in real-time or afterward. For example, Qian et al.'s [127] physical activity app tracked the user's walking speed and produced vibrations to encourage faster or slower walking. Colineau and Paris's [36] web portal provided tailored feedback (adapted to a family's situation) to encourage families to reflect upon their lifestyle and think about how to make it healthier.

A major issue with achieving behavior change is relapse: people falling back into their old behaviors. For example, Kraft et al. [78] found a relapse of 50 to 95 %. Emotional support may help to deal with negative affective states (a common cause of relapse). Several works have studied how to adapt feedback and emotional support to a. o. performance [42, 145], personality [42]; (Smith et al. [146]; considering Big 5, Resilience and Self-esteem), stressor experienced [77, 146], and culture [145].

9.3.3 Incentives and rewards

Classical economics assumes that people are rational and act to maximize their utility (payoff). In a world where behaviors have certain payoffs (negative or positive), appropriate incentives (rewards) are needed for desirable behaviors [170]. This is in agreement with the operant conditioning theory in psychology, which postulates that rewards

---

5 Serious games and gamified systems can be considered PT [162].

are essential to learn new behaviors. Therefore, rewards have been applied widely in games, education and in persuasive technology systems aiming at behavior change. Including rewards for specific actions or behaviors and using game elements in nongame environments is called "Gamification" [170].

Commonly used reward types include virtual or physical ownership, which may bring the user some privileges, (e. g., points, currency, streak freezes), status (e. g., rank, level, achievement badges) and reputation (e. g., number of followers, rating by other users). For example, points, are often used in educational online systems to incentivise participation and they can be used as a measure for awarding participation grades or status badges. For example, in I-Help [58], students earned virtual currency for helping their peers, and they could use it to "pay" for help when they needed it, or "cash" it for material objects in a lottery. UbiFit Garden, Consolvo et al. [37] used ownership of a virtual garden as a motivation, rewarding users with growth of particular flower when they performed a certain workout, and a butterfly if their goal was reached. Farzan et al. [47] used status, promoting users from *"worker bee"* to *"queen bee"* after a number of contributions to a company's information exchange platform. In the academic paper-sharing and discussion site Comtella, Cheng and Vassileva [28, 29] used ownership (points for contributing papers and ratings), status (accumulated points led to gold, silver and bronze status), and reputation (rating by other users based on the quality of contributions and quality of ratings).

Personalization is needed for the reward type provided (e. g., some people may appreciate status, others not), the reward instantiation (e. g., some may appreciate ownership, but not of flowers), and the circumstances under which a reward is provided. For example, Cheng and Vassileva [29, 30] adapted the number of points awarded for new contributions to the current needs of the community based on the number of contributions already made, the time remaining to discuss the topic at hand, and quality of the individual's contributions, capping the rewards for individual contribution depending on the user's reputation.

9.3.4 Self-monitoring and social comparison

Self-monitoring is necessary to enable an effective goal setting persuasive technique for behavior change, because without being able to track the progress toward the goal it is impossible for the user to maintain motivation for the behavior. In fact, self-monitoring is at the center of the quantified self-community/cultural phenomenon that uses the abundance of cheap sensors and trackers and the proliferation of smartwatches to engage users in self-tracking their physical activity, sleep, food and liquid intake, mental state, etc. While most of the existing self-tracking applications focus on health, self-monitoring can be applied to any target behavior, e. g., smoking cessation [76], abstinence from drinking [109], learning [169], or analysing one's interpersonal relationships online [176]. There are different ways in which the presentation of self-monitoring can be designed, with text or graphics, with a different level of precision, and showing different variables. All these offer many possible dimensions for personalization, and there exist many mundane (e. g., bar- or pie-chart visualizations) and creative examples, e. g., the UbiFit Garden [37].

Social comparison is a persuasive technique anchored in Bandura's social learning theory, which holds that people learn not only through their own experiences but also by observing the behaviors of others and their consequences. The theory suggests three forms of social learning: (1) observing others performing the behavior, (2) comparing one's behavior with that of others and (3) competing with others in achieving certain metrics for the behavior. Each of these forms can be easily implemented in a system where behavior can be measured, e. g., [112, 156]. There are several design decisions that need to be made, however, and they open possibilities for personalization. The first one is who should be in the social group which the user will compare themselves to, compete or just observe? Some options are: the users' friends (e. g., Strava [177], a group of imaginary users [115], randomly selected users, users selected from the "performance neighborhood" of the user, so that the user does not get depressed if they are underperforming [112]. Another decision is how to visualize the performance of the comparative group and the performance of the user, whether to allow for competition or not. Competition (usually designed as a leaderboard, a common game mechanic) is a very powerful motivation for some users but is a demotivator for many others [113]. The personality and culture of the user needs to be considered in choosing an appropriate social comparison technique. This needs to be done at the design stage and a tailored version to the user's preference or personality presented.

9.3.5 Persuasive messages

Persuasive messages are used to motivate, convince and remind a user. Other terms often used are prompts, nudges and signals.

9.3.5.1 Message content

Message content needs to be adapted to users' motivation and ability. Fogg [52] distinguishes three types of prompts: *spark prompts* motivate people who lack the motivation to act, *facilitator prompts* make behavior easier for motivated people with low ability, and *signal prompts* remind motivated people with high ability to act. The kind of prompt to use may depend on the current strength of habit formation (cf. [180]). Message content also needs to be adapted to a user's values and preferences [26, 56], goals (as inferred partially from user personality in Mazzotta et al. [86] and Hirsh et al. [64], or shopper types in Adaji et al. [1]), attitudes [121, 122, 152], and context [167]. For example, in Carenini and Moore [26] the strength of arguments is calculated for a particular user based on their values and preferences (e.g., when selling a house, the size of the garden may be more important to one user than another). Users are more motivated to act if they feel more involved [67]. Masthoff et al. [84] showed that the content of prompts in the charity domain therefore needs to be personalized to gender, age, religion and country affinity.

Message types

Many message types exist, most commonly based on Cialdini's seven principles of persuasion [31, 32] or argumentation schemes [174]. Thomas et al. [160] and Ruiz-Dolz et al. [138] show how argumentation schemes can be mapped onto Cialdini's principles, thereby providing an extra layer of detail with multiple argumentation schemes per principal. There has been substantial research on personalizing the message type used, e.g., on whether and how to adapt it to the user's personality[6] (e.g., [34, 35, 117, 147, 158, 161]), culture [116], and demographic factors such as gender, and age [34, 35, 159]. Most of these studies investigated Cialdini-based message types, but Thomas et al. [161] also investigated argumentation-based message types.

Message framing

Positively framed messages stress the benefits of acting as desired, while negatively framed messages stress the disadvantages of not behaving as desired. Regulatory-focus theory distinguishes four framing categories: gain, nongain, nonloss and loss [63]. Gain and non-loss messages are regarded as positively framed, and nongain and loss messages as negatively framed. Studies have shown mixed results on which framing works better; reviewing the literature on gain versus loss messages, Grazzini et al. [57] concluded that this is context (domain) dependent. Framing may also benefit from personalization: Updegraff and Rothman [164] showed that it depends on the user's risk beliefs (for high perceived risk loss-framed messages work better), motivational orientation,[7] consideration of future consequences[8] and self-efficacy (high self-efficacy means more persuaded by loss = framed compared to gain-framed).

---

6 Normally the Big Five personality traits are used.

7 People differ in their motivation to approach favorable outcomes or avoid unfavorable ones, and their sensitivity to the presence/absence of positive (promotion focus) or negative (prevention focus) events. According to Updegraf and Rothman [164], approach-motivated and promotion-focused people are more responsive to gain-framed messages, and avoidance-motivated and prevention-focused people to loss-framed messages.

8 Consideration of future consequences (CFC; Orbell, Perugini and Rakow [110]) is an individual difference in the extent to which someone is influenced by immediate or distant outcomes of decisions. According to Updegraf and Rothman [164], if there are short-term risks and safer long-term consequences (as in health screenings), then low CFC people are more likely to be persuaded by loss-framed messages, and high CFC people by gain-framed messages.

Message position
Social judgement theory [142] divides the spectrum of positions into two parts: (1) the latitude of acceptance of positions that the user finds acceptable, (2) the latitude of rejection of positions that the user finds unacceptable. For an argument to be effective, its position needs to be within the latitude of acceptance; i. e., not too far from the user's current position. There is initial research on modeling a user's position after hearing arguments, based on argument strength, position and user involvement [98]. User involvement (how important the topic is to a person) may impact the width of the latitude of acceptance. Social psychologists [67] distinguish three types of involvement: value-relevant (a person's core values/beliefs), outcome relevant (the extent to which certain outcomes are relevant to a person) and impression-relevant (concerns about the impression a person makes on others).

One-sided versus two-sided
A one-sided message provides only arguments in favor, while a two-sided message also addresses counterarguments. Carenini and Moore [26] distinguish three ways of dealing with counterarguments: omitting them, acknowledging them without directly refuting them, and acknowledging them and directly refuting them. Nuyen et al. [99] in one study found some evidence that two-sided messages worked better (they refuted a counterargument), but this was not confirmed in their second study. Carenini and Moore [26] suggest that the strength of counterarguments needs to be considered; they advocate omitting weak counterarguments, acknowledging stronger ones and refuting them depending on the user's position. It seems likely that user involvement may also play a role in whether a counterargument should be presented/refuted.

When to argue and when not
Nguyen and Masthoff [100] showed that argumentation-based messages are not always effective and that motivational interviewing [91] may be more effective. Motivational interviewing is a counseling technique in which clients make their own arguments on why they would like to change. More research is needed on the context and user characteristics that determine when motivational interviewing should be applied.

9.3.5.2 Message communication

Message source
The persuasiveness of a source is influenced by its perceived credibility, likeability and similarity [106, 154]. Research by Nguyen and Masthoff [97] shows that the message source needs to be adapted to the topic: source credibility as based on a facial photo differed per domain (why physical activity is healthy vs. what physical activity to do) and impacted the perceived credibility of the information provided. Nguyen and Masthoff

found no evidence of the source needing to be adapted to the user; similar to a recent study by ter Stal et al [151], they found some differences in appreciation based on user demographics (e. g., gender and age), but also that across demographic groups the same source images were deemed most credible. In contrast, Baylor [19] summarizes many studies by herself and others showing that users tend to be more influenced by a virtual character of their own gender, and of their own race/ethnicity. However, she notes that this is context-dependent, and also mentions studies showing different effects, e. g., one in which all middle-school students independent of gender were more persuaded toward engineering by a female character, and one where female undergraduates preferred to learn about engineering from male, older, uncool agents (confirming a stereotype of an engineer at that time). There has also been research on which perspective to use, e. g. for testimonial-based messages, should these be presented in a first-person, third-person or bystander perspective [128].

Mode of interaction

Social psychology suggests that the interaction mode can influence the effectiveness of persuasion [154].

- **One source or multiple.** Studies by Baylor and Kim [18] showed that learners were more motivated and learned more when they interacted with two virtual characters who took on different roles in supporting them instead of one for both roles; this could mean that different kinds of messages (e. g., Fogg's prompt types) need a different source. Andre et al. [7] suggested using a team of virtual characters to convey similar information in different ways, thereby reinforcing the user's beliefs. This is in line with studies in psychology, which showed the positive impact of social norms on persuasion (e. g., [48, 96]). In Nguyen et al. [99]'s study, a team of agents was however not received well, with some participants complaining that it felt like hectoring and was patronizing. Subagdja et al. [155] improved a persuasion team by paying more attention to the timing, coordination and adaptation of messages from different sources. Their study results were however inconclusive. It is likely that people's personality plays a role, such as their susceptibility to social influence [173].
- **Direct versus indirect.** Instead of virtual character(s) *directly* conversing with the user, the communication can also be indirect (also called vicarious): the user witnesses the conversation between virtual characters. This may make the source(s) more credible as the user thinks they are not trying to persuade them (e. g., [11]). Craig et al. [39] showed improved effectiveness of indirect communication in a learning domain; this was also found in one study by Ngyuen et al. [99] in a physical activity domain, but not in another. They used one character as a persuader, and a second in a similar role as the user (so persuadee). Kantharaju et al. [69] showed improved effectiveness of indirect communication with two characters

as persuaders, telling each other why a certain movie should be watched—which form of communication works best may be the user, topic and context-dependent.

– **With or without the possibility to counter-argue**. The user could be given the opportunity to counter-argue. There is a line of work on this within computational argumentation (e. g., [56, 59, 86]). For example, Hadoux and Hunter [59] show how a virtual character could argue with a user, and adapt the arguments used based on the user's concerns.

Message timing

The appropriate time to deliver a message depends on the context and user. Chaudhari et al. [27] reviewed personalized intervention timing for physical activity, as studies showed that adapting timing to the user's schedule, circadian rhythm and lifestyle could increase the likelihood of user adoption and adherence. Their review found PPTs that adapt message timing to user activity patterns (e. g., how long the user has been inactive), user availability, user location and the weather.

9.4 Application domains

Personalized Persuasive Technology (PPT) has been studied in many domains, most frequently to encourage healthy living, sustainability or user participation and engagement. Below we provide some examples.

9.4.1 Healthy living

Physical activity

Typically, physical activity PPT uses a combination of goal setting, (self-)monitoring, feedback, reminders and rewards, sometimes in combination with social comparison and persuasive messages. Often these take the form of e-coaches. For example, Nguyen and Masthoff [101] developed an e-coach that encouraged people to walk more, and used all of these techniques except social comparison. While it adapted goal setting and feedback, this was rule-based, while Vardhan et al.'s [166] e-coach *learned* what actions to take next to emulate a human walking coach. Op den Akker et al. [2] provide a literature survey on tailoring physical activity e-coaches in real-time. In addition to e-coaches, gamification is often used. For example, Altmeyer et al. [3] investigated personalizing gameful fitness applications to behavior change intentions and Hexad user types. There has also been research for particular user groups. For example, to encourage physical activity by COPD patients, Wais-Zechmann et al. [172] studied how the persuasiveness of techniques relates to a COPD patient's susceptibility to Cialdini's persuasive principles. To encourage physical activity by seniors, Kuo and Chen [79] investigated séniors' gamer types and how these relate to persuasive strategies, while Qian et al. [127] adapted feedback. Adaptation to culture has also been investigated [116]. In addition to adaptation to users, adaptation of physical activity coaches to the user's context has been investigated (e. g., [40, 45]).

Healthy diets

To encourage healthy eating, persuasive messages are frequently used (e. g., [72, 158, 159, 161]), sometimes in an argumentation-based dialogue system (e. g., [56, 86]). There is also research on recommender systems that persuade people to eat healthily by recommending healthy food they may like (e. g., [46, 54, 61]). Finally, serious games are used that include social comparison, rewards etc. (e. g., [113]).

Mental health

There are many different types of digital mental health interventions. Alqahtani et al. [4] considered these and investigated how people's Big 5 personality traits were related to the persuasiveness of features (such as relaxation exercises, self-monitoring and social support). Their work relates to the tailoring of interventions by adapting the selection of behavior change techniques. Ciocarlan et al.'s gamified *Be Kind* intervention [34, 35] encouraged users to perform small acts of kindness, which was shown to positively impact their mental well-being. They studied the personalization of activities and persuasive messages based on Cialidini's principles, so the adaptation of the techniques themselves. In addition to adaptation to users, adaptation to the user's context has been investigated. For example, Vargheese et al. [167] investigated how to encourage elderly people to engage in social activities by adapting persuasive messages to the social context. Horsch et al. [65] investigated adapting the timing of reminders in an e-coach for better sleeping to the user's context (interruptability). Hermens et al. [62] provided context-aware feedback on stress levels.

Fighting addictions

Most research in this area tends to use persuasive messaging or gamification. For example, for smoking cessation, the personalization of persuasive messages has been investigated (e. g., [43, 44, 130]) as well the adaptation of a serious game to culture [76]. To encourage responsible alcohol use, Olagunju et al. [109] added social comparison and competition strategies to the common techniques used in health-related mobile apps (self-monitoring, goal setting, feedback, reward, reminder, simulation), showing strong positive results, but did not yet personalize the application.

Disease screening and management

PT is used to encourage people to participate in screening to detect illnesses early or to adhere to treatments. For example, Smith et al. [147] studied adaptive reminders to self-check for reoccurrences of skin cancer. Hermens et al. [62] studied context-dependent feedback in an adaptive coach for people with chronic pain.

9.4.2 Sustainability

Sustainable mobility

There is a lot of work on sustainable mobility that uses PT, e. g., encouraging public transport use, car pooling, cycling and walking [55, 179]. Typically, these systems use a combination of persuasive messages, goal-setting or challenges in a gamified environment, but do not personalize the strategies or the choice of strategies used with different users. There are, however, -some exceptions. For example, it has been investigated how to adapt persuasive messages to travel attitudes [121], personality [5], and travel habits, needs and behaviors [55]. Achieving behavior change by persuasive smart city design is also being investigated (e. g., [153]) but this work is more focused on large-scale interventions/campaigns and instead of personalization–tailoring by taking into account particular groups of citizens and how to adapt their neighborhoods to persuade them.

Reduce consumption

It has, e. g., been investigated how to make diets more sustainable (e. g., [22, 149]), reduce energy consumption (e. g., [125, 152]), reduce water usage (e. g., [141]) and encourage recycling (e. g., [103]). Often persuasive messages and gamification are used.

9.4.3 Engagement and participation

Encouraging contributions to communities

Personalized rewards [58] and simulated emotions by personal agents [107] were used to motivate learners to help each other in an agent-based collaborative learning system. PPT (rewards, self-monitoring and social comparison) has been used a. o. to encourage paper sharing and student rating of papers in an online community accompanying a university course [30, 176]. The rewards for contributions were personalized based on the quality of contributions as measured by the ratings received by other users and the current needs of the community. Using a similar approach to encourage knowledge sharing in an online company platform, Farzan et al. [47] used gamification. To encourage participation in charity actions, persuasive messages are mostly used. For example, Masthoff et al. [84] showed that the causes highlighted in a persuasive message (e. g., the person to fund on Kiva, or for whom to do an Amnesty action) need to be adapted to the user's background. For charitable donations, Wang et al. [175] investigated the adaptation of persuasive message type usage (e. g., foot-in-the-door, personal story, emotion appeal, logical appeal) to users' background. To encourage good contributions, sometimes recommender systems are used. For example, Wibowo et al. [178] used a package recommender system to encourage citizens to plant flower combinations in their garden (complementing their existing flowers) that can feed bumblebees all year round, and hence support biodiversity.

Supporting learning, engagement and reflection

PPT has also been used to encourage and teach people to act more safely, for instance in cyber-space [161, 168] and driving (e. g., [24]). PPT has been used to motivate learners to study more. For example, the adaptation of emotional support to learners' personality, performance and culture has been investigated [42, 145], and the adaptation of activity difficulty to learners' personality, performance and effort [108].[9] F. Orji et al. [111, 112] investigated how to increase learner engagement tailoring a learning management system to the learners' susceptibility to three social persuasive strategies (social learning, comparison and competition), implemented as social visualizations. There has been a lot of recent work on using gamification in educational systems to increase learner engagement, e. g., Rodrigues et al. [134], and specifically on personalizing the gamification techniques to increase learner's motivation, enjoyment and flow experience [105].

E-commerce and (social) media

PPT has mainly been used to encourage people to buy or consume more. Recommender systems [131] often serve this role; while conceived to improve people's lives by making it easier to find items or services they like, they tend to also have persuasive effects. Some methods for explainable recommendation justify the recommendation using summaries of product reviews instead of explaining how the recommendation was actually generated [93]. We return to this when discussing the ethics of PPT below. More positively, PPT can be used a. o. to encourage people to shop more healthily/sustainably (e. g., [1, 46]), to accept fair recommendations (e. g., [92]), to better engage in online debates (e. g., [132]), to share knowledge (e. g., product ratings and reviews), and to be more privacy-aware online (e. g., [140]).

9.5 Evaluation

The evaluation of PPT is not straightforward, and multiple issues need to be considered.

Actual versus perceived effectiveness

It is often hard to measure *actual* effectiveness: the extent to which people change their behavior as a result of persuasive technology. For example, it can be hard to

---

9 There is a long line of research on how to adapt instruction and exercises to learners; this is beyond the scope of this chapter.

measure exactly what somebody ate in a week, and this could also be influenced by many other factors in addition to the intervention. Similarly, the use of (sustainable) transport means could depend on the weather, trips required, etc. Therefore, many studies have investigated *perceived* effectiveness: the extent to which people *believe* the intervention changed their behavior or their *intention* to behave better in future (e. g., [113, 161]). In some cases, actual persuasiveness has been measured. For example, Kaptein and van Halteren [73] measured the impact of persuasive messages on physical activity. Ciocarlan et al. [35] studied actual persuasiveness but in an artificial game setting. Effectiveness in achieving behavior change has been reported in Olagunju et al. [109] who implemented a persuasive application using social comparison and competition techniques to discourage irresponsible alcohol use. The results of a month-long study with 20 participants showed that the intervention is likely effective demonstrated by a decrease in AUDIT (Alcohol Use Disorder Identification Test) score. AUDIT is the tool recommended by the World Health Organization, and a decrease in the score indicates a substantial decrease in the number and frequency of alcohol consumption.

Layered evaluation

According to Paramythis et al. [123], the evaluation of adaptive interactive systems (such as PPT) requires a layered approach, in which adaptation is decomposed into layers, and each layer is assessed individually (in addition to assessing the system overall). They distinguish five main layers; see Figure 9.1. For example, assume that in a physical activity intervention, we want to provide a reward adapted to the user's personality and performance. First input data is collected, e. g., from sensors or surveys. This data is then interpreted, e. g., into how many steps a person made or their score on personality traits. Based on this interpreted data, a user model is constructed, e. g., of their performance or dominant personality. Based on the user model, the system decides upon the adaptation, for instance, to provide a status reward. Finally, this status reward is instantiated, for instance by adding "Super" in front of their name. Each of these steps needs to be evaluated separately. Paramythis et al. [123] also provide an overview of methods for the design and formative evaluation of adaptive interactive systems, distinguishing between three system development phases (analysis/specification, design and implementation) and the layers (or system as a whole) for which these methods are most suitable.

Direct versus indirect studies

One issue with evaluating an adaptive system through a user-based study is that adaptation takes time, often more than is available during a study [123]. One solution is an *indirect* study, where the user model is given to participants and they perform the task on behalf of a third party (one example of this is a so-called User-as-Wizard study [83].

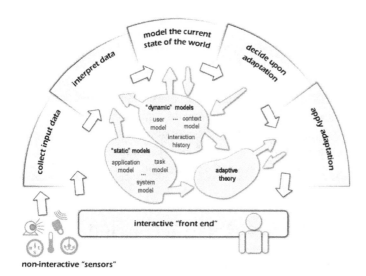

Figure 9.1: Layered evaluation of adaptive systems. Reproduced from Paramythis et al. [123].

This allows controlling the characteristics of the imaginary user, avoiding the time delay needed for populating the user model from actual user interactions. An indirect study also ensures that the input to an adaptation layer is perfect, making it suitable for layered evaluations. For example, Dennis et al. [42] studied the adaptation of emotional support to personality traits using an indirect study. Indirect studies may also be used for other reasons, e. g., when it is difficult to recruit a large enough number of target participants, such as in the work by Smith et al. [147], which studied adaptive reminders for skin cancer patients. Indirect studies can provide initial insights into what is likely effective; direct studies are still needed to confirm this with the target population.

Longitudinal versus short term
Many studies show a positive effect of behavior change interventions in the short term. However, this does not necessarily mean that the intervention is effective in the long term, given that relapse is common. There is therefore a recognized need for longitudinal studies. When systems are adaptive, this is needed even more, as adaptation happens over time [123].

Domain effects
The persuasion domain may impact the effectiveness of persuasive techniques. For example, Thomas et al. [161] found that the effectiveness of persuasive message types differed between domains. Hence, evaluations are needed in multiple domains, to see which results generalize and which are domain dependent.

Metrics and scales

Many studies use ad hoc surveys to measure perceived persuasiveness, without reporting on scale construction, validation and reliability. This makes it hard to compare between studies or domains and have confidence in measurements. Thomas et al. [161] developed a validated, cross-domain scale for measuring perceived persuasiveness based on studies in the healthy eating and cyber security domains. Kaptein et al. [70] and Busch et al. [25] also presented validated scales, but to measure people's *susceptibility* to persuasion techniques, namely to Cialdini's principles of persuasion and certain persuasive techniques (e. g., social comparison and rewards), respectively.

9.6 Ethical issues of personalized persuasion

As seen in Section 9.4, PPT has many applications aiming to help people to achieve goals they set for themselves: to exercise, learn, live healthier and adopt environmentally sustainable lifestyles. However, like any technology, PPT can be used for purposes that are harmful to individuals or have negative consequences for society. For example, PPT has been used for targeted advertising on social media sites and in search engines leading people to spend more money on online purchases. Persuasive interfaces of social networks aiming to maximize user attention can lead people to addiction, lack of real social interactions, alienation and mental health problems. To increase the effectiveness of persuasive technologies through personalization, companies hoard and commodify personal data [181], which can lead to risks of identity theft, denied services and other risks for individuals. Important ethical concerns have been raised [165] regarding the PPT deployed by large internet companies that exploit hidden cognitive biases [85, 157]. By exploiting and reinforcing existing cognitive biases, such as confirmation bias [60], filter bubbles emerge, leading to polarization of the public discourse, to a rise in populism and authoritarian leaders, trends that are detrimental to democracy [133]. Big social network platforms seek user engagement because their business model is based on selling targeted advertisements, but as a by-product of their model, they have facilitated also the spread of conspiracy theories, misinformation and propaganda , which can have deadly consequences, e. g., the antivaxxer propaganda during the Covid-19 pandemic. How do we counter these negative trends?

Personalization relies on the availability of massive amounts of user data to train machine learning and recommender system algorithms. Legislation against hoarding user data is already providing strong protections in the EU, and there are trends for strengthening privacy legislation in other countries, i. e., the US and Canada. Also, the increasing use of synthetic data instead of personal data for training algorithms can help achieve a level of personalization without compromising privacy.

The AI community has sought to achieve fairness, accountability and transparency in the AI techniques deployed in machine learning applications by designing improved algorithms and methods for unbiasing data in recommender and decision-support systems. Recently, there has been a thrust into developing methods, frameworks and techniques for Responsible AI [53] and Human-Centered AI (HCAI) [143, 144] that seeks to maintain user autonomy through safe design practice, ensuring transparency and control over the technology using methods from the Human-Computer Interaction and User Experience Design communities as well as methods for developing safe and dependable software from software engineering, certification bodies and legislation that regulates the industry.

The PT community has been concerned about the Ethics of Persuasive Technologies long before the AI community. Researchers have expressed concerns about the Ethics of PT from the very beginning of the field, in 1998–1999 [21, 50] and have proposed ethical guidelines for designers [12], e. g., performing a stakeholder analysis [50, 51], respecting privacy [71], and using value-sensitive and participatory-design methodologies [41]. In 2013, Karppinen and Oinas-Kukkonen [74] proposed a conceptual framework to help designers choose an appropriate ethical approach. The Behavior Change Wheel (BCW) [90] discussed in Section 9.3 provides a framework for developing persuasive and behavior change technology, which is at a similar level as the Human-Centered AI framework proposed by Shneiderman [144] for the development of ethical and responsible AI. All these works are focused on the design process.

With the advance of new AI applications and technologies, new concerns have been raised recently. For example, Botes [23] and Rosenberg [136] alarm about the danger of "mind-control" in the Metaverse by using PPT because of the intimate personalization due to ubiquitous sensing of psycho-physiological data about users [149, 150], the rapid advances of deep learning and generative large language model based AI tools such as ChatGPT. The advances in generative AI in sophisticated and realistic videos of conversational agents or as avatar representations of users in the Metaverse may prove to be dangerously persuasive and successful in making people trust and believe falsehoods. People tend to treat virtual agents as real people even when they are not particularly realistic [129, 148]. There seems to be no research yet [20] on developing computational techniques, tools and frameworks supporting "ethical PT" to parallel the work in the Ethical AI community, but hopes are placed on certification and regulation [137]. There is a need for methods for identifying the level of hazard of different persuasive techniques to humans and society (e. g., addictiveness, manipulation), so that the PPT industry can be regulated, and its applications certified as safe and trustworthy. Work in developing ethically certified persuasive technologies is a promising future direction of research, along with developing tools to support the regulatory and legal framework around persuasive technologies to prevent deception, coercion and manipulation. An important future research direction is to ensure that personalized persuasive technologies are supporting the best interests of all stakeholders: the individual users, the society and the environment, not just the interests of big companies.

9.7 Summary and outlook

This chapter serves as an introduction to the personalization of persuasive technology. It draws on behavior change theories from fields such as psychology and behavioral economics, which have proposed numerous behavior change techniques. The chapter provides an overview of some of the most commonly used techniques and emphasizes the importance of adapting both the technique selection and instantiation to the user, their context and the application domain for persuasive technology to be optimally effective. To illustrate this, examples are provided of the personalization that may be required, and what has already been investigated in different domains. The chapter also discusses the challenges involved in evaluating personalized persuasive technology and the ethical concerns.

Future work is required on the evaluation of personalized persuasive technology, to ensure the results of different studies can be compared, combined, reproduced and generalized. We see also future trends for personalization of PT powered by AI, e. g., generative language models and deep learning techniques, which enable PPT to dynamically adapt to the user's motivation, affective state and context. We envisage also that PPT will be applied in immersive, virtual and augmented reality contexts (a. k. a. Metaverse), using realistic generated virtual characters as coaches, advisors and simulated buddies. Research is urgently required to ensure that PPT supports the interests of all stakeholders and in methodologies for the responsible development of PPT by envisaging ways in which they can be misused, considering the risks to individuals and society. Research is needed in creating safe-guards, design methodologies and best software development practices for responsible PPT. At some point, there will be legal frameworks and legislation regulating the safe use of PPT. Software professionals can help by developing tools facilitating the regulation of the use of PPT in applications on the market and through development of tools that enable transparency and control of PPT to ensure the user's autonomy.

References

[1]   I. Adaji, K. Oyibo, and J. Vassileva. E-Commerce Shopping Motivation and the Influence of Persuasive Strategies. *Frontiers in Artificial Intelligence* 3 (2020) 67. https://doi.org/10.3389/frai.2020.00067.

[2]   H. op den Akker, V. M. Jones, and H. J. Hermens. Tailoring real-time physical activity coaching systems: a literature survey and model. *User Modeling and User-Adapted Interaction* 24 (2014) 351–392.

[3]   M. Altmeyer, S. Lessel, P. Jantwal, L. Muller, F. Daiber, and A. Krüger. Potential and effects of personalizing gameful fitness applications using behavior change intentions and Hexad user types. *User Modeling and User-Adapted Interaction* 31(4) (2021) 675–712.

[4]   F. Alqahtani, S. Meier, and R. Orji. Personality-based approach for tailoring persuasive mental health applications. *User Modeling and User-Adapted Interaction* 32 (2022) 253–295.

[5]   E. Anagnostopoulou, B. Magoutas, E. Bothos, J. Schrammel, R. Orji, and G. Mentzas. *Exploring the links between persuasion, personality and mobility types in personalized mobility applications. Persuasive*

Technology conference. LNCS, volume 10171. Cham: Springer, 2017. https://doi.org/10.1007/978-3-319-55134-0_9.

[6] E. S. Anderson, J. R. Wojcik, R. A. Winett, and D. M. Williams. Social-cognitive determinants of physical activity: the influence of social support, self-efficacy, outcome expectations, and self-regulation among participants in a church-based health promotion study. Health psychology: official journal of the Division of Health Psychology. *American Psychological Association* 25(4) (2006) 510–520.

[7] E. Andre, T. Rist, S. van Mulken, M. Klesen, and S. Baldes. The automated design of believable dialogues for animated presentation teams. In: J. Cassell, S. Prevost, J. Sullivan, and E. Churchill, editors. *Embodied Conversational Agents*. The MIT Press, 2000, pp. 220–225.

[8] M. M. Antony and D. R. Hopko. *The ABCs of behavior change: A guide to successful disease prevention and health promotion*. Oxford University Press, 2012.

[9] D. Ariely. *Predictably Irrational*. Harper-Collins, 2008.

[10] Aristotle. (350 BCE). On Rhetoric: A Theory of Civic Discourse (G. A. Kennedy, Trans.). Oxford University Press.

[11] E. Aronson. *The Social Animal*, 9th edition. New York: Worth Publishers, 2004.

[12] B. M. Atkinson. Captology: A critical review. In: *Proc. 1st International Conf. Persuasive Technology*, 2006, pp. 171–182.

[13] A. Bandura. The self system in reciprocal determinism. *The American Psychologist* 33(4) (1978) 344–358. https://doi.org/10.1037/0003-066X.33.4.344.

[14] A. Bandura. *Social foundations of thought and action: A social cognitive theory*. Prentice-Hall, 1986.

[15] A. Bandura. In: V. S. Ramachaudran, editor. *Self-efficacy. In Encyclopedia of Human Behavior*. New York: Academic Press, 1994.

[16] A. Bandura. Social cognitive theory. Annals of Child Development. In: R. Vasta, editor. *Annals of Child dDevelopment. Vol. 6. Six theories of child development*. Greenwich, CT: JAI Press, 1999, pp. 1–60.

[17] R. Bartle. Hearts, clubs, diamonds, spades: Players who suit MUDs. *Journal of MUD Research* 1(1) (1996) 19.

[18] A. L. Baylor and Y. Kim. Simulating instructional roles through pedagogical agents. *International Journal of Artificial Intelligence in Education* 15(2) (2005) 95–115.

[19] A. L. Baylor. Promoting motivation with virtual agents and avatars: role of visual presence and appearance. *Philosophical Transactions of the Royal Society B: Biological Sciences* 364(1535) (2009) 3559–3565.

[20] C. Bech. The need for focused research on coercion, deception and manipulation in persuasive use of social media. Persuasive 2020 Adjunct Proc. 2020. Available at http://ceur-ws.org/Vol-2629/.

[21] D. Berdichevsky and E. Neuenschwander. Toward an ethics of persuasive technology. *Communications of the ACM* 43(5) (1999) 51–58.

[22] D. Böhm, B. Dorland, R. Herzog, R. B. Kap, T. S. Langendam, A. Popa, M. Bueno, and R. Bidarra. How can you save the world? Empowering sustainable diet change with a serious game. In: *IEEE conference on games*. IEEE, 2021, pp. 1–7.

[23] M. Botes. Autonomy and the social dilemma of online manipulative behavior. *AI Ethics* (2022). https://doi.org/10.1007/s43681-022-00157-5.

[24] D. Braun, E. Reiter, and A. Siddharthan. SaferDrive: An NLG-based behaviour change support system for drivers. *Natural Language Engineering* 24(4) (2018) 551–588.

[25] M. Busch, J. Schrammel, and M. Tscheligi. Personalized persuasive technology - Development and validation of scales for measuring persuadability. In: *International Conference on Persuasive Technology*. Springer, Berlin, Heidelberg, 2013, pp. 33–38.

[26] G. Carenini and J. D. Moore. Generating and evaluating evaluative arguments. *Artificial Intelligence* 170 (2006) 925–952.

[27] S. Chaudhari, S. Ghanvatkar, and A. Kankanhalli. Personalization of intervention timing for physical activity. *Scoping Review JMIR Mhealth Uhealth* 10(2) (2022) e31327. https://doi.org/10.2196/31327.

[28] R. Cheng and J. Vassileva. Adaptive reward mechanism for sustainable Online learning community. In: *Proceedings of the International Conference Artificial Intelligence in Education*. Amsterdam, The Netherlands: IOS Press, 2005, pp. 152–159.

[29] R. Cheng and J. Vassileva. User motivation and persuasion strategy for peer-to-peer communities. In: *Hawaii International Conference on System Sciences (Mini-track on online communities in the digital economy/emerging technologies)*. IEEE Press, 2005.

[30] R. Cheng and J. Vassileva. Design and evaluation of an adaptive incentive mechanism for sustained educational online communities. *User Modeling and User-Adapted Interaction* 16 (2006) 321–348.

[31] R. B. Cialdini. Harnessing the science of persuasion. *Harvard Business Review* 79(9) (2001) 72–79.

[32] R. Cialdini. *Pre-Suasion: A Revolutionary Way to Influence and Persuade*. NY: Simon Schuster, 2016.

[33] A. Ciocarlan, J. Masthoff, and N. Oren. Qualitative study into adapting persuasive games for mental wellbeing to personality, stressors and attitudes. In: *Adjunct Publication of the 25th Conference on User Modeling, Adaptation and Personalization*, 2017, pp. 402–407.

[34] A. Ciocarlan, J. Masthoff, and N. Oren. Kindness is contagious: Study into exploring engagement and adapting persuasive games for wellbeing. In: *Proceedings of the 26th Conference on User Modeling, Adaptation and Personalization*, 2018, pp. 311–319.

[35] A. Ciocarlan, J. Masthoff, and N. Oren. Actual persuasiveness: impact of personality, age and gender on message type susceptibility. In: *Proceedings of the14th International Persuasive Conference*, Limassol, Cyprus: Springer International Publishing, 2019, pp. 283–294.

[36] N. Colineau and C. Paris. Motivating reflection about health within the family: The use of goal setting and tailored feedback. *User Modeling and User-Adapted Interaction* 21(4–5) (2011) 341–376.

[37] S. Consolvo, D. W. McDonald, T. Toscos, M. Y. Chen, J. Froehlich, B. Harrison, P. Klasnja, A. LaMarca, L. LeGrand, R. Libby, and I. Smith. Activity sensing in the wild: a field trial of UbiFfit garden. In: *Proceedings of the SIGCHI conference on human factors in computing systems*, 2008, pp. 1797–1806.

[38] M. Csikszentmihalyi and I. S. Csikszentmihalyi. Adventure and the flow experience. *Adventure education* (1990), 149–155.

[39] S. D. Craig, B. Gholson, M. H. Garzon, X. Hu, W. Marks, P. Wiemer-Hastings, and Z. Lu. Autor tutor and otto tudor. International Conference on AI in Education. In: *Workshop on Animated and Personified Pedagogical Agents, Le Mans, France*, 1999, pp. 25–30.

[40] S. Dantzig, M. van Bulut, M. Krans, A. Van Der Lans, and B. De Ruyter. Enhancing physical activity through context-aware coaching. In: *ACM International Conference Proceeding Series*. Association for Computing Machinery, 2018, pp. 187–190. https://doi.org/10.1145/3240925.3240928.

[41] J. Davis. Design Methods for Ethical Persuasive Computing. In: *Proceedings of the Persuasive Confence*, 2009.

[42] M. Dennis, J. Masthoff, and C. Mellish. Adapting progress feedback and emotional support to learner personality. *International Journal of Artificial Intelligence in Education* 26 (2016) 877–931.

[43] A. Dijkstra. Technology adds new principles to persuasive psychology: Evidence from health education. In: *Proceedings of the Persuasive Technology Conference*, 2006, pp. 16–26.

[44] A. Dijkstra. The persuasive effects of personalization through name mentioning in a smoking cessation message. *User Modeling and User-Adapted Interaction* 24 (2014) 393–411.

[45] X. Ding, J. Xu, H. Wang, G. Chen, H. Thind, and Y. Zhang. WalkMore: Promoting walking with just-in-time context-aware prompts 65–72, 2016. IEEE Wireless Health, WH 2016, art. no. 7764558. https://doi.org/10.1109/WH.2016.7764558.

[46] D. Elsweiler, H. Hauptmann, and C. Trattner. Food Recommender Systems. In: F. Ricci, L. Rokach, and B. Shapira, editors. *Recommender Systems Handbook*, New York, NY: Springer, 2022. https://doi.org/10.1007/978-1-0716-2197-4_23.

[47] R. Farzan, J. M. DiMicco, D. R. Millen, C. Dugan, W. Geyer, and E. A. Brownholtz. Results from deploying a participation incentive mechanism within the enterprise. In: *Proceedings of the SIGCHI conference on Human factors in computing systems*. 2008, pp. 563–572.

[48] M. Fishbein and I. Ajzen. *Belief, attitude, intention, and behavior*. Reading, MA: Addison-Wesley, 1975.

[49] M. Fishbein, H. C. Triandis, F. H. Kanfer, M. Becker, S. E. Middlestadt, and A. Eichler. Factors influencing behaviour and behaviour change. In: A. Baum, T. A. Revenson, and J. E. Singer, editors. *Handbook of health psychology*. Mahwah, NJ: Lawrence Erlbaum Associates, 2001, pp. 3–17.

[50] B. J. Fogg. Persuasive computers: perspectives and research directions. In: *Proc. SIGCHI Conference on Human Factors in Computing Systems*, Boston: ACM Press/Addison-Wesley Publishing Co., 1998, pp. 225–232.

[51] B. J. Fogg. *Persuasive Technology: Using Computers to Change What We Think and Do*. Morgan Kaufmann, 2003.

[52] B. J. Fogg. A behavior model for persuasive design. In: *Proceedings of the 4th international Conference on Persuasive Technology*, 2009, pp. 1–7.

[53] L. Floridi, J. Cowls, M. Beltrametti, R. Chatila, P. Chazerand, V. Dignum, C. Luetge, R. Madelin, U. Pagallo, F. Rossi, and B. Schafer. AI4People—an ethical framework for a good AI society: opportunities, risks, principles, and recommendations. *Minds and Machines* 28 (2018) 689–707.

[54] J. Freyne and S. Berkovsky. Intelligent food planning: personalized recipe recommendation. In: *15th international conference on Intelligent user interfaces*, 2010, pp. 321–324.

[55] S. Gabrielli, P. Forbes, A. Jylhä, S. Wells, M. Sirén, S. Hemminki, P. Nurmi, R. Maimone, J. Masthoff, and G. Jacucci. Design challenges in motivating change for sustainable urban mobility. *Computers in Human Behavior* 41 (2014) 416–423. https://doi.org/10.1016/j.chb.2014.05.026.

[56] F. Grasso, A. Cawsey, and R. Jones. Dialectical argumentation to solve conflicts in advice giving: a case study in the promotion of healthy nutrition. *International Journal of HumanComputer Studies* 53 (2000) 1077–1115.

[57] L. Grazzini, P. Rodrigo, G. Aiello, and G. Viglia. Loss or gain? The role of message framing in hotel guests' recycling behaviour. *Journal of Sustainable Tourism* 26(11) (2018) 1944–1966.

[58] J. Greer, G. McCalla, J. Vassileva, R. Deters, S. Bull, and L. Kettel. Lessons learned in deploying a multi-agent learning support system: The I-Help experience. *Proceedings of AI in Education AIED* 1 (2001) 410–421.

[59] E. Hadoux and A. Hunter. Comfort or safety? Gathering and using the concerns of a participant for better persuasion. *Argument & Computation* 10(2) (2019) 113–147.

[60] J. Haidt. *The righteous mind: Why good people disagree about politics and religion*. First Vintage Books, 2013.

[61] H. Hauptmann, N. Leipold, M. Madenach et al. Effects and challenges of using a nutrition assistance system: results of a long-term mixed-method study. *User Modeling and User-Adapted Interaction* 32 (2022) 923–975. https://doi.org/10.1007/s11257-021-09301-y.

[62] H. Hermens, H. op den Akker, M. Tabak, J. Wijsman, and M. Vollenbroek. Personalized coaching systems to support healthy behavior in people with chronic conditions. *Journal of Electromyography and Kinesiology* 24(6) (2014) 815–826.

[63] E. T. Higgins. Beyond pleasure and pain. *The American Psychologist* 52(12) (1997) 1280–1300.

[64] J. B. Hirsh, S. K. Kang, and G. V. Bodenhausen. Personalized persuasion: Tailoring persuasive appeals to recipients' personality traits. *Psychological Science* 23(6) (2012) 578–581.

[65] C. Horsch, S. Spruit, J. Lancee, R. van Eijk, R. J. Beun, M. Neerincx, and W. Brinkman. Reminders make people adhere better to a self-help sleep intervention. *Health Technology* 7 (2017) 173–188.

[66] C. S. Hulleman, K. E. Barron, J. J. Kosovich and R. A. Lazowski. Student motivation: Current theories, constructs, and interventions within an expectancy-value framework. In: *Psychosocial skills and school systems in the 21st century: Theory, research, and practice*, 2016, pp. 241–278.

[67] B. T. Johnson and A. H. Eagly. Effects of involvement on persuasion: A meta-analysis. *Psychological Bulletin* 106 (1989) 290–314.

[68] D. Kahneman and A. Tversky. Prospect Theory: An Analysis of Decision under Risk (PDF). *Econometrica* 47(2) (1979) 263–291.

[69] R. B. Kantharaju, D. De Franco, A. Pease, and C. Pelachaud. Is two better than one? Effects of multiple agents on user persuasion. In: *18th International Conference on Intelligent Virtual Agents*, 2018, pp. 255–262.

[70] M. Kaptein, P. Markopoulos, B. de Ruyter, and E. Aarts. Can You Be Persuaded? Individual Differences in susceptibility to persuasion. In: T. Gross et al., editors. *INTERACT'2009*. LNCS, volume 5726. Springer, Berlin; Heidelberg, 2009, pp. 115–118.

[71] M. C. Kaptein, D. Eckles, and J. Davis. Envisioning persuasion profiles: challenges for public policy and ethical practice. *ACM Transactions* 18(5) (2011) 66–69.

[72] M. Kaptein, B. de Ruyter, P. Markopoulos, and E. Aarts. Adaptive persuasive systems: a study of tailored persuasive text messages to reduce snacking. *ACM Transactions on Interactive Intelligent Systems (TiiS)* 2(2) (2012) 1–25.

[73] M. Kaptein and A. van Halteren. Adaptive persuasive messaging to increase service retention: Using persuasion profiles to increase the effectiveness of email reminders. *Personal and Ubiquitous Computing* 17 (2013) 1173–1185.

[74] P. Karppinen and H. Oinas-Kukkonen. Three Approaches to Ethical Considerations in the Design of Behavior Change Support Systems. In: S. Berkovsky and J. Freyne, editors. *PERSUASIVE 2013*. LNCS, volume 7822, 2013, pp. 87–98.

[75] A. Keng Kau, Y. E. Tang, and S. Ghose. Typology of online shoppers. *The Journal of Consumer Marketing* 20 (2003) 139–156. https://doi.org/10.1108/07363760310464604.

[76] R. Khaled, R. Fischer, J. Noble, and R. Biddle. A qualitative study of culture and persuasion in a smoking cessation game. In: *International Conference on Persuasive Technology*, 2008, pp. 224–236.

[77] P. Kindness, J. Masthoff, and C. Mellish. Designing emotional support messages tailored to stressors. *International Journal of Human-Computer Studies* 97 (2017) 1–22.

[78] P. Kraft, F. Drozd, and E. Olsen. Digital therapy: addressing willpower as part of the cognitive-affective processing system in the service of habit change. In: *Proceedings of the 3rd International Conference on Persuasive Technology, Oulu, Finland*, 2008, pp. 177–188.

[79] C.-M. Kuo and H.-J. Chen. The gamer types of seniors and gamification strategies toward physical activity. *LNCS* 11593 (2019) 177–188. https://doi.org/10.1007/978-3-030-22015-0_14.

[80] W. L. Leite, M. Svinicki, and Y. Shi. Attempted validation of the scores of the VARK: Learning styles inventory with multitrait–multimethod confirmatory factor analysis models. *Educational and Psychological Measurement* 70(2) (2010) 323–339.

[81] E. A. Locke and G. P. Latham. Building a Practically Useful Theory of Goal Setting and Task Motivation: A 35-Year Odyssey. *The American Psychologist* 57(9) (2002) 705–717.

[82] M. Lu. 50 cognitive biases in the modern world. Visual Capitalist. 2020, https://www.visualcapitalist.com/50-cognitive-biases-in-the-modern-world/.

[83] J. Masthoff. The user as wizard: A method for early involvement in the design and evaluation of adaptive systems. In: *Fifth workshop on user-centred design and evaluation of adaptive systems*, 2006, pp. 460–469.

[84] J. Masthoff, S. Langrial, and K. van Deemter. Personalizing triggers for charity actions. In: *Persuasive Technology: 8th International Conference, Sydney, NSW, Australia*. Springer: Berlin Heidelberg, 2013, pp. 125–136.

[85] A. Mathur, G. Acar, M. J. Friedman, E. Lucherini, J. Mayer, M. Chetty and A. Narayanan. Dark Patterns at Scale: Findings from a Crawl of 11K Shopping Websites. *Proceedings of the ACM on Human–Computer Interaction* 3(CSCW) (2019) 81. https://doi.org/10.1145/335918.

[86] I. Mazzotta, F. de Rosis, and V. Carofiglio. PORTIA: a user-adapted persuasion system in the healthy eating domain. *IEEE Intelligent Systems* 22 (2007) 42–51.

[87] R. R. McCrae and O. P. John. An introduction to the five-factor model and its applications. *Journal of Personality* 60(2) (1992) 175–215.

[88] S. Michie, M. Johnston, C. Abraham, R. Lawton, D. Parker, and A. Walker. Making psychological theory useful for implementing evidence-based practice: a consensus approach. *Quality and Safety in Health Care* 14 (2005) 26–33.

[89] S. Michie, M. Johnston, J. Francis, W. Hardeman, and M. Eccles. From theory to intervention: mapping theoretically derived behavioural determinants to behaviour change techniques. *Applied Psychology* 57 (2008) 660–680.

[90]   S. Michie, N. M. van Stralen, and R. West. The behaviour change wheel: A new method for characterising and designing behaviour change interventions. *Implementation Science* 6 (2011) 42.
[91]   W. R. Miller and S. Rollnick. *Motivational interviewing*. New York: The Guildford Press, 1991.
[92]   S. M. Mousavifar and J. Vassileva. Investigating the efficacy of persuasive strategies on promoting fair recommendations. In: *17th International Persuasive Technology conference*. Cham: Springer International Publishing, 2022, pp. 120–133.
[93]   C. Musto, M. de Gemmis, P. Lops, and G. Semeraro. Generating post hoc review-based natural language justifications for recommender systems. *User Modeling and User-Adapted Interaction* 31 (2021) 629–673.
[94]   I. B. Myers. *The Myers-Briggs Type Indicator: Manual*, 1962.
[95]   L. E. Nacke, C. Bateman, and R. L. Mandryk. BrainHex: A neurobiological gamer typology survey. *Entertainment Computing* 5(1) (2014) 55–62.
[96]   C. Nass, B. Reeves, and G. Leshner. Technology and roles: A tale of two TVs. *Journal of Communication* 46(2) (1996) 121–128.
[97]   H. Nguyen and J. Masthoff. Is it me or is it what I say? In: *Source image and persuasion. Second International Conference on Persuasive Technology, Palo Alto, CA, USA*. Berlin Heidelberg: Springer, 2007, pp. 231–242.
[98]   H. Nguyen, J. Masthoff, and P. Edwards. Modelling a receiver's position to persuasive arguments. In: *Second International Conference on Persuasive Technology, Palo Alto, CA, USA*. Berlin Heidelberg: Springer, 2007, pp. 271–282.
[99]   H. Nguyen, J. Masthoff, and P. Edwards. Persuasive effects of embodied conversational agent teams. In: *HCI International (Beijing, China)*. Berlin Heidelberg: Springer, 2007, pp. 176–185.
[100] H. Nguyen and J. Masthoff. Designing persuasive dialogue systems: Using argumentation with care. In: *Third international Persuasive Technology conference (Oulu, Finland)*. Berlin Heidelberg: Springer, 2008, pp. 201–212.
[101] H. Nguyen and J. Masthoff. Mary: A personalised virtual health trainer. In: *Adjunct Proceedings User Modeling, Adaptation and Personalization*, 2010.
[102] C. van Nimwegen, K. Bergman, and A. Akdag. Shedding light on assessing Dark Patterns: Introducing the System Darkness Scale (SDS). In: *Proceedings of the 35th British HCI and Doctoral Consortium 2022, UK*, 2022.
[103] B. S. T. O. M. Nkwo and R. Orji. Bota: A Personalized Persuasive Mobile App for Sustainable Waste Management. CEUR workshop proceedings, 2020.
[104] H. Oinas-Kukkonen and M. Harjumaa. Persuasive systems design: Key issues, process model, and system features. *Communications of the Association for Information Systems* 24(1) (2009) 28.
[105] W. Oliveira, J. Hamari, S. Joaquim et al. The effects of personalized gamification on students' flow experience, motivation, and enjoyment. *Smart Learning Environments* 9 (2022) 16. https://doi.org/10.1186/s40561-022-00194-x.
[106] J. D. O'Keefe *Persuasion: Theory and research*. Newbury Park, CA: Sage, 1990.
[107] C. Okonkwo and J. Vassileva. Affective Pedagogical Agents and User Persuasion. In: C. Stephanidis, editor. *Proc. "Universal Access in Human – Computer Interaction (UAHCI)", Proceedings of the 9th International Conference on Human- Computer Interaction, New Orleans, USA*, 2001, pp. 397–401.
[108] J. A. Okpo, J. Masthoff, M. Dennis, and N. Beacham. Adapting exercise selection to performance, effort and self-esteem. *New Review of Hypermedia and Multimedia* 24(3) (2018) 1–32.
[109] A. H. Olagunju, M. Ogenchuk, and J. Vassileva. Mobile persuasive application for responsible alcohol use: Drivers for use and impact of social influence strategies. In: *Proceedings of the 16th International Persuasive Conference*. Cham: Springer International Publishing, 2021, pp. 102–114.
[110] S. Orbell, M. Perugini, and T. Rakow. Individual differences in sensitivity to health communications: Considerations of future consequences. *Health Psychology* 23 (2004) 388–396.
[111] F. A. Orji, K. Oyibo, R. Orji, J. Greer, and J. Vassileva. Personalization of persuasive technology in higher education. In: *27th ACM Conference on User Modeling, Adaptation and Personalization*, 2019, pp. 336–340.

[112] F. A. Orji, J. Vassileva, and J. Greer. Evaluating a persuasive intervention for engagement in a large university class. *International Journal of Artificial Intelligence in Education* 31 (2021) 700–725.

[113] R. Orji, J. Vassileva, and R. L. Mandryk. Modeling the efficacy of persuasive strategies for different gamer types in serious games for health. *User Modeling and User-Adapted Interaction* 24 (2014) 453–498.

[114] R. Orji, R. L. Mandryk, and J. Vassileva. Gender, age, and responsiveness to Cialdini's persuasion strategies. In: *Persuasive Technology: 10th International Conference, PERSUASIVE 2015, Chicago, IL, USA, June 3–5, 2015, Proceedings 10*. Springer International Publishing, 2015, pp. 147–159.

[115] R. Orji, R. L. Mandryk, and J. Vassileva. Improving the efficacy of games for change using personalization models. *ACM Transactions on Computer-Human Interaction (TOCHI)* 24(5) (2017) 1–22.

[116] K. Oyibo. Designing culture-tailored persuasive technology to promote physical activity (Doctoral dissertation, University of Saskatchewan), 2020.

[117] K. Oyibo, R. Orji and J. Vassileva. Investigation of the Influence of personality traits on Cialdini's persuasive strategies. *PPT@ PERSUASIVE* (2017) 8–20.

[118] K. Oyibo, R. Orji, and J. Vassileva. Developing culturally relevant design guidelines for encouraging physical activity: A social cognitive theory perspective. *Healthcare Informatics Research* 2 (2018) 319–352.

[119] K. Oyibo, I. Adaji, and J. Vassileva. Susceptibility to fitness app's persuasive features: Differences between acting and non-acting users. In: *Adjunct proceedings of the 27th conference on user modeling, adaptation and personalization*, 2019, pp. 135–143.

[120] K. Oyibo and J. Vassileva. Persuasive features that drive the adoption of a fitness application and the moderating effect of age and gender. *Multimodal Technologies and Interaction* 4(2) (2020) 17.

[121] K. Pangbourne and J. Masthoff. Personalised messaging for voluntary travel behaviour change: Interactions between segmentation and modal messaging; Universities Transport Studies Group Conference: Bristol, UK, 2016.

[122] K. Pangbourne, S. Bennett, and A. Baker. Persuasion profiles to promote pedestrianism: Effective targeting of active travel messages. *Travel Behaviour and Society* 20 (2020) 300–312.

[123] A. Paramythis, S. Weibelzahl, and J. Masthoff. Layered evaluation of interactive adaptive systems: framework and formative methods. *User Modeling and User-Adapted Interaction* 20 (2010) 383–453.

[124] P. D. Paraschos and D. E. Koulouriotis. Game difficulty adaptation and experience personalization: a literature review. *International Journal of Human–Computer Interaction* 39(1) (2023) 1–22.

[125] P. Petkov, S. Goswami, F. Köbler, and H. Krcmar. Personalised eco-feedback as a design technique for motivating energy saving behaviour at home. In: *Proceedings of the 7th Nordic Conference on Human-Computer Interaction: Making Sense Through Design*, 2012, pp. 587–596.

[126] J. O. Prochaska and W. F. Velicer. The transtheoretical model of health behavior change. *American Journal of Health Promotion* 12(1) (1997) 38–48. https://doi.org/10.4278/0890-1171-12.1.38.

[127] H. Qian, R. Kuber, A. Sears, and E. Murphy. Maintaining and modifying pace through tactile and multimodal feedback. *Interacting with Computers* 23(3) (2011) 214–225.

[128] J. M. Quintero Johnson, A. Sangalang, and S. Y. Park. First-person, third-person, or bystander? Exploring the persuasive influence of perspective in mental health narratives. *Journal of Health Communication* 26(4) (2021) 225–238.

[129] B. Reeves and C. I. Nass. *The media equation: How people treat computers, television, and new media like real people and places*. Cambridge university press, 1996.

[130] E. Reiter, R. Robertson, and L. Osman. Lessons from a failure: Generating tailored smoking cessation letters. *Artificial Intelligence* 144 (2003) 41–58.

[131] F. Ricci, L. Rokach, and B. Shapira. *Recommender systems handbook*, 3rd edition. Springer, 2022.

[132] A. Rieger, Q. U. A. Shaheen, C. Sierra, M. Theune, and N. Tintarev. Towards healthy engagement with online debates: An investigation of debate summaries and personalized persuasive suggestions. In: *Adjunct Proceedings of the 30th ACM Conference on User Modeling, Adaptation and Personalization*, 2022, pp. 192–199.

[133] D. Robertson. The most dangerous tool of persuasion. *POLITICO* (2022). https://www.politico.com/newsletters/digital-future-daily/2022/09/14/metaverse-most-dangerous-tool-persuasion-00056681.

[134] L. Rodrigues, A. M. Toda, W. Oliveira, P. T. Palomino, J. Vassileva, and S. Isotani. Automating Gamification Personalization to the User and Beyond. *IEEE Transactions on Learning Technologies* 15(2) (2022) 199–212. https://doi.org/10.1109/TLT.2022.3162409.

[135] A. J. Rohm and V. Swaminathan. A typology of online shoppers based on shopping motivations. *Journal of Business Research* 57 (2004) 748–757. https://doi.org/10.1016/S0148-2963(02)00351-X.

[136] L. Rosenberg. The Metaverse: From Marketing to Mind Control. Future of Marketing Institute, 2022. https://futureofmarketinginstitute.com/the-metaverse-from-marketing-to-mind-control/.

[137] L. Rosenberg. Regulation of the Metaverse: A Roadmap: The risks and regulatory solutions for large scale consumer platforms. In: *Proceedings of the 6th International Conference on Virtual and Augmented Reality Simulations (ICVARS '22)*. New York, NY, USA: ACM, 2022, pp. 21–26. https://doi.org/10.1145/3546607.3546611.

[138] R. Ruiz-Dolz, J. Taverner, S. Heras, A. García-Fornes, and V. Botti. A qualitative analysis of the persuasive properties of argumentation schemes. In: *30th ACM Conference on User Modeling, Adaptation and Personalization (Barcelona, Spain)*. ACM, 2022, pp. 1–11.

[139] R. M. Ryan and E. L. Deci. Self-determination theory and the facilitation of intrinsic motivation, social development, and well-being. *The American Psychologist* 55(1) (2000) 68.

[140] J. Schäwel. How to raise users' awareness of online privacy: An empirical and theoretical approach for examining the impact of persuasive privacy support measures on users' self-disclosure on online social networking sites. PhD thesis, Universität Duisburg-Essen, Germany, 2018.

[141] P. W. Schultz, A. Messina, G. Tronu, E. F. Limas, R. Gupta, and M. Estrada. Personalized normative feedback and the moderating role of personal norms: A field experiment to reduce residential water consumption. *Environment and Behavior* 48(5) (2016) 686–710.

[142] M. Sherif and C. M. Sherif. Attitudes as the individual's own categories: The social judgment involvement approach to attitude and attitude change. In: C. W. Sherif and M. Sherif, editors. *Attitude, ego-involvement, and change*, 1967, pp. 105–139.

[143] B. Shneiderman. Human-Centered Artificial Intelligence: Reliable, Safe & Trustworthy. *International Journal of Human-Computer Interaction* 36(6) (2020) 495–504.

[144] B. Shneiderman. *Human-Centered Artificial Intelligence*. Oxford University Press, 2022.

[145] M. A. Sidi-Ali, J. Masthoff, M. Dennis, J. Kopecky, and N. Beacham. Adapting performance and emotional support feedback to cultural differences. In: *27th ACM Conference on User Modeling, Adaptation and Personalization*, 2019, pp. 318–326.

[146] K. A. Smith, J. Masthoff, N. Tintarev, and W. Moncur. The development and evaluation of an emotional support algorithm for carers. *Intelligenza Artificiale* 8(2) (2014) 181–196.

[147] K. A. Smith, M. Dennis, and J. Masthoff. Personalizing reminders to personality for melanoma self-checking. In: *Proceedings of the 2016 Conference on User Modeling Adaptation and Personalization, Halifax*, 2016, pp. 85–93.

[148] K. A. Smith and J. Masthoff. Can a virtual agent provide good emotional support? In: *32nd International BCS Human Computer Interaction Conference*, 2018, pp. 1–10.

[149] H. Spelt, E. K. V. Dijk, J. Ham, J. Westerink, and W. IJsselsteijn. Psychophysiological measures of reactance to persuasive messages advocating limited meat consumption. *Information* 10(10) (2019) 320.

[150] H. A. A. Spelt, J. H. D. M. Westerink, L. Frank et al. Physiology-based personalization of persuasive technology: a user modeling perspective. *User Modeling and User-Adapted Interaction* 32 (2022) 133–163. https://doi.org/10.1007/s11257-021-09313-8.

[151] S. ter Stal, M. Tabak, H. op den Akker, T. Beinema, and H. Hermens. Who do you prefer? The effect of age, gender and role on users' first impressions of embodied conversational agents in eHealth. *International Journal of Human–Computer Interaction* 36(9) (2020) 881–892.

[152] A. Starke, M. Willemsen, and C. Snijders. Promoting energy-efficient behavior by depicting social norms in a recommender interface. *ACM Transactions on Interactive Intelligent Systems (TiiS)* 11(3–4) (2021) 1–32.

[153] A. Stibe and K. Larson. Persuasive Cities for Sustainable Wellbeing: Quantified Communities. In: M. Younas, I. Awan, N. Kryvinska, C. Strauss, and D. Thanh, editors. *Mobile Web and Intelligent Information Systems. MobiWIS 2016*. LNCS, volume 9847. Cham: Springer, 2016.

[154] J. B. Stiff and P. A. Mongeau. *Persuasive communication*, 2nd edition. Guilford Press, 2002.

[155] B. Subagdja, A. H. Tan, and Y. Kang. A coordination framework for multi-agent persuasion and adviser systems. *Expert Systems with Applications* 116 (2019) 31–51.

[156] L. Sun and J. Vassileva. Social visualization encouraging participation in online communities. In: *Groupware: Design, Implementation, and Use: 12th International Workshop, CRIWG 2006, Medina del Campo, Spain*. Berlin Heidelberg: Springer, 2006, pp. 349–363.

[157] D. Susser, B. Roessler and H. F. Nissenbaum. Online manipulation: Hidden influences in a digital world. *Georgetown Law Technology Review* 1 (2019). https://doi.org/10.2139/ssrn.3306006.

[158] R. J. Thomas, J. Masthoff, and N. Oren. Adapting healthy eating messages to personality. In: *12th International Persuasive Technology Conference*. Amsterdam, The Netherlands: Springer International Publishing, 2017, pp. 119–132.

[159] R. J. Thomas, J. Masthoff, and N. Oren. Personalising healthy eating messages to age, gender and personality: Using Cialdini's principles and framing. In: *22nd International Conference on Intelligent User Interfaces*, 2017, pp. 81–84.

[160] R. J. Thomas, J. Masthoff, and N. Oren. Is argumessage effective? A critical evaluation of the persuasive message generation system. In: *I14th International Persuasive Technology Conference*. Limassol, Cyprus: Springer International Publishing, 2019, pp. 87–99.

[161] R. J. Thomas, J. Masthoff and N. Oren. Can I influence you? Development of a scale to measure perceived persuasiveness and two studies showing the use of the scale. *Frontiers in Artificial Intelligence* **2** (2019). https://doi.org/10.3389/frai.2019.00024.

[162] G. F. Tondello, R. Orji and L. E. Nacke. Recommender systems for personalized gamification. In: *Adjunct publication of the 25th conference on user modeling, adaptation and personalization*, 2017, pp. 425–430.

[163] G. F. Tondello, A. Mora, A. Marczewski, and L. E. Nacke. Empirical validation of the gamification user types hexad scale in English and Spanish. *International Journal of Human-Computer Studies* 127 (2019) 95–111.

[164] J. A. Updegraff and A. J. Rothman. Health message framing: Moderators, mediators, and mysteries. *Social and Personality Psychology Compass* 7(9) (2013) 668–679.

[165] US Congress Hearing. 2019. https://www.commerce.senate.gov/2019/6/optimizing-for-engagement-understanding-the-use-of-persuasive-technology-on-internet-platforms.

[166] M. Vardhan, N. Hegde, S. Merugu, S. Prabhat, D. Nathani, M. Seneviratne, N. Muhammad, P. Reddy, S. Lakshminarasimhan, R. Singh, K. Lorenzana, E. Motwani, P. Talukdar, and A. Raghuveer. Walking with PACE-Personalized and automated coaching engine. In: *30th ACM Conference on User Modeling, Adaptation and Personalization*, 2022, pp. 57–68. https://doi.org/10.1145/3503252.3531301.

[167] J. P. Vargheese, S. Sripada, J. Masthoff, and N. Oren. Persuasive strategies for encouraging social interaction for older adults. *International Journal of Human-Computer Interaction* 32(3) (2016) 190–214.

[168] J. P. Vargheese, M. Collinson, and J. Masthoff. A quantitative field study of a persuasive security technology in the wild. In: *Social Informatics: 13th International Conference, SocInfo 2022, Glasgow, UK*. Cham: Springer International Publishing, 2022, pp. 211–232.

[169] J. Vassileva. Harnessing P2P Power in the Classroom. In: J. C. Lester, R. M. Vicari, and F. Paraguaçu, editors. *Intelligent Tutoring Systems. ITS 2004*. Lecture Notes in Computer Science, volume 3220. Berlin, Heidelberg: Springer, 2004. https://doi.org/10.1007/978-3-540-30139-4_29.

[170] J. Vassileva. Motivating participation in social computing applications: a user modeling perspective. *User Modeling and User-Adapted Interaction* 22 (2012) 177–201. https://doi.org/10.1007/s11257-011-9109-5.

[171] L. van Velsen, M. Broekhuis, S. Jansen-Kosterink, and H. op den Akker. Tailoring persuasive electronic health strategies for older adults on the basis of personal motivation: Web-based survey study. *Journal of Medical Internet Research* 21(9) (2019) e11759. https://doi.org/10.2196/11759.

[172] B. Wais-Zechmann, V. Gattol, K. Neureiter, R. Orji, and M. Tscheligi. Persuasive technology to support chronic health conditions: investigating the optimal persuasive strategies for persons with COPD. In: *13th International Persuasive Technology Conference*. Waterloo, ON, Canada: Springer International Publishing, 2018, pp. 255–266.

[173] R. H. Walters and R. D. Parke. Social motivation, dependency, and susceptibility to social influence. In: *Advances in experimental social psychology*, volume 1. Academic Press, 1964, pp. 231–276.

[174] D. Walton. Enthymemes and argumentation schemes in health product ads. In: *Proceedings of the Workshop W5: Computational Models of Natural Argument, Twenty-First International Joint Conference on Artificial Intelligence*, 2009, pp. 49–56.

[175] X. Wang, W. Shi, R. Kim, Y. Oh, S. Yang, J. Zhang and Z. Yu. Persuasion for good: Towards a personalized persuasive dialogue system for social good. In: *57th Annual Meeting of the Association for Computational Linguistics*, 2019, pp. 5635–5649.

[176] A. Webster and J. Vassileva. Visualizing Personal Relations in Online Communities. In: V. P. Wade, H. Ashman, and B. Smyth, editors. *Adaptive Hypermedia and Adaptive Web-Based Systems. AH 2006*. Lecture Notes in Computer Science, volume 4018. Berlin, Heidelberg: Springer, 2006, pp. 223–233. https://doi.org/10.1007/11768012_24.

[177] L. R. West. Strava: challenge yourself to greater heights in physical activity/cycling and running. *British Journal of Sports Medicine* 49 (2015) 1024.

[178] A. T. Wibowo, A. Siddharthan, H. Anderson, A. Robinson, N. Sharma, H. Bostock, A. Salisbury, R. Comont, and R. Van Der Wal. Bumblebee friendly planting recommendations with citizen science data. In: *International Workshop on Recommender Systems for Citizens*, 2017, pp. 1–6.

[179] M. Wunsch et al. What makes you bike? Exploring persuasive strategies to encourage low-energy mobility. In: T. MacTavish and S. Basapur, editors. *Persuasive Technology. PERSUASIVE 2015*. LNCS, volume 9072. Chicago, IL, USA: Springer, Cham, 2015. https://doi.org/10.1007/978-3-319-20306-5_5.

[180] C. Zhang, J. Vanschoren, A. van Wissen et al. Theory-based habit modeling for enhancing behavior prediction in behavior change support systems. *User Modeling and User-Adapted Interaction* 32 (2022) 389–415.

[181] S. Zuboff. *The age of surveillance capitalism*. Profile Books, 2019.

Chiara Luisa Schleu and Mirjam Augstein

10 Personalization approaches for remote collaborative interaction

Abstract: In the past years, work settings became more flexible, involving a drastically increased share of remote work and collaboration. Remote collaborative interaction where teams might not only be spatially distributed but also involve highly diverse members with different interests, backgrounds and attitudes, require elaborated system support to turn out successful for the team. In the domain of computer-supported cooperative work, there exist numerous approaches that can be used by systems to support collaborative interaction, such as communication and coordination tools, awareness mechanisms or sharing options. Although rich in functionality, out-of-the-box solutions are often not able to adapt to individual needs of the people in a team and specific needs of a team as a whole. Many related challenges can be attempted to be overcome by means of personalization, either user-driven or system-driven, based on either the explicit collection of user requirements or on the automated interpretation of interaction data. Yet, personalized support often does not consider the specific ad hoc situations a team might be in. Thus, in this chapter, we discuss a phenomenological approach, driven by identification and analysis of particular, potentially critical team situations, combined with traditional personalization concepts. We present a qualitative interview study with seven experts of different related fields who were asked to suggest personalization approaches for selected team situations in a remote collaboration setting. The exemplary team situations were derived from a prestudy data elicitation with a team of four persons interacting on a collaborative task. Experts' statements were thematically coded, categorized and compiled to a taxonomy of personalized collaboration support measures. Further, we derive design implications for personalized collaborative systems based on this taxonomy.

Keywords: Collaborative interaction, collaboration support, personalization, taxonomy

10.1 Introduction

Remote forms of collaboration and fully distributed teams in the work context have become widespread in recent years [28, 33] while at the same time, mainly colocated settings have become less common [50], at least in domains, which do not per se require onsite presence (e. g., due to a need for specialized infrastructure such as production machinery). For instance, Hamersly and Land suggest that employing distributed

Acknowledgement: Part of the work reported in this chapter has been conducted within the scope of the Hybrid Collaboration Spaces (HYCOS) project, funded by the Austrian Science Fund (FWF) [P 34928].

https://doi.org/10.1515/9783110988567-010

teams in organizations is becoming a prerequisite for growth and business success [21]. The global trend toward remote work and collaboration has been further reinforced by the COVID-19 pandemic. With this trend, also the need for systems and tools facilitating and supporting remote collaboration drastically increased. In the domain of Computer-Supported Cooperative Work (CSCW), a lot of research has already been done on different approaches that enable such support and that can be built into *collaborative systems* (i. e., computer-based systems, tools and services providing an infrastructure for collaborative interaction). These approaches include very basic *communication and coordination tools* (e. g., audio and videoconferencing or messaging services, shared calendars or voting tools), but also advanced concepts enabling mutual *awareness of activities* (e. g., through notifications of others' activities, highlighting changes in artefacts or indications of others' presence in certain regions of shared workspaces), or *information sharing facilities* across different personal and shared parts of a workspace.

Current CSCW software is rich in functionality and widely used, and a lot of research, including both conceptual work and user studies, has been conducted to substantiate the underlying ideas. Yet, existing tools often cannot adapt to the specific needs and requirements of individual members of a team or the team as a whole. This is a known challenge (not only) for collaborative systems, which can be generally approached by the introduction of *personalization*. Personalization, according to Augstein and Neumayr [2] generally stands for the concept of "supporting users individually and according to their individual needs and prerequisites" and can be implemented with different foci, e. g., by means of *configuration* (involving "initiative of the user him or herself," also often denoted as *adaptability* [40]) or by means of "system-initiated adaptation to the user's needs" (which is often also described under the notion of *adaptivity*) [2]. This fundamental dichotomy is also the basis of Opperman et al.'s scale [40], which introduces a "spectrum of adaptation in computer systems" concretely naming five distinct manifestations of personalization while remaining interpretable as continuum between two extremes.

The extent and quality of personalization approaches in computer systems including collaborative ones is strongly dependent on the amount and level of detail of available information about the users. Such information, which forms the basis for personalization, is usually collected either explicitly (e. g., via surveys querying user requirements) or implicitly (e. g., via logging, analysis and interpretation of interaction data). Both concepts, however, focus on longer-term user (or team) requirements and usually do not consider specific situations a user or a team of users might be in during the interaction with the system. Thus, a new strategy has recently evolved under the notion of *phenomenological approaches* [43]. Saatçi et al. [43] state that especially for support of collaboration, the needs of collaborative situations rather than the individual requirements of participating users should be in the focus. Their approach is fundamentally new in several aspects and it significantly differs from the traditional views of user-centered design and personalization. They argue that "designing truly valuable experiences for hybrid meetings requires moving from the traditional, essentialist and perception-obsessed user-centered design approach to a phenomenological approach to the needs of meetings themselves" [43].

In this chapter, we aim at establishing a link between the situation-based concept of collaboration support and those traditionally based on user- and group-focused personalization. We see huge potential in both of them, and thus consider a combination as promising. The concrete research questions we attempt to answer are: *RQ1: How can traditional personalization approaches be used to support remote collaboration in certain critical situations? RQ2: How can the identified measures be categorized? RQ3: What can designers of collaborative systems do to comply with the suggested measures?* Therefore, we first identified exemplary distinctive team situations in a small-scale prestudy, focusing on such which can be considered "critical" (e. g., situations in which a team's work might be ineffective, conflictual or otherwise compromised); see Section 10.3.1. The resulting collection of distinctive and potentially critical team situations then became the basis for a qualitative interview study conducted with seven experts of different fields who were asked to envision methods of personalized support suitable for the respective situations (see Section 10.3.2). As a major contribution of this chapter, we then present a *taxonomy of situation-focused personalized collaboration support measures* derived from the experts' suggestions (see Section 10.4) and propose a number of *design implications* based on this taxonomy (see Section 10.5).

10.2 Background literature

In the context of our work presented in this chapter, we provide background literature related to the following topics most relevant: *personalization and collaboration support approaches* (see Section 10.2.1), and related *methodological approaches* (see Section 10.2.2). The latter comprises work around (i) the *identification of critical situations in collaboration settings* (see Section 10.2.2.1) and (ii) the *thematic coding of interview data and data-driven derivation of a categorization scheme* (see Section 10.2.2.2).

10.2.1 Personalization and collaboration support approaches

In this section, we describe different categorization possibilities for personalization or collaboration support measures. We consider these relevant because they provide an overview of how such categorization schemes might look like and what different approaches are currently available. In our work (specifically, the taxonomy presented in Section 10.4), we however intendedly did not rely on any existing categorization scheme as a basis for classifying experts' suggestions. The reason for this decision is that we did not want to restrict experts' ideas in any way a priori and expected inherent limitations and compromises related to correct assignment of measures to categories (e. g., in case suggested measures do not really fit to any of the available categories).

10.2.1.1 Personalization approaches

Often, methods and techniques of system- or user-initiated personalization are rooted in answers to Knutov et al.'s six major "questions of adaptation" [27]: *What can we adapt? What can we adapt to? Why do we need adaptation? Where can we apply adaptation? When can we apply adaptation?* and *How do we adapt?* Knutov et al. [27], based on Brusilovsky [8], distinguish between *content adaptation techniques* (e. g., inserting, removing or altering fragments), *adaptive presentation techniques* (e. g., dimming fragments, zooming or scaling, arrangement of elements) and *adaptive navigation techniques* (e. g., link hiding, link generation or guidance). Partly, these categories overlap and some techniques might be related to more than one category (e. g., link sorting is mainly associated with adaptive presentation techniques but also related to adaptive navigation techniques). This can make it very hard to disambiguate the idea behind a concrete technique and correctly assign it to one of the available categories. Further, this established and prominent categorization is strongly linked to adaptive hypermedia and nonexhaustive when it comes to alternative application domains. For instance, Augstein and Neumayr [2] already suggested *adaptive interaction techniques* (e. g., including automated selection and configuration of input and output devices, modalities and activities or user interface adaptation) to be added as a distinct branch in the categorization. In the context of our work, the categorization lacks concrete techniques related to *collaboration support*. Even if many of the traditional techniques are also applicable for personalized support of groups (or individuals in a group, which might benefit the group as well), they do not explicitly capture the focus on the collaborative setting. This drawback has been partially already been addressed in a recent review of personalized collaborative systems [35] where the authors suggest a taxonomy of related work mainly based on the respective collaboration scenario (colocated, remote or hybrid). This taxonomy, since it aims at roughly categorizing existing work rather than classifying in detail different support approaches, is however too general and not of sufficient level of detail for our use case.

10.2.1.2 (Personalized) collaboration support approaches

Explicit collaboration support might either concentrate on the process of *collaboration establishment* or on the *collaboration process* itself. The former, e. g., includes group formation [1, 32, 42], task assignment [13] or configuration of available collaboration media [15]. The latter, e. g., includes dynamic role assignment [48, 56], adjusting group size or changing the availability of elements [29, 42].

In the context of the work presented in this chapter, we focus on *support of the collaboration process*. According to Brusilovsky and Peylo [9], personalized collaboration support systems might have a knowledge base of "good and bad collaboration patterns," which are either hard-coded into the system or learned from interaction with the system over time. Our approach is a combination of both: on one hand, we apply human expertise to identify solutions to critical situations in a collaboration process (i. e., domain knowledge which could be hard coded into the system in the future) (see Section 10.3.2); on the other hand, we conduct an analysis of an exemplary collaboration process a priori to identify such potentially critical situations (see Section 10.3.1), which is a step that could at least be partly automatized in the future.

Collaboration support systems that focus on the collaboration process itself can offer dedicated collaboration support on different levels. For instance, Niederman et al. [37] suggest a categorization distinguishing between measures on the *design level* (i. e., selecting tools and techniques, structuring the process so that a team may complete their tasks most efficiently), *execution level* (i. e., guiding a team through a process), *activity level* (i. e., providing context-aware adaptations to a team's activities to increase effectiveness and efficiency) and *behavior level* (i. e., inspiring more collaborative behavior among team members through analysis of interactions and rewards). In the context of our work, we generally consider this categorization sufficiently generic to not introduce severe drawbacks if used for assigning support measures to the existing categories. In fact, many of the collaboration support measures suggested by the experts (see Section 10.4) could be assigned to the levels suggested by Niederman et al. We however did not want to exclusively rely on their scheme because it is not intended to explicitly capture personalization techniques, and thus might not sufficiently represent measures that target the individual in a team rather than the team itself.

10.2.2 Methodological approaches

In this section, we summarize methodological foundations that guided our work during the steps of identifying critical situations in the given group interaction setting (see Section 10.2.2.1) and conducting the thematic analysis leading to the taxonomy presented in Section 10.4 (see Section 10.2.2.2).

10.2.2.1 Identification of critical situations in collaborative settings

One traditional observation-based method for the identification of critical situations is the Critical Incident Technique (CIT). Flanagan [16] describes it as a "procedure for gathering certain important facts concerning behavior in defined situations." He further points out that CIT "does not consist of a single rigid set of rules governing such data collection" but it "should be thought of as a flexible set of principles, which must be modified and adapted to meet the specific situation at hand." In essence, CIT comprises that (i) only simple types of judgements are required of an observer, (ii) reports from only qualified observers are included and (iii) all observations are evaluated by the observer in terms of an agreed upon statement of the purpose of the activity [16]. CIT also includes classification of observed critical incidents, which is, "[i]n the absence of an adequate theory of human behavior," an "inductive" and "relatively subjective" step [16]. A subsequent step (i. e., "after a classification system has been developed") then involves "inferences regarding practical procedures for improving performance based on the observed incidents" [16]. Flanagan further suggests collecting the "ideas of a number of well-qualified authorities," e. g., in the form of an interview, pointing out that the acquired statements might be "fairly lengthy and detailed." He points out the importance of selecting observers who are familiar with the respective task at hand and specifies that in case groups should be observed, the following information should be collected: general description, location, persons, times and conditions. Further, regarding the behaviors to be observed, the following is important: general type of activity, specific behaviors, criteria of relevance to general aim, criteria of importance to general aim (critical points). CIT has been applied for the identification of critical incidents in numerous settings including collaborative interaction. For instance, Kvarnström in her study identified critical incidents in collaboration such as "contribution not valued, not put to use," "lack of concensus" or "[t]eam decides over the individual" (see [30]).

In the context of our work, the CIT is highly relevant because it significantly inspired our methodology described in Section 10.3. We followed the steps of first identifying critical situations in a collaborative interaction setting via multifaceted data collection including observation but also analysis of further factors relevant for the "general aim," such as behaviors and activities, before we conducted an interview study with renown experts ("well-qualified authorities" [16]). Further, we established a classification system (see Section 10.4) before we deducted design implications for collaborative systems ("inferences regarding practical procedures for improving performance based on the observed incidents" [16]); see Section 10.5.

Another methodological concept of high relevance is Saatçi et al.'s work around the identification of "disruptive situations" in hybrid meetings [43]. Saatçi et al., whose idea behind a "phenomenological approach" is to place the requirements of a meeting itself rather than the individual needs of users in the focus of interest, describe an indepth micro analysis of a single hybrid meeting. They focus on technological troubles and three specific disruptive moments in the meeting, which included a status update and brainstorming activities in the context of a global software company. Example disruptive moments they identified are situations where colocated team members tried to make sure that a remote participant had video on, or asked a remote participant to turn off video due to apparent network trouble. The recording of the meeting was analyzed using Ethnomethodology and Conversation Analysis (EM/CA) and a number of design and practice suggestions for hybrid meetings (e. g., related to improvement of technical state awareness, communication of expected behavior or communication of meeting format) were drawn from the analysis.

In the context of our work, Saatçi et al.'s is relevant because first, it inspired us to specifically focus on the requirements of the collaborative situation, and second, we also conducted an analysis of critical situations in a team scenario based on a single meeting followed by an in-depth analysis to derive a solid basis for later identification of design implications. Our concrete methodology is similar in terms of data collection but differs in the means of analysis (e. g., involving collaborative coupling behavior [25, 36, 51], territorial functioning [31, 46, 52, 53] and team activities).

10.2.2.2 Thematic analysis and categorization

A second strand of relevant methodological foundations for our work is related to the thematic analysis and categorization of collected field data. We consider the Contextual Design (CD) methodology coined by Holtzblatt and Beyer [4, 5, 24], specifically focusing on its Affinity Building (AB) process, as most important.

CD comprises a framework of methods for planning and implementing a user-centered design process throughout different phases of a project. One of these phases is the process of requirements elicitation, which according to Holtzblatt and Beyer is a nontrivial task because humans are often not sufficiently able to describe their requirements and regularly fail in uncovering "hidden factors" (especially when they are personally affected) [23, 24]. Instead of simply asking people for their requirements, Holtzblatt and Beyer suggest conducting Contextual Inquiry (CI) including observation of users in their natural (work) setting combined with an interview.

In the CD framework, CI is usually followed by AB, which includes the generation of so-called affinity notes, i. e., short descriptions of meaningful events, problems, issues or statements, that capture the key issues about the data [5]. These affinity notes are then systematically hierarchically clustered to form a so-called affinity diagram. During the manual clustering process, it is important to neither relate to any predefined categories (but let the categories evolve from the given data) nor assign single notes to groups based on keywords (but refer to the semantic concepts behind the notes). After grouping the notes to clusters, shared categories are derived for each group, which are then further aggregated by adding top-level categories (the AB process as defined by Holtzblatt and Beyer utilizes a number of four hierarchical levels with the concrete notes constituting the lowest one). Subsequently, requirements but also design ideas are derived from the affinity diagram. The CD methodology comprises many further steps to guide a full user-centered design process.

In our work, we mainly referred to its AB concept during the construction of our taxonomy for the following reasons: (i) we did not want to rely on any predefined set of categories in order not to lose any information, which does not fully fit into this scheme and (ii), we aimed at deriving the categories but also concrete support measures directly from the data (in our case, experts' ideas gathered through interviews). This, together with our previous and extensive very positive experiences with the CD framework (and specifically, AB), motivated our methodological decision.

10.3 Qualitative study

In this section, we describe our empirical work to (i) identify exemplary yet typical critical situations in collaborative interaction, (ii) obtain support measures for collaborative systems combining user-centered (personalization-based) and phenomenological approaches (cf. Sections 10.1 and 10.2) and (iii) derive design implications for collaborative systems. Our endeavors comprise a prestudy in form of an observed and recorded team experiment (cf. Section 10.3.1) and an expert interview, which we consider the core of our empirical work (cf. Section 10.3.2).

10.3.1 Prestudy team experiment

The prestudy experiment with a team of four persons remotely collaborating on a joint task, provided a foundation for the identification of exemplary yet typical critical team situations. In this section, we describe the setting, procedure, task and methods applied, as well as the four participants and our findings related to critical situations.

10.3.1.1 Collaborative task

The task selected for the prestudy is related to collaboratively planning a joint 5-day holiday to a destination of the participants' choice. According to McGrath's task taxonomy, the task could be considered as a "Type 1: Planning task" and a "Type 4: Decision-making task" [34]. The task is predestined to involve a number of different activities: in order to complete it, the team would have to find new information, make sense of it collaboratively and then come to a joint decision. It was stated as a clear condition that in the end, the team should come to an agreement on which activities they would like to realize. The task was chosen because it does not require any domain-specific or comparable level of prior knowledge, we expected the participants to be quickly able to identify with it and because it could easily trigger potentially critical situations in the form of disagreement and lively discussion/debates.

10.3.1.2 Setting

The four participants collaborated in a fully distributed manner and were asked to collaboratively plan their joint holiday in a remote Skype call. Additionally, they were provided access to the online whiteboard tool MetroRetro,[1] a WYSIWIS environment that enables users to write virtual post-it notes, move them around, cluster them and react to them via comments, emojis or votes. The participants only made used of Skype's audio connection and did not activate their video streams, which was neither intended nor prespecified by the study design but the participants' decision. It might have resulted from their routines and their familiarity among each other, which would be line with the observations of Samrose et al. [44] who studied team dynamics during video conferencing sessions.

10.3.1.3 Procedure

After the participants had signed an informed consent, they were introduced to Metro-Retro, which not all of them were familiar with. They had to collect notes in a shared workspace, interact with each other's notes, list places they would like to visit and then vote on everyone's suggestions. The team's favorite destination—Iceland—was carried over to the main task as the team's holiday destination. After the introduction phase, the team collaborated on the main task, which was declared as complete after 28:10 minutes once the team had decided on a few activities per day and potential backup activities in case of bad weather. Following the experiment, all participants individually completed an anonymous questionnaire on their perception of the task and the collaboration. No time limit was set for the questionnaires.

10.3.1.4 Methods and data collection

The team session was systematically observed by an experienced observer and additionally audio- and screen-recorded for each participant for reasons of subsequent in-depth analysis. These recordings were not only used for the analysis of the team session but also as a basis for the expert interview (see Section 10.3.2). In addition to the observation and recordings, we collected demographic information (not linkable to the rest of the data) as well as participants' answers to a questionnaire containing eight open and ten closed questions (5-point Likert-scale, with one exception of a yes/no question). The questions focused on (i) participants' perception of the collaboration in general and (ii) their ideas regarding personalized support mechanisms a system could have provided

---

1 https://metroretro.io, last accessed on 28 December 2022.

to aid the collaboration. The recordings of the team experiment were analyzed with a focus on (i) the group's activities, (ii) the team's collaborative coupling behavior and, most importantly, (iii) critical situations which arose.

For the *analysis of group activities*, we used a two-stage thematic coding process: first, the video recordings were analyzed to identify all different types of activities the team exhibited; second, this list was used to selectively code the recordings. Regarding *collaborative coupling behavior*, we referred to Neumayr et al.'s list of coupling styles [36] and systematically analyzed the recordings to identify all occurrences of these coupling styles. Regarding the *identification of critical situations*, we made use of the basic CIT ideas (see Section 10.2.2.1) during observation and post hoc analysis. We chose this diverse set of methods to gain a good overview of the collaboration process and be able to richly describe it qualitatively in addition to the list of critical situations, which are of highest relevance for the following expert interviews. We expected that it might be necessary to draw connections between specific collaborative situations (e. g., during specific activities or certain coupling styles) and certain critical incidents.

10.3.1.5 Participants

Four participants (coded as P1–P4 in the remainder of this chapter) were recruited for the prestudy. They were between 24 and 38 years old, three male and one female. The participants were selected according to the following inclusion criteria: They should know and be sufficiently familiar with each other so that they would not feel uncomfortable to raise concerns or initiate debate. This was additionally reasonable in the context of the chosen task because strangers would not usually plan a joint holiday. Further, all participants should be generally familiar with remote collaboration infrastructure such as conferencing and brainstorming tools.

Further, we wanted to recruit a group not too homogeneous but also not too diverse regarding personality types (roughly based on the dimensions of the OCEAN model [14]). Additionally, we aimed at a certain diversity among the participants regarding their interests and preferences relevant for planning a holiday (e. g., adventure vs. relaxing, different dietary requirements, etc.). Finally, the participants should be comfortable with conducting the experiment in the English language (to allow for integration of international experts later, see Section 10.3.2).

10.3.1.6 Findings

We mainly consider the findings of our prestudy as a basis for the expert interviews but shortly summarize them in the following.

Collaboration characteristics
The systematic manual coding process related to the team's *collaborative coupling* behavior (using Neumayr et al.'s Domino framework [36]) revealed a clear preference for the coupling style DISC (Active Discussion), which made up about half of the total collaboration time, followed by SGP (Same General Problem, meaning that the participants individually worked on the same problem from different starting points), which made up about 20 % of the total time.

Subgroup formation can be described as rather volatile (since the participants engaged in direct collaboration with other team members in different and varying constellations). The findings related to collaborative coupling are also confirmed by our *analysis of activities*, which revealed that discussion made up the by far largest part of the collaboration, followed by information foraging, decision-making and clustering of notes by theme. Almost the full collaboration time was spent on task-related activities—only a very small share was spent on administrative or technological issues.

Challenges and critical situations
The participants concretely named challenges related to the following issues (which largely overlap with the observer's assessment): lack of awareness or confusion related to others' activities, limited domain knowledge, difficulties in agreeing on methods to use, unsatisfactory efficiency caused by large amounts of manual work (e. g., for clustering activities), embarrassment and audio conflicts. In total, we identified eight *Critical Situations (CS1–CS8)* that are collaboration- rather than activity-focused and generalize well to other settings: *CS1: A user shares their contributions later than the others, CS2: Users are talking over each other, CS3: Users a taking comparatively long for a task or start working on a new one before the other has been completed, CS4: Not all users' contributions seem to be valued equally, CS5: A user is not able to follow another user's activities, CS6: A user is not heard by the others (in the sense of being given attention),* and *CS7: There is seemingly unnecessary idle time.* Further, we identified one critical collaboration-related issue, which might affect the whole process rather than a specific, time-constrained situation: *CS8: Certain users are more quiet while others are verbally stronger.*

In addition to the critical situations focused on general collaboration aspects listed above, we (again, in accordance with the participants' direct feedback and suggestions) identified three situations where a personalized system could have provided task-specific[2] support. We name them as *Personalization Situation (PS) 1–3. PS1: A system could help a team choosing the next activities after finishing collecting initial information,*

---

2 By task-specific in this context, we do not refer to holiday planning but the more general activities carried out by the team.

PS2: A system could help a team with making decisions and *PS3: A system could support the general process a team is following.* PS3, similar to CS8, is a more overarching one related to the whole process, not constrained to a time-constrained situation.

10.3.2 Expert interviews

The main part of our qualitative research comprised interviews with seven experts based on recordings and the 11 identified critical or personalization situations. In this section, we describe our procedure, method and participants, and provide a high-level summary before Section 10.4 is dedicated to the in-depth presentation of the taxonomy we derived from the experts' statements.

10.3.2.1 Method and procedure

The expert interviews were conducted in a fully remote manner and in the English language, in order to ensure that participation would be possible also for international experts. During the individual interview sessions, experts signed an informed consent related to collection and use of their data. Next, they were shown a video stream combining the individual screen recordings of the four pre-study participants arranged in a 2x2 matrix underlain with the audio recording, providing them with full control over the video. The video was further available to the experts in beforehand to account for potential network problems. The video was annotated with the critical situations identified during the analysis process and by the participants themselves (see CS1–CS8 and PS1–PS3 introduced above) and related questions: after a critical situation occurred, a blank frame was inserted showing a question to be answered by the experts (e. g., "How could an automated system prevent them talking over each other?"). The experts were asked to voice their thoughts on the collaboration and answer the questions regarding the CS and PS, but also to mention anything in addition that they noticed.

The following questions Q1–Q9 appeared in the video: *Q1: P3 only shares their notes later than the others. Should an automated system take action here? How? When?* (related to CS1), *Q2 How could an automated system prevent them talking over each other? How could it help them recover from this issue?* (related to CS2), *Q3 How could an automated system support the team members when they have finished collecting some initial information for their interests?* (related to PS1, PS3), *Q4 Should an automated system remind them that they have not finished their previous task (identifying duplicates)?* (related to CS3, PS1, PS3), *Q5 How could an automated system have supported their decision-making process? How would you characterize a "good" decision?* (related to PS2), *Q6 How could an automated system support here and ensure that all members' ideas are valued equally?* (related to CS4), *Q7 How could an automated system have prevented P2 not being able to follow P4's actions?* (related to CS5), *Q8 How could an automated system have helped P1 to be heard just now?* (related to CS6), *Q9 How could an automated system reduce the group's idle time?* (related to CS7).

The additional questions (Q10–Q13) asked after viewing the video were as follows: *Q10 How could an automated system support users like P1 and P2, who are more quiet, against verbally stronger users and help them get their points across?* (related to CS8), *Q11 How could an automated system support the general process that a team is following (i. e., to help a team stay on track, or suggest a more efficient way to do something)?* (related to PS3), *Q12 What could be some limitations that an automated system should abide by? What things should not be adapted under any circumstances?* and *Q13 What other more general observations have you made, and what implications would you draw from these observations for an automated system?*. The last two questions Q12 and Q13 are not directly related to the critical and personalization situations identified before but should open room for experts' own ideas independent of the recordings.

The interviews were all extensive and revealed a multitude of ideas (see Section 10.4). The duration of the individual interviews ranged between 60 and 100 minutes. They ended with a thank you and farewell to the respective expert.

10.3.2.2 Participants

The aim of our research was to join the concepts of personalization-based as well as situation-based ("phenomenological") support in remote collaboration in order to answer our research questions RQ1–RQ3 (see Section 10.1). Thus, we considered expertise in different domains as highly relevant, foremost *HCI* (bringing in a broad understanding of user needs, User Experience (UX) and user-centered design), *CSCW* (contributing fundamental knowledge of remote collaboration, related potentials and challenges as well as methods of supporting collaborative interaction), *Personalization, Adaptive and Adaptable Systems* (contributing an extensive background in methods of personalized support for individuals and teams) and *Design Thinking (DT)* (bringing in a particularly open mindset related to solution ideation, conceptualization and related methodology, as well as a broad view not dominated by a certain domain).

In addition to the broad view we hoped to gain through considering expertise in the named fields, we expected experts with a researcher's as well as a practitioner's background to address the matter from different perspectives. For example, we anticipated that experts with a rather scientific background would have broad knowledge on the fundamentals of methods and concepts to contribute, and that experts with a rather practical background would focus particularly strongly on user needs and requirements and quickly have concrete design ideas in mind.

In total, we recruited the following seven experts:

Expert 1 (39 years, male, German): E1 is a professor of HCI with 15 years working experience with collaborative systems, both in research and industry. His main focus is on interaction design for colocated or hybrid settings.

Expert 2 (40 years, female, Brazilian): E2 is a UX Designer with 8 years experience in UX design and a background in Architecture and Urban Planning. She also has 5 years of experience teaching HCI at a university.

Expert 3 (51 years, male, German): E3 is a UX designer with 25 years of expertise in UX design and a DT coach. He has 35 years of work experience as a designer.

Expert 4 (34 years, male, Austrian): E4 is a final stage PhD candidate for HCI and CSCW, who has been researching in the HCI field for 8 years, with an additional background in personalization and web development.

Expert 5 (43 years, male, German): E5 is a professor of HCI with 15 years of research experience in interaction design, information visualization, CSCW and ubiquitous computing.

Expert 6 (46 years, female, American): E6 is a UX designer with 16 years of experience, with a large focus on user research.

Expert 7 (48 years, male, Greek): E7 holds a PhD in computer science, with a specialization in HCI and personalization. He has done extensive work on the research, development and evaluation of adaptive systems in the domains of accessibility and e-learning (e. g., adaptive online collaborative learning activities). He is not active in this field any more but retains an overview of recent work.

10.3.2.3 Data collection and analysis

All interviews were conducted by the same interviewer who also took notes during the interviews. For reasons of later in-depth analysis and to not miss anything important, the sessions were additionally recorded and later transcribed. We aimed at (i) capturing the broad overview inherently provided by the diverse expertise present in the selection of interview partners and (ii) not letting any predefined categorization scheme bias the overview gained in the study. Thus, we followed the ideas of the CD methodology, which suggests building an affinity diagram based on affinity notes (see Section 10.2.2.2 [5]) as a foundation for further steps. As suggested by Beyer and Holztblatt [5, 24], we converted the interview transcriptions to unique statements, which then constituted our pool of affinity notes. All statements were randomly arranged in the pool, clustered and then themes and subthemes were derived from the clusters. This step finally led to the taxonomy presented in Section 10.4.

10.3.2.4 Descriptive statistics and summary

In total, 307 statements related to personalized collaboration support in the team setting under investigation, were compiled by the involved experts. Out of that, experts repeated a statement 27 times, and on 87 occurrences, a statement was made by more than one expert. This leaves a total of 193 unique statements across all seven experts. We further observed that experts with a similar background tended to make more similar statements, i. e., a scientific background (E1, E4, E5, E7) vs. a practitioner's background (E2, E3, E6), and that the experts with a scientific background gave more statements on average than the experts with a practitioner's background. Regarding the level of system versus user initiative in experts' suggestions for personalized support, we can summarize that they considered a minimum of user control highly important. Thus, while an automated system should show some initiative, the majority of its features should be initiated, approved or selected by users, according to the experts. A detailed thematic analysis of experts' statements is provided in Section 10.4.

10.4 Thematic coding and taxonomy

In this section, we present (i) the qualitative insights we gained through the expert interviews, and (ii) the resulting taxonomy. The taxonomy was established through a systematic coding process of the experts' statements, which followed the AB procedure as described in Section 10.2.2.2 and involved two coders: an experienced primary coder who was mainly responsible for the coding task, and a secondary one with rich theoretical and methodological knowledge as well as practical experience with the CD methodology and AB, who carefully reviewed the results. The resulting categorization underwent several iterations in which borderline cases or cases in which the categorization was unclear, were discussed. Parts of the taxonomy were thus repeatedly revised. This process was inspired by Beyer's and Holtzblatt's idea of a "Wall Walk" where the Affinity Diagram is reviewed (and, if necessary, complemented or revised, see [5]). These iterations helped the researchers to ensure that the categorization was done according to the CD methodology, e. g., avoiding keyword-based or other undesired ways of coding. The final structure of the taxonomy on the top level of our hierarchy can be seen in Figure 10.1. The detailed branches for each topic can be found in the Appendix; see Figures 10.2 to 10.9. The design implications resulting from the experts' statements are presented in Section 10.5.

As can be seen in the figures and the following sections, many of the experts' ideas and suggestions match or are similar to traditional CSCW topics such as awareness support measures [18, 20, 41, 45], management of collaborative coupling [7, 25, 36, 51, 54], management of different territories and smooth transfer between them [31, 47, 52], as well as motivational measures [6, 10–12, 17, 22, 26]. This was in part expected and confirms the high relevance of these topics in collaborative systems. However, we intentionally did not use them as the top level of our hierarchical organization as we did not want to overlook any other arising topics or introduce a priori limitations. The need for an unbiased categorization was one of the major reasons why we chose the AB process

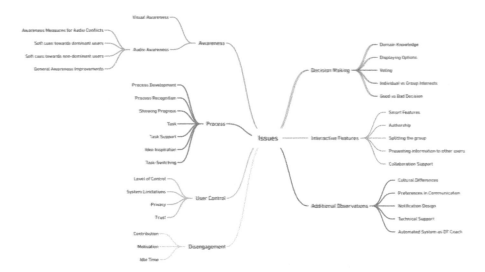

Figure 10.1: The top levels of the taxonomy of collaboration support measures.

rooted in the CD methodology for our research. This way, less traditional topics could be presented with equal significance, if represented accordingly in the interviews. As the results summarized in the following sections indicate, this seems to have been a good decision since the experts' ideas are broad, including also less popular concepts, which is also reflected by the taxonomy.

The taxonomy itself is intended as a tool for researchers which can be used in several ways, e.g., to gain a structured overview of collaboration support methods, as a guideline when ideating or implementing new collaboration support measures, or for the systematic classification or evaluation of existing measures (also see the discussion in Section 10.6, inspired by other taxonomies such as the ones described in [3, 19, 39]). In the following Sections 10.4.1 to 10.4.7, we describe in detail the major branches of the taxonomy, as well as the experts' related statements on which the respective parts of the taxonomy are based on.

10.4.1 Awareness

The topic *Awareness* consists of two subtopics: *Visual Awareness* (see Figure 10.2) and *Audio Awareness* (see Figure 10.3). Within *Visual Awareness*, the experts discussed how workspace awareness could be maintained, in particular awareness for activities in the shared workspace and shared attention. For a team to achieve awareness of each member's activities, each of the members need to share what they are working on and the results of their work, i. e., sharing their notes. In the observed collaboration session, one user shared their notes significantly later while the others had already begun discussing each other's notes. While the experts acknowledged that making notes public before the user is ready to share them can be detrimental [**E1, E4, E5, E7**], they made a few suggestions as to how users could be encouraged to share their notes, i. e., through pop-ups [**E1, E4, E5, E6, E7**] appearing at the beginning of the session [**E6**], or after someone suggests to share notes [**E1, E6**].

Furthermore, it was discussed how the participants could be made implicitly aware of the size and limits (or the lack thereof) of their workspace. Online whiteboard workspaces tend not to have no spatial limits, unlike their real-life counterparts, which increases the likelihood that a team is not aware of a member's actions. Users could be made aware of a team mate's actions happening outside of their view-port, i. e., through indicating everyone's view-port through rectangles [**E5**]. If users have not yet discovered the entirety of their workspace, an automated system could show a zooming-out animation [**E5**]. Nevertheless, users can only be aware of what happens in the shared workspace, not what happens in the other tabs of their teammates [**E5**] (i. e., their personal territories). This, according to [**E5**], leads to discrepancies.

An automated system should also try to support shared attention and give users an easy overview of changes at the "right" moment [**E7**]. The changes could be displayed in a specific "overview space," i. e., a column next to the document itself [**E7**]. This space should highlight where users are performing actions (i. e., displaying the actions via icons) [**E7**]. Users should also be able to call unto their team members when they want to discuss a specific item. The system should let users navigate to their team member's position and return to their own previous position easily [**E7**].

The second topic, *Audio Awareness*, is divided into different subthemes: *Awareness Measures for Audio Conflicts, Soft Cues toward Dominant Users, Soft Cues toward Non-dominant Users* and *General Awareness Improvements*. The term *Audio Conflicts* refers to users talking over each other and thereby missing what the others have said. The term *Recovery from Audio Conflicts* refers to the social recovery of such conflicts through users asking each other to repeat themselves, and deciding who should talk first afterwards. The experts agreed that a system should never interrupt the conversation of users [**E1, E2, E4, E5, E6, E7**], it should also neither decide which user gets to talk nor mute users automatically [**E1, E2, E4, E5, E7**], as this would "detract from the social quality of the interaction" [**E7**]. A less intrusive version of this would be to have users "raise their hands" in order to talk [**E2, E3, E5**], however, the experts recognized that the effectiveness of this would greatly depend on the type of session [**E3, E4, E5**]. It might work well for discussions [**E4**], but less so for collaborative work [**E5**].

The reason that most audio conflicts occur in general was identified as missing visual cues in online settings compared to a colocated setting [**E1, E2, E5, E7**]. When colocated, people use visual cues (face, posture, movement) to judge when others are about to talk [**E1, E7**]. For virtual settings, we would need similar cues, either through video or animated characters, or ambient light or background changes [**E1, E2, E5**]. A user's cursor could also show an animation (i. e., an animated pulse) if the user is speaking [**E7**]. While it would be difficult for a system to prevent users from experiencing audio conflicts, it could help users in the recovery, i. e., through highlighting everyone who was speaking [**E1, E5, E7**], through replaying individual user's audio track after an audio conflict has occurred [**E4**], or providing a transcript of the audio conflict [**E4**]. This would work in a similar way as replaying the audio snippets, without disrupting the conversational flow. One expert suggested that users talking over each other could also have positive effects, especially if users have a similar hierarchical position [**E3**]. It can "really start a conversation within the group," and make users active and excited; however, this strongly depends on the group [**E3**].

Automatically lowering the volume of a very dominant user could be a way to make sure others are also heard, however, it would also be a very disruptive action [**E7**]. It would impair the user's rights and their feeling of control, and thereby is also likely to decrease user acceptance [**E7**]. Instead, a system could show a small pop-up to a dominant user, with the suggestion to speak more slowly [**E3, E5**]. If a less dominant user is being talked over, a system should generally try to help that user getting their point heard [**E2**]. Before taking any action, such as sending a notification to other users, the system should ask the user to confirm this action [**E1, E2, E**]. The user might, in retrospect, decide that their comment was not as relevant, or the conversation might have already moved on [**E2, E4**]. A user might also feel embarrassment by needing system support [**E2**]. A system could also encourage more passive users to speak up through providing a nudge at the right moment [**E7**].

10.4.2 Process

The better the process, the more effectively a team can work. However, teams can face a number of challenges due to their processes. The experts responded to the team's struggles observed in the experiment and provided a number of ideas regarding *Process Development*, *Process Recognition* through a system, *Showing the Process, Tasks, Task Support* and *Task-Switching* (see Figure 10.4).

Regarding *Process Development* and whether it could be automated to some extent, the experts' opinions were split between providing a structure, similarly to a Design Thinking workshop structure, and not providing any structure, as it might impose on users and take away the dynamic element of collaboration. On the one hand, supporting a team's organizational tasks could make them more efficient [**E1, E6**]. The system could support users in creating a time-boxed agenda for themselves in the beginning [**E1, E6**]. If the collaboration is task-oriented, the system could recognize and support subtasks such as brainstorming, sorting, categorization of ideas, voting, prioritization, decision-making and guide users along to the next step [**E4**]. On the other hand, a lot of *Process Development* happens ad hoc and can change dynamically during the collaboration [**E5**]. Improvisation is a very human trait, defining the individual steps of a process and their order would thereby impose on users [**E5**]. To automate a process, one would need to strictly model the collaboration and thereby forcing users to only work one way—"this could be detrimental," warned one expert strongly [E5]. "The assumption that collaboration can be formalized is heavily flawed" [E5]. Predicting or modeling future collaborations would be near impossible, since users develop their working style dynamically within the group [E5]. Performing creative tasks within a tightly structured process could create an "assembly-line" feeling within users and severely harm their creative flow and their quality of ideas [E5]. Users preconfiguring some process support within an automated system for themselves might be a better solution for creative tasks [E5].

Even if a system cannot entirely recognize a team's process, it should still show some kind of basic structure to the team, e. g., an outline that the team has previously agreed upon [E7]. If the system displays the overall progress, seeing how they are getting closer to their goal might increase motivation and feeling of accomplishment [E2, E7]. However, in order to do so, a system would need to know the tasks required for a project—creating and agreeing on a task list before starting a project is in itself a challenging task [E7]. It might be a good alternative to let users choose from templates [E7]. An automated system will probably be limited in the extent of support it can give, and in the types of tasks it can support, i. e., "creating a document—possible vs. designing a new logo— not possible" [E7]. Outlining the current step would support users in keeping track of their current task, and allow them to be more efficient [E1, E2, E3, E6, E7]. Helping a team to keep track of tasks is especially helpful the larger the group is [E7].

Regarding tasks, the experts discussed how a system might adapt itself to different tasks, or how it could support a team during a task. If individual tasks are time-boxed, either by the system or by the users, the system could check in with users once they finished the previous task [E3, E4]. It would help users to work more efficiently if they utilize timers for individual subtasks, whether or not this is automated [E1, E6]. However, if users then decide to switch tasks in the middle of such a time frame, the system should support this type of dynamic process development [E1]. The users will have good reasons to switch strategies [E1]. It might even be possible for users to parallelize tasks [E5]. In such a case, awareness support would be very important to help users align and catch up with each other after a task [E5].

In order to support users during tasks, the system could add additional information to notes through domain knowledge, i. e., the location or duration of activities [E1, E7]. This way the system could detect potential conflicts earlier than humans [E1]. When users are taking notes, a system could cluster notes based on the vocabulary used, or it could identify duplicate notes [E1, E4, E7]. The system could also offer users different views for the data, based on its type, i. e., viewing locations on a map [E1].

Instead of relying on the system to try and recognize what users are working on, users could also just indicate to the system what they are working on, which tasks are up next, postponed or done [E1, E2, E5, E7]. This would be more accurate [E1, E2, E5, E7]. Changes in user activity are unlikely to always be a reliable indicator of task completion [E5]. If the system thinks that a team might be done with their overall task, it could prompt the team to save or export their result [E4]. If that is done nonintrusively, the message can be easily ignored [E4].

10.4.3 User control

When using a system, the user should always feel like they are in control, as stated by design guidelines by Nielsen [38] or Shneiderman [49]. When automating a system, ensuring user control can be an issue. The experts discussed this issue and raised different aspects of it, such as the *Level of Control, System Limitations, Privacy* and *Trust toward the System* (see Figure 10.5). The experts described how a user's privacy should be handled by an adaptive system, and how an such a system might inspire user trust (and which factors might impair it).

To make sure a user is always in control, the system should never take away a user's tools, and restrain a user's activities, especially not in their private, personal space [E7]. An automated system should never just execute an action, but rather make suggestions for users to choose from [E5, E7]. The user should always be and feel in control [E1, E4]. An automated system should "not act like the director of the band, but more as a musician playing in the band" [E7]. One expert argued strongly in favor of leaving as much manual control with the users as possible, since this can greatly enrich their collaboration [E5]. If the system in fact pretends to be an equal member of the team, the users "might start hating the system," which would negatively impact their productivity [E1]. An automated system should never tell users what to do [E1, E3] or give users the impression that they are lacking intelligence or competence [E2]. Further, an automated system cannot police the collaboration [E7] and, therefore, should also accept humans failing to complete a task [E3]. It should never embarrass or shame users [E2]. If users willfully ignore someone or something, there is nothing that a system could really do to alleviate that [E7]. Regarding transparency, it was noted that the system should never use data without informing the users [E2]. In order for users to build trust toward the system, it should be very explicit in what it is and is not capable of [E1]. An automated system should also never hide content from users [E4]. It should only ever dim and highlight in order to help users focus on the relevant information [E4].

The issue of *Privacy* touches group awareness in some aspect, as creating awareness of others' activities may be in some form a breach of privacy. Sharing everyone's desktop would be a definite breach of privacy [E5], as would making notes publicly visible before the user is ready to do so [E1, E4, E5, E7]. There should be strict limits to what kind of user activities may be broadcast to the team. Users might even want to decide per item, whether they want to share it [E4]. The system could also enable more and more functionality over time, so that users have time to learn about the system and build trust toward it [E1]. If the users have learned that the system is using data about the users to create value for them, they might then be more inclined to give the system access to additional data in the future [E1]. If the system can analyze the audio space, it should only react to instructions that users are giving to the system [**E1**]. If the system analyzes what users say to each other, this might be considered "creepy" and be detrimental toward user trust in the system [**E1**]. Furthermore, a voice-based assistant might be useful in enabling user trust toward automated systems, similar to Voice UIs [**E2**].

10.4.4 Disengagement

Users disengaging from a collaborative session can pose a very serious problem for a team's success. When discussing *Disengagement*, the experts covered the topics of *Contribution*, *Motivation* and *Idle Time* (see Figure 10.6).

In order to stop a minority of users from dominating the conversation while others can barely get a word in, the system could display each user's talking time [**E4, E5, E7**], and notify more dominant users. It is important that users are nudged to talk more/less at the right moment where they might be the most motivated to follow the system's nudge [**E7**]. Such a nudge could be either displayed publicly or privately [**E7**]. For a private notification, it could show the user's own talking time in relation to the others, without showing the exact talking time, e.g., "You're talking 50 % more than your team mates" [**E4, E5**]. The system could also show each team member's activity publicly to show the team if someone is overly dominant or passive. Then the team themselves could nudge the more passive team members themselves [**E7**]. The system could also nudge more dominant users to include quiet users into the conversation more by prompting to ask the more quiet user's opinion [**E1, E4**]. This way, the more dominant user would still be nudged to talk less and not talk over others, without being told they "talk too much" [**E1, E4**]. This might work better, since it would be less negative toward the dominant user [**E1. E4**].

Further, to ensure equal treatment for members and their ideas, the system could highlight ideas that have not yet been included [**E1, E5**]. An indicator for that could be the number of interactions with an object, and how many members of the team interacted with the object [**E1, E5**]. However, if the system then highlights ideas which the users have discussed and rejected before, it would be detrimental to users—the system would be highlighting the "bad" ideas they have rejected, and by extension, dimming the "better" ideas that they have accepted [**E5**]. If the system asked for explicit confirmation, which ideas are accepted or rejected, would be annoying to users, since that type of information is expressed implicitly beforehand [**E5**]. If the users had to inform the system every step of the way, the system would only add to the workload of users [**E5**]. Gamification could also be a good way to encourage users to contribute more: through visualizing all user actions [**E1, E2**] and calculating scores based on the different types of contribution (talking, notes, classification, voting, etc.) [**E2**]. This would also enable soft competition, and let users see how much they contributed to the whole team effort [**E2, E6, E7**]. Showing the contribution in such a way would give users a more realistic idea of their own contribution and seeing the progress meter filling up could make the team more productive and energetic [E2].

The experts were also asked about the *Idle Time* that occurred in the team session. While some thought it might be due to the experimental setting [E5], or the deliverables perhaps not being clear enough [E2], others thought the "idle" time was rather time spent to learn the tool better [E5], or a well-needed pause for users to collect their thoughts [E3, E7]. Depending on what the reason for the idle time is, the system could support the users in different ways. If users are taking a moment to collect their thoughts and figuring out the next step, it would be a good opportunity for the system to display recommendations to help them with exactly that [E7]. Idle time can also be a needed break for users to help them come up with new ideas [E3]. To evaluate how the idle time was used, the system could measure the change in productivity afterwards [E3]. Idle time can occur naturally in both colocated and remote settings, but in remote settings the threshold to freeloading might be lowered, since the other team members are not physically there [E1]. To some extent, reduced participation should be accepted, because no one can give 100 % all the time [E1]. Even in colocated settings, a drop in participation is common toward the end of the session [E1]. If the system detects such a drop in participation, it should not respond with obtrusive nudges like, e. g., "Don't you want to do this?" [E1].

10.4.5 Decision-making

The experts listed several aspects of *Decision-making* and how it might be supported through an adaptive system (see Figure 10.7). In particular, the experts discussed the aspects of *Domain Knowledge* for decision-making, how *Displaying Options* might support users, and the importance of *Voting*. The experts also commented on the interplay of *Individual vs. Group Interests* and how a system might support a team with conflicting interests, as well as how a decision might be characterized as either a *Good vs. Bad Decision* and whether a system could support users in making better decisions.

To support any kind of decision-making, an automated system would need detailed *Domain Knowledge* in order to evaluate and judge the decision [E2, E6]. It would also need to be able to assess the different dimensions of the options that the users can decide between—and since keeping a good overview over different options can also be difficult for users [E7], the system could explicitly display the options [E7]. Adding a visual representation of options would be a great support for users [E7]. Moreover, to reduce the possibility of a dominant person influencing other team members during the decision-making process, the system could try to calculate other options and present them to the team as alternatives [E4]. Anonymous *Voting* would help to ensure that the team knows every member's opinions and priorities [E2, E3, E4, E6, E7]. The system would also need to know how the individual team members rate the priorities of the different options and their dimensions [**E1, E4, E5, E7**]. If users expressed their interests explicitly, then the system could calculate a quality measure of how close the individual preferences are to the collective decision [**E4, E5, E6**]. However, there are several problems with this approach. First of all, asking users to enter their preferences into the system would be a burden to them, since they also have to tell their team mates about their preferences at the same time [**E5**]. Moreover, asking the team to enter their priorities and constraints for each option could also lead to discussions for every point, because the team members probably do not agree with each other on each point [**E1**]. Finally, people only really formulate their preferences over time—this makes it harder for the system to learn their preferences, if the users themselves are also only just developing their own preferences [**E5**]. A user's preferences will likely change over time depending on new input by other team members, so they would have to enter their preferences multiple times, which would multiply the effort [**E5**].

The experts had different opinions on what made a *Good or a Bad Decision*, or whether such a judgment could even be made. Overall, it seems that it would be very difficult to generate a best-decision model—a compromise between everyone's ideas would suffer if one person maybe does not have any good ideas [**E1, E2, E4**]. A good decision could also be defined as requiring as little concessions per team member as possible [**E5**]. Although creating a generic model might be difficult, a system could build a nongeneric model specific to a team over time [**E4**]. Through reviewing past decisions made by the team, the system could learn for future decisions and help the team improve their decisions [**E4**]. One expert took a very different approach. He stated that the system should not try to influence the team's decision in any way [**E3**]. At most, the system could question the team's decision, and suggest a new idea [**E3**]. Furthermore, if the team makes a "bad decision," this should still be accepted as the team's decision. It can serve as a learning opportunity for the team or be an indicator that the team discussion was based on false assumptions [**E3**].

10.4.6 Interactive features

The experts also discussed how an adaptive system's *Interactive Features* might be able to support the team. The following topics were covered here: *Smart Features, Authorship, Forming Subgroups, Presenting Information to other Users* and more generally *Collaboration Support* (see Figure 10.8).

One expert noted that a lot could already be done to improve CSCW through simply improving the interaction design of tools such as MetroRetro [**E5**]. Collaborative systems should be able to support different types of drag and drop, i. e., moving single notes vs. moving clusters while preserving the spatial orientation and distances of the items [**E5**]. It might be possible to analyze the semantic relationship of notes through comparing their time of creation, and their proximity of their position to each other [**E5**]. If the system classifies notes as more similar than average, it could then move the related notes together [E5]. If the users do not want this to happen, they should have an easy way to undo it, otherwise user control will be impacted negatively [E5].

Displaying the creator of an object, i. e., through the background color of a post-it note can have different effects at different times of the collaboration. While the team is grouping notes, or during the decision-making process, the system could automatically anonymize the notes [E6], so that the influence of personal relations on the decision is reduced [E6]. [E7] had a different opinion: they stated that users were more likely to dismiss anonymous notes, than eponymous notes. A system should therefore show who created a note permanently and not, i. e., only while hovering [E2, E6, E7]. This could also be a way a system could help users with realizing if they are overlooking one person's ideas to always show who created the note [E7].

If team members form subgroups to work on a specific topic in greater detail, the team on a whole can become more effective. During individual research, users might not be aware of what everyone else is working on [E4]. If the system can pick up that two members are working on similar topics, it can inform them of similar notes added elsewhere in the workspace, and encourage them to form a subgroup [E4]. Splitting the group could also be helpful for dissolving conflict between team members through forming subgroups of dominant and nondominant users [E3].

If a user wants to show a part of the workspace to others, they should have the option to broadcast this part to users who can then accept or decline to view [E1, E3]. If a team consists of team members and moderators, the moderators should be able to force others to view a specific section of the workspace [E3]. To enable users to follow each others' actions more easily, the system could highlight objects that are (a) being manipulated by users that are currently talking [E2] or (b) being manipulated regardless of whether the user is also talking [E2]. The system could recognize a user trying to show something to others through recognizing mouse movements around an object or certain audio cues (i. e., "Hey, look here!") [E7]. When this occurs, the system could highlight the object or nudge other users to look at another part of the workspace [E7]. If the system recognized a user saying "I didn't see that," it could offer that user a replay of the actions of the last few seconds [E1]. The system could even offer this functionality independent of any such audio cues [E1, E4]. A potential problem of this functionality could be that users are missing something new happening while they were watching the replay [E1]—two experts warned that recovering from this problem of not seeing something happening outside of one's own view-port might only be possible through social interaction [E1, E4].

10.4.7 Additional observations

Finally, all of the experts' statements that did not fit into any of the aforementioned categories, which emerged through thematic clustering, were collected in this topic, including *Cultural Differences, Preferences in Communication, Notification Design, Idea Inspiration* and *Automated System as Design Thinking Coach* (see Figure 10.1).

Experts noted that due to *Cultural Differences*, an automated system would probably not work as well for all cultures. It would have to have to be very flexible and include cultural differences in its' user model [E3, E4, E7].

Moreover, people have different *Preferences* in how they want to *Communicate* [E1]. An expert shared a story about a colleague who prefers to write in the chat during a Zoom call rather than speak, and is often overlooked because of that [E1]. A system should offer support for the different ways in which people want to collaborate [E1]. To do so, a system might highlight the message sent by a quiet user more to raise special attention [E1]. Yet, shy users might be embarrassed by the extra attention and thus communicate even less [E1, E5].

If the system were to show some kind of score for team member's contributions, then different ways of contribution and different skill sets should be taken into account [E2].

While reminders can be helpful, visual cues by the system should avoid forcing a lot of attention on them. If the system "acts like a pedantic annoying team member" user acceptance will be impacted negatively [E1]. Based on the previous input of users, the system could show other new information to users that appears to be relevant to the users' topic [E1, E2, E3]. However, the system should not overload users with thousands of search results but instead present new information in an easy-to-digest format, one occasional idea at a time [E1, E2]. In order to show users a new direction or offer a new perspective, the system could formulate this nudge as a question [E3].

One expert, who is a DT coach himself, envisioned automated systems to act very much like a facilitator in a DT session [E3]. The facilitator could set up the system before a session, i. e., setting the overarching goal, so that the automated system might identify gaps and offer support to the facilitator during the session [E3]. He noted that the system's frequency of interaction should depend on the activity level of the team, just as is advised for DT coaches: if the team is very active, the coach should not be, and vice versa [E3]. Another expert suggested that an automated system specifying singular steps for users might work best in a DT type of session, which is anyway very tightly structured [E5]. However, an automated system would not be able to replace a facilitator completely. Further, the system should not be in conflict with the facilitator [E5].

10.5 Design implications

In this section, we present design implications derived from the results of the expert interview presented in Section 10.4 and organized according to the taxonomy's top layer.

We consider the taxonomy itself (see Section 10.4) a tool for researchers, e. g., as a classification scheme for collaboration support measures (also see Section 10.6) and, together with the underlying qualitative findings of our study, the major scientific contribution of this chapter (cf. RQ1 and RQ2). The design implications presented here are, on the other hand, mainly targeted toward practitioners designing or implementing collaborative systems (cf. RQ3). Some of the design implications furthermore seem rather obvious while others are potentially new (or at least, less well known to designers). For reasons of completeness and to keep with the structure of the taxonomy, we nevertheless list all design implications in the order specified by the taxonomy. Those we consider most interesting are highlighted in italic font.

Design implications for awareness (AW)
→ **AW1:** Enable workspace awareness, with particular focus on team member's activities.
→ *AW2: Encourage users to share information.*
→ **AW3:** Make users aware of the size of their workspace and their position within the workspace, as well as their team members' position, even and especially when things are happening outside of a user's view-port.
→ *AW4: Support shared attention and give users an overview of changes.* The timing of displaying these changes is particularly important.
→ **AW5:** Be aware that remote team members cannot know what happens in other tabs of their colleagues, and provide support if needed.
→ **AW6:** Depending on the type of collaboration that a system should support, provide a structure for audio collaboration (raising hands, queue, free talking).
→ *AW7: Focus on supporting users in recovering from audio conflicts.*
→ *AW8: If equal participation is important for the type of collaboration that a system should support, provide nudges to dominant and nondominant users to engage more/less.*

Design implications for process development (PD)
→ **PD1:** Depending on the task domain, it might be possible to predefine a structure for users.
→ *PD2: Automatically detecting a team's process and current tasks will generally not be reliable. A better approach may be to offer easy-to-use and effective tools to help users improve their process themselves, i. e., timers.*
→ *PD3: An automated system should not impair human improvisation during collaboration.*
→ **PD4:** If a system recognizes the users' current task, it should display this and offer support particular to this task.
→ **PD5:** A system could support note-taking through automatic clustering based on vocabulary or identifying of duplicate or similar notes.

Design implications for user control (UC)

→ **UC1:** An automated system should never take away a user's tools, restrain a user's activities or stop users from doing something in their private space. An automated system should never just execute an action, but rather make suggestions for users to choose from.

→ *UC2: An automated system cannot police the collaboration and, therefore, should also accept human failure.* It should never embarrass or shame users.

→ **UC3:** If users willfully ignore someone or something, there is nothing that a system could really do to alleviate that.

→ *UC4: In order for users to build trust toward the system, it should be very explicit in what it is and is not capable of.* The system could also enable more and more functionality over time, so that users have time to learn about the system and build trust toward it.

Design implications for disengagement (DE)

→ **DE1:** To keep less active team members engaged, the system could nudge more dominant users to involve them more, or nudge the less active members to participate more. This could be done by displaying the relative talking time compared to the rest of a team as a whole, or through publicly showing everyone's activity to encourage less active members to contribute.

→ **DE2:** Gamification could also be valuable to keep users engaged, i. e., through calculating scores based on different kinds of contributions.

→ *DE3: Idle time in and of itself is not just wasted time, but can be a useful time for users to collect their thoughts.* A system should therefore support idle time, and could measure the success of idle time through measuring the productivity following such a drop in activity.

→ **DE4:** It should also be accepted that users are still humans and cannot be 100 % active all the time. Occasional drops in participation are natural.

Design implications for decision making (DM)

→ **DM1:** To support a team in decision-making, a system will need to have domain knowledge and be able to assess different dimensions of possible options.

→ *DM2: To help users keep an overview of possible options, a system could display possible options explicitly to the users.* An automated system could also attempt to calculate other related options and offer these alternatives to the team.

→ **DM3:** Before making a decision, a team should hold an anonymous voting session to ensure all opinions have been heard.

→ *DM4: A system should not take strong influence on the team's decision, even an objectively "bad decision" should still be accepted as it may serve as a learning opportunity for the team.* The system may help the team reflect on past decisions or offer them alternative options when making new decisions, but it should not interfere.

Design implications for interactive features (IF)

→ **IF1:** *Extend drag and drop functionality to support moving multiple objects simultaneously while preserving the spatial relationships between them.*

→ **IF2:** An automated system could calculate the similarity between notes (thematic, time and place of creation) and cluster them accordingly. This action should be easily reversible.

→ **IF3:** *While users should in general be able to see who created an object, it might make sense to hide this information while the team is making a decision or clustering notes.* The anonymity of the object may have positive or negative effects on the team work, depending on the situation.

→ **IF4:** *Subgroups can make team work more effective.* An automated system could initiate subgroups, e. g., during a research phase upon detecting that two team members are working on related topics.

→ **IF5:** Forming subgroups may also be a helpful tool to solve conflicts between team members.

→ **IF6:** *Users should be able to share something with others, i. e., through highlighting or broadcasting their view-port.* To support shared attention, a system could automatically highlight objects that are being manipulated by users that are currently talking, or highlight them regardless of whether the user is talking. It may also react to cues such as "look here" and highlight the object the user is talking about.

→ **IF7:** A system could also offer a replay tool to allow users to rewatch something that just happened, in case they were unable to see something. This could however pose the additional issue that during the time spent rewatching something, users may miss what happens next.

Miscellaneous design implications (MISC)

→ **MISC1:** *An automated system that includes a user model should also have knowledge about cultural differences.*

→ **MISC2:** If a system counts the users' contributions and calculates a score from these, it should take into account different ways to contribute, preferences and varying skill sets.

→ **MISC3:** *An automated system could offer new information relevant to the users' topic. This should be done in an easy-to-digest way, one occasional idea at a time.*

10.6 Discussion and conclusion

In this chapter, we attempted to establish a link between traditional user-based personalization-driven approaches of collaboration support and phenomenological ones. Further, we strove to answer three related research questions around (i) *personalized yet also typical (critical-) situation-based support measures for remote collaboration* (see

RQ1), (ii) *categorization of these measures* (see *RQ2*) and (iii) *implications and sugges-tions for designers of future collaborative systems* (see *RQ3*). The core of our empirical work is a qualitative interview study with seven experts of different fields, based on a prestudy data elicitation through a team experiment involving the identification of exemplary yet typical and critical situations in (remote) collaborative interaction. The interview study revealed a rich set of qualitative insights in the form of detailed answers to questions based on the recordings of the team experiment but also open discussion with the individual experts. These data were then converted to affinity notes according to the contextual inquiry method and thematically clustered based on the AB process (both originating from the CD methodology [5]). The clustering process then finally re-sulted in a taxonomy of personalized and situation-based support measures for remote collaborative interaction.

We consider the taxonomy a main contribution of this chapter and a profound an-swer to both RQ1 (support measures) as well as RQ2 (categorization of these measures). While we do not necessarily regard it as complete (but extensible by other researchers, e. g., based on the analysis of different collaborative use cases), it is already extremely rich in detail and scope. We expect it to succeed in inspiring other researchers with dif-ferent backgrounds and perspectives working on (remote) collaborative systems. We intend the taxonomy to be applicable as follows: (i) to gain a profound overview of col-laboration support possibilities, (ii) for the description of (existing) collaboration sup-port measures, (iii) for the systematic classification of such collaboration support mea-sures, (iv) for the evaluation of such measures and (v) for the ideation and development of new collaboration support measures. Additionally, it can serve as a basis for future extensions by other researchers.

Since the taxonomy is targeted mainly toward an audience of scientists, we addition-ally derived *implications for future designers of collaborative systems* from the taxonomy in order to provide a *concrete set of suggestions for practitioners*, which is a secondary contribution of our chapter as well as an answer to *RQ3*.

While we clearly see a contribution of our work for the research community but also practitioners, we want to acknowledge and discuss potential limitations as follows. One might argue that although the results gained through the expert interview are mul-tifaceted and rely on a wide range of different perspectives, the foundation for these interviews is limited in scope. The identification of critical situations in remote collab-oration is based on a single team scenario involving a group of four participants col-laborating on one prespecified kind of task, which might seem sparse at first glance. However, first, it is not unusual to analyze only one single interaction scenario (but in a fine-grained way) for such and similar purposes (see, e. g., [43]). Second, the critical sit-uations we identified can be argued to generalize well to other scenarios (as discussed in Section 10.3.1.6) and to be typical for (remote) collaboration, as also explicitly stated by one of the involved experts (E5). Third, we considered potentially arising limitations due to lack of relevant situations (such that can be considered critical as well as typical) already throughout the full process of study design. This can, e. g., be seen in the selection of participants (see Section 10.3.1.5) and collaborative task (see Section 10.3.1.1) for the prestudy team experiment. Regarding the participants, we considered candidates' demographic background but also their personality, collaboration attitudes, preferences and behavior before finally selecting them. Regarding the task, we made sure it was generally suitable to provoke discussion and disagreement but also required a high amount of interaction. The results of the team experiment suggest that our selection strategy was successful.

Nevertheless, we acknowledge that the resulting taxonomy might not be complete in the sense of fully exhaustive, which is why we constructed it in a way that allows for simple extension. We thus explicitly want to encourage other researchers to apply the taxonomy to their respective settings in one or more of the above mentioned ways and to add to it if necessary. For instance, results gained from in-depth analysis of collaboration settings including video streams might be of particular interest (since the participants of our prestudy did not use video features) and lead to extensions of the taxonomy. However, many elements of the taxonomy in its current form already fit such settings. For instance, many concepts and design implications discussed by Xu et al. [55], who investigated simulated gaze of remote participants using a system with asymmetric awareness, can be well located in the taxonomy.

References

[1] Ewa Andrejczuk, Filippo Bistaffa, Christian Blum, Juan A. Rodríguez-Aguilar, and Carles Sierra. Synergistic team composition: A computational approach to foster diversity in teams. *Knowledge-Based Systems* 182 (2019) 104799.

[2] Mirjam Augstein and Thomas Neumayr. Automated personalization of input methods and processes. In: Mirjam Augstein, Eelco Herder, and Wolfgang Wörndl, editors. *Personalized Human-Computer Interaction*. Berlin, Germany: De Gruyter Oldenbourg, 2019.

[3] Mirjam Augstein and Thomas Neumayr. A human-centered taxonomy of interaction modalities and devices. *Interacting with Computers* 31(1) (2019).

[4] Hugh Beyer and Karen Holtzblatt. *Contextual Design: Defining Customer-Centered Systems*, 1st edition. Morgan Kaufmann, 1997.

[5] Hugh Beyer, Karen Holtzblatt, and Lisa Baker. An agile customer-centered method: rapid contextual design. In: *Conference on extreme programming and agile methods, Heidelberg, Germany*. Berlin, Heidelberg: Springer, 2004, pp. 50–59.

[6] Rupert Brown. Social identity theory: Past achievements, current problems and future challenges. *European Journal of Social Psychology* 30(6) (2000) 745–778.

[7] Frederik Brudy, Joshua Kevin Budiman, Steven Houben, and Nicolai Marquardt. Investigating the role of an overview device in multi-device collaboration. In: *Proceedings of the 2018 CHI Conference on Human Factors in Computing Systems, CHI'18*. New York, NY, USA: Association for Computing Machinery, 2018, pp. 1–13.

[8] Peter Brusilovsky. Methods and techniques of adaptive hypermedia. *User Modeling and User-Adapted Interaction* 6(2–3) (1996) 87–129.

[9] Peter Brusilovsky and Christoph Peylo. Adaptive and Intelligent Web-based Educational Systems. *International Journal of Artificial Intelligence in Education* 13(2–4) (2003) 156–169.

[10] Brian Butler, Lee Sproull, Sara Kiesler, and Robert Kraut. Community effort in online groups: Who does the work and why. *Leadership at a Distance Research in Technologically Supported Work* 1 (2007) 171–194.

[11] Terry Connolly and Brian K. Thorn. Discretionary databases: Theory, data, and implications. *Organizations and Communication Technology* 219 (1990) 219–233.

[12] Terry Connolly, Brian K. Thorn, and Alan Heminger. Discretionary databases as social dilemmas. *Social Dilemmas: Theoretical Issues and Research Findings* 7 (1992) 199–207.

[13] Stavros Demetriadis and Anastasios Karakostas. Adaptive collaboration scripting: A conceptual framework and a design case study. In: *2008 International Conference on Complex, Intelligent and Software Intensive Systems, Los Alamitos, CA, USA*. IEEE Computer Society, 2008, pp. 487–492.

[14] John M. Digman. Personality structure: Emergence of the five-factor model. *Annual Review of Psychology* 41 (1990) 417–440.

[15] Pierre Dillenbourg, Michael Baker, Agnès Blaye, and Claire O'Malley. The Evolution of Research on Collaborative Learning. In: Peter Reiman and Hans Spada, editors. *Learning in Humans and Machine: Towards an Interdisciplinary Learning Science*. Oxford, United Kingdom: Elsevier, 1995, pp. 189–211.

[16] John C. Flanagan. The critical incident technique. *Psychological Bulletin* 51(4) (1954).

[17] Janet Fulk, Rebecca Heino, Andrew J. Flanagin, Peter R. Monge, and François Bar. A test of the individual action model for organizational information commons. *Organization Science* 15(5) (2004) 569–585.

[18] Nitesh Goyal, Gilly Leshed, Dan Cosley, and Susan R. Fussell. Effects of implicit sharing in collaborative analysis. In: *Proceedings of the SIGCHI Conference on Human Factors in Computing Systems, CHI '14*. New York, NY, USA: Association for Computing Machinery, 2014, pp. 129–138.

[19] Jonathan Grudin and Steven Poltrock. Taxonomy and theory in computer supported cooperative work. *The Oxford Handbook of Organizational Psychology* 2 (2012) 1323–1348.

[20] Carl Gutwin and Saul Greenberg. A Descriptive Framework of Workspace Awareness for Real-Time Groupware. *Computer Supported Cooperative Work* 11(3–4) (2002) 411–446.

[21] Bill Hamersly and Denise Land. Building productivity in virtual project teams. *Revista de Gestão e Projetos-GeP* 6(1) (2015) 01–13.

[22] Guido Hertel, Udo Konradt, and Borris Orlikowski. Managing distance by interdependence: Goal setting, task interdependence, and team-based rewards in virtual teams. *European Journal of Work and Organizational Psychology* 13(1) (2004) 1–28.

[23] Karen Holtzblatt and Hugh Beyer. *Contextual Design. Design for Life*, 2nd edition. Morgan Kaufmann, 2017.

[24] Karen Holtzblatt, Jessamyn Burns Wendell, and Shelley Wood. *Rapid Contextual Design. A How-To Guide to Key Techniques for User-Centered Design*. Morgan Kaufmann, 2005.

[25] Petra Isenberg, Danyel Fisher, Sharoda A. Paul, Meredith Ringel Morris, Kori Inkpen, and Mary Czerwinski. Co-Located Collaborative Visual Analytics Around a Tabletop Display. *IEEE Transactions on Visualization and Computer Graphics* 18(5) (2012) 689–702.

[26] Steven J. Karau and Jason W. Hart. Group cohesiveness and social loafing: Effects of a social interaction manipulation on individual motivation within groups. *Group Dynamics: Theory, Research, and Practice* 2(3) (1998) 185.

[27] Evgeny Knutov, Paul De Bra, and Mykola Pechenizkiy. Ah 12 years later: a comprehensive survey of adaptive hypermedia methods and techniques. *New Review of Hypermedia and Multimedia* 15(1) (2009) 5–38.

[28] Abdullah Konak and Sadan Kulturel-Konak. Impact of online teamwork self-efficacy on attitudes toward teamwork. *International Journal of Information Technology Project Management (IJITPM)* 10(3) (2019) 1–17.

[29] Florian König and Alexandros Paramythis. Adaptive collaboration scripting with ims ld. In: Thanasis Daradoumis, Stavros Demetriadis, and Fatos Xhafa, editors. *Intelligent Adaptation and Personalization Techniques in Computer-Supported Collaborative Learning*. Berlin, Heidelberg: Springer, 2012, pp. 47–84.

[30] Susanne Kvarnström. Difficulties in collaboration: A critical incindet study of interprofessional healthcare teamwork. *Journal of Interprofessional Care* 22(2) (2008) 191–203.

[31] Ida Larsen-Ledet and Henrik Korsgaard. Territorial Functioning in Collaborative Writing. *Computer Supported Cooperative Work (CSCW)* 28(3) (2019) 391–433.

[32] Richard A. Layton, Misty L. Loughry, Matthew W. Ohland, and George D. Ricco. Design and validation of a web-based system for assigning members to teams using instructor-specified criteria. *Advances in Engineering Education* 2(1) (2010) n1.

[33] Rachel Lindner and Dónal O'Brien. In: *The Global Virtual Teams Project: Learning to Manage Team Dynamics in Virtual Exchange*. Voillans, France: Research-publishing.net, 2019, pp. 81–89.

[34] Joseph Edward McGrath. *Groups: Interaction and performance, volume 14*. Prentice-Hall Englewood Cliffs, NJ, 1984.

[35] Thomas Neumayr and Mirjam Augstein. A systematic review of personalized collaborative systems. *Frontiers in Computer Science* 2 (2020) 43.

[36] Thomas Neumayr, Hans-Christian Jetter, Mirjam Augstein, Judith Friedl, and Thomas Luger. Domino: A descriptive framework for hybrid collaboration and coupling styles in partially distributed teams. *Proceedings of the ACM on Human-Computer Interaction* 2(CSCW) (2018) 1–24.

[37] Fred Niederman, Robert O. Briggs, Gert Jan de Vreede, and Gwendolyn L. Kolfschoten. Extending the contextual and organizational elements of adaptive structuration theory in gss research. *Journal of the Association for Information Systems* 9(10) (2008) 4.

[38] Jakob Nielsen. Heuristic evaluation. In: *Usability inspection methods*. John Wiley & Sons, Inc., 1994, pp. 25–62.

[39] Ingrid Nunes and Dietmar Jannach. A systematic review and taxonomy of explanations in decision support and recommender systems. *User Modeling and User-Adapted Interaction* 27(3–5) (2017) 393–444.

[40] Reinhard Oppermann, Rossen Rashev, and Kinshuk. Adaptability and Adaptivity in Learning Systems. *Knowledge Transfer* 2 (1997) 173–179.

[41] Mai Otsuki, Keita Maruyama, Hideaki Kuzuoka, and Yusuke Suzuki. Effects of Enhanced Gaze Presentation on Gaze Leading in Remote Collaborative Physical Tasks. In: *Proceedings of the ACM International Conference on Human Factors in Computing Systems (CHI)*, 2018.

[42] Alexandros Paramythis. Adaptive Support for Collaborative Learning with IMS Learning Design: Are We There Yet? In: *Proceedings of the Adaptive Collaboration Support Workshop*, 2008.

[43] Banu Saatçi, Kaya Aküz, Sean Rintel, and Clemens Nylandsted Klokmose. (re)configuring hybrid meetings: Moving from user-centered design to meeting-centered design. *Computer Supported Cooperative Work (CSCW)* 29 (2020) 769–794.

[44] Samiha Samrose, Ru Zhao, Jeffery White, Vivan Li, Luis Nova, Yichen Lu, Mohammad Rafayet Ali, and Mohammed (Ehsan) Hoque. Coco: Collaboration coach for understanding team dynamics during video conferencing. *Proceedings of the ACM on Interactive Mobile Wearable and Uniquitous Technologies* 1(4) (2018).

[45] Christian Schlösser, Benedikt Schröder, Linda Cedli, and Andrea Kienle. Beyond Gaze Cursor: Exploring Information-based Gaze Sharing in Chat. In: *Proceedings of the Workshop on Communication by Gaze Interaction (COGAIN), Warsaw, Poland*, 2018.

[46] Stacey D. Scott, M. Sheelagh, T. Carpendale, and Kori M. Inkpen. Territoriality in collaborative tabletop workspaces. In: *Proceedings of the 2004 ACM conference on Computer-Supported Cooperative Work*, 2004, pp. 294–303.

[47] Stacey D. Scott, M. Sheelagh, T. Carpendale, and Kori M. Inkpen. Territoriality in Collaborative Tabletop Workspaces. In: *Proceedings of the ACM International Conference on Computer-Supported Cooperative Work (CSCW)*, 2004.

[48] Yin Sheng, Haibin Zhu, Xianzhong Zhou, and Wenting Hu. Effective Approaches to Adaptive Collaboration via Dynamic Role Assignment. *IEEE Transactions on Systems, Man, and Cybernetics: Systems* 46(1) (2016) 76–92.

[49] Ben Shneiderman and Pattie Maes. Direct manipulation vs. interface agents. *Interactions* 4(6) (1997) 42–61.

[50] Gretchen M. Spreitzer, Lindsey Cameron, and Lyndon Garrett. Alternative work arrangements: Two images of the new world of work. *Annual Review of Organizational Psychology and Organizational Behavior* 4 (2017) 473–499.

[51] Anthony Tang, Melanie Tory, Barry Po, Petra Neumann, and Sheelagh Carpendale. Collaborative Coupling over Tabletop Displays. In: *Proceedings of the ACM International Conference on Human Factors in Computing Systems (CHI), Montréal, Québec, Canada,* 2006.

[52] Jennifer Thom-Santelli, Dan Cosley, and Geri Gay. What's mine is mine: territoriality in collaborative authoring. In: *Proceedings of the SIGCHI Conference on Human Factors in Computing Systems,* 2009, pp. 1481–1484.

[53] Philip Tuddenham and Peter Robinson. Territorial coordination and workspace awareness in remote tabletop collaboration. In: *Proceedings of the SIGCHI Conference on Human Factors in Computing Systems,* 2009, pp. 2139–2148.

[54] Philip Tuddenham and Peter Robinson. Territorial Coordination and Workspace Awareness in Remote Tabletop Collaboration. In: *Proceedings of the ACM International Conference on Human Factors in Computing Systems (CHI),* 2009.

[55] Bin Xu, Jason Ellis, and Thomas Erickson. Attention from afar: Simulating the gazes of remote participants in hybrid meetings. In: *Proceedings of the ACM International Conference on Designing Interactive Systems (DIS17), Edinburgh, Scotland, United Kingdom,* 2017, pp. 101–113.

[56] Haibin Zhu. Adaptive Collaboration Systems: Self-Sustaining Systems for Optimal Performance. *IEEE Systems, Man, and Cybernetics Magazine* 1(4) (2015) 8–15.

Appendix A. Taxonomy

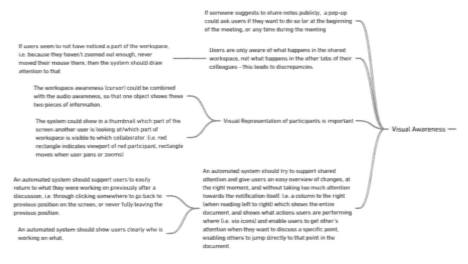

Figure 10.2: Detailed overview for the theme Visual Awareness.

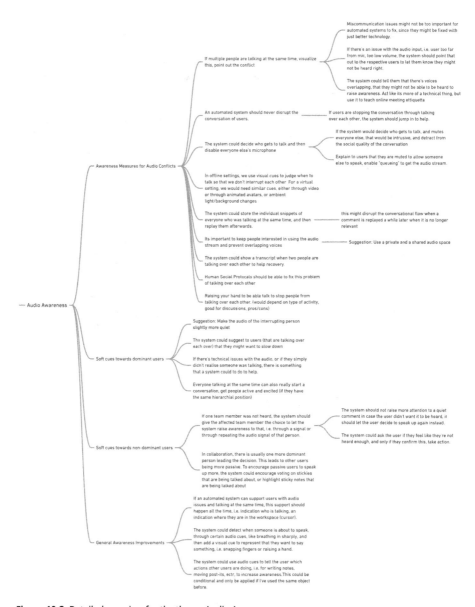

Figure 10.3: Detailed overview for the theme Audio Awareness.

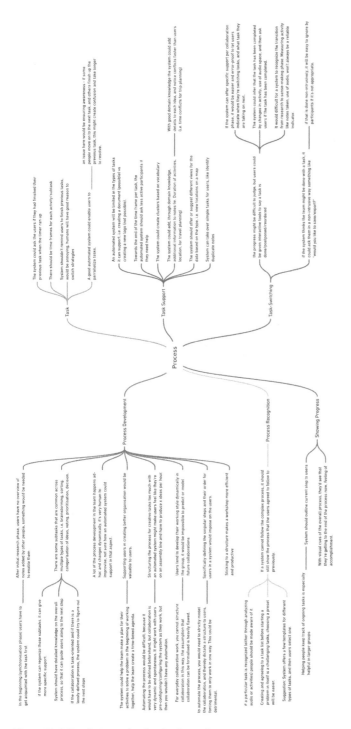

Figure 10.4: Detailed overview for the theme Process.

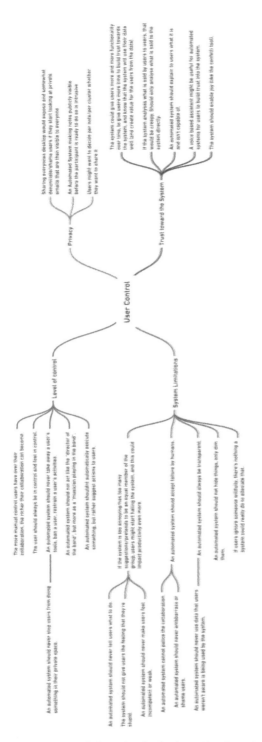

Figure 10.5: Detailed overview for the theme User Control.

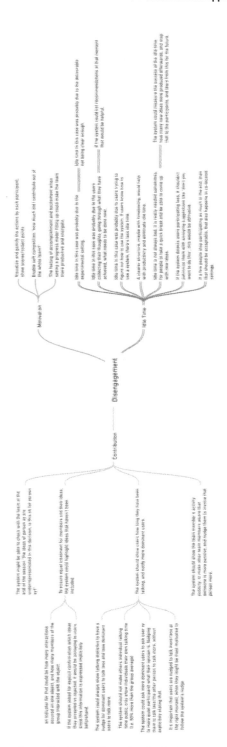

Figure 10.6: Detailed overview for the theme Disengagement.

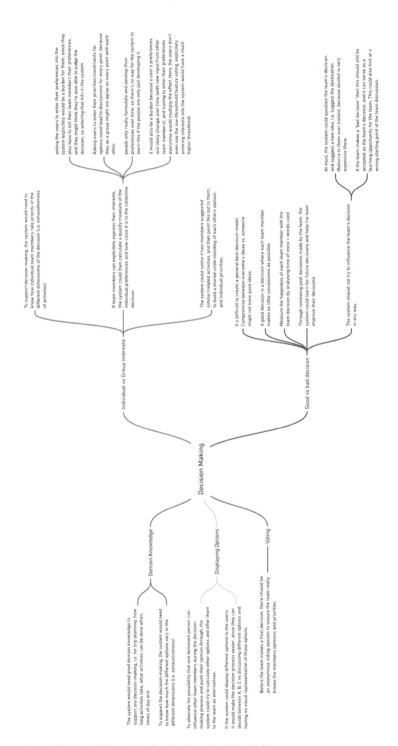

Figure 10.7: Detailed overview for the theme Decision Making.

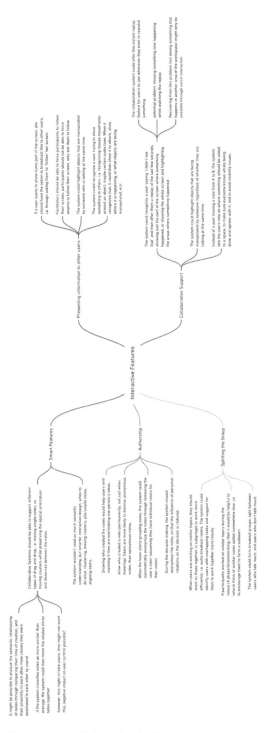

Figure 10.8: Detailed overview for the theme Interactive Features.

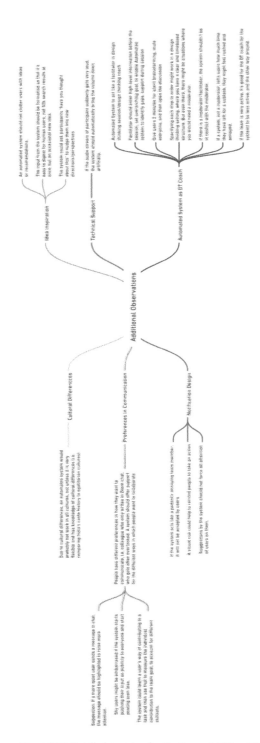

Figure 10.9: Detailed overview for the theme Additional Observations.

Part IV: **Personalization domains**

Peter Knees, Markus Schedl, Bruce Ferwerda, and Audrey Laplante

11 Listener awareness in music recommender systems: directions and current trends

Abstract: Music recommender systems are a widely adopted application of personalized systems and interfaces. By tracking the listening activity of their users and building preference profiles, a user can be given recommendations based on the preference profiles of all users (collaborative filtering), characteristics of the music listened to (content-based methods), meta-data and relational data (knowledge-based methods; sometimes also considered content-based methods) or a mixture of these with other features (hybrid methods). In this chapter, we focus on the listener's aspects of music recommender systems. We discuss different factors influencing relevance for recommendation on both the listener's and the music's side and categorize existing work. In more detail, we then review aspects of (i) listener background in terms of individual, i. e., personality traits and demographic characteristics, and cultural features, i. e., societal and environmental characteristics, (ii) listener context, in particular modeling dynamic properties and situational listening behavior and (iii) listener intention, in particular by studying music information behavior, i. e., how people seek, find and use music information. This is followed by a discussion of user-centric evaluation strategies for music recommender systems. We conclude the chapter with a reflection on current barriers, by pointing out current and longer-term limitations of existing approaches and outlining strategies for overcoming these.

Keywords: Music recommender systems, personalization, user modeling, user context, user intent

11.1 Introduction

Music recommender systems are a widely adopted application of personalized systems and interfaces [138]. On a technical level, large-scale music recommender systems became feasible through online music distribution channels and collective platforms that track users' listening events.[1] By tracking the listening activity of their users and build-

---

1 Early examples from the prestreaming era are peer-to-peer networks and platforms like Last.fm (http://last.fm).

Acknowledgement: We thank Fabien Gouyon for the discussions leading to the updated factor model. This research was funded in whole, or in part, by the Austrian Science Fund (FWF) [P33526]. For the purpose of open access, the author has applied a CC BY public copyright license to any Author Accepted Manuscript version arising from this submission.

https://doi.org/10.1515/9783110988567-011

ing preference profiles, a user can be given recommendations based on the pool of preference profiles of all users (collaborative filtering, e. g., [18, 145]), characteristics of the music listened to (content-based methods, e. g., [15, 150]), expert- and user-generated (relational) meta-data (knowledge-based methods, e. g., [80, 120, 158]; sometimes also considered content-based methods), or a mixture of these, potentially extended by other features (hybrid methods, e. g., [29, 67, 111]).

The main research area exploring these opportunities, i. e., music information retrieval (MIR), historically, has predominantly followed content-based approaches [81]. This can facilitate music recommendation starting from preferred examples and then following the query-by-example paradigm, which is central to information retrieval tasks. While aspects of user adaptivity and relevance feedback can be addressed, e. g., [83, 121], modeling of the listener was underrepresented in the majority of work [135].

For developing recommender systems, traditionally, static collections and recorded user interactions have served as offline ground truth. This permits researchers to optimize retrieval and recommendation system performance, e. g., by maximizing precision or minimizing error; cf. [19, 140]. More recently, with the establishment of dedicated online music streaming platforms such as Spotify[2] and Pandora,[3] more dynamic and user-oriented criteria, assessed by means of massive online A/B testing, have driven the industrial development; cf. [1, 147]. However, both offline and online approaches operate on the basis of a system-centric view and, therefore, neglect user- and usage-centric perspectives on the process of music listening. Such perspectives involve, e. g., factors of listening context such as activity or social setting, listening intent or the listener's personality, background and preferences. Incorporating this information can enhance the process of music recommendation in a variety of situations, from mitigating cold-start scenarios, i. e., when usage data of new users is missing, to mood- and situation-tailored suggestions, to adaptive and personalized interfaces that support the listener in his or her music information-seeking activities.

In this chapter, we focus on aspects of the listener in music recommendation. In Section 11.2, we discuss different factors that influence the relevance of recommendations. This covers both aspects of the listener and of the musical items to recommend. Additionally, we briefly outline the development from search scenarios to approaches to personalization and user adaptation. Section 11.3 deals with aspects of *listener background* and discusses variables that influence differences in music preferences of listeners, divided into individual (i. e., personality traits and demographic characteristics) and cultural features (i. e., societal and environmental characteristics). In Section 11.4, we focus on the *listener context*, i. e., contextual and situational listening behavior. To this end, we elaborate on the modeling and elicitation of the listener's emotion, on the

---

2 http://www.spotify.com

3 http://www.pandora.com

emotion assigned to music items, and on the relationship between these two. We further discuss methods that exploit various sensor data for user modeling. Section 11.5 then focuses on *listener intention*, in particular by studying music information behavior, i. e., how people seek, find and use music information. This includes studies conducted in the information science field on how people discover new music artists or new music genres in everyday life, as well as studies that examine how people use and perceive music recommender systems.

To round this chapter off, we give an overview of user-centric evaluation strategies for music recommender systems in Section 11.6, before concluding with a discussion of current barriers in Section 11.7, where we point out current and longer-term limitations of existing approaches and outline strategies for overcoming these. Despite presenting existing technical academic work, we highlight findings from nontechnical disciplines to call attention to currently missing facets of music recommender systems. These identified but yet not technically covered requirements should help the reader in identifying potential new research directions.

11.2 Relevant factors in music recommendation

In the field of recommender systems research, the interaction of two factors is relevant for making recommendations: the user and the item, i. e., in our case a music entity, such as a track, an artist or a playlist. In traditional recommender systems, based on previous interactions of users and items, future interactions are predicted, either by identifying similar users or items (memory-based collaborative filtering) or by learning latent representations of users and items by decomposing the matrix of interactions (model-based collaborative filtering). While model-based methods have the advantage of resulting in representations of users and items that permit effective prediction of future interactions, a major drawback of these latent representations is that they are hard to interpret and, while describing the data, typically cannot be connected to actual properties of neither users nor items. In an attempt to connect models to such properties (e. g., rating biases of users, popularity biases of products or domain-specific properties like preference for the music genre of a track), more factors and degrees of freedom are included to fit the observed data (e. g., [31, 64, 86]). However, particularly in scenarios where no prior interaction data has been observed ("cold start"), such purely data-driven models show their weakness, making explicit modeling of user properties, usage context, etc. and their effects desirable. In this data-driven scenario, the service (e. g., the streaming platform) that connects users and items must also not be forgotten, as only interactions that are possible using the service can be observed. As a consequence, this biased data shapes the models of user-item interactions deployed for recommendation.

While different aspects of music items are well covered by research in MIR, modeling different facets of the listener have found less entry into recommendation systems.

For all, user, service and item, we can identify different categories of these facets that impact recommendations, namely *intrinsic* properties, *goal* and *external* aspects [79]. Figure 11.1 shows these nine finer grained factors underlying the interaction between users and items.[4]

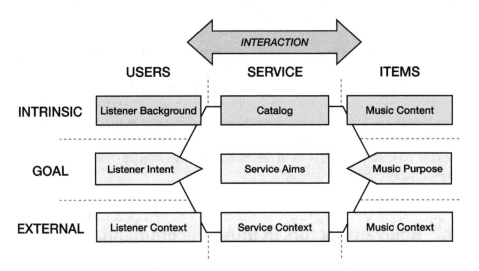

Figure 11.1: User, service and item factors influencing recommendations [79]. Recommender systems typically model and predict the interaction between users and items as it is observed on a specific platform/service. Users, service and items can be described by factors that can be categorized into *intrinsic properties*, *goal* and *external factors*. While intrinsic factors refer to mostly stable features, goal and external factors are more dynamic.

In terms of *item factors*, we can distinguish between:

Music content referring to everything that is contained in or, more pragmatically, that can be extracted from the audio signal itself, such as aspects of rhythm, timbre, melody, harmony, structure or even the mood of a piece.

Music purpose] referring to the intended usage of the music, which can have a spiritual or political purpose (e. g., an anthem) or created for the purpose of playing in the background (e. g., muzak). This also relates to aspects of *associative coding* in Juslin's theory [70], which conveys connotations between the music and other "arbitrary" events or objects. The role of this facet for recommendation has remained largely unexplored, apart from special treatment of certain events, such as offer-

---

4 This extends the model presented in the previous edition of this chapter [82] by the dimension of the service, which was an extension of the four categories of influences of music similarity perception by Schedl et al. [135] integrating aspects of the model of music perception and conveyed emotions by Juslin [70].

ing special playlists for holiday seasons like Christmas, containing tracks usually filtered out during the remaining time.

Music meta-data (and cultural context) referring to aspects of the music that cannot be inferred directly from the audio signal, such as meta-data like year of recording or country of origin, as well as different types of community meta-data: user-generated content such as reviews or tags; additional multimodal contextual information such as album artwork, liner notes or music videos; and diverse outcomes and impacts of marketing strategies. This also captures elements categorized as associative coding (see above).

Correspondingly, in terms of *service factors*, we can distinguish between:

Catalog referring to music being made available to users, e. g., commercially licensed tracks (cf. Spotify) or content that is provided by users (cf. SoundCloud).

Service aims describing the intention, market niche or unique selling point of the service. This can be manifest in particular "products" or functionality (e. g., a focus on discovery), specific goals (e. g., exclusively promoting certain artists or providing higher quality audio), or a particularly lucrative business model.

Service context referring to the operational circumstances. Based on the context, catalog and service aims might differ, e. g., through country-specific licensing restrictions or the service might offer different services, e. g., in a mobile app versus a desktop app.

In terms of *user facets*, we focus on a specific group of users, namely the end-consumers of music services, i. e., the music listeners.[5] For the listener as the user, we can distinguish between:

Listener background referring to the listener's personality traits, such as preference and taste, musical knowledge, training and experience, as well as to demographics and cultural background. Generally, this comprises more static and stable characteristics of the user.

Listener intent referring to the goal of the listener in consuming music. Potential goals span from evocation of certain emotions, i. e., emotional self-regulation, to the desire to demonstrate knowledge, musical sophistication or musical taste in a social setting.

Listener context referring to the current situation and setting of the user, including location, time, activity, social context or mood. This generally describes more dynamic aspects of the listener.

In the following, we focus on the listener and review work dealing with these different dimensions. First, considering aspects of listener background, we give an overview

---

5 In a multistakeholder scenario such as music recommendation, the user could also refer to, e. g., the artists providing the tracks or advertisers aiming to find suited soundtracks for promoting their goods.

of work exploring music preference, personality and cultural characteristics. Second, we focus on contextual and more dynamic factors, namely modeling the listener's emotional state, as well as deriving a listener's context from sensor data of personal devices. Finally, we deal with the least explored area in terms of music recommender systems, i. e., the listener's intent, in the context of music information behavior.

11.3 Correlates of music preferences

Music plays an important part in our lives. We actively use music as a resource to support us in everyday life activities. Hence, music can have different functions (cf. Section 11.5). Merriam and Merriam [112] defined several functions of music among which are: emotion expression, aesthetic enjoyment, entertainment, communication and symbolic representation. Given the different functions of music, the kind of music that is appropriate for a certain function may be a personal matter. What we like to listen to is shaped by our personal tastes and preferences as well as by our cultural preconceptions [117]. Although there is ample research done in traditional psychology on individual differences of music preferences, it is important to investigate to what extent these findings still hold in a technological mediated context as well as investigating new relationships that have become available through new interaction opportunities that technologies facilitate. In the sections below, we discuss work on music preferences in a technological setting that deals with preference correlations with individual as well as cultural aspects with which we try to draw parallels with results from traditional psychology.

11.3.1 Individual aspects

The existence of individual differences in music preferences has been investigated quite extensively in traditional psychological research already (for an overview see [127]). However, with recent technological advances, current online music systems (e. g., online music streaming services) provide their users with an almost unlimited amount of content that is directly at their disposal. This abundance of available music may have deviating effects on our prior knowledge of how people listen to music. For example, users may be prone to try out different content more than they would do in the offline world and even their preference may change more often or becomes more versatile [49].

Prior psychological work argued that age may play an important role in identifying individual differences in music preferences due to varying influences that shape music preferences across the course of life. For example, an individual may develop their music taste through the influence of parents in the early ages, but get influenced by the taste of peers later on in life [128]. Recent work investigated the change of music preferences over age by analyzing the music listening histories of an online music streaming service [48]. By being able to trace back the music listening histories, a mapping was able to be made on the change of music preferences. Although the online music listening behaviors reflected more diversity and versatility, the general trends are in line with prior psychological work [128]. The results showed that over time music preferences became more stable, while in the younger age groups music preferences are more exploratory and scattered across genres. Recent work has shown that, conversely, demographic information of users can also be predicted from online listening behavior [88] as well as the musical sophistication of music listeners [37].

Aside of the identification of age differences, another way that is often used to segment online music listeners is based on their personality. Personality has shown to be a stable construct and is often used as a general model to relate behavior, preferences and needs of people to [69]. A common way to segment people on personality traits is being done based on the five-factor model (FFM). The FFM describes personality traits based on five general dimensions: openness to experience, conscientiousness, extraversion, agreeableness and neuroticism (see Table 11.1).

Table 11.1: Five-factor model, adopted from [69].

General dimensions	Primary factors
Openness to experience	Artistic, curious, imaginative, insightful, original, wide interest
Conscientiousness	Efficient, organized, planful, reliable, responsible, thorough
Extraversion	Active, assertive, energetic, enthusiastic, outgoing, talkative
Agreeableness	Appreciative, forgiving, generous, kind, sympathetic, trusting
Neuroticism	Anxious, self-pitying, tense, touchy, unstable, worrying

Several works have shown the relationship between personality traits and online music preferences, but mainly investigated the relationship of personality traits with ways of interacting within a system. Although these results do not allow for a comparison with results from traditional psychology, they do provide new insights in user interactions with music systems and how these interactions can be personalized. Ferwerda et al. [45] investigated how personality and emotional states influence the preference for certain kinds of music. Other studies have shown that personality is related to the way we browse (i. e., by genre, mood or activity) for online music [51]. In their study, they simulated an online music streaming service in which they observed how users navigated through the service to find music that they liked to listen to. Tkalčič et al. [149] investigated the relationship between personality traits and digital concert notes. They looked at whether personality influences the preferences of the amount of content presented. Others looked at the music diversity needs based on personality traits [38], and have proposed ways to incorporate personality traits into music recommender systems to improve music recommendations to users [40, 42].

These aforementioned works on individual differences in music listening behaviors mainly relied on smaller scale studies in which the authors created their own experimental platforms. In a meta-analysis study by Schäfer and Mehlhorn [131], they argue that individual differences such as personality traits play an negligible role in music listening preferences due to the small effect sizes that are normally reported. However, Anderson et al. [2] showed that individual differences do play an important role. In their study, they used a large-scale Spotify data set in which they mapped individual differences with distinguishable music listening behaviors.

11.3.2 Cultural aspects

Aside from individual aspects, preference differences can already occur on a cultural level. The environments that we are exposed to have a big influence in how our preferences are shaped [117, 134]. Especially with services being online and widespread, analyses of more global behaviors are possible. For example, artist preference differences have been found based on linguistic distance [107]. A known way to investigate cultures is by relying on Hofstede's cultural dimensions [62]. Although this model originates from 1968, it is still being actualized. Hofstede's cultural dimensions are based on data of 97 countries. The data showed patterns that resulted in the following six dimensions: power distance index, individualism, uncertainty avoidance index, masculinity, long-term orientation and indulgence, as described in the following.

Power distance defines the extent to which power is distributed unequally by less powerful members of institutions (e. g., family). High power distance indicates that a hierarchy is clearly established and executed in society. Low power distance indicates that authority is questioned and power attempted to be distributed equally.

Individualism defines the degree of integration of people into societal groups. High individualism is defined by loose social ties—the main emphasis is on the "I" instead of the "we"—while this is the opposite for low individualistic cultures.

Masculinity defines a society's preference for achievement, heroism, assertiveness and material rewards for success (countries scoring high in this dimension). Conversely, low masculinity represents a preference for cooperation, modesty, caring for the weak and quality of life.

Uncertainty avoidance defines a society's tolerance for ambiguity. High scoring countries in this scale are more inclined to opt for stiff codes of behavior, guidelines and laws, whereas more acceptance of different thoughts and/or ideas are more common for those scoring low in this dimension.

Long-term orientation is associated with the connection of the past with the current and future actions and/or challenges. Lower scoring countries tend to believe that traditions are honored and kept, and value steadfastness. High scoring countries believe more that adaptation and circumstantial, pragmatic problem-solving are necessary.

Indulgence defines in general the happiness of a country. Countries scoring high in this dimension are related to a society that allows relatively free gratification of basic and natural human desires related to enjoying life and having fun (e. g., be in control of their own life and emotions), whereas low scoring countries show more controlled gratification of needs and regulate it by means of strict social norms.

Studies that looked at Hofstede's cultural dimensions found differences on several aspects, e. g., diversity in music listening. Countries scoring high on the power distance tend to show less diversity in the artists and genres they listened to. The individualism dimension was found to negatively correlate with music diversity [50]. Extended analysis can be found in [41]. Others have shown that Hofstede's cultural dimensions and socioeconomic factors can be used to predict genre preferences of music listeners [108, 139, 143]. By applying a random forest algorithm, they were able to achieve an improvement of 16.4 % in genre prediction over the baseline [143]. Hofstede's cultural dimensions have also been used to better understand how conformity in group decision-making occurs. For example, several studies investigated how groups collaboratively create music playlist and they found that people from individualist cultures tend to conform less than collectivist cultures [9, 36].

The identification of individual and cultural differences with regards to music contributes to new and deeper understanding of behaviors, preferences and needs in online music environments. Aside of that, the findings also provide insights on how these differences can be exploited for personalizing experiences. For example, a persistent problem for personalized systems is implicit preference elicitation for new users. Relying on identified individual and cultural differences may contribute to mitigate these preference elicitation problems. For example, research has shown that personality can be predicted from behavioral trails on social media (e. g., Facebook [17, 42, 57], Twitter [56, 126], Instagram [43, 44, 46, 47, 95] and a combination of social media sources [144]). With the increased implementation of single sign-on (SSO) mechanisms[6] allow users to easily login and register to an application, but also let applications import user information from the connected application. Hence, these personalization prediction methods could play an important role in personalization strategies to mitigate preference elicitation for new users. When there are no external information sources available to extract user information from, personalization strategies based on cultural findings may be the second best option for personalization. Country information often already consists in a standard user profile and is therefore easy to acquire.

---

6 Buttons that allow users to register or login with accounts of other applications. For example, social networking services: "Login with your Facebook account."

11.4 Contextual and situational music listening behavior

The situation or context a person is in when listening to music—or deciding what to listen to—is known to strongly affect the music preferences as well as consumption and interaction behavior [10, 27]. To give an example, a person is likely to listen to different music or create a different playlist when preparing for a romantic dinner than when preparing to go out on a Saturday night [55].

The most frequently considered types of context include *location* (e. g., listening at workplace, when commuting or relaxing at home) [74] and *time* (typically categorized into, e. g., morning, afternoon and evening) [16]. In addition, context may also relate to the listener's *activity* [155], *weather* [123], *listening device*, e. g., earplugs on a smartphone versus hi-fi stereo at home [55], and various *social aspects* [24, 118], just to name a few.

Another type of context is *interactional context* with sequences, which is particularly important for the tasks of session-based recommendation and sequence-aware recommendation. In this case, context refers to the sequence of music pieces a listener decides to consume consecutively. In the music domain, such tasks are often referred to as automatic playlist generation or automatic playlist continuation [13, 20]. Sequence learning and natural language processing techniques applied to playlist names are typically used to infer contextual aspects.

A particularly important situational characteristic is that of *mood and emotion*, both from a user's perspective [132] and song annotations [161]. In the following, we therefore first introduce in Section 11.4.1 the most common approaches to model listeners' moods and emotions, emotions perceived while listening to music, and ways to connect listeners and music pieces through affective cues, and in turn to build emotion-aware recommender systems. In Section 11.4.2, we subsequently review methods that exploit various sensor data for user modeling in music recommender systems, e. g., from sensors built into smart devices. Such sensor data can either be used directly to learn contextual music preferences, or to infer higher-level context categories such as the target user's activity.

11.4.1 Emotion and mood: connecting listeners and music

The affective state of the listener has a strong impact on his or her short-time musical preferences [73]. Vice versa, music strongly influences our affective state. It therefore does not come as a surprise that affect regulation is regarded as one of the main reasons why people listen to music [109, 132]. As an example, people may listen to completely different musical genres or styles when they are sad in comparison to when they are happy. Indeed, prior research on music psychology discovered that people usually choose the type of music, which moderates their affective condition [85]. More recent findings show that music is often chosen for the purpose of augmenting the emotional situation perceived by the listener [116].

Note that in psychology—often in contrast to recommender systems or MIR research, but also everyday use—it is common to distinguish between *mood* and *emotion* as two different affective constructs. The most important differences are that a mood is characterized as an experience of longer but less intense duration without a particular stimulus, whereas an emotion is a short experience with an identifiable stimulus event that causes it.

In order to build affect-aware music recommenders, it is necessary to (i) infer the emotional state or mood the listener is in, (ii) infer emotional concepts from the music itself and (iii) understand how these two interrelate. These three tasks are detailed below. In the context of (i), we also introduce the most important ways to describe emotions.

11.4.1.1 Modeling the listener's emotional state

The emotional state of a human can be elicited explicitly or implicitly. In the former case, the person is typically presented a questionnaire or user interface that maps the user's explicit input to an emotion representation according to one of the various *categorical models* or *dimensional models*. Categorical models describe emotions by distinct words such as happiness, sadness, anger or fear [61, 164], while dimensional models described emotions by scores with respect to two or three dimensions. One of the most prominent dimensional models is Russel's two-dimensional circumplex model [129], which represents valence and arousal as orthogonal dimensions; cf. Figure 11.2 (top). Into this model, categorical models can be integrated, e. g., by mapping emotion terms to certain positions within the continuous emotion space. The exact positions are commonly determined through empirical studies with humans. For a more detailed elaboration on emotion models in the context of music, we refer to [136, 161]. One prominent example is the Geneva emotion wheel,[7] depicted in Figure 11.2 (bottom). It is a hybrid model that uses emotion terms as dimensions and describes the intensity of each of these emotions on a continuous scale.

Besides explicit emotion elicitation, the implicit acquisition of people's emotional states can be effected, for instance, by analyzing user-generated text [28], speech [34] or facial expressions in video [32] as well as a combination of audio and visual cues [75, 115].

11.4.1.2 Modeling the emotion perceived in music

Music can be regarded as an emotion-laden content and can hence also be described by emotion words, similar to listeners. The task of automatically assigning to a given music

---

7 http://www.affective-sciences.org/gew

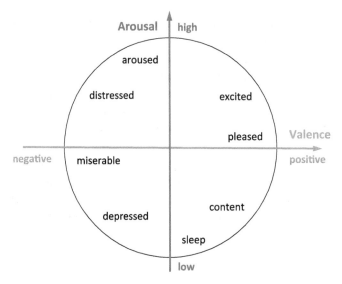

Figure 11.2: Emotion models. Top: emotional terms expressed in the valence-arousal space, according to [129]. Bottom: Geneva emotion wheel, according to [141].

piece such emotion terms (in case of categorical emotion models) or intensities (in case of dimensional models) is an active research area, typically refereed to as music emotion recognition (MER), e. g., [8, 65, 76, 162, 164]. If categorical emotion models are adopted, the MER task is treated as a classification task, whereas it is considered a regression task in case of dimensional models. Even though a variety of data sets, feature modeling approaches and machine learning methods have been created, devised and applied, respectively, integrating the emotion terms or intensities predicted by MER tools into a music recommender system is, however, not an easy task due to several reasons.

In the beginning of MER research, the problem was approached from a pure machine learning perspective, taking audio features as input to predict labels, which in this case constituted emotion terms. These approaches were agnostic of the actual meaning of the emotion terms as they failed to distinguish between *intended emotion, perceived emotion*, and *induced or felt emotion* [140]. Intended emotion refers to the emotion the composer, songwriter or performer had in mind when creating or performing the music piece; perceived emotion refers to the emotion recognized by a person listening to a piece; induced emotion refers to the emotion felt by the listener. Current MER approaches commonly target perceived or induced emotions.

Second, the ways musical characteristics reflected by content descriptors (rhythm, tonality, lyrics, etc.) influence the emotional state of the listener remains highly subjective, even though some general rules have been identified [89]. For instance, a musical piece in major key is typically perceived brighter and happier than a piece in minor key. A fast piece is perceived more exciting or more tense than a slow one. However, the perception of music emotion also depends on other psychological constructs such as the listener's personality [45, 136]; cf. Section 11.3.1.

11.4.1.3 Relating human emotions and music emotion annotations

As a result of the previous discussion on the relationship between listeners and emotions (Section 11.4.1.1) and between music pieces and emotions (Section 11.4.1.2), we assume to have information about user-emotion assignments and item-emotion assignments. Toward building emotion-aware music recommender systems, we next have to connect users and items through emotions, which is a challenging endeavor, in particular since such relations can also be influenced by the user's intent.

Three fundamental intents or purposes of music listening have been identified in a decent study conducted by Schäfer et al. [132]: *self-awareness* (e. g., stimulating a reflection of people on their identity), *social relatedness* (e. g., feeling closeness to friends and expressing identity) and *arousal and mood regulation* (e. g., managing emotions). Several studies found that affect regulation is indeed the most important purpose why people listen to music [12, 109, 132]. Nevertheless, modeling music preferences as a function of the listener's mood, listening intent and affective impact of listening to a certain emotionally laden music piece is a highly challenging endeavor.

11.4.1.4 Toward emotion-aware music recommender systems

Full-fledged emotion-aware music recommender systems are still rare. Preliminary approaches integrate content and mood-based filtering [3] or implement cross-modal recommendation, such as matching the mood of an input video with that of music pieces and recommending matching pieces [130]. Other work infers the user's emotional state from sensor data (cf. Section 11.4.2) and matches it with explicit user-specific preference indications. For instance, Park et al. [122] gather information about temperature, humidity, noise, light level, weather, season and time of day and subsequently use these features to predict whether the user is depressed, content, exuberant or anxious. Based on explicit user preference feedback about which type of music he or she prefers in a given emotional state, the proposed system then adapts recommendations.

More recently, Deng et al. [26] proposed an emotion-ware music recommender system that extracts affective cues and music listening data from popular Chinese microblogging service Sina Weibo (https://www.weibo.com). The authors combine various text resources and emoticons to create a lexicon, and in turn predict the emotions in posted messages. Their approach models emotions via different categorical models, ranging from 2 to 21 emotion categories. Leveraging these models, a user's emotional context is represented as a vector over the dimensions of the emotion model, each dimension containing the term frequency of words belonging to each emotion category in the user's most recent microblogs. Deng et al.'s approach then creates relations between emotions and songs for a given user by considering the emotions in the user's posts directly before posting a music listening event. Each pair of user and song is, therefore, attached an emotion vector. Exploiting these relations, the authors propose a user-based and an item-based collaborative filtering model, as well as a hybrid of the two. All models are based on emotional similarity between users and songs. The user-based collaborative filtering model recommends songs to the target user u based on the product of two components: overall emotional similarity to other users v (irrespective of their music preferences) and similarity between u's current emotion and the emotion v expressed when listening to the song under consideration. The item-based collaborative filtering model selects the emotionally most similar songs to the songs s already listened to by the target user u, and weighs them with the similarity between u's current emotion and u's emotion when listening to s. The proposed hybrid system linearly combines the scores predicted by the user-based and the items-based recommender. Deng et al. further investigate a random walk approach that creates a bipartite graph of users, emotional contexts and songs, and adapts a variant of PageRank to traverse the graph and create recommendations.

To conclude, research on emotion-aware music recommendation is still at an early stage. Creating systems that make recommendations that truly satisfy the user requires a decent psychological understanding of the listener's affective state, listening intent and affective impact of a song on the listener. Gaining such insights, elaborating methods to create respective listener profiles, and subsequently devising approaches to integrate them into systems can be considered open research challenges. This especially entails understanding and modeling the dynamics of emotions during music listening processes. For a more detailed discussion of these and other aspects, the reader is referred to the surveys by Lex et al. [104] and Assunção et al. [4].

11.4.2 Sensor data for context modeling

Contextual modeling for music recommender systems can also be achieved by exploiting various sensor data, where we understand sensors in a broad sense, not only as physical or hardware devices, but also including virtual sensors like active apps or running background tasks on a personal device. Today's smart devices are packed with sensors, ranging from motion to proximity to light sensors. It has therefore become easier than ever to gather large amounts of sensor data and exploit them for various purposes, such as gait recognition [154], human activity classification [90] or personal health assistance [105].

Table 11.2 provides a categorization of some sensor data that can be gathered from smart devices [55]. Data attributes are either of categorical or numerical type. In addition to the frequently used temporal, spatial and motion signals, the table lists hardware-specific attributes (device and phone data), environmental information about the sur-

Table 11.2: Categories of common sensor data used in context modeling, adapted from [55]. Letters in parenthesis indicate whether the attribute is **C**ategorical or **N**umerical.

Category	Attributes
Time	day of week (N), hour of day (N)
Location	provider (C), latitude (C), longitude (C), accuracy (N), altitude (N)
Weather	temperature (N), wind direction (N), wind speed (N), precipitation (N), humidity (N), visibility (N), pressure (N), cloud cover (N), weather code (N)
Device	battery level (N), battery status (N), available internal/external storage (N), volume settings (N), audio output mode (C)
Phone	service state (C), roaming (C), signal strength (N), GSM indicator (N), network type (N)
Task	recently used tasks/apps (C), screen on/off (C), docking mode (C)
Network	*mobile network*: available (C), connected (C);
	active network: type (C), subtype (C), roaming (C);
	Bluetooth: available (C), enabled (C);
	Wi-Fi: enabled (C), available (C), connected (C), BSSID (C), SSID (C), IP (N), link speed (N), RSSI (N)
Ambient	light (N), proximity (N), temperature (N), pressure (N), noise (N)
Motion	acceleration force (N), rate of rotation (C), orientation of user (N), orientation of device (C)
Player	repeat mode (C), shuffle mode (C), *sound effects*: equalizer present (C), equalizer enabled (C), bass boost enabled (C), bass boost strength (N), virtualizer enabled (C), virtualizer strength (N), reverb enabled (C), reverb strength (N)

rounding of the user (ambient), connectivity information (network), information about used applications (task) and application-specific information (in our context, of a music player).

Such sensor data has been exploited to some extent to build user models that are subsequently integrated into context- or situation-aware music recommender systems. Most earlier approaches are characterized by taking only a single category of context sensors into account though, most often spatial and temporal features. To give a few examples, Lee and Lee [100] exploit weather conditions alongside listening histories. Cebrian et al. [16] use temporal features. Addressing the task of supporting sports and fitness training, a considerable amount of work uses sensors to gauge steps per minute or heart rate to match the music played with the pace of the listener, or to stimulate a particular exercising behavior, e. g., Biehl et al. [11], Elliott and Tomlinson [33], Dornbush et al. [30], Cunningham et al. [21], de Oliveira and Oliver [25] and Moens et al. [113]. Besides the use case of sports and exercising, there further exists research work that targets other specific task, e. g., music recommendation while working [160], driving a car [6] or for multiple activity classes such as running, eating, sleeping, studying, working or shopping [153, 155]. An approach to identify music to accompany the daily activities of relaxing, studying and workout is proposed in [159].

More recent research works integrate a larger variety of sensor data into user models. For instance, Okada et al. [119] present a mobile music recommender that exploits sensor data to predict the user's activity, environment and location. Activity is inferred from the device's accelerometer and classified into idle, walking, bicycling, running, etc. The user's environment is predicted by recording audio on the device and matching it to a database of audio snippets, which are labeled as meeting, office, bus, etc. As for location, latitude and longitude GPS data is clustered into common user locations. Integrating activity, environment, location and quantized temporal data with respect to time of day and week days, the proposed system learns rules such as "Every Sunday afternoon, the user goes jogging and listens to metal songs," which are used among other information to effect recommendations.

Wang et al. [155] present a system, which records time of day, accelerometer data and ambient noise. Using these features, the recommender predicts the user's activity, i. e., running, walking, sleeping, working or shopping. Activity-aware recommendations are eventually effected by matching music pieces labeled with activity tags with the user's current activity.

Schedl et al. [133] propose a mobile music recommender called Mobile Music Genius, which acquires and monitors various context features during playback. It uses a decision tree classifier to learn to predict music preferences for given contexts. The user preference is modeled at various levels, i. e., genre, artist, track and mood; the context is modeled as an approximate 100-dimensional feature vector, including the attributes listed in Table 11.2. While playing, the user context is continuously monitored and compared to the temporally preceding context vector. If context changes exceed a sensitivity parameter, a track that fits the new context is requested from the classifier and added as next track to the playlist.

Hong et al. [63] exploit day of the week, location, weather and device vibration as features to build a bipartite graph, in which nodes either represent contexts or music pieces. Edges connect the two categories of nodes and the weight of an edge indicates how often a user has listened to a certain piece in a certain context. A random walk with restart algorithm is then used to identify music pieces that fit a given context. This algorithm takes into account the number, lengths and edge weights of paths between the given context node and the music nodes.

In summary, early works that exploit sensor data for context modeling for music recommendation focused on single and typically simple sensors, such as time or weather, while more recent ones consider a variety of sensor data, extending the above by motion, environment or location information, among others. Context models are then created either based on the entirety of the considered sensor data [63, 133], or based on inferred information such as the user's activity [119, 153, 155] or mood [122].

11.5 Music information behavior

To deepen our understanding the listeners' perception and uses of music recommender systems, we should also examine their music information behavior in everyday life. The term "information behavior" encompasses a wide range of activities including seeking, finding, using, selecting, avoiding and stumbling upon information [14]. The information can come from formal sources (e. g., books, magazines, music recordings) or from informal ones (e. g., friends, family members). In other words, information behavior research does not limit its scope to users' interaction with information systems. It also looks more broadly at the information practices that surround the use (or nonuse) of these systems.

In this section, we look at the music-related information behavior of people in everyday life. In the first subsection, we review the literature on how people discover music in their daily life and the place music recommender systems play in it; in the second, we focus more specifically on studies on users' perception of music recommender systems; lastly, we look into the use of playlists for organizing music on streaming platforms to gain a better understanding of use cases and playlists as a source of information for recommender systems.

11.5.1 Discovering music in everyday life

Task-based experiments and transaction logs are useful for identifying usability problems in a system. However, the intent and experience of users can only be inferred from the traces of their interactions with the system. To know about the true users' needs, we need to take a step back to get a broader perspective on information practices in real life. To understand how music recommender systems can better support their users, we suggest looking at the studies on how people discover music in their daily life. For the most part, these studies have been conducted by researchers in information sciences and employ qualitative interviewing, observations, diaries and surveys, with the objective of learning about the real-life behaviors of real-life users, oftentimes in real-life settings.

11.5.1.1 Importance of friends and families

Consistently and across age groups, studies show that friends, family and acquaintances were and remain the main source of music discovery in everyday life [68, 77, 91, 148]. Even as music streaming services are pervasive, people prefer approaching friends and relatives to ask for music suggestions rather than seeking recommendations in online services. In a survey conducted by Lee and her colleagues [96], 82.8 % reported turning to friends or family members when searching for music information. Qualitative studies reveal that people do not only turn to people out of convenience. They appreciate receiving recommendations specifically tailored to their tastes from a source they trust, that is a close friend, a relative or an acquaintance they consider as being more knowledgeable in the music domain than they are and whose music tastes they value [68, 91, 92].

And these knowledgeable friends do not usually need to be arm-twisted to provide recommendations: people who rank high on the mavenism scale were found to be more likely to provide (and receive) music recommendations [152]. Additionally, along with the recommendations, the informant will often willingly provide information about the artist and the music, and convey their appreciation and enthusiasm along the way, thus turning the social interaction into a "musical experience in its own right" [77].

11.5.1.2 Prevalence of serendipitous encounters

Research on music information behavior also uncovered that people often discover music by chance. People do not typically go to music streaming services with the specific objective of looking for the perfect gem. They stumble upon it during their daily routine (e. g., music heard on the radio or television, in a cafe, in a friend's car) or en route, while looking for something else. Indeed, studies with younger adults show music discoveries are often the result of passive information behavior or serendipitous encounters [23, 91, 152]. Music has become a nearly constant soundtrack in many people's lives. Opportunities for encountering music are numerous. However, the strong engagement adolescents and young adults have with music might also explain the prevalence of these events. Research suggests that serendipitous encountering of information does not occur completely randomly, "but from circumstances brought about by unconscious motives, which lead ultimately to the serendipitous event" [53]. In [91], it was found that many avid music listeners were also "superencounterers," for they regularly engaged in activities likely to produce serendipity (e. g., wandering in a music festival) and were constantly monitoring their environment for interesting music.

11.5.1.3 The role of music recommender systems

Although all surveys converge to show the widespread adoption of music streaming services, the recommendations they offer have yet to convince all users. In a survey conducted by Lee et al. [96], 64.6 % of the participants reported using cloud music services to discover music. Other surveys conducted at the same period yielded similar results: Legault-Venne et al. [101] found that 67.1 % of respondents used music streaming services to discover new music, and Liikkanen and Åman [106] found that 65 % used YouTube.[8] Lee et al.'s [96] survey also revealed that a much smaller proportion of women (36.4 %) used these functionalities compared with men (77.1 %). Interestingly, for people who use streaming services to find new music, system recommendations have not displaced traditional ways to discover music. Instead, qualitative studies show that people

---

8 https://www.youtube.com

often use a combination of strategies. For instance, interviews with users revealed what seems to be a common pattern: people first get introduced to new music in their daily life (e. g., in the mass media, through friends), then they use music recommender systems to expand their exploration to other songs and/or artists [68, 77].

11.5.2 User studies of music recommender systems

Considering the rapid and widespread adoption of music streaming services, several recent user studies on these systems have been published. In this section, we put our main focus on the studies on users' experience with and perception of music recommendations provided by these systems. These studies consist mainly in qualitative research conducted by social scientists and user experience studies on music streaming services conducted by researchers in information sciences.

11.5.2.1 Users' perception of music recommendations

Since the major players in the music streaming industry have comparable (and very extensive) catalogs, the branding of these services now lies in the services they offer, including personalized recommendations and curated playlists [35, 114]. Therefore, it comes with no surprise to find that "Exposure to new things/serendipity" is the most important quality for a music service for users [96]. But how are these recommendations perceived by users? Studies do not provide a clear answer to that question, mainly because the perception seems to vary from user to user. In general, users have been found to have an overall positive perception of the recommendations provided by music streaming services [106, 110]. Many users report relying on system recommendations to navigate the amount of music available [106, 110, 156]. Similarly, heavy music service users appreciate the fact that system recommendations reduce their load by assisting them in digital curation tasks [58]. Results from a large-scale study by Avdeeff [5] highlight another interesting advantage of system recommendations from the users' perspective: for younger people who often perceive music genres as being confusing, the suggestions YouTube provides represent a useful alternative for discovery. Research also shows that many users consider that system recommendations have led them to expand their music taste, helping them to "traverse musical boundaries that they would previously have avoided for fear of being seen as 'uncool' or 'out of place' " [156], hence "nudging their pre-Spotify taste boundaries of music" [110]. Certain users even develop a sense of ownership or intimacy with the system. They talk about "their algorithm," the one that knows their taste and has an understanding of them as listeners, and worry about others using their account to listen to music, thus "ruining" their algorithm [156].

But users are not always as enthusiastic about system recommendations. One of the main criticisms target the lack of novelty and true exploration, which prompted one user to say that she felt "stuck in [her] own circles" [68]. Likewise, Kjus found that users "lose interest in the large databases after a period of initial fascination," a symptom he attributes to the inability of recommender systems to lead users to long tail items [77]. Some users also complain about the system playing songs they dislike or making recommendations they do not understand [58, 142]. In the same line, several studies reveal a general lack of trust toward music recommender systems. Lee and Price [98] found that most users want more transparency: they want the systems to explain the recommendations. For some users, when Spotify partnered with artists and labels, distrust came with the realization that some services infuse their own commercial interests into their algorithms [77, 114]. As a result of these perceived weaknesses or inaccuracies, Siles et al. [142] found that some users employed various strategies to "train, cajole, mould or steer the system" to receive better recommendations. Finally, and for very different reasons, opinion leaders were also found to show a less enthusiastic attitude toward the personalized recommendations music streaming services provide. The fact that curation and discovery can be outsourced to the system represents for them a lost opportunity to demonstrate social distinction through display of their discriminatory judgment [156].

11.5.2.2 Users' engagement with music recommender systems

Many studies have focused, voluntarily or not, on avid music listeners. Recent large-scale studies and smaller qualitative studies with more diversified samples have uncovered a wider array of engagement practices with music streaming services. Users' engagement appears to vary in accordance with the importance music plays in their life [54, 58, 87, 110, 156, 157]. A group of researchers conducted a qualitative study [98], followed by a large-scale survey [54] on the behavior and preferences of music streaming services users. Their analysis resulted in seven personas with various levels of music expertise and involvement with music systems. These personas include the "Active Curator" who "cares about organizing collection and [is] willing to spend time for it," as well as the "Guided Listener" who "wants to engage with a music streaming service minimally." Indeed, studies on opinion leaders [157] and music mavens [110] found that users with a higher level of music expertise were more willing than others to invest the time and effort required to manually curate their own playlists. On the contrary, users for whom music is not as important do not show the same level of engagement. Studies demonstrate that many users wish to be able to listen to music continuously, without interacting much with the system. Johansson [68] reports on young users feeling "lazy" or "less active," who do not want to make the effort of creating playlists or browsing to find music to listen to. Webster [156] observes gender differences in users' engagement: "music connoisseurs" are predominantly (young) men and are thus more likely to show a higher level of control when selecting music.

The tendency of many users to adopt a passive or "lean-back" attitude might be the consequence of the abundance (or overabundance) of choices in music services. Having access to such large music collections can seem exhilarating at first, but it can also be intimidating to some. Users have expressed feeling "stressed" or "overwhelmed" by the number of items to chose from, or have used the term "drowning" to refer to how they felt [68, 77], a problem known in psychology as choice overload. According to research, strategies for dealing with choice overload include withdrawing/escaping or surrendering the selection to someone else [66]. In this context, for lesser-engaged users, recommender systems become their gateway to music, which is why it is important to also take the needs of these users into consideration in the design of music recommender systems.

11.5.3 Personal structures and music organization on streaming platforms

The term *music recommendation* may actually refer to a variety of use cases with quite diverse requirements, such as discovery, automatic radio stations or playlist completion, to name a few; cf. [137]. The diversity of potential use cases and desiderata for music services is also shown in a study by Lehtiniemi and Holm [103], who have investigated the features that users expect from the "ultimate" music player. Apart from previously discussed features for serendipitous music discovery and mood-based search (Sections 11.5.1 and 11.4.1, resp.) and contextual awareness (Section 11.4), these also comprise the "storing, editing and fine-tuning [of] playlists." This points to a frequently utilized functionality of platforms, which despite promoting the paradigm of *accessing music* over *owning* it, cater to a need for organizing tracks and even maintaining some sort of "personal collections" through playlists; cf. [22, 58, 97]. Often these again reflect existing concepts of music organization, such as (sub)genres, or according to mood or activity, i. e., how people use music [52, 109]. As playlist data is a potential source for training of collaborative filtering models, understanding better what user intents stand behind them and whether this can be observed in the data is a relevant question.

In a qualitative study, Hagen [58] has analyzed how listeners use and organize playlists, and which common needs and factors can be identified. In terms of usage, a playlist can be categorized into *static, dynamic* and *temporal.* For static playlists, users basically retain the original aggregation of music for the life of the list. This often follows or incorporates existing structures, such as albums. Dynamic playlists change their composition; however, this change is mostly characterized by growth, rarely by deletions. Temporary playlists are highly dynamic and possibly quickly deleted. Playlists, in particular dynamic and temporal, are extended, e. g., through random plays or encounters on automatic radio stations or through other recommendations. As such, a bias through algorithmic selection might exist but the final selection is curated manually.

With regard to categorization and organizational "themes," established *"standardized" categories* adopting, e. g., the above mentioned album structures, but also artists or "genres" as common denominator can be observed. Beside this, users resort to organization into *individual categories*, which split up these existing structures based on personal preference. This can comprise concepts like the tuning of tracks or TV series and films, etc. The previously discussed *context sensitivity* marks another category, e. g., by creating playlists for sleep, exercise, study, work or commuting. Context-oriented playlists also comprise seasonally relevant aggregations, as found in the playlist such as "Alternative Christmas," "Upcoming Summer," "Spring-Like Winter" or "Summery Sun 2013." Not least, Hagen identifies the theme "The Self and Others" for contextual playlists, comprising various temporally important tracks linked to personal events ("soundtrack of life"). In conclusion, across all taken angles, the themes of fluidity, curation and control are important and reoccurring factors in the creation of playlists.

Comparing these qualitative findings to quantitative analyses of playlist data reveals similar trends. Modeling user created playlists published on the website, Art of the Mix,[9] McFee and Lanckriet [111] identify various types of categorical labels. The top 25 categories analyzed comprise standardized categories like "Single Artist," as well as various genres (e. g., "Rock," "Jazz," "Folk" or "Reggae"), individual categories ("Theme," "Cover," "Alternating DJ") and context-oriented playlists ("Romantic," "Break Up," "Road Trip," "Depression"), as well as "soundtrack of life" playlists ("Narrative"). In an analysis of the *#nowplaying* data set [163], Pichl et al. [124] identify "contextual clusters" of usage intents from playlist titles. Mentioned examples comprise playlists named "party," "workout" or 'Christmas.". An identified seasonal cluster for "summer" contains playlists such as "my summer playlist," "summer 2015 tracks," "finally summer" and "hot outside." Individual playlists can be found in clusters containing keywords such as "favorites," "random" or "playlist." Individual playlists, as described by Hagen [58], that focus on TV shows or movie soundtracks, are also part of an explanation of atypical playlist compositions, e. g., with respect to record label distributions; cf. [78].

11.6 User-centric evaluation of music recommender systems

Most evaluation approaches in current music recommender systems research and recommender systems research in general focus on quantitative measures, both geared toward retrieval accuracy (e. g., precision, recall, F-measure or NDCG) and qualities beyond pure accuracy that cover further factors of perceived recommendation quality (e. g., spread, coverage, diversity or novelty) [140]. While such beyond-accuracy measures aim to quantify and objectively assess parameters desired by users, they cannot fully capture actual user satisfaction with a recommender system. For instance, while

---

9 https://www.artofthemix.org

operational measures have been defined to quantify serendipity and diversity, they can only capture certain criteria. Serendipity and diversity as *perceived* by the user, however, can differ substantially from these measures, since they are highly subjective concepts [151]. Thus, despite the advantages of facilitating automation of evaluation and reproducibility of results, limiting recommender systems evaluation to such quantitative measures means to forgo essential factors related to user experience (UX).

Hence, in order to improve user awareness in music recommender systems, it is essential to incorporate evaluation strategies that consider factors of UX. To overcome the tendency to measure aspects such as user satisfaction or user engagement [59, 102] individually, evaluation frameworks for recommender systems aim at providing a more holistic view. One such framework is the ResQue model by Pu et al. [125], which proposes to evaluate the perceived qualities of recommender systems according to 15 constructs pertaining to four evaluation layers. The first layer deals with perceived system qualities and aims at evaluating aspects of recommendation quality, namely *accuracy, novelty* and *diversity, interaction adequacy, interface adequacy, information sufficiency* and *explicability*. The second layer deals with beliefs, evaluating *perceived ease of use, control, transparency* and *perceived usefulness*. Layers three and four deal with attitudes (*overall satisfaction* and *confidence and trust*) and behavioral intentions (*use intentions* and *purchase intentions*), respectively. These constructs are evaluated using questionnaires consisting of up to 32 questions to be rated on a Likert scale.

Another evaluation framework is presented by Knijnenburg et al. [84]. In contrast to the model by Pu et al., which focuses on outcome experience of recommender systems, Knijnenburg et al. aim at providing insight into the relationships of six constructs that impact user experience: objective system aspects (OSA), subjective system aspects (SSA), subjective user experiences (EXP), objective interaction (INT) and personal and situational characteristics (PC and SC). This includes considerations of users' expertise of the domain or concerns for privacy, which are not reflected in the model by Pu et al. In particular, Knijnenburg et al. explicitly link INT, i. e., observable user behavior such as clicks, to OSA, i. e., unbiased factors such as response time or user interface parameters, through several subjective constructs, i. e., SSA (momentary, primary evaluative feelings evoked during interacting with the system [60]) and EXP (the user's attitude toward the system), and argue that EXP is caused by OSA (through SSA) and PC (e. g., user demographics, knowledge or perceived control) and/or SC (e. g., interaction context or situation-specific trust or privacy concerns). To assess subjective factors, such as perceived qualities of recommendations and system effectiveness, variety, choice satisfaction or intention to provide feedback, Knijnenburg et al. also propose a questionnaire.

Both frameworks can be applied to music recommender systems, however, neither is specifically designed for modeling the processes particular to these systems. Therefore, some of the assumptions do not hold for the requirements of today's music recommender systems. For instance, the ResQue model by Pu et al. has a strong focus toward commercial usage intentions, which in music recommender systems, are by far more complex than the mere goal of using the system or intending to purchase (cf. Section 11.5). In particular with flat-rate streaming subscriptions being the dominating business model, selecting items does not have the same significance as a purchase. On a higher level, the commercial usage intention could be translated into or interpreted as continued subscription or monthly renewal of the service.

The model by Knijnenburg et al. can be easier adapted, as it was built around multimedia recommender systems therefore offering more flexibility to incorporate the factors discussed in Section 11.2 and exemplarily detailed throughout this chapter. For instance, the INT aspects in the model can be adapted to refer to typical observable behavior of the user like favoring a song or adding it to a playlist, while PC aspects should reflect psychological factors, including affect and personality (as described in Sections 11.4.1 and 11.3, resp.), social influence, musical training and experience and physiological condition, to mention a few more examples. SC, on the other hand, should be adapted to the particularities of music listening context and situations. To get a better understanding of the various evaluation needs in the specific scenario of music recommendation and tailor new strategies, researchers in music recommender systems should therefore increasingly resort to the findings of user-centric evaluations, in situ interviews and ethnographic studies; cf. [7, 23, 39, 71, 72, 93, 94, 96, 99, 146].

11.7 Conclusions

In this chapter, we have identified different factors relevant for making music recommendations, namely intrinsic aspects, external factors and goals of both users and items. Focusing on the listener's aspects, we have highlighted exemplary technical approaches to model these factors and exploit knowledge about them for recommendation scenarios.

Regarding intrinsic aspects, i. e., the listener's background, we have reviewed work investigating the connection between a user's demographic information, personality traits or cultural background on one hand, and musical preference, interest in diversity and browsing preference on the other. While correlations of different user characteristics with music consumption behavior could be uncovered, for a lack of comprehensive data, it has not yet been explored whether these findings are consistent over different experiments. Hence it needs to be investigated if these or other interactions emerge when evaluating several indicators simultaneously in a larger study and with the same subjects. Exploiting more diverse data sources, such as from social media and other online activities, should give a more holistic picture of the user. In practice, the resulting challenge is to connect and match user activities across different platforms. While single sign-on options have facilitated the tracing of individuals across several services for the syndicated platforms, impartial academic research does not have comparable means. It remains, however, at least ethically questionable to which extent such profiling of users is justifiable and necessary on the premise of providing improved user experience, specifically music listening experiences.

Similar considerations can be taken on matters of modeling external factors, i. e., the listener's context. We have reviewed work dealing with estimating the current emotional state of listeners and connecting this to the emotions estimated to be conveyed by a piece, as well as work dealing with estimation of situational context of the listener based on sensor data. Both aspects can be highly dynamic and obtaining a ground truth and a general basis for repeatable experiments is challenging, if not elusive. Explicit assessments of mood and context requires introspection and reflection by the user and might be considered intrusive. On the other hand, taking a purely data-driven approach and exploring a wealth of accessible logging data to uncover latent patterns without proper means of validation might give rise to false assumptions and models and further raise issues concerning privacy.

To gain a better understanding of listeners' intents, we have reviewed work dealing with music information behavior to examine how people discover music in their daily life, how users perceive system recommendations in music streaming services, and how they organize music on streaming platforms. The key role friends and family play in discovering music suggest that people highly value the trustworthiness of the source of a music recommendation. Indeed, one of the most important criticisms leveled at music recommender systems is their lack of transparency and a breach of trust that comes from the role some services have taken in the promotion of specific artists. This impression contributes to the perception that music recommender systems are not the independent discovery tools they pretend to be. In terms of system design, this means that music recommender systems should pay close attention to building and maintaining the trust of their users, for instance, by providing explanations to users as to why items are being recommended to them and by clearly identifying promotional recommendations. Furthermore, music information behavior studies revealed the prevalence of passive information behavior and serendipitous encounters in discovering music in daily life. In the same line, the review of studies on users' perception of and experience with music streaming services showed that users have various expectations regarding how much they want to engage with music recommender systems. Although certain users, especially the highly devoted music fans, are willing to spend time actively engaging with a system to keep a high level of control, others feel submerged by the millions of tracks available in a music service and prefer giving out a larger part of the control to the system in order to interact only minimally with it. This means that user-centered music recommender systems should let the users decide how much control they want to surrender to the system in order to cater to all users.

To conclude, we believe that a deepened understanding of the different factors of both user and music and their interplay is the key to improved music recommendation services and listening experiences. User awareness is therefore an essential aspect to adapt and balance systems between exploitation and exploration settings and not only identify the "right music at the right time," but also help in discovering new artists and styles, deepening knowledge, refining tastes, broadening horizons—and generally be a catalyst to enable people to enjoy listening to music.

References

[1]   X. Amatriain and J. Basilico. Recommender systems in industry: A netflix case study. In: F. Ricci, L. Rokach, and B. Shapira, editors. *Recommender Systems Handbook*. Boston, MA: Springer US, 2015, pp. 385–419.

[2]   I. Anderson, S. Gil, C. Gibson, S. Wolf, W. Shapiro, O. Semerci, and D. M. Greenberg. "just the way you are": Linking music listening on spotify and personality. *Social Psychological and Personality Science* 12(4) (2021) 561–572.

[3]   I. Andjelkovic, D. Parra, and J. O'Donovan. Moodplay. Interactive mood-based music discovery and recommendation. In: *Proceedings of the 2016 Conference on User Modeling Adaptation and Personalization, UMAP'16*. New York, NY, USA: ACM, 2016, pp. 275–279.

[4]   W. Assunção, L. S. G. Piccolo, and L. A. M. Zaina. Considering emotions and contextual factors in music recommendation: a systematic literature review. *Multimedia Tools and Applications* 81(6) (2022) 8367–8407.

[5]   M. Avdeeff. Technological engagement and musical eclecticism: An examination of contemporary listening practices. *Participations: Journal of Audience and Reception Studies* 9(2) (2012) 265–285.

[6]   L. Baltrunas, M. Kaminskas, B. Ludwig, O. Moling, F. Ricci, K.-H. Lüke, and R. S. InCarMusic. Context-Aware Music Recommendations in a Car. In: *International Conference on Electronic Commerce and Web Technologies (EC-Web), Toulouse, France*, 2011.

[7]   L. Barrington, R. Oda, and G. Lanckriet. Smarter than genius? human evaluation of music recommender systems. In: *Proceedings of the 10th International Society for Music Information Retrieval Conference, ISMIR'09, Nara, Japan*, 2009.

[8]   M. Barthet, G. Fazekas, and M. Sandler. Multidisciplinary perspectives on music emotion recognition: Implications for content and context-based models. In: *Proceedings of International Symposium on Computer Music Modelling and Retrieval* 2012, pp. 492–507.

[9]   C. Bauer and B. Ferwerda. The effect of ingroup identification on conformity behavior in group decision-making: the flipping direction matters. In: *Proceedings of the 56th Hawaii International Conference on System Sciences*. University of Hawaii, 2023, pp. 2242–2251.

[10] C. Bauer and A. Novotny. A consolidated view of context for intelligent systems. *Journal of Ambient Intelligence and Smart Environments* 9(4) (2017) 377–393.

[11] J. T. Biehl, P. D. Adamczyk, and B. P. B. DJogger. A Mobile Dynamic Music Device. In: *Proceedings of the 24th Annual ACM SIGCHI Conference on Human Factors in Computing Systems Extended Abstracts (CHI EA), Montréal, QC, Canada*, 2006.

[12] D. Boer and R. Fischer. Towards a holistic model of functions of music listening across cultures: A culturally decentred qualitative approach. *Psychology of Music* 40(2) (2010) 179–200.

[13] G. Bonnin and D. Jannach. Automated generation of music playlists: Survey and experiments. *ACM Computing Surveys (CSUR)* 47(2) (2015) 26.

[14] D. O. Case. *Looking for information: a survey of research on information seeking needs, and behavior*, 3rd edition. Bingley, UK: Emerald Group Publishing, 2012.

[15] M. A. Casey, R. Veltkamp, M. Goto, M. Leman, C. Rhodes, and M. Slaney. Content-based music information retrieval: Current directions and future challenges. *Proceedings of the IEEE* 96(4) (2008) 668–696.

[16] T. Cebrián, M. Planagumà, P. Villegas, and X. Amatriain. Music Recommendations with Temporal Context Awareness. In: *Proceedings of the 4th ACM Conference on Recommender Systems (RecSys), Barcelona, Spain*, 2010.

[17]   F. Celli, E. Bruni, and B. Lepri. Automatic personality and interaction style recognition from facebook profile pictures. In: *Proceedings of the 22nd ACM international conference on Multimedia*. ACM, 2014, pp. 1101–1104.

[18]   Ò. Celma. *Music Recommendation and Discovery – The Long Tail, Long Fail, and Long Play in the Digital Music Space*. Berlin, Heidelberg, Germany: Springer, 2010.

[19]   Ò. Celma and P. Herrera. A New Approach to Evaluating Novel Recommendations. In: *Proceedings of the 2nd ACM Conference on Recommender Systems (RecSys), Lausanne, Switzerland*, 2008.

[20]   C.-W. Chen, P. Lamere, M. Schedl, and H. Zamani. RecSys Challenge 2018: Automatic Music Playlist Continuation. In: *Proceedings of the 12th ACM Conference on Recommender Systems, RecSys'18*. New York, NY, USA: ACM, 2018, pp. 527–528.

[21]   S. Cunningham, S. Caulder, and V. Grout. Saturday Night or Fever? Context-Aware Music Playlists. In: *Proceedings of the 3rd International Audio Mostly Conference: Sound in Motion, Piteå, Sweden*, 2008.

[22]   S. J. Cunningham, D. Bainbridge, and A. Bainbridge. Exploring personal music collection behavior. In: S. Choemprayong, F. Crestani, and S. J. Cunningham, editors. *Digital Libraries: Data, Information, and Knowledge for Digital Lives*. Cham: Springer International Publishing, 2017, pp. 295–306.

[23]   S. J. Cunningham, D. Bainbridge, and D. Mckay. Finding new music: A diary study of everyday encounters with novel songs. In: *Proceedings of the 8th International Conference on Music Information Retrieval, Vienna, Austria, September 23–27*, 2007, pp. 83–88.

[24]   S. J. Cunningham and D. M. Nichols. Exploring Social Music Behaviour: An Investigation of Music Selection at Parties. In: *Proceedings of the 10th International Society for Music Information Retrieval Conference (ISMIR 2009), Kobe, Japan*, 2009.

[25]   R. de Oliveira and N. O. TripleBeat. Enhancing Exercise Performance with Persuasion. In: *Proceedings of the 10th International Conference on Human Computer Interaction with Mobile Devices and Services (Mobile CHI), Amsterdam, the Netherlands*, 2008.

[26]   S. Deng, D. Wang, X. Li, and G. Xu. Exploring User Emotion in Microblogs for Music Recommendation. *Expert Systems with Applications* 42(23) (2015) 9284–9293.

[27]   A. K. Dey. Understanding and using context. *Personal and Ubiquitous Computing* 5(1) (2001) 4–7.

[28]   L. Dey, M. U. Asad, N. Afroz, and R. P. D. Nath. Emotion extraction from real time chat messenger. In: *2014 International Conference on Informatics, Electronics Vision (ICIEV)* 2014, pp. 1–5.

[29]   J. Donaldson. A hybrid social-acoustic recommendation system for popular music. In: *Proceedings of the ACM Conference on Recommender Systems (RecSys), Minneapolis, MN, USA*, 2007.

[30]   S. Dornbush, J. English, T. Oates, Z. Segall, and A. Joshi XPod. A Human Activity Aware Learning Mobile Music Player. In: *20th International Joint Conference on Artificial Intelligence (IJCAI): Proceedings of the 2nd Workshop on Artificial Intelligence Techniques for Ambient Intelligence, Hyderabad, India*, 2007.

[31]   G. Dror, N. Koenigstein, and Y. K. Yahoo!. Music Recommendations: Modeling Music Ratings with Temporal Dynamics and Item Taxonomy. In: *Proceedings of the 5th ACM Conference on Recommender Systems (RecSys), Chicago, IL, USA*, 2011.

[32]   S. Ebrahimi Kahou, V. Michalski, K. Konda, R. Memisevic, and C. Pal. Recurrent neural networks for emotion recognition in video. In: *Proceedings of the 2015 ACM on International Conference on Multimodal Interaction, ICMI'15*. New York, NY, USA: ACM, 2015, pp. 467–474.

[33]   G. T. Elliott and B. Tomlinson. PersonalSoundtrack. Context-aware playlists that adapt to user pace. In: *Proceedings of the 24th Annual ACM SIGCHI Conference on Human Factors in Computing Systems Extended Abstracts (CHI EA), Montréal, QC, Canada*, 2006.

[34]   M. Erdal, M. Kächele, and F. Schwenker. Emotion recognition in speech with deep learning architectures. In: F. Schwenker, H. M. Abbas, N. El Gayar, and E. Trentin, editors. *Proceedings of Artificial Neural Networks in Pattern Recognition: 7th IAPR TC3 Workshop*. Springer International Publishing, 2016, pp. 298–311.

[35]   M. Eriksson, R. Fleischer, and A. Johansson. *Spotify Teardown: Inside the black box of streaming music*. MIT Press, 2019.

[36]   B. Ferwerda and C. Bauer. To flip or not to flip: Conformity effect across cultures. In: *CHI Conference on Human Factors in Computing Systems Extended Abstracts*, 2022, pp. 1–7.

[37]   B. Ferwerda and M. Graus. Predicting musical sophistication from music listening behaviors: A preliminary study, 2018. arXiv preprint. Available at arXiv:1808.07314.

[38]   B. Ferwerda, M. Graus, A. Vall, M. Tkalčič, and M. Schedl. The influence of users' personality traits on satisfaction and attractiveness of diversified recommendation lists. In: *4th Workshop on Emotions and Personality in Personalized Systems 43, EMPIRE, 2016*, 2016.

[39]   B. Ferwerda, M. P. Graus, A. Vall, M. Tkalcic, and M. Schedl. How item discovery enabled by diversity leads to increased recommendation list attractiveness. In: *Proceedings of the Symposium on Applied Computing*. ACM, 2017, pp. 1693–1696.

[40]   B. Ferwerda and M. Schedl. Enhancing music recommender systems with personality information and emotional states: A proposal. In: *UMAP Workshops*, 2014.

[41]   B. Ferwerda and M. Schedl. Investigating the relationship between diversity in music consumption behavior and cultural dimensions: A cross-country analysis. In: *UMAP (Extended Proceedings)*, 2016.

[42]   B. Ferwerda and M. Schedl. Personality-based user modeling for music recommender systems. In: *Joint European Conference on Machine Learning and Knowledge Discovery in Databases*. Springer, 2016, pp. 254–257.

[43]   B. Ferwerda, M. Schedl, and M. Tkalcic. Predicting personality traits with instagram pictures. In: *Proceedings of the 3rd Workshop on Emotions and Personality in Personalized Systems 2015*. ACM, 2015, pp. 7–10.

[44]   B. Ferwerda, M. Schedl, and M. Tkalcic. Using instagram picture features to predict users' personality. In: *International Conference on Multimedia Modeling*. Springer, 2016, pp. 850–861.

[45]   B. Ferwerda, M. Schedl, and M. Tkalčič. Personality & Emotional States: Understanding Users' Music Listening Needs. In: *Extended Proceedings of the 23rd International Conference on User Modeling, Adaptation and Personalization (UMAP), Dublin, Ireland, June–July*, 2015.

[46]   B. Ferwerda and M. Tkalcic. Predicting users' personality from instagram pictures: Using visual and/or content features? In: *The 26th Conference on User Modeling, Adaptation and Personalization, 2018, Singapore*, 2018.

[47]   B. Ferwerda and M. Tkalcic. You are what you post: What the content of instagram pictures tells about users' personality. In: *The 23rd International on Intelligent User Interfaces*, 2018.

[48]   B. Ferwerda, M. Tkalčič and M. Schedl. Personality traits and music genre preferences: How music taste varies over age groups. In: *Proceedings of the 1st Workshop on Temporal Reasoning in Recommender Systems (RecTemp) at the 11th ACM Conference on Recommender Systems, Como, August 31, 2017*, 2017.

[49]   B. Ferwerda, M. Tkalčič, and M. Schedl. Personality traits and music genres: What do people prefer to listen to? In: *Proceedings of the 25th Conference on User Modeling, Adaptation and Personalization*. ACM, 2017, pp. 285–288.

[50]   B. Ferwerda, A. Vall, M. Tkalčič, and M. Schedl. Exploring music diversity needs across countries. In: *Proceedings of the 2016 Conference on User Modeling Adaptation and Personalization*. ACM, 2016, pp. 287–288.

[51]   B. Ferwerda, E. Yang, M. Schedl, and M. Tkalčič. Personality traits predict music taxonomy preferences. In: *Proceedings of the 33rd Annual ACM Conference Extended Abstracts on Human Factors in Computing Systems*. ACM, 2015, pp. 2241–2246.

[52]   B. Ferwerda, E. Yang, M. Schedl, and M. Tkalčič. Personality Traits Predict Music Taxonomy Preferences. In: *ACM CHI '15 Extended Abstracts on Human Factors in Computing Systems, Seoul, Republic of Korea*, 2015.

[53]   A. Foster. Serendipity and information seeking: an empirical study. *Journal of Documentation* 59(3) (2003) 321–340.

[54]   J. Fuller, L. Hubener, Y.-S. Kim, and J. H. Lee. Elucidating user behavior in music services through persona and gender. In: *Proceedings of the 17th International Society for Music Information Retrieval Conference*, 2016, pp. 626–632.

[55] M. Gillhofer and M. Schedl. Iron Maiden While Jogging, Debussy for Dinner? - An Analysis of Music Listening Behavior in Context. In: *Proceedings of the 21st International Conference on MultiMedia Modeling (MMM), Sydney, Australia*, 2015.

[56] J. Golbeck, C. Robles, M. Edmondson, and K. Turner. Predicting personality from twitter. In: *Privacy, Security, Risk and Trust (PASSAT) and 2011 IEEE Third Inernational Conference on Social Computing (SocialCom), 2011 IEEE Third International Conference on*. IEEE, 2011, pp. 149–156.

[57] J. Golbeck, C. Robles, and K. Turner. Predicting personality with social media. In: *CHI'11 extended abstracts on human factors in computing systems*. ACM, 2011, pp. 253–262.

[58] A. N. Hagen. The playlist experience: Personal playlists in music streaming services. *Popular Music and Society* 38(5) (2015) 625–645.

[59] J. Hart, A. G. Sutcliffe, and A. di Angeli. Evaluating user engagement theory. In: *CHI Conference on Human Factors in Computing Systems, 6 May 2012. Paper presented in Workshop 'Theories behind UX Research and How They Are Used in Practice'*, 2012.

[60] M. Hassenzahl. The thing and i: Understanding the relationship between user and product. In: M. A. Blythe, K. Overbeeke, A. F. Monk, and P. C. Wright, editors. *Funology: From Usability to Enjoyment*. Netherlands, Dordrecht: Springer, 2005, pp. 31–42.

[61] K. Hevner. Expression in Music: A Discussion of Experimental Studies and Theories. *Psychological Review* 42 (1935).

[62] G. Hofstede, G. J. Hofstede, and M. Minkov. *Cultures and Organizations: Software of the Mind*, 3rd edition. New York, NY, United States: McGraw-Hill, 2010.

[63] J. Hong, W.-S. Hwang, J.-H. Kim, and S.-W. Kim. Context-aware music recommendation in mobile smart devices. In: *Proceedings of the 29th Annual ACM Symposium on Applied Computing, SAC'14*. New York, NY, USA: ACM, 2014, pp. 1463–1468.

[64] Y. Hu, Y. Koren, and C. Volinsky. Collaborative Filtering for Implicit Feedback Datasets. In: *Proceedings of the 8th IEEE International Conference on Data Mining (ICDM), Pisa, Italy*, 2008.

[65] A. Huq, J. Bello, and R. Rowe. Automated Music Emotion Recognition: A Systematic Evaluation. *Journal of New Music Research* 39(3) (2010) 227–244.

[66] S. S. Iyengar and M. R. Lepper. When choice is demotivating: Can one desire too much of a good thing? *Journal of Personality and Social Psychology* 79(6) (2000) 995–1006.

[67] D. Jannach, L. Lerche, and I. Kamehkhosh. Beyond "hitting the hits": Generating coherent music playlist continuations with the right tracks. In: *Proceedings of the 9th ACM Conference on Recommender Systems, RecSys'15*. New York, NY, USA: ACM, 2015, pp. 187–194.

[68] S. Johansson. Music as part of connectivity culture. In: S. Johansson, A. Werner, P. Åker, and G. Goldenzwaig, editors. *Streaming Music: Practices, Media, Cultures*. Milton, United Kingdom: Taylor & Francis Group, 2018.

[69] O. P. John, E. M. Donahue and R. L. Kentle. The big five inventory—versions 4a and 54, 1991.

[70] P. N. Juslin. What Does Music Express? Basic Emotions and Beyond. *Frontiers in Psychology* 4(596) (2013).

[71] I. Kamehkhosh and D. Jannach. User perception of next-track music recommendations. In: *Proceedings of the 25th Conference on User Modeling, Adaptation and Personalization, UMAP'17*. New York, NY, USA: ACM, 2017, pp. 113–121.

[72] I. Kamehkhosh, D. Jannach, and G. Bonnin. How Automated Recommendations Affect the Playlist Creation Behavior of Users. In: *Joint Proceedings of the 23rd ACM Conference on Intelligent User Interfaces (ACM IUI 2018) Workshops: Intelligent Music Interfaces for Listening and Creation (MILC), Tokyo, Japan*, 2018.

[73] M. Kaminskas and F. Ricci. Contextual music information retrieval and recommendation: State of the art and challenges. *Computer Science Review* 6(2) (2012) 89–119.

[74] M. Kaminskas, F. Ricci, and M. Schedl. Location-aware Music Recommendation Using Auto-Tagging and Hybrid Matching. In: *Proceedings of the 7th ACM Conference on Recommender Systems (RecSys), Hong Kong, China*, 2013.

[75]   H. Kaya, F. Görpinar, and A. A. Salah. Video-based emotion recognition in the wild using deep transfer learning and score fusion. *Image and Vision Computing* 65 (2017) 66–75.

[76]   Y. E. Kim, E. M. Schmidt, R. Migneco, B. G. Morton, P. Richardson, J. Scott, J. Speck, and D. Turnbull. Music emotion recognition: A state of the art review. In: *Proceedings of the International Society for Music Information Retrieval Conference*, 2010.

[77]   Y. Kjus. Musical exploration via streaming services: The norwegian experience. *Popular Communication* 14(3) (2016) 127–136.

[78]   P. Knees, A. Ferraro, and M. Hübler. Bias and feedback loops in music recommendation: Studies on record label impact. In: *Proceedings of the 2nd Workshop on Multi-Objective Recommender Systems co-located with 16th ACM Conference on Recommender Systems (MORS@RecSys'22)*, volume 3268. CEUR-WS, 2022.

[79]   P. Knees and M. Hübler. Towards Uncovering Dataset Biases: Investigating Record Label Diversity in Music Playlists. In: *Proceedings of the 1st Workshop on Designing Human-Centric Music Information Research Systems, Delft, the Netherlands*, 2019.

[80]   P. Knees and M. Schedl. A survey of music similarity and recommendation from music context data. *ACM Transactions on Multimedia Computing Communications and Applications* 10(1) (2013) 2:1–2:21.

[81]   P. Knees and M. Schedl. *Music Similarity and Retrieval – An Introduction to Audio- and Web-based Strategies*. The Information Retrieval Series, volume 36. Springer, 2016.

[82]   P. Knees, M. Schedl, B. Ferwerda, and A. Laplante. User awareness in music recommender systems. In: M. Augstein, E. Herder, and W. Wörndl, editors. *Personalized Human-Computer Interaction*. Berlin, Boston: De Gruyter, 2019, pp. 223–252.

[83]   P. Knees and G. Widmer. Searching for music using natural language queries and relevance feedback. In: N. Boujemaa, M. Detyniecki, and A. Nürnberger, editors. *Adaptive Multimedia Retrieval: Retrieval, User, and Semantics*. Berlin, Heidelberg: Springer, 2008, pp. 109–121.

[84]   B. P. Knijnenburg, M. C. Willemsen, Z. Gantner, H. Soncu, and C. Newell. Explaining the user experience of recommender systems. *User Modeling and User-Adapted Interaction* 22(4–5) (2012) 441–504.

[85]   V. J. Konecni. Social interaction and musical preference. *Psychology of Music* (1982) 497–516.

[86]   Y. Koren. Factorization Meets the Neighborhood: A Multifaceted Collaborative Filtering Model. In: *Proceedings of the 14th ACM SIGKDD International Conference on Knowledge Discovery and Data Mining (KDD), Las Vegas, NV, USA*, 2008.

[87]   A. E. Krause and A. C. North. Music listening in everyday life: Devices, selection methods, and digital technology. *Psychology of Music* 44(1) (2016) 129–147.

[88]   T. Krismayer, M. Schedl, P. Knees and R. Rabiser. Predicting user demographics from music listening information. *Multimedia Tools and Applications* (2018).

[89]   F.-F. Kuo, M.-F. Chiang, M.-K. Shan, and S.-Y. Lee. Emotion-based music recommendation by association discovery from film music. In: *Proceedings of the 13th annual ACM international conference on Multimedia*. ACM, 2005, pp. 507–510.

[90]   J. R. Kwapisz, G. M. Weiss, and S. A. Moore. Activity recognition using cell phone accelerometers. *ACM SIGKDD Explorations Newsletter* 12(2) (2011) 74–82.

[91]   A. Laplante. Everyday life music information-seeking behaviour of young adults: An exploratory study. Doctoral dissertation, McGill University, 2008.

[92]   A. Laplante. Who influence the music tastes of adolescents? a study on interpersonal influence in social networks. In: *Proceedings of the 2nd International ACM Workshop on Music information retrieval with user-centered and multimodal strategies (MIRUM)*, 2012, pp. 37–42.

[93]   A. Laplante. Improving music recommender systems: What we can learn from research on music tastes? In: *15th International Society for Music Information Retrieval Conference, Taipei, Taiwan*, 2014.

[94]   A. Laplante and J. S. Downie. Everyday life music information-seeking behaviour of young adults. In: *Proceedings of the 7th International Conference on Music Information Retrieval, Victoria (BC), Canada, October 8–12*, 2006.

[95]   A. Lay and B. Ferwerda. Predicting users' personality based on their 'liked' images on instagram. In: *The 23rd International on Intelligent User Interfaces*, 2018.

[96]   J. H. Lee, H. Cho, and Y.-S. Kim. Users' music information needs and behaviors: Design implications for music information retrieval systems. *The Journal of the Association for Information Science and Technology* 67(6) (2016) 1301–1330.

[97]   J. H. Lee, Y.-S. Kim, and C. Hubbles. A Look at the Cloud from Both Sides Now: An Analysis of Cloud Music Service Usage. In: *Proceedings of the 17th International Society for Music Information Retrieval Conference, ISMIR, New York City, United States*, 2016, pp. 299–305.

[98]   J. H. Lee and R. Price. Understanding users of commercial music services through personas: Design implications. In: *Proceedings of the 16th International Society for Music Information Retrieval Conference (ISMIR 2015)*, 2015, pp. 476–482.

[99]   J. H. Lee, R. Wishkoski, L. Aase, P. Meas, and C. Hubbles. Understanding users of cloud music services: Selection factors, management and access behavior, and perceptions. *The Journal of the Association for Information Science and Technology* 68(5) (2017) 1186–1200.

[100] J. S. Lee and J. C. Lee. Context Awareness by Case-Based Reasoning in a Music Recommendation System. In: H. Ichikawa, W.-D. Cho, I. Satoh, and J. Youn, editors. *Ubiquitous Computing Systems*. LNCS volume 4836. Springer, 2007.

[101] A. Legault-Venne, A. Laplante, S. Leblanc-Proulx and D. Forest. Du vinyle à youtube: les habitudes de consommation et de recherche de musique des jeunes adultes québécois. *Partnership: The Canadian Journal of Library and Information Practice and Research* 11(2) (2016).

[102] J. Lehmann, M. Lalmas, E. Yom-Tov, and G. Dupret. Models of user engagement. In: *Proceedings of the 20th International Conference on User Modeling, Adaptation, and Personalization, UMAP'12*. Berlin, Heidelberg: Springer-Verlag, 2012, pp. 164–175.

[103] A. Lehtiniemi and J. Holm. Designing for music discovery: Evaluation and comparison of five music player prototypes. *Journal of New Music Research* 42(3) (2013) 283–302.

[104] E. Lex, D. Kowald, P. Seitlinger, T. N. T. Tran, A. Felfernig, and M. Schedl. Psychology-informed recommender systems. *Foundations and Trends in Information Retrieval* 15(2) (2021) 134–242.

[105] H. Li and M. Trocan. Deep learning of smartphone sensor data for personal health assistance. *Microelectronics Journal* (2018).

[106] L. A. Liikkanen and P. Åman. Shuffling services: Current trends in interacting with digital music. *Interacting with Computers* 28(3) (2016) 352–371.

[107] M. Liu, X. Hu and M. Schedl. Artist preferences and cultural, socio-economic distances across countries: A big data perspective. In: *The 18th International Society for Music Information Retrieval Conference, Suzhou, China, October 23–27, 2017*, 2017.

[108] M. Liu, X. Hu, and M. Schedl. The relation of culture, socio-economics, and friendship to music preferences: A large-scale, cross-country study. *PLoS ONE* 13(12) (2018) e0208186.

[109] A. J. Lonsdale and A. C. North. Why do we listen to music? A uses and gratifications analysis. *British Journal of Psychology* 102(1) (2011) 108–134.

[110] M. Lüders. Pushing music: People's continued will to archive versus spotify's will to make them explore. *European Journal of Cultural Studies* 24(4) (2021) 952–969.

[111] B. McFee and G. Lanckriet. Hypergraph Models of Playlist Dialects. In: *Proceedings of the 13th International Society for Music Information Retrieval Conference (ISMIR), Porto, Portugal*, 2012.

[112] A. P. Merriam and V. Merriam. Uses and functions. In: *The Anthropology of Music, chapter 11*. Northwestern University Press, 1964.

[113] B. Moens, L. van Noorden, and M. Leman. D-Jogger. Syncing Music with Walking. In: *Proceedings of the 7th Sound and Music Computing Conference (SMC), Barcelona, Spain*, 2010.

[114] J. W. Morris and D. Powers. Control, curation and musical experience in streaming music services. *Creative Industries Journal* 8(2) (2015) 106–122.

[115] F. Noroozi, M. Marjanovic, A. Njegus, S. Escalera and G. Anbarjafari. Audio-visual emotion recognition in video clips. *IEEE Transactions on Affective Computing* (2017) 1.

[116] A. C. North and D. J. Hargreaves. Situational influences on reported musical preference. *Psychomusicology: A Journal of Research in Music Cognition* 15(1–2) (1996) 30.

[117] A. C. North, D. J. Hargreaves, and J. J. Hargreaves. Uses of music in everyday life. *Music Perception: An Interdisciplinary Journal* 22(1) (2004) 41–77.

[118] K. O'Hara and B. Brown. *Consuming Music Together: Social and Collaborative Aspects of Music Consumption Technologies*. Computer Supported Cooperative Work, volume 35. Netherlands: Springer, 2006.

[119] K. Okada, B. F. Karlsson, L. Sardinha, and T. N. Contextplayer. Learning contextual music preferences for situational recommendations. In: *SIGGRAPH Asia 2013 Symposium on Mobile Graphics and Interactive Applications, SA'13*, New York, NY, USA: ACM, 2013, pp. 6:1–6:7.

[120] S. Oramas, V. C. Ostuni, T. D. Noia, X. Serra, and E. D. Sciascio. Sound and music recommendation with knowledge graphs. *ACM Transactions on Intelligent Systems and Technology* 8(2) (2016) 21:1–21:21.

[121] E. Pampalk, T. Pohle, and G. Widmer. Dynamic Playlist Generation Based on Skipping Behavior. In: *Proceedings of the 6th International Conference on Music Information Retrieval (ISMIR), London, UK*, 2005.

[122] H.-S. Park, J.-O. Yoo, and S.-B. Cho. A context-aware music recommendation system using fuzzy Bayesian networks with utility theory. In: *Proceedings of the 3rd International Conference on Fuzzy Systems and Knowledge Discovery (FSKD), Xi'an, China*, 2006.

[123] T. Pettijohn, G. Williams and T. Carter. Music for the seasons: Seasonal music preferences in college students. *Current Psychology* (2010) 1–18.

[124] M. Pichl, E. Zangerle, and G. Specht. Understanding playlist creation on music streaming platforms. In: *Proceedings of the 2016 IEEE International Symposium on Multimedia (ISM)*, 2016, pp. 475–480.

[125] P. Pu, L. Chen, and R. Hu. A user-centric evaluation framework for recommender systems. In: *Proceedings of the Fifth ACM Conference on Recommender Systems, RecSys'11*, New York, NY, USA: ACM, 2011, pp. 157–164.

[126] D. Quercia, M. Kosinski, D. Stillwell, and J. Crowcroft. Our twitter profiles, our selves: Predicting personality with twitter. In: *Privacy, Security, Risk and Trust (PASSAT) and 2011 IEEE Third Inernational Conference on Social Computing (SocialCom), 2011 IEEE Third International Conference on* IEEE, 2011, pp. 180–185.

[127] P. J. Rentfrow. The role of music in everyday life: Current directions in the social psychology of music. *Social and Personality Psychology Compass* 6(5) (2012) 402–416.

[128] P. J. Rentfrow and S. D. Gosling. The do re mi's of everyday life: The structure and personality correlates of music preferences. *Journal of Personality and Social Psychology* 84(6) (2003) 1236.

[129] J. A. Russell. A Circumplex Model of Affect. *Journal of Personality and Social Psychology* 39(6) (1980) 1161–1178.

[130] S. Sasaki, T. Hirai, H. Ohya, and S. Morishima. Affective music recommendation system based on the mood of input video. In: X. He, S. Luo, D. Tao, C. Xu, J. Yang, and M. A. Hasan, editors. *MultiMedia Modeling*. Cham: Springer International Publishing, 2015, pp. 299–302.

[131] T. Schäfer and C. Mehlhorn. Can personality traits predict musical style preferences? a meta-analysis. *Personality and Individual Differences* 116 (2017) 265–273.

[132] T. Schäfer, P. Sedlmeier, C. Städtler, and D. Huron. The psychological functions of music listening. *Frontiers in Psychology* 4(511) (2013) 1–34.

[133] M. Schedl, G. Breitschopf, and B. Ionescu. Mobile Music Genius: Reggae at the Beach, Metal on a Friday Night? In: *Proceedings of the 4th ACM International Conference on Multimedia Retrieval (ICMR), Glasgow, UK*, 2014.

[134] M. Schedl and B. Ferwerda. Large-scale analysis of group-specific music genre taste from collaborative tags. In: *The 19th IEEE International Symposium on Multimedia (ISM2017), Taichung, December 11–13, 2017*, 2017.

[135] M. Schedl, A. Flexer and J. Urbano. The neglected user in music information retrieval research. *Journal of Intelligent Information Systems* (2013).

[136] M. Schedl, E. Gómez, E. Trent, M. Tkalčič, H. Eghbal-Zadeh and A. Martorell. On the Interrelation between Listener Characteristics and the Perception of Emotions in Classical Orchestra Music. *IEEE Transactions on Affective Computing* **PP(99)** (2017).

[137] M. Schedl, P. Knees, B. McFee, and D. Bogdanov. Music recommendation systems: Techniques, use cases, and challenges. In: F. Ricci, L. Rokach, and B. Shapira, editors. *Recommender Systems Handbook.* New York, NY: Springer US, 2022, pp. 927–971.

[138] M. Schedl, P. Knees, B. McFee, D. Bogdanov, and M. Kaminskas. Music Recommender Systems. In: F. Ricci, L. Rokach, B. Shapira, and P. B. Kantor, editors. *Recommender Systems Handbook*, 2nd edition. Springer, 2015, pp. 453–492. Chapter 13.

[139] M. Schedl, F. Lemmerich, B. Ferwerda, M. Skowron, and P. Knees. Indicators of country similarity in terms of music taste, cultural, and socio-economic factors. In: *The 19th IEEE International Symposium on Multimedia (ISM2017), Taichung, December 11–13, 2017*, 2017.

[140] M. Schedl, H. Zamani, C.-W. Chen, Y. Deldjoo and M. Elahi. Current challenges and visions in music recommender systems research. *International Journal of Multimedia Information Retrieval* (2018).

[141] K. Scherer. What are emotions? And how can they be measured? *Social Science Information* 44(4) (2005) 693–727.

[142] I. Siles, A. Segura-Castillo, R. Solís and M. Sancho. Folk theories of algorithmic recommendations on spotify: Enacting data assemblages in the global south. *Big Data and Society* 7(1) (2020).

[143] M. Skowron, F. Lemmerich, B. Ferwerda, and M. Schedl. Predicting genre preferences from cultural and socio-economic factors for music retrieval. In: *Proceedings of the 39th European Conference on Information Retrieval (ECIR)*, 2017.

[144] M. Skowron, M. Tkalčič, B. Ferwerda, and M. Schedl. Fusing social media cues: personality prediction from twitter and instagram. In: *Proceedings of the 25th international conference companion on world wide web, International World Wide Web Conferences Steering Committee*, 2016, pp. 107–108.

[145] M. Slaney and W. White. Similarity Based on Rating Data. In: *Proceedings of the 8th International Conference on Music Information Retrieval (ISMIR), Vienna, Austria*, 2007.

[146] L. Spinelli, J. Lau, L. Pritchard, and J. H. Lee. Influences on the social practices surrounding commercial music services: A model for rich interactions. In: *Proceedings of the 19th International Society for Music Information Retrieval Conference (ISMIR), Paris, France*, 2018.

[147] H. Steck, R. van Zwol, and C. Johnson. Interactive recommender systems: Tutorial. In: *Proceedings of the 9th ACM Conference on Recommender Systems, RecSys'15*. New York, NY, USA: ACM, 2015, pp. 359–360.

[148] S. J. Tepper and E. Hargittai. Pathways to music exploration in a digital age. *Poetics* 37(3) (2009) 227–249.

[149] M. Tkalčič, B. Ferwerda, D. Hauger, and M. Schedl. Personality correlates for digital concert program notes. In: *International Conference on User Modeling, Adaptation, and Personalization*. Springer, 2015, pp. 364–369.

[150] A. van den Oord, S. Dieleman, and B. Schrauwen. Deep Content-based Music Recommendation. In: C. Burges, L. Bottou, M. Welling, Z. Ghahramani, and K. Weinberger, editors. *Advances in Neural Information Processing Systems 26 (NIPS)*. Curran Associates, Inc., 2013.

[151] S. Vargas, L. Baltrunas, A. Karatzoglou, and P. Castells. Coverage, redundancy and size-awareness in genre diversity for recommender systems. In: *Proceedings of the 8th ACM Conference on Recommender Systems, RecSys'14*, New York, NY, USA: ACM, 2014, pp. 209–216.

[152] M. Verboord. Music mavens revisited: Comparing the impact of connectivity and dispositions in the digital age. *Journal of Consumer Culture* 21(3) (2021) 618–637.

[153] S. Volokhin and E. Agichtein. Understanding music listening intents during daily activities with implications for contextual music recommendation. In: *Proceedings of the 2018 Conference on Human Information Interaction & Retrieval, CHIIR'18*. New York, NY, USA: ACM, 2018, pp. 313–316.

[154] W. Wang, A. X. Liu, and M. Shahzad. Gait recognition using wifi signals. In: *Proceedings of the 2016 ACM International Joint Conference on Pervasive and Ubiquitous Computing, UbiComp'16*. ACM, New York, NY, USA, 2016, pp. 363–373.

[155] X. Wang, D. Rosenblum, and Y. Wang. Context-aware Mobile Music Recommendation for Daily Activities. In: *Proceedings of the 20th ACM International Conference on Multimedia, Nara, Japan*. ACM, 2012, pp. 99–108.

[156] J. Webster. The promise of personalisation: Exploring how music streaming platforms are shaping the performance of class identities and distinction. *New Media & Society* (2021).

[157] A. Werner. Organizing music, organizing gender: algorithmic culture and spotify recommendations. *Popular Communication* 18(1) (2020) 78–90.

[158] B. Whitman and S. Lawrence. Inferring Descriptions and Similarity for Music from Community Metadata. In: *Proceedings of the 2002 International Computer Music Conference (ICMC), Göteborg, Sweden*, 2002.

[159] K. Yadati, C. C. Liem, M. Larson, and A. Hanjalic. On the automatic identification of music for common activities. In: *Proceedings of the 2017 ACM on International Conference on Multimedia Retrieval, ICMR'17*. New York, NY, USA: ACM, 2017, pp. 192–200.

[160] H. Yakura, T. Nakano, and M. Goto. Focusmusicrecommender: A system for recommending music to listen to while working. In: *23rd International Conference on Intelligent User Interfaces, IUI'18*. New York, NY, USA: ACM, 2018, pp. 7–17.

[161] Y.-H. Yang and H. H. Chen. *Music Emotion Recognition*. CRC Press, 2011.

[162] Y.-H. Yang and H. H. Chen. Machine recognition of music emotion: A review. *ACM Transactions on Intelligent Systems and Technology* 3(3) (2012) 40:1–40:30.

[163] E. Zangerle, M. Pichl, W. Gassler, and G. Specht. #nowplaying music dataset: Extracting listening behavior from twitter. In: *Proceedings of the First International Workshop on Internet-Scale Multimedia Management, WISMM '14*. New York, NY, USA: Association for Computing Machinery, 2014, pp. 21–26.

[164] M. Zentner, D. Grandjean, and K. R. Scherer. Emotions evoked by the sound of music: characterization, classification, and measurement. *Emotion* 8(4) (2008) 494.

Daniel Herzog, Linus W. Dietz, and Wolfgang Wörndl

12 Tourist trip recommendations – foundations, state of the art and challenges

Abstract: Tourist Trip Design Problems (TTDPs) deal with the task to support tourists in creating a trip composed of a set or sequence of points of interests (POIs) or other items related to travel. This is a challenging problem for personalized recommender systems (RSs), because it is not only needed to discover interesting POIs matching the preferences and interests, but also to combine these destinations to a practical route. In this chapter, we present the TTDP and show how it can be modeled using different mathematical problems. We present trip RSs with a focus on recommendation techniques, data analysis and user interfaces. Finally, we summarize important current and future challenges that research in the field of tourist trip recommendations faces today. The chapter concludes with a short summary.

Keywords: Tourist trip design problem, recommender systems, group recommendation, context-aware recommender systems, mobility patterns, public displays, orienteering problem

12.1 Introduction

Recommender systems (RSs) are software tools and techniques, which support users in finding products, services or information that are useful for them [79]. RSs have been successfully applied in many domains, such as e-commerce, movies or news to help users to make decisions and to increase sales.

Another well-established application field for RSs is tourism. The travel and tourism domain is one of the main contributors to global economy. In 2017, the sector contributed directly or indirectly 8.3 trillion USD to the global economy and supported 313 million jobs, which is equal to 10.4 % of the world's Gross Domestic Product (GDP) and 1 in 10 of all jobs [102]. RSs can support users in identifying travel destinations and attractions they would like to visit. Furthermore, they can be used for comprehensive travel planning, e. g., by combining travel destinations, transport connections and activities. In addition, RSs can support the user with proactive recommendations when already traveling, e. g., while exploring a city [84, 101]. While there are some approaches on commercial websites to suggest package tours or try to inspire customers with predefined trip proposals, there are limited options for independent travelers to receive personalized trip recommendations.

The research focus of RSs in tourism is shifting toward the recommendation of complex items, such as itineraries composed of multiple points of interest (POIs). The latter

https://doi.org/10.1515/9783110988567-012

has become a popular example for a travel-related item that can be recommended by solving the Tourist Trip Design Problem (TTDP). In its simplest formulation, the TTDP is identical with the Orienteering Problem (OP), an optimization problem, which aims to combine as many locations as possible along a route to maximize the value of the route for the user [97]. An abstract model for solving the TTDP comprises two steps: (i) collecting relevant items such as POIs and analyzing travel-related data and (ii) developing algorithms using these data to generate recommendations [105]. There are several variants of the TTDP, most of them being based on the OP. In this work, however, we use a broader definition of the TTDP, which allows us to recommend tourist trips and routes on different granularities, such as trips composed of multiple travel regions, which can represent countries. An important aspect when integrating the TTDP into practical tourism applications is the development of specialized user interfaces to display the recommendations to individuals and groups of travelers and also facilitate gathering feedback from users.

While other surveys review the TTDP as an optimization problem [40, 42, 63, 81, 98], we focus our discussion from the perspective of a tourist trip recommender system. In this chapter, we first present the TTDP and show how it can be modeled in different travel-related scenarios. We then summarize the current state of the art in tourist trip RSs with a focus on recommendation techniques, data analysis and user interfaces. We also highlight important current and future challenges that research in the field of tourist trip recommendations is facing. The chapter concludes with a short summary.

12.2 The tourist trip design problem

Tourists exploring a city usually want to visit as many interesting POIs as possible. However, visiting all attractions is not an option due to practical constraints, such as time. Hence, algorithms solving the TTDP try to find a route containing some of the POIs maximizing the route's value for the user without violating the given constraints.

According to Vansteenwegen and van Oudheusden, mobile tourist guides need to consider the following information to solve the TTDP: (i) a user profile with the user's travel preferences, (ii) additional user requirements, such as the amount of time and money the user intends to spend and (iii) information about the POIs that can be visited [97]. Having obtained a set of candidate items, scores have to be assigned to the POIs according to the user's preferences and constraints. Then TTDP algorithms can be used to combine POIs with high scores to enjoyable routes, which are suggested to the user.

Vansteenwegen and van Oudheusden introduced the TTDP as an extension of the OP. In our work, we broaden this definition, allowing us to recommend tourist trips and routes on different granularities, such as trips composed of multiple travel regions, which can represent countries. For this purpose, we introduce our extended definition of the TTDP by presenting different travel-related scenarios. We show how the OP and similar graph-theoretic routing problems, namely the Traveling Salesman Problem (TSP) with its specializations, but also the Knapsack Problem (KP), can be used to solve variants of the TTDP.

12.2.1 The traveling salesman problem

The TSP is a classic routing problem that optimizes the route of a traveler visiting all nodes in a graph exactly once before returning to the original position. Being an NP-hard problem, computing optimal solutions becomes intractable soon; however, heuristics usually provide sufficiently good approximations [56]. The TSP has many practical applications. In logistics, it can be used to plan routes of vehicles that have to visit a fixed set of locations, before they return to the depot. In tourism, this problem is suitable to model round trips, where the user wants to visit all locations of a static set and eventually return to the starting point. Visiting all national parks of the US in an optimal route would be a typical example for this [74].

However, given myriad destinations and POIs to visit, travelers usually have to choose which attractions to include in their trip. Ergo, the pure formulation is not well suited for most tourist recommenders. Instead, most variants of the TTDP use special cases of the TSP, where not all locations have to be visited and the overall value of the trip is determined by nonbinary profits.

12.2.2 The orienteering problem

The OP is a special form of the TSP [54], where the origin and destination do not have to be identical. All locations are associated with a profit and may be visited at most once. The OP is also referred to as the Selective TSP [57]. The aim is to maximize the overall profit gained on a single tour limited by constraints, such as time and money [93] (see Figure 12.1a). Hence, it can be used to model the aforementioned scenarios in which the user expects a route containing some of the most interesting locations without violating constraints. The majority of tourist recommendation literature uses the OP and its variants to model the TTDP [40]. In the following, we present specializations of the OP, which serve as more complex models for the TTDP. Furthermore, we briefly present some algorithms and heuristics solving these problems.

The goal of the Team Orienteering Problem (TOP) is to find k routes at the same time maximizing the total profit of all routes [23] (see Figure 12.1b). The name of this problem is derived from a team in which each team member selects one route in an attempt to avoid overlaps of the locations visited by each team member. In a tourism scenario, a team member is commonly interpreted as one day in a multiday trip. Exact algorithms

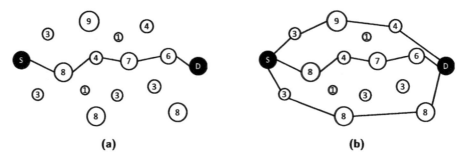

Figure 12.1: Example paths from a start S to a destination D solving (a) the OP (a) and (b) the TOP with $k = 3$ teams. The numbers denote the locations' scores.

solving the TOP have been proposed [20], but the main research focus is on developing faster heuristics to make it applicable in real-world scenarios. The first heuristic, MAX-IMP, was introduced by Butt and Cavalier [19]. Souffriau et al. propose the Greedy Randomized Adaptive Search Procedure (GRASP) for the TOP [87] and subsequently improve their work with a Path Relinking extension to the GRASP algorithm [88]. Friggstad et al. present efficient algorithms to solve the TOP, not by optimizing for the overall benefit, but maximizing the benefits of the worst day, which lead to similar user satisfaction as curated lists by travel experts [34].

In the Orienteering Problem with Time Windows (OPTW), each location can only be visited within a defined time window [53]. These time windows can represent the opening hours of an attraction. Kantor and Rosenwein [53] were the first to solve the OPTW [95]. If the TOP is extended by time windows, it is called the Team Orienteering Problem with Time Windows (TOPTW) [96]. Vansteenwegen et al. developed an iterated local search (ILS) heuristic solving the TOPTW [96]. In a recent approach, a three-component heuristic for the TOPTW is proposed [50].

The Time-Dependent Orienteering Problem (TDOP) assumes that the time needed to travel between two locations depends on the time the traveler leaves the first location [33]. This extension can be used to model different modes of transportation in a tourist trip recommendation. For example, a tourist can leave a location later than planned when a bus connection to the next location is available; hence, the traveling time between the two locations decreases. Fomin and Lingas provide a $(2 + \epsilon)$-approximation algorithm to solve the TDOP [33]. Combining the TDOP with time windows and multiple routes leads to the Time-Dependent Team Orienteering Problem with Time Windows (TDTOPTW) [35]. Garcia et al. developed different heuristics solving the TDTOPTW [35, 36].

The Multiconstrained Team Orienteering Problem with Time Windows (MCTOPTW) introduces additional thresholds besides the time budget, which a path is not supposed to exceed [37]. A common example of such a constraint is money. In this case, the vertices come with a fixed cost and the routing algorithm has to find a path, which exceeds neither the financial threshold, nor the time budget. Garcia et al. were the first to solve the MCTOPTW [37] using a meta-heuristic based on the ILS heuristic of Vansteen-wegen et al. [96]. Souffriau et al. extend the MCTOPTW to the Multiconstrained Team Orienteering Problem with Multiple Time Windows (MCTOPMTW) [89], which allows defining different time windows on different days and more than one time window per day.

Some problems dynamically assign the reward of visiting a location, depending on certain events or the order in which the attractions are visited. This allows a more re-alistic modeling of the TTDP. In the Generalized Orienteering Problem (GOP), every lo-cation is assigned multiple scores representing different goals of the visitor [41]. Hence, the user's travel purpose can be modeled. The objective function in the GOP is nonlin-ear; thus, it penalizes paths including two similar attractions, such as two restaurants in a row [45]. In the Team Orienteering Problem with Decreasing Profits (DPTOP), the profit of each node decreases with time [3]. Hence, the DPTOP can be used to model a variant of the TTDP, where the value of locations for the user is lower the later the trav-eler arrives there. In the Clustered Orienteering Problem (COP), the score of a node can only be gained if all nodes of a group of nodes are part of the path [5]. The Orienteering Problem with Stochastic Profits (OPSP) assumes that the locations' profits are stochastic with a known distribution and their values are not revealed before the locations are vis-ited [51]. Campbell et al. [21] introduce the Orienteering Problem with Stochastic Travel and Service Times (OPSTS), in which the traveler is punished if they do not reach a lo-cation before a deadline.

Until today, the OP research mostly focuses on the creation of tourist trips for single users. Recent work introduces a variant of the OP, which tries to find routes for a group of users [47, 91].

12.2.3 The knapsack problem

The KP offers a different perspective on the TTDP. It is useful when the costs of travel between the locations are unknown or negligible. In the traditional 0–1 KP, each travel item can be packed into a bag with limited size, i. e., be part of the final recommendation, exactly once or not at all. Each item comes with a profit and a cost that are independent of the other items and the route to be taken. While the profits are to be maximized, the sum of costs is not allowed to exceed the knapsack's capacity [55]. It should be noted that using the KP to select items, the result is an unordered set of items. The obtain a route, the items can be fed into a TSP solver after the KP algorithm selected the locations that have to be visited. Hence, the problem is not suitable when the routing costs between the items are important.

A variant of the KP is the Oregon Trail Knapsack Problem (OTKP) [18]. In this formu-lation, the value of a region is not only determined by the user query, but also depends on the presence or absence of other regions in the recommended composite trip. This allows to penalize travel items that do not fit together. The OTKP has been used to improve item diversity by decreasing the values of similar items in the same trip [46].

12.3 State of the art in tourist trip recommendations

Having defined and explained the TTDP as a mathematical problem, we now present the state of the art in tourist trip recommendations. We review several approaches for recommending different types of travel-related items and present practical applications solving the TTDP. Furthermore, we focus on two topics particularly important for the development of tourist trip RSs: group recommendations (Section 12.3.2), item diversity (Section 12.3.3) and efforts to learn from past trips (Section 12.3.4). The summary of the state of the art in tourist trip recommendations helps us to identify current and future challenges in the development of next generation tourist trip RSs.

12.3.1 Recommender systems in tourism

Most RSs in tourism recommend ranked lists of single items. We refine the categorization of items recommended by tourism RSs introduced by Borràs et al. [13] and Gavalas et al. [39] as follows: (i) a set of travel items, such as multiple POIs or travel destinations, (ii) a travel plan (also called travel bag or travel bundle) combining coherent travel items, such as destinations, activities, accommodation and other services, in one recommendation and (iii) a sequence of items, such as a sequence of POIs along an enjoyable route for a single or multiday trip. In the following, we present some of the most important examples in each of these categories.

12.3.1.1 Recommendation of sets of travel items

GUIDE is a tourist guide recommending POIs considering different personal and environmental context factors, such as the user's age or the time of the day [25]. Another example of a context-aware RS for POIs is South Tyrol Suggests (STS), which takes various context factors, such as the weather, into account to recommend POIs in South Tyrol, Italy [14]. Furthermore, a personality questionnaire is used to mitigate the cold start problem. Benouaret and Lenne recently presented an RS for travel packages, where each package is composed of a set of different POIs [11]. Another promising idea to find POIs is presented by Baral and Li [10], but it has not yet been implemented in a practical application. Their approach combines different aspects of check-in information in location-based social networks (LBSNs), such as categorical, temporal, social and spatial information in one model to predict the most potential check-in locations.

In previous work, we developed a system for combining travel regions to recommend a composite trip [46, 104]. The user is asked to specify their interests, e. g., *nature and wildlife*, *beach* or *winter sports* along with potential travel regions and monetary and temporal limitations. The underlying problem for picking the regions is the OTKP [18]. Every additional week the user is staying in the same region, the region's score decreases. The destination information is manually modeled by expert knowledge. Messaoud et al. extend this approach by focusing on the diversity of activities within a composite trip [69]. They use hierarchical clustering to improve the heterogeneity of activities. The underlying data set is the same as in the original approach [46], but extended by seasonal activities that have been rated in correspondence to specific regions and traveler types.

12.3.1.2 Recommendation of tourist plans

Lenz was first to develop a case-based RS for holiday trips [60]. The case description of CABATA contains features such as the type of holiday, the travel region or intended means of transportation. The case solutions present recommendations that fulfill all user requirements and others that are at least similar to the user query. CABATA is a prototypically implemented part of an architecture for travel agent systems called IMTAS and was presented to the public in 1994 [61]. Other early examples of case-based travel RSs for tourist plans are DieToRecs [77] and Trip@dvice [100]. DieToRecs allows the recommendation of single items, such as destinations or hotels, and bundling of travel items for a personalized travel plan [77]. The case base of Trip@dvice contains travel plans created by the community [100]. It has been selected by the European Union and by the European Travel Commission as a travel RS in the European tourism destination portal http://visiteurope.com. Ricci presents TripMatcher and VacationCoach [78], two of the early travel RSs using content-based approaches to match the user preferences with potential destinations. VacationCoach explicitly asks the user to choose a suitable traveler type, such as *culture creature* or *beach bum*. TripMatcher uses statistics on past user queries and guesses the importance of attributes not explicitly mentioned by the user to come up with recommendations. A conversational RS for travel planning is presented by Mahmood et al. [64].

Vathis et al. present a solution to what they call the Vacation Planning Problem (VPP) [99]. The authors have extended the simpler TTDP with scenarios for exploring larger geographical area, recommending intermediate destinations and accommodation areas along a trip, and determining the optimal distribution of trip days among different destinations. They have designed a clustering scheme to group POIs together and an efficient dynamic programming approach for solving this complex problem.

12.3.1.3 Recommendation of sequences of travel items

The aforementioned context-aware RS GUIDE was also one of the first applications that recommends personalized tourist trips [25]. For this purpose, the user has to choose POIs they would like to visit. Then the system calculates a route considering contextual information, such as the opening hours of the selected POIs. GUIDE is also able to update the recommended routes dynamically when the user decides to stay longer than planned at a POI. De Choudhury et al. use photo streams to estimate where users were and how much time they spent at a POI and traveling between POIs [26]. Based on this information, their approach creates a POI graph and recommends tourist trips. Another solution using photos is presented by Brilhante et al. Their application, TripBuilder, uses unsupervised learning for mining common patterns of movements of tourists in a given geographic area [16].

City Trip Planner is a web application that recommends multiday tourist trips [94]. It respects certain limitations, like opening hours, and can also include a lunch break into the trip. Gavalas et al. present Scenic Athens, a context-aware, mobile tourist guide for personalized tourist trip recommendations in Athens, Greece [38]. Compared to similar applications, Scenic Athens can also incorporate scenic routes into the trip recommendations. Quercia et al. introduce a different approach for route recommendation [76]. Instead of recommending shortest paths between two directions or maximizing attraction values of POIs, their trip recommender suggests routes that are perceived as pleasant. The authors collect crowd-sourced ratings to identify pleasant routes.

Often users are in need for recommendations when they are already on the go. Thus, several smartphone applications for tourist trip planning have been published in the last years. Google Trips[1] offers a day plans functionality, which suggests thematic tourist trips such as *The Museum Mile* in New York. In addition, it automatically collects reservations and booking confirmations from the user's Gmail account to collect all travel-related items in the app. In our previous work, we developed TourRec, a mobile trip RS, which uses a multitier web service to recommend tourist trips composed of multiple POIs [43, 59]. It allows the user to rate different categories, such as *Food* or *Outdoors and Recreation*, on a scale from 0 to 5. The higher a category's rating is, the more likely POIs of this category appear in the recommended trip. Furthermore, the user has the option to overwrite the ratings of subcategories. For instance, users can rate all *Food* POIs with a 0, but rate cafés with a 5 if they want to avoid restaurants, but not cafés. Then the user specifies an origin, a destination, the starting time and the maximum duration of the trip to request a new recommendation. Based on this information, TourRec calculates a route and visualizes it as a list or on the map (see Figure 12.2). The recommendations are context-aware, which is a particular challenge when sequences

---

1 https://get.google.com/trips/

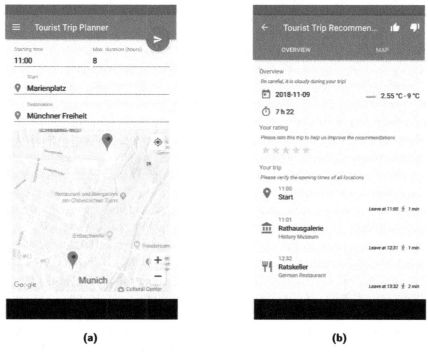

      (a)   **(b)**

Figure 12.2: User interfaces of the TourRec application allowing the user to (a) request a new trip recommendation and (b) display it on a map or in a list view.

instead of single items are recommended [58]. We present this challenge and our own solutions in Section 12.4.1.

12.3.2 Group recommendations

The vast majority of work in the field of tourist trip RSs focuses on recommendations for single users, but in practice tourists often travel in groups. A group recommender system (GRS) for tourist trips has to consider the preferences and constraints of all group members. GRSs have been applied in various domains such as movies, music or news [65]. In the tourism domain, applications have been presented that suggest lists of POIs [6] or travel packages tailored for groups [66].

A GRS for tourist trips on mobile devices can be implemented in various ways that can be differentiated by the way consensus is established [44]. For example, the group can use only one device. In this scenario, one person of the group has to enter the group's preferences before a recommendation can be made. Existing applications can be used by groups without any additional development effort; however, the group must agree on the preferences on their own, which can be a difficult and time-consuming task. Another option is to have one device per group member, allowing the group members to state their preferences separately. One the one hand, hiding preferences from other group members can avoid manipulation and social embarrassment [52]. One the other hand, an open discussion can be impeded and a strategy to aggregate the individual preferences is required. Finally, a group can also interact with a mutual display, which may facilitate an open discussion between the group members to establish consensus. We present the challenges and opportunities of public displays in RSs in Section 12.4.4.

When preferences are collected separately, a group recommendation can be generated by combining each user's individual recommendations to one single group recommendation or by aggregating the distinct preferences into a recommendation for a so-called *virtual user*. Many preference aggregation strategies are inspired by the social choice theory [65]. Simple approaches, such as calculating the average of user preferences, are easy to implement but can lead to unhappy group members when one person dislikes an item that is liked by the majority of the group members. Other strategies filter out items that are disliked by at least one person or assign different weights for users. In this case, the preferences of an important person, e. g., a child, can be prioritized. Research has shown that there is no perfect way to aggregate the individual preferences. Instead, the group's intrinsic characteristics and the problem's nature have to be considered [27, 48].

We have extended the TourRec application with group recommendations [47, 48]. The idea is to allow each user to state their preferences separately on a personal device and then send the group recommendation back to every user. We use Google Nearby Connections² to connect multiple smartphones. It uses Bluetooth and Wi-Fi to find other devices in the vicinity and to establish a connection between devices running TourRec [43].

We implemented solutions for both group recommendation strategies: aggregating user preferences and merging recommendations. We integrated the *Average*, *Average without Misery* and *Most Pleasure* preference aggregation strategies into the TourRec application.

Furthermore, we developed different approaches where individual recommendations are merged to one trip for the group. These approaches first calculate one route for each group member using the individual's travel preferences. Then a group recommendation is generated using a social choice strategy. Only POIs, which are part of at least one of these individual recommendations, are candidates for a recommendation. POIs that are part of more than one individual recommendation, receive a greater weight, which makes it more likely that these are part of the aggregated route, which is recommended to the group. Another approach selects segments (e. g., three POIs in a row) from every individual recommendation. In addition, we developed an alternative approach considering splitting groups for some time so that each homogeneous subgroup can pursue their interests before merging back with the other group members.

---

2 https://developers.google.com/nearby/connections/overview

A major drawback of previous research in the field of GRS is that studies often use synthetic groups, which can lead to falsified results [65]. We have conducted a user study with 120 participants in 40 real groups. The results showed significant differences with regard to the quality of recommendations generated by the various strategies. Most groups were willing to split temporarily during a trip, even when they were traveling with persons close to them. In this case, this split group generated the best recommendations for different evaluation criteria [47].

12.3.3 Item diversity

One natural requirement for a RS for composite trips is to adjust the diversity of the items to the user's preferences [22]. In typical tourism RSs, where only n out of k items can be recommended, the algorithm should consider skipping some high-ranked recommendations in favor of variety in the recommended itinerary. For example, even if the user's preference model shows high interest for one specific activity, such as culinary attractions, it is suboptimal to only recommend numerous restaurants and cafés.

Wu et al. present a study [103] in which they assess user satisfaction based on the diversity level of the recommendations. They use the five-factor model for personality [67] to capture the user's need for diversity. That model is commonly used in RSs to personalize recommendations [71, 92]. Another strategy to improve recommendation diversity is to group items by their features via clustering algorithms. Messaoud et al. propose a variety seeking model using semantic hierarchical clustering to establish diversity in a set of recommended activities [69]. Diversity can also be expressed as a constraint. Savir et al. measure the diversity level based on attraction types and ensure that the trip diversity level is above a defined threshold [82].

This level of variety needs to be personalized to fit the user needs. Some travelers want to obtain an exhaustive impression of the travel destination; others who are up for relaxing at the beach do not profit from diverse recommendations. Therefore, the level of expected diversity within the trip must be elicited and incorporated into the user model. Furthermore, the recommendations should not only be diverse, but be calibrated to reflect the user's various interests. If the user has visited 60 % outdoor, 30 % culture and 10 % entertainment attractions, recommendations should reflect this distribution. To overcome this problem, Steck has proposed a reranking algorithm in the domain of music recommendations [90].

12.3.4 Learning from past tourist trips

With nowadays' ubiquity of GPS modules in mobile phones, a vast amount of spatiotemporal data is being collected. Such data become publicly available if users choose to publish them, as often done in LBSNs. The general adoption of LBSNs opened many opportunities for researchers to analyze human mobility in general and in combination with their social activities, such as traveling. Capturing the mobility and social ties of users in mathematical models is the basis to derive features that can then be used to influence the ranking and composition of items. Song et al. develop and evaluate mathematical models for human mobility and its predictability [85, 86]. Further analysis of human mobility in LBSNs reveals that not only geographic and economic constraints affect mobility patterns, but also the individual social status [24]. However, an analysis of another LBSN, Gowalla, shows that the number of check-ins and the number of places a user has visited follow log-normal distributions, while connecting to friends is better described by a double Pareto law [83]. LBSN data have also been used to capture cross-border movement [12]. The authors demonstrate how mobility dynamics of people in a country can be analyzed; however, this study is not about tourists and is limited to one country, Kenya. Noulas et al. analyze activity patterns of Foursquare users in urban areas, like the spatial and temporal distances between two check-ins [72]. They uncover recurring patterns of human mobility that can be used to predict or recommend future locations of users.

Data from LBSNs has already been analyzed to improve RSs [9]. This is not surprising since the user's locations and social graph tells a lot about individual preferences. Spatial cooccurrences have been used to identify similar users and generate implicit ratings for collaborative filtering algorithms [107]. In another approach [8], travelers in a foreign city are matched to local experts based on their respective home behavior to recommend Foursquare venues. Hsieh et al. use past LBSN data to recommend travel paths along POIs in cities [49]. For this purpose, they present solutions to derive the popularity, the proper time of day to visit, the transit time between venues and the best order to visit the places. In our previous work, we mined trips from Foursquare check-ins to analyze global travel patterns [29]. They reveal the distribution of the duration of stay per country and which countries are frequently visited together [31].

12.4 Current and future challenges

In the following, we present some of the most important challenges in the development of next-generation tourist trip RSs, which we identified from previous work (see Section 12.3). Furthermore, we present ideas of how to tackle these challenges and first results from our own work.

12.4.1 Context-aware tourist trip recommendations

Incorporating contextual information into the recommendation process can have a significant effect on the quality of a recommendation [2]. It is particularly important for mobile tourist RS [39], which have to adapt the recommendations to the current weather, for example. Existing research focuses on context-aware recommendations of single POIs. When recommending itineraries, additional context factors have to be considered. In our previous work, we explored two context factors particularly important for sequences of POIs: the time of day and previously visited POIs [58]. The optimal time to visit a POI influences the order of POIs in a tourist trip. For example, a restaurant receives a higher score when recommended during lunchtime or in the evening than in the early morning. Furthermore, the previously visited POIs influence the perceived quality of a POI in a trip. When a proposed trip contains two restaurant recommendations in a row, the second restaurant may not be appreciated by the user. Our suggested approach is to calculate the influence of a previously visited POI on a candidate POI subject to the number of POIs visited in between. This influence is called item dependence [45].

We conducted an online questionnaire to determine the influence of the context factors on the user's decision of visiting a POI and the ratings of the POIs under these conditions [58]. The results of the questionnaire show that the time of day is highly relevant for a music event, while the previously visited POI is less important, for example. Furthermore, shopping POIs receive a very high rating when visited in the afternoon and music events are not appreciated in the morning.

We integrated the context factors for sequences as well as other factors, such as weather, into the trip composition algorithms of our mobile application TourRec. Figure 12.2b illustrates the context awareness of TourRec. The weather data are directly presented using an icon and the expected temperature range. The previously visited POI and the time of day context factors are considered in the recommended trip. A museum is recommended during a cold and cloudy morning. Then a restaurant is suggested for lunch.

We compared the quality of the context-aware recommendations to the previous version ignorant of contextual information in a small user study [58]. The context-aware version outperformed the baseline version especially in terms of diversity and recommending POIs at suitable times of the day. However, one disadvantage of our initial approach was the possible equalizing of two or more extreme contextual conditions due to the weighted arithmetic mean. An outdoor activity can be recommended even if it rains and storms, if the other context factors are very positive for a specific POI. We tackle this issue by defining thresholds for every context factor. If context factors exceed their threshold values, the corresponding POIs are not considered for a recommendation.

12.4.2 Duration of item consumption

Traditionally, RSs came up with an ordered list of recommendations, of which the user would choose one. When it comes to RSs for composite trips, typically several items are recommended in sequence. In such a scenario, it is worthwhile to suggest a duration of stay for each attraction, instead of proposing equal amounts of time [28]. When recommending POIs in urban areas, service providers like Google already have rich information about the distribution of the durations of stay. Therefore, a first refinement step would be to assign the median visit time of each venue as duration of stay [34]. In Section 12.3.1, we discussed several approaches to plan an optimal trip in a city within temporal constraints. However, to the best of our knowledge, none adjusts the durations of stay with respect to the personal fit of the venue. If the distribution of the duration of stay shows a high variance, the recommendations should be personalized so that the duration of stay is prolonged if the venue has a high score, and shortened otherwise.

In our travel region RS, we propose to gradually decrease the score of a region by 5–10 % per week, selecting the next region from the result list as soon as the score surpasses the one of the former [46]. While this score adjustment is already a form of personalization of the duration of item consumption, it is indirect and given the weekly interval quite coarse-grained.

An ideal solution would consider three aspects to calculate the duration of item consumption; first, the typical time needed to visit one location, second, the personalized score of the location, and finally, further context information such as the total trip time and the type of traveler. The first two are already widely used in tourist RSs; however, the third is largely unexplored, mainly because it requires more information about the user. A recent approach investigates typical tourist travel patterns on country level with a focus on the durations of stay [29]. While the concrete approach lacks generality, mobility patterns can both be used to derive the typical durations of stay. Based on this approach, a cluster analysis of the mobility patterns of global trips revealed four groups of travelers [30]. To determine the pace at which a user usually travels, their past trips could be derived from an LBSN they are using and then classified into one of these groups.

12.4.3 Deriving tourist mobility patterns

In Section 12.3.4, we have already discussed how past trips can be used to improve recommendations to new users. We argue that in the future this avenue should be pursued to learn about realistic trips and user preferences. However, the evaluations of many contributions discussed in this chapter are rarely based on field data and almost none of the suggested algorithms is used within a commercial context. As researchers in the area of tourist trip recommendations we should ask ourselves: *"Would we realistically go on a trip as recommended by our approach?"* So, if the user requests a city trip of 5 hours, is it appropriate to recommend 36 items, just because the algorithms computed that in theory somebody could visit those in the given time frame?

Tourist mobility patterns can be derived by analyzing traveler trajectories [29, 31]. Single trips can be aggregated and characterized with metrics, such as the number of visited places in a certain time, photos taken and modes of transportation used. Also, the typical routes can be derived to learn how tourists move in the city. This information could be used to verify that the recommended trips are within a 90 % interval of the analyzed past trips. Data sources can be LBSNs [9, 29, 31], regional smartphone applications [15], but also image meta-data [106]. Furthermore, tourist mobility patterns help to understand the dynamics of the durations of stay as we have discussed in Section 12.4.2.

12.4.4 Tourist trip recommendations on public displays

Public displays are ubiquitous today. They are used to display arrival and departure times of public transport, weather reports, news or advertisements. While these applications are examples for public displays with an information-only purpose, advances in technology enable interactive and personalized content. For example, the content can be personalized based on the user's stereotypes [73]. Interactive displays in shopping malls can highlight relevant shops the user is interested in, instead of only showing static maps [62]. Tourist trip RSs on personal mobile devices, such as the TourRec application, can be used in conjunction with kiosk systems that are deployed at touristic areas [44]. The integration of public displays is particularly interesting for group travelers since they provide a larger and mutual screen for all group members to facilitate the discussion among the group members, and hence finding consensus.

The sizes of public displays range from small TV screens for displaying information, such as visitor information in museums, to large multiuser wall displays in public spaces [75]. Besides size, public displays can be differentiated based on their interaction paradigms. Users can either directly interact with the touchscreen or keys attached to the display, or they can use speech or gestures captured by cameras [70].

Two factors may prevent people from interacting with a public display: social embarrassment and privacy. Public display applications have to be designed in a way that they attract users to interact with the display and also to protect their information when entering personal data. When designing interactive systems, *shoulder-surfing*, where passersby can identify sensitive content not meant for their eyes, such as a recommendation for the next POI the user should visit, should be hindered [17]. The user can pair his or her mobile phone with the public display to reduce the effects of *shoulder-surfing* by keeping the individual travel preferences on the personal device and displaying only the group recommendation on the public screen. It has been shown that using a mobile device to enter personal information is a promising solution to overcome privacy issues [4].

While many RSs for mobile devices have been developed and evaluated, only few examples use public displays or hybrid approaches combining smartphones and public displays. We have integrated public displays into the TourRec application [44]. Compared to the smartphone version, the public display application can show all relevant information on one single screen, as shown in Figure 12.3. We conducted a large user study with real groups to evaluate our approach [48]. Our results show that public displays are

Figure 12.3: The TourRec application running on a kiosk system.

attractive for users who prefer a more open discussion of their preferences. However, decisions on group preferences often tend to be unfair for some group members, especially when they do not know each other very well. A distributed recommender system aggregating the individual preferences of group members was the most appreciated solution in our study [48].

12.4.5 Fairness and multistakeholder issues

So far in this chapter and in most of the corresponding literature, the discussion is from the perspective of users or groups of users. However, recommendation in the domain of travel and tourism is a multisided concept that needs to take into account the needs and perspectives of multiple stakeholder groups [1]. Balakrishnan and Wörndl [7] identify the following stakeholder classes that may be important in this scenario:

- *User*: receive recommendations to plan their trips, e. g., travelers, airline passengers, tourists, hikers, park visitors, festival attendees.
- *Providers*: provide the recommended service or facility, e. g., hotels, resorts, rentals, amusement parks, airlines, tour operators.
- *System*: intermediates or booking platforms, e. g., flight or hotel booking services, vacation recommenders, city information systems, travel sites.
- *Society*: representative of local communities or the society as a whole, e. g., destination management organizations (DMOs), regional and local authorities, municipal councils, airports, national parks.

The notion of fairness has recently gained attention in the recommender systems research community [32]. The general idea is that no stakeholder should be harmed by the outcome of a recommendation. When recommending tourist trips, however, popular places may be recommended that already suffer from high visitor numbers and overtourism. On the other hand, it would be desirable to promote underexplored POIs and services. In addition, tourism recommendation need to incorporate the environmental impact, e. g., by recommending places that can be comfortably visited using public transportation. Merinov et al. [68] proposes a utility model for travel itinerary optimization based on simulated visitor behavior. But as of now, there is very limited work in considering multistakeholder fairness in tourist trip recommender systems.

12.5 Conclusions

In this chapter, we presented foundations, the current state of the art and ongoing research challenges concerning the TTDP. Compared to related work, we use a broader definition of the TTDP. Instead of only using the OP and its variants to model the TTDP, we showed how other mathematical problems, namely the TSP and KP, can be used to recommend tourist trips and routes on different granularities, such as inner-city routes, road trips and trips composed of multiple countries. Furthermore, we provided an overview of the state of the art of RSs in tourism, TTDP algorithms, group recommendations and aspects of item diversity and we showed how to analyze past tourist trips to come up with more realistic recommendations.

The main goal of our work is to make research on recommending tourist trips more applicable in practical scenarios. For this purpose, we highlighted some of the most important challenges in the development of next-generation tourist trip RSs. In practical applications, algorithms solving the TTDP should not only connect a set of nodes with fixed scores to come up with the best solution from a pure mathematical point of view. Instead, the nodes have to be perceived as travel items, such as POIs or travel regions, with certain characteristics that have to be taken into account when recommended to the user. This is why tourist trip RSs solving the TTDP should become more context-aware and take into account factors such as weather, time of day and previously visited POIs. They should come up with a recommended sequence of POIs that is not only optimized by an algorithm, but also a pleasure to follow. Therefore, we argue that solutions to the TTDP should be evaluated more from a user's perspective.

Nowadays, many data about tourist mobility are available. We argue that analyzing mobility patterns can provide insights into preferences of individual travelers and the ideal time and duration to visit a given POI or region. Incorporating such information can potentially improve the quality of recommendations.

Particularly in view of group recommendations, alternative user interfaces for tourist trip recommendations are an important issue. While smartphones are very popular devices today to receive recommendations everywhere, larger displays, such as public displays, should be integrated into the recommendation process to facilitate the discussion among group members. Finally, tourism recommender systems raises issues of fairness and the needs of different stakeholder classes have to be considered in future applications.

References

[1] H. Abdollahpouri and R. Burke. Multistakeholder recommender systems. In: *Recommender systems handbook*. Springer, 2021, pp. 647–677.

[2] Gediminas Adomavicius and Alexander Tuzhilin. Context-aware recommender systems. In: Francesco Ricci, Lior Rokach, and Bracha Shapira, editors. *Recommender Systems Handbook*. New York, NY, USA: Springer US, 2015, pp. 191–226.

[3] H. Murat Afsar and Nacima Labadie. Team orienteering problem with decreasing profits. *Electronic Notes in Discrete Mathematics* 41 (2013) 285–293.

[4] Florian Alt, Alireza Sahami Shirazi, Thomas Kubitza, and Albrecht Schmidt. Interaction techniques for creating and exchanging content with public displays. In: *Proceedings of the SIGCHI Conference on Human Factors in Computing Systems, CHI '13*. New York, NY, USA: ACM, 2013, pp. 1709–1718.

[5] E. Angelelli, C. Archetti, and M. Vindigni. The clustered orienteering problem. *European Journal of Operational Research* 238(2) (2014) 404–414.

[6] Liliana Ardissono, Anna Goy, Giovanna Petrone, Marino Segnan, and Pietro Torasso. Tailoring the recommendation of tourist information to heterogeneous user groups. In: *Revised Papers from the Nternational Workshops OHS-7, SC-3, and AH-3 on Hypermedia: Openness, Structural Awareness, and Adaptivityf*. London, UK: Springer-Verlag, 2002, pp. 280–295.

[7] G. Balakrishnan and W. Wörndl. Multistakeholder recommender systems in tourism. In: *Proc. Workshop on Recommenders in Tourism (RecTour 2021)*, 2021.

[8] Jie Bao, Yu Zheng, and Mohamed F. Mokbel. Location-based and preference-aware recommendation using sparse geo-social networking data. In: *Proceedings of the 20th International Conference on Advances in Geographic Information Systems, SIGSPATIAL '12*. New York, NY, USA: ACM, 2012, pp. 199–208.

[9] Jie Bao, Yu Zheng, David Wilkie, and Mohamed Mokbel. Recommendations in location-based social networks: a survey. *Geoinformatica* 19(3) (2015) 525–565.

[10] Ramesh Baral and Tao Li. Maps: A multi aspect personalized POI recommender system. In: *Proceedings of the 10th ACM Conference on Recommender Systems, RecSys '16*. New York, NY, USA: ACM, 2016, pp. 281–284.

[11] Idir Benouaret and Dominique Lenne. A package recommendation framework for trip planning activities. In: *Proceedings of the 10th ACM Conference on Recommender Systems, RecSys '16*. New York, NY, USA: ACM, 2016, pp. 203–206.

[12] Justine I. Blanford, Zhuojie Huang, Alexander Savelyev, and Alan M. MacEachren. Geo-located tweets. enhancing mobility maps and capturing cross-border movement. *PLoS ONE* 10(6) (2015) 1–16.

[13] Joan Borràs, Antonio Moreno, and Aida Valls. Intelligent tourism recommender systems: A survey. *Expert Systems with Applications* 41(16) (2014) 7370–7389.

[14] Matthias Braunhofer, Mehdi Elahi, Mouzhi Ge, and Francesco Ricci. Sts: Design of weather-aware mobile recommender systems in tourism. In: *Proceedings of the 1st Workshop on AI*HCI: Intelligent User Interfaces (AI*HCI 2013)*, 2013.

[15] Matthias Braunhofer, Mehdi Elahi, and Francesco Ricci. Usability assessment of a context-aware and personality-based mobile recommender system. In: *International conference on electronic commerce and web technologies*. Springer International Publishing, 2014, pp. 77–88.

[16] Igo Brilhante, Jose Antonio Macedo, Franco Maria Nardini, Raffaele Perego, and Chiara Renso. Where shall we go today?: Planning touristic tours with tripbuilder. In: *Proceedings of the 22Nd ACM International Conference on Information & Knowledge Management, CIKM '13*. New York, NY, USA: ACM, 2013, pp. 757–762.

[17] Frederik Brudy, David Ledo, Saul Greenberg, and Andreas Butz. Is anyone looking? mitigating shoulder surfing on public displays through awareness and protection. In: *Proceedings of The International Symposium on Pervasive Displays, PerDis '14*. New York, NY, USA: ACM, 2014, pp. 1:1–1:6.

[18] Jennifer J. Burg, John Ainsworth, Brian Casto, and Sheau-Dong Lang. Experiments with the "oregon trail knapsack problem". *Electronic Notes in Discrete Mathematics* 1 (1999) 26–35. CP98, Workshop on Large Scale Combinatorial Optimisation and Constraints.

[19] Steven E. Butt and Tom M. Cavalier. A heuristic for the multiple tour maximum collection problem. *Computers & Operations Research* 21(1) (1994) 101–111.

[20] Steven E. Butt and David M. Ryan. An optimal solution procedure for the multiple tour maximum collection problem using column generation. *Computers & Operations Research* 26(4) (1999) 427–441.

[21] Ann M. Campbell, Michel Gendreau, and Barrett W. Thomas. The orienteering problem with stochastic travel and service times. *Annals of Operations Research* 186(1) (2011) 61–81.

[22] Pablo Castells, Neil J. Hurley, and Saul Vargas. Novelty and diversity in recommender systems. In: Francesco Ricci, Lior Rokach, and Bracha Shapira, editors. *Recommender Systems Handbook*. New York, NY, USA: Springer US, 2015, pp. 881–918.

[23] I-Ming Chao, Bruce L. Golden, and Edward A. Wasil. The team orienteering problem. *European Journal of Operational Research* 88(3) (1996) 464–474.

[24] Zhiyuan Cheng, James Caverlee, Kyumin Lee, and Daniel Z. Sui. Exploring millions of footprints in location sharing services. In: *Proceedings of the Fifth International Conference on Weblogs and Social Media, ICWSM '11*. Palo Alto, CA, USA: AAAI, 2011, pp. 81–88.

[25] Keith Cheverst, Nigel Davies, Keith Mitchell, Adrian Friday, and Christos Efstratiou. Developing a context-aware electronic tourist guide: Some issues and experiences. In: *Proceedings of the SIGCHI Conference on Human Factors in Computing Systems, CHI'00*. New York, NY, USA: ACM, 2000, pp. 17–24.

[26] Munmun De Choudhury, Moran Feldman, Sihem Amer-Yahia, Nadav Golbandi, Ronny Lempel, and Cong Yu. Automatic construction of travel itineraries using social breadcrumbs. In: *Proceedings of the 21st ACM Conference on Hypertext and Hypermedia, HT'10*. New York, NY, USA: ACM, 2010, pp. 35–44.

[27] Sérgio R. de M. Queiroz and Francisco de A. T. de Carvalho. Making collaborative group recommendations based on modal symbolic data. In: Ana L. C. Bazzan and Sofiane Labidi, editors. *Advances in Artificial Intelligence – SBIA 2004: 17th Brazilian Symposium on Artificial Intelligence, Sao Luis, Maranhao, Brazil, September 29–Ocotber 1, 2004. Proceedings*. Berlin, Heidelberg: Springer Berlin Heidelberg, 2004, pp. 307–316.

[28] Linus W. Dietz. Data-driven destination recommender systems. In: *Proceedings of the 26th Conference on User Modeling, Adaptation and Personalization, UMAP '18*, New York, NY, USA: ACM, 2018.

[29] Linus W. Dietz, Daniel Herzog, and Wolfgang Wörndl. Deriving tourist mobility patterns from check-in data. In: *Proceedings of the WSDM 2018 Workshop on Learning from User Interactions, Los Angeles, CA, USA*, 2018.

[30] Linus W. Dietz, Rinita Roy, and Wolfgang Wörndl. Characterization of traveler types using check-in data from location-based social networks. In: *Proceedings of the 26th ENTER eTourism Conference*, 2019.

[31] L. W. Dietz, A. Sen, R. Roy, and W. Wörndl. Mining trips from location-based social networks for clustering travelers and destinations. *Information Technology & Tourism* 22 (2020) 131–166.

[32] M. D. Ekstrand, A. Das, R. Burke, and F. Diaz. Fairness in recommender systems. In: *Recommender systems handbook*. Springer, 2021, pp. 679–707.

[33] Fedor V. Fomin and Andrzej Lingas. Approximation algorithms for time-dependent orienteering. *Information Processing Letters* 83(2) (2002) 57–62.

[34] Zachary Friggstad, Sreenivas Gollapudi, Kostas Kollias, Tamas Sarlos, Chaitanya Swamy, and Andrew Tomkins. Orienteering algorithms for generating travel itineraries. In: *Proceedings of the Eleventh ACM International Conference on Web Search and Data Mining, WSDM '18*. New York, NY, USA: ACM, 2018, pp. 180–188.

[35] Ander Garcia, Olatz Arbelaitz, Maria Teresa Linaza, Pieter Vansteenwegen, and Wouter Souffriau. Personalized tourist route generation. In: *Proceedings of the 10th International Conference on Current Trends in Web Engineering, ICWE'10*. Berlin, Heidelberg: Springer-Verlag, 2010, pp. 486–497.

[36] Ander Garcia, Pieter Vansteenwegen, Olatz Arbelaitz, Wouter Souffriau, and Maria Teresa Linaza. Integrating public transportation in personalised electronic tourist guides. *Computers & Operations Research* 40(3) (2013) 758–774. Transport Scheduling.

[37] Ander Garcia, Pieter Vansteenwegen, Wouter Souffriau, Olatz Arbelaitz, and Maria Linaza. Solving multi constrained team orienteering problems to generate tourist routes. Tech. rep., Centre for Industrial Management/Traffic & Infrastructure, Katholieke Universiteit Leuven, Leuven, Belgium, 2009.

[38] Damianos Gavalas, Vlasios Kasapakis, Charalampos Konstantopoulos, Grammati Pantziou, and Nikolaos Vathis. Scenic route planning for tourists. *Personal and Ubiquitous Computing* 1–19, 2016.

[39] Damianos Gavalas, Charalampos Konstantopoulos, Konstantinos Mastakas, and Grammati Pantziou. Mobile recommender systems in tourism. *Journal of Network and Computer Applications* 39 (2014) 319–333.

[40] Damianos Gavalas, Charalampos Konstantopoulos, Konstantinos Mastakas, and Grammati Pantziou. A survey on algorithmic approaches for solving tourist trip design problems. *Journal of Heuristics* 20(3) (2014) 291–328.

[41] Zong Woo Geem, Chung-Li Tseng, and Yongjin Park. Harmony search for generalized orienteering problem: best touring in china. In: Lipo Wang, Ke Chen, and Yew Soon Ong, editors. *Advances in natural computation*. Berlin, Heidelberg: Springer Berlin Heidelberg, 2005, pp. 741–750.

[42] A. Gunawan, H. C. Lau, and P. Vansteenwegen. Orienteering problem: A survey of recent variants, solution approaches and applications. *European Journal of Operational Research* 255(2) (2016) 315–332.

[43] Daniel Herzog, Christopher Laß, and Wolfgang Wörndl. TourRec: A Tourist Trip Recommender System for Individuals and Groups. In: *Proceedings of the 12th ACM Conference on Recommender Systems, RecSys '18*. New York, NY, USA: ACM, 2018, pp. 496–497.

[44] Daniel Herzog, Nikolaos Promponas-Kefalas, and Wolfgang Wörndl. Integrating Public Displays into Tourist Trip Recommender Systems. In: *Proceedings of the 3rd Workshop on Recommenders in Tourism co-located with 12th ACM Conference on Recommender Systems (RecSys '18)*, 2018, pp. 18–22.

[45] Daniel Herzog and Wolfgang Wörndl. Exploiting item dependencies to improve tourist trip recommendations. In: *Proceedings of the Workshop on Recommenders in Tourism co-located with 10th ACM Conference on Recommender Systems (RecSys 2016), Boston, MA, USA, September 15, 2016*, 2016, pp. 55–58.

[46] Daniel Herzog and Wolfgang Wörndl. A travel recommender system for combining multiple travel regions to a composite trip. In: *CBRecSys@RecSys, Foster City, Silicon Valley, California, USA*. CEUR Workshop Proceedings, volume 1245. CEUR-WS.org, 2014, pp. 42–48.

[47] D. Herzog and W. Wörndl. User-centered evaluation of strategies for recommending sequences of points of interest to groups. In: *Proceedings of the 13th ACM Conference on Recommender Systems*, 2019, pp. 96–100.

[48] D. Herzog and W. Wörndl. A user study on groups interacting with tourist trip recommender systems in public spaces. In: *Proceedings of the 27th ACM Conference on User Modeling, Adaptation and Personalization*, 2019, pp. 130–138.

[49] Hsun-Ping Hsieh, Cheng-Te Li, and Shou-De Lin. Exploiting large-scale check-in data to recommend time-sensitive routes. In: *Proceedings of the ACM SIGKDD International Workshop on Urban Computing, UrbComp'12*. New York, NY, USA: ACM, 2012, pp. 55–62.

[50] Qian Hu and Andrew Lim. An iterative three-component heuristic for the team orienteering problem with time windows. *European Journal of Operational Research* 232(2) (2014) 276–286.

[51] Taylan Ilhan, Seyed M. R. Iravani, and Mark S. Daskin. The orienteering problem with stochastic profits. *IIE Transactions* 40(4) (2008) 406–421.

[52] Anthony Jameson. More than the sum of its members: Challenges for group recommender systems. In: *Proceedings of the Working Conference on Advanced Visual Interfaces, AVI '04*. New York, NY, USA: ACM, 2004, pp. 48–54.

[53] Marisa G. Kantor and Moshe B. Rosenwein. The orienteering problem with time windows. *Journal of the Operational Research Society* 43(6) (1992) 629–635.

[54] Imdat Kara, Papatya Sevgin Bicakci, and Tusan Derya. New formulations for the orienteering problem. *Procedia Economics and Finance* 39 (2016) 849–854.

[55] Hans Kellerer, Ulrich Pferschy, and David Pisinger. *Knapsack Problems*. Berlin: Springer, 2004.

[56] Gilbert Laporte. The traveling salesman problem: An overview of exact and approximate algorithms. *European Journal of Operational Research* 59(2) (1992) 231–247.

[57] Gilbert Laporte and Silvano Martello. The selective travelling salesman problem. *Discrete Applied Mathematics* 26 (1990) 193–207.

[58] Christopher Laß, Daniel Herzog, and Wolfgang Wörndl. Context-aware tourist trip recommendations. In: *Proceedings of the 2nd Workshop on Recommenders in Tourism co-located with 11th ACM Conference on Recommender Systems (RecSys 2017), Como, Italy, August 27, 2017*, 2017, pp. 18–25.

[59] Christopher Laß, Wolfgang Wörndl, and Daniel Herzog. A multi-tier web service and mobile client for city trip recommendations. In: *The 8th EAI International Conference on Mobile Computing, Applications and Services (MobiCASE)*. ACM, 2016.

[60] Mario Lenz. Cabata: Case-based reasoning for holiday planning. In: *Proceedings of the International Conference on Information and Communications Technologies in Tourism*. Secaucus, NJ, USA: Springer-Verlag New York, Inc., 1994, pp. 126–132.

[61] Mario Lenz. Imtas: Intelligent multimedia travel agent system. In: Stefan Klein, Beat Schmid, A. Min Tjoa, and Hannes Werthner, editors. *Information and Communication Technologies in Tourism*. Vienna: Springer Vienna, 1996, pp. 11–17.

[62] Marvin Levine. You-are-here maps: Psychological considerations. *Environment and Behavior* 14(2) (1982) 221–237.

[63] K. H. Lim, J. Chan, S. Karunasekera, and C. Leckie. Tour recommendation and trip planning using location-based social media: A survey. *Knowledge and Information Systems* 60 (2019) 1247–1275.

[64] Tariq Mahmood, Francesco Ricci, and Adriano Venturini. Improving recommendation effectiveness: Adapting a dialogue strategy in online travel planning. *Information Technology & Tourism* 11(4) (2009) 285–302.

[65] Judith Masthoff. Group recommender systems: Aggregation, satisfaction and group attributes. In: Francesco Ricci, Lior Rokach, and Bracha Shapira, editors. *Recommender Systems Handbook*. Boston, MA: Springer US, 2015, pp. 743–776.

[66] Kevin McCarthy, Lorraine McGinty, Barry Smyth, and Maria Salamó. The needs of the many: A case-based group recommender system. In: *Proceedings of the 8th European Conference on Advances in Case-Based Reasoning, ECCBR'06*. Berlin, Heidelberg: Springer-Verlag, 2006, pp. 196–210.

[67] Robert R. McCrae and Oliver P. John. An introduction to the five-factor model and its applications. *Journal of Personality* 60(2) (1992) 175–215.

[68] P. Merinov, D. Massimo and F. Ricci. Sustainability driven recommender systems, 2022.

[69] Montassar Ben Messaoud, Ilyes Jenhani, Eya Garci, and Toon De Pessemier. SemCoTrip: A variety-seeking model for recommending travel activities in a composite trip. In: *Advances in Artificial Intelligence: From Theory to Practice, Arras, France*. Springer International Publishing, 2017, pp. 345–355.

[70] Jörg Müller, Florian Alt, Daniel Michelis, and Albrecht Schmidt. Requirements and design space for interactive public displays. In: *Proceedings of the 18th ACM International Conference on Multimedia, MM '10*. New York, NY, USA: ACM, 2010, pp. 1285–1294.

[71] Julia Neidhardt, Leonhard Seyfang, Rainer Schuster, and Hannes Werthner. A picture-based approach to recommender systems. *Information Technology & Tourism* 15(1) (2015) 49–69.

[72] Anastasios Noulas, Salvatore Scellato, Cecilia Mascolo, and Massimiliano Pontil. An empirical study of geographic user activity patterns in foursquare. In: *Proceedings of the Fifth International Conference on Weblogs and Social Media, ICWSM '11*, volume 11. Palo Alto, CA, USA: AAAI, 2011, pp. 70–573.

[73] Sebastian Oehme and Linus W. Dietz. Affective computing and bandits: Capturing context in cold start situations. In: *Proceedings of the RecSys Joint Workshop on Interfaces and Human Decision Making for Recommender Systems, Vancouver, Canada*, 2018.

[74] Randall S. Olson. The optimal U. S. national parks centennial road trip. Online, 2016. http://www.randalolson.com/2016/07/30/the-optimal-u-s-national-parks-centennial-road-trip.

[75] Peter Peltonen, Esko Kurvinen, Antti Salovaara, Giulio Jacucci, Tommi Ilmonen, John Evans, Antti Oulasvirta, and Petri Saarikko. It's mine, don't touch!: Interactions at a large multi-touch display in a city centre. In: *Proceedings of the SIGCHI Conference on Human Factors in Computing Systems, CHI '08*. New York, NY, USA: ACM, 2008, pp. 1285–1294.

[76] Daniele Quercia, Rossano Schifanella, and Luca Maria Aiello. The shortest path to happiness: Recommending beautiful, quiet, and happy routes in the city. In: *Proceedings of the 25th ACM Conference on Hypertext and Social Media, HT '14*. New York, NY, USA: ACM, 2014, pp. 116–125.

[77] F. Ricci, D. R. Fesenmaier, N. Mirzadeh, H. Rumetshofer, E. Schaumlechner, A. Venturini, K. W. Wöber, and A. H. Zins. Dietorecs: a case-based travel advisory system. In: D. R. Fesenmaier, K. W. Wöber, and H. Werthner, editors. *Destination recommendation systems: behavioural foundations and applications*. CABI, 2006, pp. 227–239.

[78] Francesco Ricci. Travel recommender systems. *IEEE Intelligent Systems* (2002) 55–57.

[79] Francesco Ricci, Lior Rokach, and Bracha Shapira. Recommender systems: Introduction and challenges. In: Francesco Ricci, Lior Rokach, and Bracha Shapira, editors. *Recommender Systems Handbook*. Boston, MA: Springer US, 2021, pp. 1–35.

[80] F. Ricci, L. Rokach, and B. Shapira. Recommender systems: Techniques, applications, and challenges. *Recommender Systems Handbook* (2021) 1–35.

[81] J. Ruiz-Meza and J. R. Montoya-Torres. A systematic literature review for the tourist trip design problem: extensions, solution techniques and future research lines. *Operations Research Perspectives* (2022) 100228.

[82] Amihai Savir, Ronen Brafman, and Guy Shani. Recommending improved configurations for complex objects with an application in travel planning. In: *Proceedings of the 7th ACM Conference on Recommender Systems, RecSys '13*. New York, NY, USA: ACM, 2013, pp. 391–394.

[83] Salvatore Scellato and Cecilia Mascolo. Measuring user activity on an online location-based social network. In: *2011 IEEE Conference on Computer Communications Workshops*. IEEE, 2011, pp. 918–923.

[84] Alexander Smirnov, Alexey Kashevnik, Andrew Ponomarev, Nikolay Shilov, and Nikolay Teslya. Proactive recommendation system for m-tourism application. In: Björn Johansson, Bo Andersson, and Nicklas Holmberg, editors. *Perspectives in Business Informatics Research*. Springer International Publishing, Cham, 2014, pp. 113–127.

[85] Chaoming Song, Tal Koren, Pu Wang, and Albert-László Barabási. Modelling the scaling properties of human mobility. *Nature Physics* 6(10) (2010) 818–823.

[86] Chaoming Song, Zehui Qu, Nicholas Blumm, and Albert-László Barabási. Limits of predictability in human mobility. *Science* 327(5968) (2010) 1018–1021.

[87] Wouter Souffriau, Pieter Vansteenwegen, Greet Vanden Berghe, and Dirk Van Oudheusden. A greedy randomised adaptive search procedure for the team orienteering problem. In: *EU/MEeting*, 2008, pp. 23–24.

[88] Wouter Souffriau, Pieter Vansteenwegen, Greet Vanden Berghe, and Dirk Van Oudheusden. A path relinking approach for the team orienteering problem. *Computers & Operations Research* 37(11) (2010) 1853–1859.

[89] Wouter Souffriau, Pieter Vansteenwegen, Greet Vanden Berghe, and Dirk Van Oudheusden. The multiconstraint team orienteering problem with multiple time windows. *Transportation Science* 47(1) (2013) 53–63.

[90] Harald Steck. Calibrated recommendations. In: *Proceedings of the 12th ACM Conference on Recommender Systems, RecSys '18*. New York, NY, USA: ACM, 2018, pp. 154–162.

[91] Kadri Sylejmani, Jürgen Dorn, and Nysret Musliu. Planning the trip itinerary for tourist groups. *Information Technology & Tourism* 17(3) (2017) 275–314.

[92] Marko Tkalcic, Matevž Kunaver, Jurij Tasic, and Andrej Kosir. Personality based user similarity measure for a collaborative recommender system. In: Christian Peter, Elizabeth Crane, Lesley Axelrod, Harry Agius, Shazia Afzal, and Madeline Balaam, editors. *5th Workshop on Emotion in Human-Computer Interaction-Real World Challenges, Fraunhofer*, 2009, pp. 30–37.

[93] Theodore Tsiligirides. Heuristic methods applied to orienteering. *Journal of the Operational Research Society* (1984) 797–809.

[94] Pieter Vansteenwegen, Wouter Souffriau, Greet Vanden Berghe, and Dirk Van Oudheusden. The city trip planner. *Expert Systems with Applications* 38(6) (2011) 6540–6546.

[95] Pieter Vansteenwegen, Wouter Souffriau, and Dirk Van Oudheusden. The orienteering problem: A survey. *European Journal of Operational Research* 209(1) (2011) 1–10.

[96] Pieter Vansteenwegen, Wouter Souffriau, Greet Vanden Berghe, and Dirk Van Oudheusden. Iterated local search for the team orienteering problem with time windows. *Computers & Operations Research* 36(12) (2009) 3281–3290.

[97] Pieter Vansteenwegen and Dirk Van Oudheusden. The mobile tourist guide: an OR opportunity. *OR Insight* 20(3) (2007) 21–27.

[98] P. Vansteenwegen, A. Gunawan, P. Vansteenwegen, and A. Gunawan. State-of-the-art solution techniques for optw and toptw. *Orienteering Problems: Models and Algorithms for Vehicle Routing Problems with Profits* (2019) 67–81.

[99] N. Vathis, C. Konstantopoulos, G. Pantziou, and D. Gavalas. The vacation planning problem: A multi-level clustering-based metaheuristic approach. *Computers & Operations Research* 150 (2023) 106083.

[100] Adriano Venturini and Francesco Ricci. Applying trip@dvice recommendation technology to www.visiteurope.com. In: *Proceedings of the 2006 Conference on ECAI 2006: 17th European Conference on Artificial Intelligence August 29 – September 1, 2006, Riva Del Garda, Italy*. Amsterdam, The Netherlands: IOS Press, 2006, pp. 607–611.

[101] Wolfgang Woerndl, Johannes Huebner, Roland Bader, and Daniel Gallego-Vico. A model for proactivity in mobile, context-aware recommender systems. In: *Proceedings of the fifth ACM conference on Recommender systems, RecSys '11*. ACM, 2011.

[102] World Travel and Tourism Council. Travel & Tourism Global Economic Impact & Issues 2018, March 2018.

[103] Wen Wu, Li Chen, and Liang He. Using personality to adjust diversity in recommender systems. In: *Proceedings of the 24th ACM Conference on Hypertext and Social Media, HT '13*. New York, NY, USA: ACM, 2013, pp. 225–229.

[104] Wolfgang Wörndl. A web-based application for recommending travel regions. In: *Adjunct Publication of the 25th Conference on User Modeling, Adaptation and Personalization, UMAP '17*. New York, NY, USA: ACM, 2017, pp. 105–106.

[105] Wolfgang Wörndl, Alexander Hefele, and Daniel Herzog. Recommending a sequence of interesting places for tourist trips. *Information Technology & Tourism* 17(1) (2017) 31–54.

[106] Liu Yang, Lun Wu, Yu Liu, and Chaogui Kang. Quantifying tourist behavior patterns by travel motifs and geo-tagged photos from flickr. *ISPRS International Journal of Geo-Information* 6(11) (2017) 345.

[107] Yu Zheng and Xing Xie. Learning travel recommendations from user-generated GPS traces. *ACM Transactions on Intelligent Systems and Technology* 2(1) (2011) 1–29.

Wilfried Grossmann, Mete Sertkan, Julia Neidhardt, and
Hannes Werthner

13 Pictures as a tool for matching tourist preferences with destinations

Abstract: Usually descriptions of touristic products comprise information about accommodation, tourist attractions or leisure activities. Tourist decisions for a product are based on personal characteristics, planned vacation activities and specificities of potential touristic products. The decision should guarantee a high level of emotional and physical well-being, considering also some hard constraints like temporal and monetary resources, or travel distance. The starting point for the design of the described recommender system is a unified description of the preferences of the tourist and the opportunities offered by touristic products using the so-called seven-factor model. For the assignment of the values in the seven-factor model a predefined set of pictures is the pivotal instrument. These pictures represent various aspects of the personality and preferences of the tourist as well as general categories for the description of destinations, i. e., certain tourist attractions like landscape, cultural facilities, different leisure activities or emotional aspects associated with tourism. Based on the picture selection of a customer a so-called factor algorithm calculates values for each factor of the seven-factor model. This is a rather fast and intuitive method for acquisition of information about personality and preferences. The evaluation of the factors of the products is obtained by mapping descriptive attributes of touristic products onto the predefined pictures and afterwards applying the factor algorithm to the pictures characterizing the product. Based on this unified description of tourists and touristic products a recommendation can be defined by measuring the similarity between the user attributes and the product attributes. The approach is evaluated using data from a travel agency. Furthermore, other possible applications are discussed.

Keywords: Tourism, seven-factor model, travel behavior, user modeling

13.1 Introduction

The purpose of a recommender system is usually characterized as providing "suggestions for items that are most likely of interest to a particular user" [25]. Thus, in order to be capable of accurately delivering personalized recommendations, an appropriate user model is required at the core of such a system. As a consequence, various ways to introduce a more comprehensive view of the users, their needs and their preferences have been explored. In this context, personality-based approaches are increasingly gaining attention. It has been shown that in a number of domains user preferences can be re-

https://doi.org/10.1515/9783110988567-013

lated to the personality of a user and that recommender systems can successfully exploit these relationships [31], also in the context of tourism [3].

Providing accurate recommendations for travel and tourism is particularly challenging as the touristic product typically possesses a considerably high complexity. Usually, the product consists of a bundle of different but interrelated components, e. g., means of transport, accommodations and attractions and activities at the destination [32]. In the early phase of the travel decision-making process, moreover, people are often not capable of phrasing their tourism preferences explicitly, so they might rather be intangible and implicitly given [35]. In addition, traveling is emotional, and this aspect should also be considered within a computational model [33]. In an ideal case, the model should capture the user preferences and the product characteristics in a comparable way.

The goal of this chapter is to describe in detail how user preferences and touristic products can be represented in a 7D space of latent properties and how this representation can be used for delivering personalized recommendations. A typical application scenario of this approach is the following one: A travel agency offers various products to their customers, e. g., short-term city trips, round trips, family holiday trips, cruises or event trips (e. g., attendance of sport or cultural events). For better marketing and customer relationship management (CRM), the agency is interested in personalized offers for already existing customers (based on the existent customer information). In addition to providing a better service to existing customers, the agency is also interested in attracting new customers and providing suitable products for them. Hence, the agency is mainly interested in developing a recommender system for the inspiration and planning phase of customers.

For achieving this goal, the starting point of the approach is the already existing system, which was introduced in [18]. The system addresses users at a nonverbal and emotional level where a predefined set of pictures is used to elicit user preferences. These preferences are modeled by combining 17 tourist roles from literature and the "Big Five" personality traits [19] and result in a 7D representation of tourist preferences. Note that these pictures are not destination-specific but show the various aspects of preferences and personalities in a prototypical way.

The novel feature in this paper is the innovative use of the pictures for characterization of not only user preferences but also the offered products. These products can be described in different ways and to distinguish between the different descriptions we use the notation <Product>, <Factor|Picture|Category>, <Profile>, indicating which type of attributes are used for the description. For the description of the customers in the seven-factor model, we use the notation *User Factor Profile*.

The approach is based on a three-step procedure. Starting point is a set of descriptors of touristic products. It should be mentioned that these descriptors can encompass not only facts about a destination but also opinions of former tourists about a destination. In the first step, the descriptors of the products are collected and mapped onto a unified system of categories. The result is a so-called *Product Category Profile* for a product. In the second step, the categories are mapped onto the set of pictures, which are used for characterization of the customer preferences. The results is a so-called *Product Picture Profile*. In the third step, a *Product Factor Profile* is computed using the same algorithm, which calculates the *User Factor Profile*.

The chapter is organized as follows: After the presentation of related work in Section 13.2, we illustrate in Section 13.3 the key concepts of the picture-based recommender system. In Section 13.4, the first results of an empirical validation are presented. This evaluation shows that the approach is both valid and well performing in a domain, where implicit and emotional factors strongly impact the decision-making process. In Section 13.5, we discuss further work.

13.2 Related work

The main objective of our work is providing an innovative and enjoyable support in describing user needs and preferences (for details, see [18, 19]). Critique-based recommender techniques pursue a similar goal [17], but their focus is on the conversational process, where first results are refined iteratively. Although users do not have to specify all their preferences from the very beginning, some initial input is required, e. g., by answering some questions or with the help of initial examples, e. g., pictures of hotels [26]. For the latter, similarities to our approach exist, but their pictures clearly refer to products, whereas in our case the pictures capture user types and prototypical product characteristics. Our approach is supported by [22] as their work related to the design of preference elicitation interfaces shows that (i) low cognitive effort (e. g., due to pictures) can lead to high user liking, and (ii) affective feedback can increase the willingness to spend more effort. In some sense, our approach fits the idea of reciprocal recommender systems, where the preferences of both sides involved are expressed and matched [15] using the same personality-centered measurement instrument.

The first steps in this direction have already been introduced. Glatzer et al. [12] propose a method to categorize hotels into the seven factors using text-mining on hotel descriptions. Sertkan et al. [27, 28] show that a tourism destination's seven-factor representation can be determined by their hard facts. Furthermore, Sertkan et al. [29, 30] achieve promising results in determining users' seven-factors by employing deep learning on their pictures.

Despite its high complexity, tourism has been an important application domain for recommender systems since the 2000s [24], and it is becoming increasingly relevant as more and more travelers are relying on information and communication technology in all phases of their tourist experiences [2, 9, 21]. In [13], it is shown that tourist types can be used to predict activities of travelers during vacations as these types are distinguishable regarding travel style (e. g., variety seeking), travel motivations (e. g., social contacts) and travel values (e. g., active versus passive). This associations can be exploited when proposing appropriate tourism objects. In [1], a relation is established between tourist types and representative tourism-related pictures, implying that tourist types can be assigned to users based on their selected pictures. Our work builds upon these results.

A web-based application of a picture-based recommender system is provided by Cruneo [4]. On the website of this company, cruises can be compared, and to determine the travel style of a user, 12 pictures are used. However, this application is focusing on a very specific segment and it is not clear whether a theoretical framework is given. Other systems use pictures for a more fine-grained recommendation like route planning from a more emotional perspective [23] or guides for visiting a city [5].

13.3 The picture-based approach

In this section, we describe the three cornerstones of the picture-based approach:
- The seven-factor model;
- The determination of *User Factor Profiles* (i. e., seven-factor representation of users);
- The determination of *Product Factor Profiles* (i. e., seven-factor representation of products), expressed either directly in terms of the seven factors or by pictures.

13.3.1 Seven-factor model

Much research has already been conducted in order to develop comprehensive user models of tourists capable of capturing respective preferences, needs and interest. A well-established and known framework in this sense is introduced in [11], namely the 17 tourist roles. The mentioned framework captures the short-term preferences of tourists, i. e., preferences which might change depending on the context (e. g., seasonality such as summer or winter, special occasions or single/group) [18, 19]. On the other side, personality traits tend to be more stable over time and can, in general, be considered as long-term preferences and behavior [16, 34]. A well-known, widely used and domain-independent framework in this context is the five-factor model, also known as the "Big Five" personality traits [14]. The seven-factor model [19] was obtained from 997 questionnaires, using existing standardized questions for assessing and measuring the 17 tourist roles and the "Big Five" personality traits of the respondents. Using the collected data, a factor analysis was conducted, which reduced the initial 22 dimensions (i. e., 17 tourist roles plus the "Big Five" personality traits) and resulted in seven independent factors, i. e., the seven-factor model, which is briefly summarized in Table 13.1.

The resulting seven factors are easier to interpret and to process cognitively and computationally compared to the initial 22 dimensions. It has been shown that based on

Table 13.1: Seven-factor model [18, 19].

Factor	Description
Sun and chill-out	a neurotic sun lover, who likes warm weather and sun bathing and does not like cold, rainy or crowded places
Knowledge and travel	an open-minded, educational and well-organized mass tourist, who likes traveling in groups and gaining knowledge, rather than being lazy
Independence and history	an independent mass tourist, who is searching for the meaning of life, is interested in history and tradition and likes to travel independently, rather than organized tours and travels
Culture and indulgence	an extroverted, culture and history loving high-class tourist, who is also a connoisseur of good food and wine
Social and sports	an open-minded sportive traveler, who loves to socialize with locals and does not like areas of intense tourism
Action and fun	a jet-setting thrill seeker, who loves action, party and exclusiveness and avoids quiet and peaceful places
Nature and recreation	a nature and silence lover, who wants to escape from everyday life and avoids crowded places and large cities

different demographic characteristics different user groups can be well distinguished within the seven-factor model [20].

13.3.2 Determination of *user factor profiles*

Figure 13.1 illustrates both the "traditional" and the picture-based way of eliciting a user's profile, which is, in our case, the representation of a user in the seven-factor model. Note that a user is represented as a mixture of these factors.

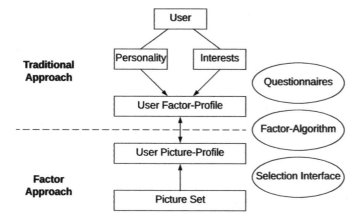

Figure 13.1: Traditional- versus picture-based approach to user profiling.

In the literature, most common approaches to obtain a user's preferences, needs and personality are critique-based. Thus, to obtain preference, needs and personality, users have to communicate with the system or fill out questionnaires (upper path of Figure 13.1). The seven factors of a user were originally obtained in such a conventional way as outlined in Section 13.3.1.

Many people have difficulties in explicitly expressing their preferences and needs [35] and usually travel decisions (e. g., where to go, how to travel) are rather not rationally taken but implicitly given [19]. Thus, by a simple method of picture selection (lower path of Figure 13.1), the picture-based approach avoids tedious communication with the system and addresses also the implicit and emotional level of the decision-making.

For the development of the factor approach (lower part of Figure 13.1), several steps were carried out. First, travel-related pictures were preselected and it was evaluated in a workshop whether they fit to the seven factors. This resulted in a set of 102 pictures. In a second study, 105 people were asked to select and rank a number of pictures out of the 102 travel-related pictures by considering their next hypothetical trip. Furthermore, the participants had to fill out the same questionnaires, which were used for the development of the seven-factor model. It turned out that people tend to select between three and seven pictures. The initial set of 102 travel-related pictures, moreover, was reduced by simply omitting the most and least frequently chosen pictures. This resulted in a more concise set of 63 travel-related pictures (i. e., those that were capturing most of the information). With the help of experts, further relations between the seven factors and the pictures were established. These relations, moreover, were quantified through multiple regression analysis (ordinary least squares). This regression analysis resulted in seven equations, one for each of the seven factors, denoted in Figure 13.1 by the term factor algorithm. Application of these equations to a given *User Picture Profile* obtained from the selection interface gives the *User Factor Profile*, as shown in the lower part of Figure 13.1 [18, 19].

Note that the *User Factor Profile* obtained either by the traditional approach using a questionnaire or by the factor Approach, as well as by the factor approach using the selection interface, is a mixture of the seven factors. This corresponds to the well-known fact that people can have a variation of travel preferences simultaneously [13].

Overall, this nonverbal way of obtaining people's preferences and needs through a simple picture selection not only counteracts the mentioned difficulties in explicitly expressing one's preferences and needs, but also gamifies the way of interaction with the system, which is experienced as interesting, exciting and inspiring by the users.

13.3.3 Development of the *product factor profile*

The computational model for the *Product Factor Profile* is depicted in Figure 13.2.

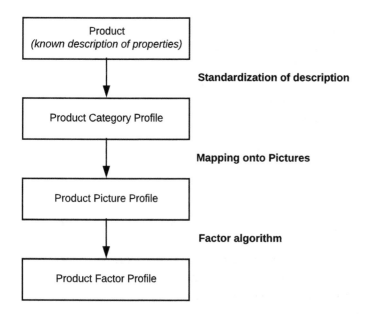

Figure 13.2: Development of the *Product Factor Profile*.

Starting point for the development of the *Product Factor Profile* are known descriptors for the products, which were collected from different sources. The following sources of information were used:

- Classification of products according to the travel agency: The agency has defined a coarse classification of products using terms like "city trip," "round trip" and "event visit."
- Information from the *GIATA* database [10]: The *GIATA* database offers information about accommodations including not only detailed descriptions of the accommodations but also information about possible touristic activities in their neighborhood, like sports facilities. Furthermore, the database offers information about distances to places of interest like city centers, beaches or ski lifts.
- Information from customer evaluations: The agency stores product bookings, customer information and opinions.

In the following we describe the steps of Figure 13.2 in detail.

Step 1: Determination of a *product category profile*
The *Product Category Profile* is defined as a numeric vector of 37 dimensions representing the importance of each category for a product. The categories define a standardized description of a product using the following terminology:

- Topographic categories describing the landscape of the product: Mountains, sea and coast and beach, lakes, cities and nature and landscape.

- Infrastructure categories describing the touristic infrastructure of the product: Spas and fitness, arts and culture, points of interest (POIs), gastronomy, night-life, history, excursions, markets and events.
- Activity categories referring to touristic activities related to the product: Winter sports, summer sports, extreme sports, recreational sports, dining, drinking, sight-seeing, shopping, entertainment, walking, wellness, observing nature, workshops and cultural activities.
- Customer needs categories referring to emotional aspects related to the product: Relaxing and recreative, exciting and thrilling, family-friendly, calming, entertaining, exclusive and luxurious, alternative, romantic and adventurous.

In the following, we describe the procedure for obtaining the values in these categories from different sources.

First of all, based on the previously mentioned information sources various tourism product attributes were extracted. This process of attribute generation was carried out in dependence of the structure of the sources. The following basic methods were used for defining (generating) the product attributes:

- In the case of the textual descriptions of destinations, attributes were defined by keyword extraction. For example, for the term "fly and drive," the attributes "individual product" and "travel by plane" were extracted. This was done mainly interactively using the R text mining environment.
- The travel agency's classifications of products were directly used as attributes.
- Relevant information in the *GIATA* database was either used directly as attributes or transformed (i. e., numerical into categorical) beforehand. For example, information about the distance d to the beach in meters was translated into weights w according to the following rules:
  if $(d \leq 400)$, **then** $w = 3$; **if** $(400 < d \leq 1000)$, **then** $w = 2$; **if** $(1000 < d \leq 3000)$, **then** $w = 1$; **if** $(d > 3000)$, **then** $w = 0$.
- Based on the information of the user evaluations, attributes were defined by keyword extraction, resulting mainly in attributes, which describe the emotional feelings of the tourists. Typical examples are "quiet," "exciting," "child-friendly" or "wellness."

This process resulted in a vector of 400 product attributes, i. e., 58 obtained from the travel agency, 212 from the *GIATA* database and 130 from the user evaluations. The entries of such a vector are weights of the attributes. Those weights are either results of the binning process (i. e., categorization of numerical information) in the *GIATA* database or a consequence of the fact that some of the keywords are used in more than one source. For example, "child-friendly" can occur in the description of the product but also in the evaluation of the users. The higher the value of the attribute the more important is the attribute for the characterization of the product.

Next, the existing list of attributes was mapped onto the 37 categories. This mapping was done by five tourist experts from the university and the travel agency, which provided the data. In most cases, the assignment was straightforward by expert knowledge and the results showed a high degree of consistency. Only for 17 attributes (about 5 %) there was disagreement in a first round, and the results were unified after discussion. The final assignment is represented as a 400 × 37 matrix A indicating the relation between descriptor attributes and categories. Multiplying the row vector $\vec{p}$ of descriptor attributes with A results in the *Product Category Profile* $P_{CP} = \vec{p}A$, which is a 37-dimensional vector where each component gives an integer weight for the importance of the category for the product. In order to avoid overestimation of some categories, a cut-off of the attributes was done. Here, the cut-off value 5 was used.

Note that this profile encompasses from the first three top-level categories (topography, infrastructure and activities) an abstract profile of the product and from the categories of the fourth top-level category information about the emotional aspects and customer needs of the product.

In addition to the categories, five constraint variables were defined for each product, i. e., price, means of transport, travel time, weather and distance of the product from the customer's home.

Step 2: Determination of a *product picture profile*
For each product, the *Product Picture Profile* is a vector of dimension 63, where each component of the vector represents the importance of the picture for characterization of the product. In the following, the calculation of the *Product Picture Profile* is outlined.

First of all, pictures are assigned to the 37 categories. The same 63 pictures as in the determination of the *User Profile* are used. In this assignment, multiple attributions of pictures to different categories are possible. For example, a picture showing a hiking tourist may be assigned to the topographic category *nature & landscape*, to the activity categories *walking* and *recreational sports*, and to the customer needs category *relaxing and recreative*. Consequently, the picture assignment to the categories can be represented as a 37 × 63 matrix B, indicating the relation between categories and pictures. Note that due to the multiple assignments of pictures to different categories matrix B has multiple nonzero entries in each row.

The assignment was done independently by three tourist experts and by eight test persons. As a result, we obtained 11 possible assignment matrices B. Averaging of these matrices resulted in the final assignment matrix $\bar{B}$. The *Product Picture Profile* is now defined by the vector $P_{PP} = \vec{p}A\bar{B}$.

Step 3: Determination of a *product factor profile*
The *Product Factor Profile* is a 7D vector where each component of the vector defines the aptitude of the product for the factors defined in Table 13.1. The transformation of the *Product Picture Profile* into the *Product Factor Profile* is done by application of the factor algorithm used in the computation of the *User Factor Profile* from pictures. In this step,

not all pictures assigned to a product are used but only the pictures with the highest weight. Here, the seven highest weighted pictures of each product are used.

As a result, one obtains a profile, which uses the same seven factors as the *User Factor Profile* for all touristic products under consideration. Note that the mapping of product characteristics onto the language of the categories and the assignment of the pictures to the categories is done only once. As soon as these results are available, one can compute the *Product Factor Profile* automatically when there is input about the attributes for the touristic product. Moreover, it should be mentioned that a profile can be obtained also by incomplete information about the product.

13.4 Validity of the picture-based approach

The factor model can be used in different ways. As mentioned in the Introduction, the main usage scenario of interest lies in the development of an enhanced CRM for a travel agency. For this scenario, we describe four different types of evaluation. The first one considers the validity of the approach with respect to a ground truth defined by experts of the tourist agency. The second evaluation considers the application of the method for recommendation of a product to a potential customer with known *User Factor Profile* and the third evaluation refers to the use of the method for recommendation to customers who have already booked a product in the past. Finally, we consider a simple application of the methods for recommendation based on product clustering.

13.4.1 Evaluation 1: validation of the *product factor profiles*

For validation of the algorithm, which computes the *Product Factor Profiles* according to the steps described in Section 13.3.3, the procedure was applied to 1221 products offered by an Austrian travel agency. The values of the seven factors for these products were also assessed by experts from the travel agency according to their knowledge about the products. The experts assessed each of the seven factors on a percent scale resulting in a value between 0 and 100 for each factor of the *Product Factor Profile*. These assessments correspond to the idea that the factors are orthogonal and allow for an interpretation of a conditional probability for the fit of the product to a factor. For the evaluation of the *Product Factor Profile*, it was assumed that the expert assessment is the ground truth. The question is how far the computed profiles match with these profiles. For matching the cosine, similarity of the two profiles was used. This measure has the advantage that it can be interpreted as the correlation between the two profile vectors and allows in this way for a well-known interpretation. A disadvantage of the measure is probably that the profiles are normalized in length and the norm of the profiles is not considered. This means that it is possible that the experts assess the relations between the seven factors for two products in a similar way but the level of the assessment is different.

The results of the comparison are shown in Table 13.2 and Figure 13.3. Note that we use the term "similarity" for the measure calculated for each pair (*Product Factor Profile* due to experts and *Product Factor Profile* due to the algorithm) and we do not display separate curves for the two profiles.

Table 13.2: Similarity distribution of *product factor profiles* and expert profiles.

Min	First quartile	Median	Mean	Third quartile	Max
0.04	0.53	0.70	0.65	0.80	0.97

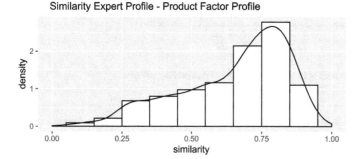

Figure 13.3: Similarity distribution of *Product Factor Profiles* and expert profiles.

The summary measures and the skewness of the distribution indicate that for 25 % of all products there is a high or very high correlation between the expert assessment and the outcome of the algorithm and for 25 % of all products the correlation is low.

13.4.2 Evaluation 2: comparison of *product factor profiles* and *user factor profiles*

A second method for validation of the approach is to compare *Product Factor Profiles* of purchased products with the *User Factor Profiles* of the customers obtained from the selection interface (see Section 13.3.2). Overall, 81 *User Factor Profiles* were available. For comparison of the booked profiles and the user profiles, the same method was used as in the first evaluation. The results of the comparison are shown in Table 13.3 and Figure 13.4. The number of cases is rather small but the results lead to similar conclusions as in Section 13.4.1. The lower values of the similarity can be explained by the fact that customer decisions depend on a number of facts not captured in the profiles. Hence, a higher variability can be expected.

Table 13.3: Similarity distribution of *Product Factor Profiles* and *User Factor Profiles*.

Min	First quartile	Median	Mean	Third quartile	Max
0.15	0.44	0.64	0.59	0.72	0.90

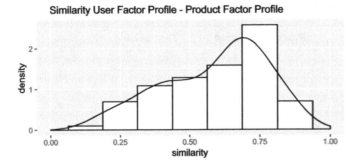

Figure 13.4: Similarity distribution of *User Factor Profiles* and *Product Factor Profiles*.

13.4.3 Evaluation 3: comparison of the booked products from users with multiple bookings

The third evaluation concerns the question in how far the *Product Factor Profiles* of products purchased by a user are similar and depend on user preferences. From the database of the tourist agency, 982 customers were filtered who booked two different products at different times. Again, the similarity of the two bookings was computed by the cosine similarity. The summary measures and the shape of the similarity distribution are shown in Table 13.4 and Figure 13.5.

Table 13.4: Similarity distribution of *Product Factor Profiles* for multiple bookings.

Min	First quartile	Median	Mean	Third quartile	Max
0.00	0.53	0.83	0.72	0.97	1.00

The results confirm the hypothesis that tourists have the tendency to book products with a rather similar *Product Factor Profile*. This fact shows that usage of the picture-based approach can be applied in direct marketing activities: If one proposes potential customers products, which are similar to those previously booked the conversion rate of such a recommendation will be higher than in the case of proposing an arbitrary product. It should be noted that in this case we use only an implicit determination of the *User Factor Profile* from previous bookings.

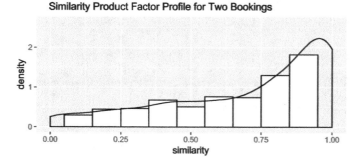

Figure 13.5: Similarity distribution of *Product Factor Profiles* for multiple bookings.

13.4.4 Evaluation 4: evaluation of the product clusters defined by product factor profiles

This evaluation involves the application of a cluster analysis onto the *Product Factor Profiles* in which the products can be grouped into and, furthermore, representatives of product clusters are shown to the potential customer. If the customer decides for one of the products further recommendations can be made by selection of products from this cluster.

For defining clusters, different methods of cluster analysis for 1946 products in the database of the travel agency were examined. Figure 13.6 shows a summary of the results of a hierarchical cluster analysis using the similarity matrix based on the cosine similarity and the Ward method for cluster aggregation. The choice of the number of clusters, the cluster method and the use of the similarity matrix was the result of a number of experiments with different settings of the parameters.

As one can see for some of the factors the relation to the clusters is evident. For example, products with high adequacy for customers interested in factor 1 (i. e., *Sun and chill-out*) occur mainly in cluster 2 (475 products), products for customers interested in properties described by factor 6 (i. e., *Action and fun*) occur mainly in cluster 1 (72 products) and products with high adequacy for customers interested in factor 7 (i. e., *Nature and recreation*) can be found mainly in cluster 4 (619 products) and cluster 5 (275 products). In some cases, the distinction is not so clear but recommendation of a product, which belongs to the same cluster as a previously booked product definitely increases the probability of booking compared to a random recommendation.

13.5 Conclusions and further development

In this chapter, we showed further development of the picture-based approach not only for obtaining user preferences with pictures but also for characterizing touristic prod-

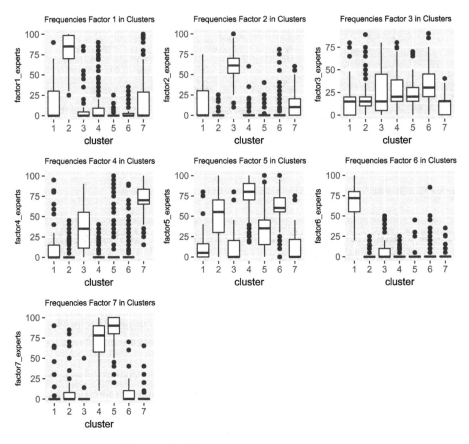

Figure 13.6: Distribution of factors in the clusters.

ucts with respect to the seven-factor model using pictures. The empirical results show that this approach is valid, as judged by the evaluation of products by experts, and can be applied in different application scenarios. A demonstration for the realization of the potential of the approach by using an A/B test is planned in the future.

A number of further developments of the system are planned. In particular, work for the following improvements and modifications have already started:

- Development of a user-friendly interface for mobile devices: At the moment, the system presents all 63 pictures for the selection on one screen. This it not very convenient for the much smaller screen size of a mobile device. A new interface, which is based on a sequential presentation of the pictures, is under development. At the moment, two different scenarios are tested, i. e., presentation of four pictures and presentation of two pictures.
- Extension of the picture set: In the actual version of the system, the picture set is static and cannot be changed. A first analysis of the coefficients of the pictures in the factor algorithm showed that the pictures can be grouped according to the impor-

tance for the decision by the factor algorithm. This clustering can be used for augmentation of pictures. In connection with the new interface with sequential picture presentation, the augmentation offers the opportunity to present only a selection of pictures from a larger set. This offers users a higher degree of variety and more entertainment in multiple usage of the system.

- Extension of the user interface for customer acquisition: As previously outlined, the system can be used for customer acquisition and CRM without performing the picture test. An extension of the interface for better support of these usage scenarios is planned.
- Application of the model in other domains: The approach is of interest whenever recommendation includes not only hard facts but also users' tastes and emotions. First, results of an application in the domain of event marketing showed promising results.
- Adapting the system for groups: Traveling is an activity, which is predominantly experienced by groups of people (e. g., family, friends, colleagues) rather than individuals. It has been shown that the satisfaction of group members to group decisions not only depends on the similarity to the respective individual preferences, but also on the personality of the individual group members. The picture-based approach, and thus the seven-factor model, is a good starting point for capturing and aggregating preferences, needs and personality of individual group members. In this context, further adaptations, improvements and evaluations are planned, especially for dealing with group dynamics [6–8].
- Breaking the data source (data structure) and expert knowledge dependence: Neural networks, in particular convolutional neural networks, can be used to identify concepts out of tourism product pictures. In turn, these learned concepts can be exploited for mapping the respective tourism products onto the defined categorization (see Section 13.3.3, Step 1). In this way, we can omit the one-time manual expert allocation of tourism product attributes (given by the used data source) onto the defined categories. Furthermore, this approach would lead to a more generalized solution by easing the dependence on heterogeneous data sources (data structures).

Bibliography

[1] H. Berger, M. Denk, M. Dittenbach, D. Merkl, and A. Pesenhofer. Quo vadis homo turisticus? towards a picture-based tourist profiler. *Information and Communication Technologies in Tourism* 2007 (2007) 87–96.

[2] J. Borras, A. Moreno, and A. Valls. Intelligent tourism recommender systems: A survey. *Expert Systems with Applications* 41(16) (2014) 7370–7389.

[3] M. Braunhofer, M. Elahi, M. Ge, and F. Ricci. Context dependent preference acquisition with personality-based active learning in mobile recommender systems. In: *International Conference on Learning and Collaboration Technologies*. Springer, 2014, pp. 105–116.

[4] Cruneo GmbH (2017). https://www.cruneo-kreuzfahrtvergleich.de.

[5] M. De Chouhdury, M. Feldman, S. Amer-Yahia, N. Golbandi, R. Lempel, and C. Yu. Automatic construction of travel itineraries using social breadcrumbs. In: *HT '10 Proceedings of the 21st ACM conference on Hypertext and hypermedia*. ACM, 2010, pp. 35–44.

[6] A. Delic, and J. Neidhardt. A comprehensive approach to group recommendations in the travel and tourism domain. In: *Adjunct publication of the 25th conference on user modeling, adaptation and personalization*. ACM, 2017, pp. 11–16.

[7] A. Delic, J. Neidhardt, T. N. Nguyen, F. Ricci, L. Rook, H. Werthner, and M. Zanker. Observing group decision making processes. In: *Proceedings of the 10th ACM conference on recommender systems*. ACM, 2016, pp. 147–150.

[8] A. Delic, J. Neidhardt, L. Rook, H. Werthner, and M. Zanker. Researching individual satisfaction with group decisions in tourism: experimental evidence. In: *Information and Communication Technologies in Tourism 2017*. Springer, 2017, pp. 73–85.

[9] D. Gavalas, C. Konstantopoulos, K. Mastakas, and G. Pantziou. Mobile recommender systems in tourism. *Journal of Network and Computer Applications* 39 (2014) 319–333.

[10] GIATA GmbH (2018). https://https://www.giata.com/.

[11] H. Gibson, and A. Yiannakis. Tourist roles: Needs and the lifecourse. *Annals of Tourism Research* 29(2) (2002) 358–383.

[12] L. Glatzer, J. Neidhardt, and H. Werthner Automated assignment of hotel descriptions to travel behavioural patterns. In: *Information and Communication Technologies in Tourism 2018*. Springer, 2018, pp. 409–421.

[13] U. Gretzel, N. Mitsche, Y.-H. Hwang, and D. R. Fesenmaier. Tell me who you are and I will tell you where to go: use of travel personalities in destination recommendation systems. *Information Technology & Tourism* 7(1) (2004) 3–12.

[14] O. P. John, and S. Srivastava. The big five trait taxonomy: History, measurement, and theoretical perspectives. *Handbook of personality: Theory and Research* 2 (1999) 102–138.

[15] I. Koprinska, and K. Yacef. People-to-people reciprocal recommenders. In: *Recommender Systems Handbook*. Springer, 2015, pp. 545–567.

[16] G. Matthews, I. J. Deary, and M. C. Whiteman. *Personality traits*. Cambridge University Press, 2003.

[17] L. McGinty, and J. Reilly. On the evolution of critiquing recommenders. In: *Recommender Systems Handbook*. Springer, 2011, pp. 419–453.

[18] J. Neidhardt, R. Schuster, L. Seyfang, and H. Werthner. Eliciting the users' unknown preferences. In: *Proceedings of the 8th ACM Conference on Recommender systems*. ACM, 2014, pp. 309–312.

[19] J. Neidhardt, L. Seyfang, R. Schuster, and H. Werthner. A picture-based approach to recommender systems. *Information Technology & Tourism* 15(1) (2015) 49–69.

[20] J. Neidhardt, and H. Werthner. Travellers and their joint characteristics within the seven-factor model. In: *Information and Communication Technologies in Tourism 2017*. Springer, 2017, pp. 503–515.

[21] J. Neidhardt, and H. Werthner. IT and tourism: still a hot topic, but do not forget it. *Information Technology & Tourism* 20(1) (2018) 1–7.

[22] A. Pommeranz, J. Broekens, P. Wiggers, W.-P. Brinkman, and C. M. Jonker. Designing interfaces for explicit preference elicitation: a user-centered investigation of preference representation and elicitation process. *User Modeling and User-Adapted Interaction* 22(4–5) (2012) 357–397.

[23] D. Quercia, R. Schifanella, and Luca M. Aiello. The shortest path to happiness: Recommending beautiful, quiet and happy routes in the city. In: *HT '14 Proceedings of the 25th ACM conference on Hypertext and social media*. ACM, 2014, pp. 116–125.

[24] F. Ricci. Travel recommender systems. *IEEE Intelligent Systems* 17(6) (2002) 55–57.

[25] F. Ricci, L. Rokach, and B. Shapira. Recommender systems: Introduction and challenges. In: *Recommender Systems Handbook*. Springer, 2015, pp. 1–34.

[26] F. Ricci, K. Woeber, and A. Zins. Recommendations by collaborative browsing. In: *Information and Communication Technologies in Tourism 2005*. Springer, 2005, pp. 172–182.

[27] M. Sertkan, J. Neidhardt, and H. Werthner. Mapping of tourism destinations to travel behavioural patterns. In: *Information and Communication Technologies in Tourism 2018*. Springer, 2018, pp. 422–434.

[28] M. Sertkan, J. Neidhardt, and H. Werthner What is the "personality" of a tourism destination? *Information Technology & Tourism* (2018).

[29] M. Sertkan, J. Neidhardt, and H. Werthner. Eliciting Touristic Profiles: A User Study on Picture Collections. In: *Proceedings of the 28th ACM Conference on User Modeling, Adaptation and Personalization*. ACM, 2020, pp. 230–238.

[30] M. Sertkan, J. Neidhardt, and H. Werthner. PicTouRe - A Picture-Based Tourism Recommender. In: *Proceedings of the 14th ACM Conference on Recommender Systems*. ACM, 2020, pp. 597–599.

[31] M. Tkalcic, and L. Chen. Personality and recommender systems. In: *Recommender systems handbook*. Springer, 2015, pp. 715–739.

[32] H. Werthner, and S. Klein. *Information technology and tourism: a challenging relation*. Springer-Verlag Wien, 1999.

[33] H. Werthner, and F. Ricci. E-commerce and tourism. *Communications of the ACM* 47(12) (2004) 101–105.

[34] A. B. Woszczynski, P. L. Roth, and A. H. Segars. Exploring the theoretical foundations of playfulness in computer interactions. *Computers in Human Behavior* 18(4) (2002) 369–388.

[35] A. Zins. Exploring travel information search behavior beyond common frontiers. *Information Technology & Tourism* 9(3–1) (2007) 149–164.

Index

https://doi.org/10.1515/9783110988567-014

Printed in the USA
CPSIA information can be obtained
at www.ICGtesting.com
LVHW081946160524
780451LV00005B/515